Broken Soldiers

BROKEN
Soldiers

Raymond B. Lech

University of Illinois Press

Urbana and Chicago

Library of Congress Cataloging-in-Publication Data
Lech, Raymond B., 1940–
Broken soldiers / Raymond B. Lech.
p.   cm.
Includes bibliographical references and index.
ISBN 0-252-02541-5 (cloth : alk. paper)
1. Korean War, 1950–1953—Prisoners and prisons, North Korean.
2. Prisoners of war—United States.
I. Title.
DS921.L43   2000
951.904'27—dc21   00-008208

C 5 4 3 2 1

To Richard N. Stravino,
a friend for life

and

my four beautiful granddaughters,
Nicole Renee Jimenez, Denise Adriana Jimenez,
Natalie Michele Lech, and Allyson Marie Lech

CONTENTS

Appendixes

ILLUSTRATIONS FOLLOW PAGE 144

ACKNOWLEDGMENTS

The bulk of the primary source documents concerning army personnel were obtained during 1984 and 1985, and the transcripts were forwarded to me by the Department of the Army, United States Army Judiciary, in Falls Church, Virginia. My appreciation to the U.S. Army Judiciary and to Mary B. Dennis, deputy clerk of court and my primary contact. Not only did she get material to me in an orderly manner, but she also followed up on declassification reviews.

The U.S. Navy was also cooperative in finding, declassifying, and making available the three volumes of Col. Frank Schwable's court of inquiry. I particularly appreciate the efforts of the Office of the Judge Advocate General in Alexandria, Virginia.

Noel Parsons, editor-in-chief at Texas A&M University Press, has been a kind friend to this work. His interest in *Broken Soldiers* never faded. A former Air Force officer, he was extremely helpful concerning technical Air Force matters, and he advised me in developing the Epilogue of this volume.

George Billy, library director at the U.S. Merchant Marine Academy, Kings Point, New York, was only a telephone call away when I needed assistance with citations and, more important, archiving. He was particularly kind about providing minute details. I am grateful to him for allowing me immediate access to his office, at any time and with any question.

Bonnie McGuirk, as usual, played a supportive role and constantly provided a shoulder to lean on. Tom Smith read the original manuscript and pointed out the forest when I was looking at trees. Mike Daly was there when I had to move well over five hundred pounds of documents from one archive to another. It never took more than a telephone call to get his help.

Irene Mandra, who has a brother missing from the Korean War, is vice president and treasurer of the Coalition of Families and provided valuable help in getting documents to me, specifically those concerning missing Americans who allegedly were not repatriated.

At the University of Illinois Press, my thanks go to Mary Giles and to Richard Wentworth, the Press's former editor-in-chief and director, who was the first at the Press to review the manuscript and recommend its publication.

NOTE ON SOURCES

The only way to discover what really went on in North Korean and Chinese prisoner of war camps was to speak with—and interrogate—the men who were there and had lived through the horror of the years between 1950 and 1953. Furthermore, these exchanges had to take place when memories were fresh rather than thirty-five to forty years after the event. Finally, the charge of perjury (and the subsequent penalty thereof) had to be imposed upon the interviewed for misstatements.

I personally did not interview former POWs of the Korean War because doing so would require an army of individuals—which is how the interviews were conducted. Reading them, as well as the letters, memoranda, appellate reviews, and the trial proceedings themselves, however, provided a feeling of being there, of actually being present in the room with the interrogator and in the courtroom with the judge, jury, lawyers, and accused.

Army investigators, interrogators, and lawyers talked with the former Korean POWs, under oath, as soon as they got out of the camps—often within days. Many army interrogators were tough men and didn't hesitate to ask embarrassing questions and demand answers. During the pretrial interviews, no judges or juries were present, no objections were made (hearsay evidence was admissible), and answers were demanded and given. After studying transcripts of the interviews and interrogations, I couldn't come up with one question that I wish had been asked.

After the men had been repatriated, fourteen of them were court-martialed. In reviewing these transcripts, which the army furnished, the actual courtroom dramas were the meat between the bread. Included in what the army calls "the transcripts" were all pretrial interviews on one side, as well as exhibits, appellate reviews, memos, letters, and anything else imaginable concerning POWs. The army threw nothing away.

Upon my initial request to the army, I was eventually sent sixteen cartons of transcripts and supporting documents. Each carton weighed approximately thirty pounds and held five or more volumes, with nearly four hundred (and sometimes up to a thousand) pages per volume. Therefore, the original papers from the army, now in my possession, come to 480 pounds, eighty volumes, and more than sixty thousand legal-sized, single-spaced pages.

Pages were missing from many of the transcripts, sometimes hundreds of pages at a time, because they contained classified information. Therefore, I requested and received still another carton, which weighed thirty pounds and contained previously secret documents concerning the Korean POWs. To the best of my knowledge, the army has no more classified material in its possession concerning this subject.

To make everything tangible (and clarify the written documents), the army also provided six, seven-inch reel-to-reel tape recordings of broadcasts made by U.S. soldiers and airmen from Radios P'yŏngyang and Peking. To hear their voices after knowing what they had been through was a sad experience.

The National Archives located, declassified, and provided 325 pages of previously secret documents (Record Group 340) from the files of the secretary of the air force concerning air force prisoners. The U.S. Navy forwarded the entire court of inquiry transcript of Col. Frank Schwable, USMC (three volumes containing many previously classified documents), which transcript also contained numerous exhibits, and supporting documents.

>«

After the war, fourteen U.S. Army courts-martial and one marine corps court of inquiry were held. All of the documents from those proceedings are in my possession (approximately sixty thousand pages, much of which has been declassified at my request), including but not limited to the entire courts-martial proceedings themselves and pretrial investigations (interviews), Counter Intelligence Corps interrogations, appellate reviews, and both internal and external (public) letters and memoranda.

When reviewing a citation, that reference does not necessarily mean that the particular quotation was specifically extracted from the court-martial (trial) proceeding. If a complete transcript contains three thousand pages, for example, only one thousand may be relevant to the actual courtroom. The remaining two thousand pages could be any number of sources, such as interviews (pretrial investigations), letters, memoranda, and exhibits. The army kept everything, although in the end it filed all into one bulk of papers containing many volumes. That aggregate was called the court-martial "transcripts."

Each U.S. Army transcript is formally known by the name of the person being tried, and, for many, ten or more volumes (some volumes have well over a thousand pages) cover a single court-martial. For example, the source of epigraph at the beginning of the Introduction is "Lt. Col. Harry Fleming, USA, Transcripts, 10:1212" (i.e., it is from the court-martial record of Lt. Col. Harry Fleming, volume 10, page 1212). All secondary sources have been noted in the traditional manner and can also be found in the bibliography.

Broken Soldiers

INTRODUCTION

You must adhere to one side, or else you will perish. There is the side of war and aggression to which the capitalists and warmongers of America belong, and the other side is the side of truth and righteousness and of the people to which we belong. If you do not see the truth, if you do not believe the truth, you will perish.

    —Major Han, North Korean army, in Lt. Col. Harry Fleming, USA, Transcripts, 10:1212

       It was an ugly little war that began during the summer of 1950 and lasted three years. The result of the bitter fight was that no one won, yet nearly thirty-five thousand American families lost sons, fathers, and husbands in the struggle. Their lives were sacrificed for a cause that many have written about and judged. This book will not repeat those efforts. For some, however, the war took something just as precious as their lives—their minds and their sacred honor. That process is the subject of this book.

    Prisoners are taken during the course of every conflict, and the Korean War was no different. Surrender, especially during the first nine months of the war, was not uncommon; 7,190 Americans laid down their arms rather than their lives.* Yet approximately three thousand of these same men died anyway. Most of the remaining four thousand who returned home from Chinese camps along the Manchurian border bore emotional scars that would never heal. Pak's Palace, Pike's Peak, Bean Camp, Death Valley, the Caves, and many other places in North Korea were the sources of horrors never before inflicted on Americans. Camp 5 on the south bank of the Yalu River near Pyoktong (and also the north bank in Manchurian territory) still contains the bodies of more than 1,500 GIs. What went on up there?

>«

The uniqueness of the POW situation during the Korean War lies in two arenas: the percentage of deaths to the total prisoner population and indoctrination toward communist meanings, values, and way of life. Hardly any war since the turn of the twentieth century has caused the number of prisoner deaths that occurred in Korea, based on total POW population. As for indoctrination, nothing like what took place in Korea had ever happened before.

Forty-three percent of all American POWs in Korea died in captivity—through starvation—in a period of six months. Although the numbers of prisoners in Korea were not as large as those of other wars, three thousand deaths in such a short period is staggering.

Four percent of the Americans held captive by the Germans and Italians died during World War II, as did 34 percent of those held by the Japanese. The only theater of operations that came close to comparing with Korea was the Eastern Front during World War II. There, the German POW casualty rate under the Russians was 45 percent, and that for Russians under the Germans was 60 percent.

During the American Civil War, the Andersonville prison camp at Anderson Station, Georgia, was notorious, especially between February 1864 and April 1865, when the Confederates amassed forty-one thousand Union soldiers, 32 percent of whom perished. North Vietnam claimed to hold 766 Americans during that long war, with a death rate of nearly 14 percent (106 men died). It is rare, however, for Korea to even be mentioned during conversations about POWs, although the death rate there statis-

_____

* There were 6,656 from the U.S. Army; 263 from the Air Force; 231 marines; and 40 from the U.S. Navy.

tically surpassed that of any other conflict save the one between Russia and Germany. Korea was truly the "forgotten war."

>«

The United States did not train its citizen-soldiers very well about what to do if captured. Everyone learned in boot camp to give only name, rank, and service number, but that wasn't sufficient against a ruthless enemy who, when he didn't kill the body, strove to transmute the spirit. Comdr. Ralph Bagwell, USN, testified that "the conduct we exhibited was completely through lack of guidance or lack of prior instruction. . . . In retrospect, and even at that time, [that conduct] might not have seemed the logical thing to do. However, it was the best we could muster."[1] What they mustered, however, frequently was insufficient to the challenge.

The majority of the captive Americans did practically everything their North Korean and Chinese captors told them to do. They did so because they feared death. It was rarely a clean, fast death that threatened, but a slow, agonizing one. The enemy used a weapon that didn't cost a penny but achieved its purpose with remarkable efficiency: starvation. After they had cleaned the body of its meat, after they had living skeletons in their cages, they began to "cleanse" the mind.

The starvation months were between November 1950 and April 1951, when nearly three thousand men died. "I have never seen human beings come so close to being animals as we were in January, February, March, and most of April, 1951," said Lt. Col. Charles Fry, an inmate at Camp 5. Another prisoner reported, "We could almost look at one another and tell just about when one of us was going to die."[2] In their focus on food, many captives shed a logical defense, and all that we call civilization collapsed. It was at this point, in April 1951, that great numbers of officers and enlisted, young and old, white and black, turned their backs on the West and began to embrace the enemy. There were exceptions, but they were the minority.

>«

In 1949 Soviet Foreign Minister Andri Vishinsky gave a speech to celebrate Stalin's seventieth birthday. "We shall conquer the world not with atomic bombs," he said, "but with our ideas, our brains, and our doctrines." One year later, at the beginning of the Korean War, the high command of the North Korean army issued orders that mandated "all efforts will be made to destroy the enemy in thought and politically."[3] Those efforts worked so well that when the conflict ended in 1953 twenty-three captured soldiers refused to come home.

Propaganda is nothing new in war or peace. Psychological manipulation goes on all the time. Advertising is a form of propaganda—why buy one brand of toothpaste instead of another? Xerxes employed rumormongering more than 2,500 years ago, and American colonials used a frontline propaganda leaflet at Bunker Hill to encourage the opposing Redcoats to defect. What happened in Chinese POW camps, however, was not propaganda but a forced indoctrination of communist doctrine and practice. The Chinese even refused to recognize their captives as prisoners and called them students. Soon, many captive "students" began to cooperate with the enemy.

The North Koreans and Chinese (for the United Nations had two enemies in Korea) conceived and carried out a methodical and calculated program of torture. Diabolical as they were, captured marine pilot Frank Schwable said, "Let me emphasize that those people over there are . . . intelligent at this game, they know what they are doing and they don't fool with us."[4]

The captors' initial master plan was to destroy the individuality of their prisoners. The technique was simple, Pavlovian conditioning by turning captives into "starving dogs." The Russians began the study of these methods in the service of the state and quickly discovered how to employ identical methods on human beings: Starve them then train them.

When the training* began, prisoners split into three principal groups: progressives, middle-of-the-roaders, and reactionaries. Every POW in Korea carried one of the three labels. The middle-of-the-roaders were in the majority. They did little or nothing to fight their captors and little or nothing to help them. They studied communism because they were told to, they signed appeals because they were directed to, and they wrote procommunist articles because they were ordered to. They swayed with the wind, but never too far in either direction. The Chinese classified them as Class B prisoners.

---

* The term *brainwashing* is not employed frequently in this book because it has been subjected to so many differing definitions.

The next-largest group was the progressives. These were Class A prisoners, or, as the Chinese preferred, "peace loving prisoners." Such a captive apparently accepted the political, economic, and social gospel of Marx, Engels, Lenin, and Stalin, even if he was not sure what doing so meant. He reputedly assisted the enemy in almost every way possible by spreading propaganda in the camps and informing on other Americans. As Sgt. Donnell Adams put it, "In my opinion, a Progressive is a type of man that would deny his country, deny his God, and every time they say something he squatted and done it, and done it in such an emotional way that his whole heart and soul was in it."[5] The progressive can be described as a collaborator, in the commonly understood sense of that word if not in the legal sense.

The smallest but bravest group was the reactionaries, who were hated by the Chinese and detested by the progressives. They actively resisted indoctrination, resisted study sessions, resisted cooperation, resisted writing, resisted signing, and resisted making every other concession their captors demanded. It is hard to be a hero when you're a POW, but these are the men who came back heros.

>«

When the soldiers came home after three years of captivity, they were asked, "What do you think of communism?" A common answer was, "Although communism won't work in America, I think it's a good thing for Asia." That answer meant that the "student" had received a passing grade from his Chinese mentors. After Frank Schwable, a pilot, arrived in the United States, he said, "I trust that in the minds of my own countrymen there will be an intelligent understanding of what has happened and that at least some value may evolve from my misfortune."[6] We shall see.

Notes

1. Maj. Ronald Alley, USA, Transcripts, 4:126.
2. Lt. Col. Paul Liles, USA, Transcripts, 4b:1760; Lt. Col. Harry Fleming, USA, Transcripts, 9:962.
3. Col. Frank Schwable, USMC, Transcripts, 3:1290; Middleton, *Compact History of the Korean War,* 94.
4. Schwable Transcripts, 3:1026.
5. Sgt. James Gallagher, USA, Transcripts, 4:315.
6. Schwable Transcripts, 3:1262.

PART 1
Hell

To you my friends I say: Do not be afraid of those who kill the body and after that can do no more. I will tell you whom to fear: Fear him who, after he has killed, has the power to cast into hell.

—Luke XII:4

ONE

Enter the Tiger

From this moment there will be no question of virtue or morality; for despotism, cui ex honesto nulla est spes, *wherever it prevails, admits no other master; it no sooner speaks than probity and duty lose their weight and blind obedience is the only virtue which slaves can still practice.*

—Rousseau, *On the Origin of Inequality*

During the early morning hours of Sunday, June 25, 1950, a North Korean army of ninety thousand men crossed the 38th Parallel and attacked South Korea. Caught flat-footed, the defending Republic of Korea (ROK) forces, less than half as numerous as the invaders, were no match for the heavily armed, tank-supported troops from the north. Almost immediately the ROK forces began to retreat.

Approximately 120 miles across the Korea Strait in a more or less southerly direction from the South Korean port of Pusan lies the Japanese island of Kyushu. There, on this fateful Sunday, forty-year-old Maj. Ambrose Nugent, U.S. Army, staff duty officer with the 52d Field Artillery Battalion of the 24th Infantry Division, was having lunch. The prematurely gray-haired career officer from Merrill, Wisconsin, had been on Kyushu for only a month, having requested assignment in the Far East after completing a two-year tour of recruiting duty with the Fifth Army in southern Illinois. Half-way through his leisurely Sunday meal, a messenger approached the table and asked him to report immediately to battalion headquarters.[1]

When he reached headquarters, the meeting of senior officers was already underway, and Major Nugent heard secret orders: a portion of the artillery battalion would be shipped to Korea in support of an infantry element that would be flown to the peninsula from Kyushu within the week.* When he heard that, Nugent, the eldest of six children, volunteered to go with the artillery "in an effort to stem the Red tide."[2]

It took the entire week to prepare one firing battery and portions of headquarters and service battery for the move, but by the following Saturday night, July 1, 1950, all was in order. Six 105-mm howitzers together with seventy-three vehicles and 106 artillerymen were loaded aboard an LST at Fukuoka harbor. The next morning, the ship released its lines from the safe Japanese shore and made the short voyage across the strait to war, reaching Pusan at 7 P.M.[3]

Major Nugent had received custody of his two minor children when he and his first wife were divorced in 1943; he had remarried in 1947. He had also stopped smoking when he was on recruiting duty in Illinois. As he set foot on Korean soil on the evening of July 2, he weighed 215 pounds, somewhat overweight for his average height and frame. He didn't know it then, but within a few weeks he would begin to lose weight rapidly.[4]

Once ashore, Nugent's unit was immediately ordered to move northwesterly across the peninsula to the opposite coast. All night the officers pieced together rail transportation, and on Monday, July 3, men, guns, and vehicles were loaded. The train chugged toward the battle. By 5 P.M. they had entered the city of Taejon, about fifty miles from the west coast; there they loaded ammunition and headed almost due north. Shortly after midnight the train trip ended, and the unit unloaded and boarded their vehicles. Just as dawn was breaking on the morning of Tuesday, July 4, the battalion moved into P'yongt'aek, a town astride the main north-south road on the west coast of the peninsula. They were about thirty-five miles south of Seoul, the South Korean capital now in the hands of the North Koreans.[5]

---

* This element was the understrength 1st Battalion (consisting of B and C Companies and half of Headquarters Company), 21st Infantry Regiment, 24th Infantry Division, commanded by Lt. Col. Charles Bradford Smith.

Ambrose Nugent was assigned as a liaison officer, coordinating artillery fire with the infantry. He constantly remained with the foot soldiers but was linked to his own unit by radio. During the late afternoon of July 4, Lt. Col. Charles B. Smith, commanding officer of the 430 infantrymen who composed his "Task Force Smith," ordered the troops to move a mile or so north of P'yongt'aek into the hills siding the road leading from Seoul. In their southward attack, the North Korean 4th Division would have to use this route as the axis of advance, and Colonel Smith was hoping to stop them.[6]

Major Nugent moved with the infantry, and while advancing toward the action he saw "the remnants of a ROK division, perhaps five or six thousand . . . hell-bent for the rear in complete disorder, abandoning weapons and their wounded." The major made every effort to get them to turn around, go back, and make a stand with these few Americans, but the South Koreans were too disorganized. After perhaps thirty minutes the GIs did manage to clear the road sufficiently to get some of their own vehicles through, and the American troops pulled into the hills.[7]

Shortly before midnight, Brig. Gen. George Barth, a forward representative of Maj. Gen. William F. Dean's headquarters, which commanded all American and ROK troops, called a meeting of the principal officers of Task Force Smith and its artillery support. The general decided to go forward himself for some night reconnaissance. Colonel Smith hopped into Nugent's jeep, and, followed by Barth in his, they drove north. Major Nugent recalled that they passed over two or three bridges, stopping at Barth's order to remove explosives that had been put in place by the South Koreans. The American commander believed that keeping the bridges intact eventually would facilitate moving other Allied units forward.

"At this particular point," Nugent says, "every one of the Americans there were convinced that we were going to hold them up there until such time as other elements of the 24th Division could pull in." But the only force backing the small group of Americans at P'yongt'aek was 1,981 men of the 34th Infantry Regiment, and they had independent orders to block the one eastern road to Ansong.[8]

While the senior officers made their northern reconnaissance, the two rifle companies that made up the bulk of Task Force Smith completed their deployment into the low hills along each side of the highway. Major Nugent thought it "an excellent defense because we had fifteen to twenty thousand yards of vision from there . . . , excellent observation for artillery fire."[9]

As first light began to peek through the heavily overcast sky on Wednesday, July 5, the general arrived again for one last meeting with the defenders. Major Nugent's directive was simple: "The orders from General Barth were that this position would be held at all costs, and he didn't say it once, he said it two or three times." After giving the no-retreat order, Barth left the area and drove south to the headquarters of the 34th Infantry Regiment.[10]

At approximately 9:00 A.M., Nugent recalled that "suddenly we heard a rumble from the north." Thirty-one Soviet-built T-34 tanks were moving south on the road "followed by a great number of trucks loaded with infantry." Nugent was at the infantry command post (CP) and put in charge of three .50–caliber machine guns and three 2.36-inch bazooka teams. When the enemy armor came within range, he ordered the antitank rockets to take them under fire, but the rounds bounced off the steel monsters. Six tanks passed and continued south down the road. It was the first American battle of the war in Korea, and the first American death of the conflict occurred during the fight.[11]

Seeing that his bazookas couldn't do the job, Nugent called upon the artillery CP at his rear to fire on the enemy. The tanks were momentarily stopped when the heavy shells began to fall, and the following North Korean infantry jumped off their trucks and scattered to the west side of the road. Watching the action from the crest of a small hill, Major Nugent looked to his right and was shocked to see a column of perhaps two thousand North Koreans coming down a trail in the eastern hills. He was slowly being flanked by two North Korean regiments, one that had scattered from the trucks and dispersed to the left of the road and the other in the hills to his right.[12]

Quickly, the major reported to artillery that two regiments were coming down on him and the troops of Task Force Smith, but "the order from there was to hang on." Wire communication between the infantry and artillery was lost as perhaps a hundred shells fell on the invaders. "I then attempted radio communication," said Nugent, "but it was raining quite heavily at the time and the darn radio didn't work. It was impossible to get communication with the artillery."[13]

Losing the support of the big guns was a serious matter, and the infantry officers decided to set up a defensive perimeter around the command post. Nugent stayed with them, but "we were surrounded on three sides." The fighting around the perimeter was heavy, and casualties mounted rapidly. A makeshift aid station was established on the hill's opposite slope, and wounded Americans were brought in throughout the day.[14]

Sometime during the afternoon, withdrawal orders were received, but Major Nugent, either elsewhere at the time or otherwise failing to hear them, found himself alone at the command post. Knowing something was wrong, he left his position and began to run south. He had gone only a short distance, however, when he noted no other GIs and therefore assumed that no withdrawal order had been issued after all. He turned and headed back to the command post. "I managed to get back up to quite near the CP," he remembered, "but I couldn't make it because there was a little too much fire coming in there from the enemy mortars." Staying hidden in brush, Nugent watched the North Korean infantry sweep through the command post and aid station.[15]

From where he was hiding, by 3 P.M. he could clearly observe thirty-three wounded GIs in the aid station. "The enemy came in shooting and bayoneting those people," he recalled. He assumed that the same thing happened to an additional forty wounded who were out of sight.[16]*

As the North Koreans moved by him, it became very quiet, and Nugent, who had served during World War II in both the Pacific and European theaters, decided to follow the enemy south. At 4:20 P.M. he found some brush about three feet high and decided to hide in it until nightfall; then he planned to continue his retreat toward friendly lines. Because he was out of ammunition, he stripped his pistol and flung the various parts in opposite directions. He had laid still for only a short time when three enemy soldiers passed his hideout. "Two of them passed by me," said the major, "but the third one spotted me, evidentially, and fired his rifle from the hip twice and it shook me up pretty much around the head. I made a move to roll over but by that time, with his yelling, there were about ten or twelve of them on me and I became a prisoner of the Koreans."[17]

He was stripped of everything except his basic clothing. Then "they

---

* Indeed, wounded had been left behind. Joseph Goulden notes that "abandoning the wounded on the battlefield also violated American military doctrine. If a soldier knows he will not be left on the ground when hurt, he understandably fights better. Smith's wounded, unfortunately, were not . . . the last to be abandoned to the enemy" (*Korea*, 123).

just beat the hell out of me," using fists, rifle butts, and feet. Bloodied and afraid, Nugent had his hands tied behind his back with telephone wire. He was then marched south, in the direction of the attack.[18]

Around 6 P.M., the major was shoved into a shack, where he found three enlisted men: Sgt. Marvin Talbert, a Sergeant DuBois from St. Petersburg, Florida, and a soldier named King. The four Americans had their biceps and ankles tied, causing excruciating pain, and were forced to stand against a mud wall.[19] In walked a North Korean officer. "UN troops?" he asked. They didn't answer. He pulled a bullet from his cartridge case, took a towel, shined the bullet's nose, held it up, looked at it, shined it some more, looked at it again, and pointed it at Major Nugent. Then he placed the bullet on a low table in front of him. He took a second bullet, a third bullet, and a fourth bullet. At dusk in the dingy mud shack the officer performed this identical ritual three more times for the benefit and terror of his captives. He next unholstered his pistol and gently inserted the shined bullets into the cylinder.

Walking up to him, the officer placed the black, cold muzzle of the weapon against Nugent's forehead. "Sayonara, okay? Sayonara, okay?" The major could only murmur, "No, no." At that moment, he recalled, "I did silently say a prayer or two, maybe three or four." The middle-aged man from Wisconsin believed he would never see his wife and two children again. The officer stared at Nugent for a moment, then gracefully side-stepped to King.

"Sayonara, okay?" Still, there was not a word in reply. He next moved to Sergeant Talbert. "Sayonara, okay?" "No," the American whispered, and then, after a brief pause, he said, "Okay." Hesitating briefly, the sadist slipped over to DuBois. "Sayonara, okay?" Defeated, the GI stared at the Korean and dared, "Go ahead and shoot you yellow bastard, you're going to kill us anyway." At that moment a senior officer entered the room and ordered the prisoners bound together and marched north.[20]

The fourteen-mile trudge in the fast-darkening evening led them past their old position, and they noticed four knocked-out North Korean tanks. They also saw the bodies of five young Americans lying on their stomachs with hands tied behind their backs.

Soon they had to urinate, but the guard with a tommy gun refused to untie their bonds. He pushed them to the side of the dirt road, unzipped their trousers and, in turn, removed and held their penises while they each relieved themselves.

The amount of military traffic headed south was enormous. Although Nugent thought of escape, his hands were tied and the enemy was all about. "It was only a fool's dream to attempt an escape under these conditions," he concluded. The group reached the city of Suwon after dark and were thrust into a small cell.[21]

The following morning they noticed five Koreans, wearing civilian clothes, in the jail with them. The floor was carpeted with blood and human excrement. The door opened a crack, and little rice balls were rolled in. The guard amused himself by aiming the balls to roll through the blood and feces. They ate.[22]

Early that morning of July 6, the four American soldiers were put on a yellow school bus going to Seoul. Also on board were thirty-seven other frightened American GIs. Their decrepit transportation went nearly a mile before breaking down, and everyone debarked into pouring rain and began to walk toward the capital. Southbound traffic was still heavy, and the forty-one prisoners were constantly being forced to the side of the road. During one such delay, as Major Nugent was standing amid the other dripping prisoners, his gray-haired head bowed, a southbound truck suddenly halted and a North Korean soldier jumped off. He ran to Nugent, grabbed the gold-framed spectacles off his face, shoved them into his pocket, and leaped back aboard the waiting vehicle.[23]

They continued walking, and Major Nugent vividly remembers one other experience that day. He saw an American lying on the side of the road. "He had black hair, looked to be pretty well built, quite near six feet I would say. He had his hands wired or tied behind his back and a hole through the back of his head, behind the right ear."[24]

On the evening of his second day of captivity, Major Nugent entered Seoul. During the entire course of the day, since his breakfast of contaminated rice balls, he had been given three small crackers to eat. In times to come he would remember that as a feast.[25]

≫≪

During the morning of July 7, Nugent was escorted to a sparsely furnished room somewhere in Seoul. His interrogation began. For more than twenty-four hours he sat at attention in a straight-backed chair and was asked military questions. He was provided no food, water, or access to toilet facilities and had to relieve himself in his trousers. But in the end he told them nothing, and the following day, worn but still proud, he was sent to the white capitol building in the heart of Seoul.[26]

Prisoners from points south were being funneled into the conquered city, and when Nugent walked into the building he counted seventy-two Americans packed into one room. He quickly discovered that he was the senior officer, and he took command. The remainder of the day passed uneventfully.[27]

Around 7 A.M., guards came into the room and pulled out six men, including Nugent. They were taken into a vacant office and questioned by six newspaper correspondents, apparently communists, including an Englishman named Shapiro. The interview was short, and soon the six Americans were left sitting alone at a long table facing a bare wall. Someone in the background was typing.

Soon a Korean came in, placed blank sheets of paper in front of them, and ordered them to sign their names. They refused, and one American told the Korean, "Go fuck yourself." That seemed not to impress the interpreter, who calmly told them that they were going to make a radio broadcast. They refused again, and the Korean told them to please think about it. They had ten minutes. If, when he came back, the six still refused to cooperate, he was going to shoot all seventy-two Americans.

Nugent was afraid, for "they had convinced me, among others, that they meant what they said. They did that by shooting our people, beating them to death, which they had done and I had seen, and I had seen a lot of it." As the senior officer responsible for the well-being of the group, the major agreed to cooperate. They first signed the blank paper.* M. Sgt. Harvey Baily, also present, felt "pretty sick at heart because I had just signed a piece of paper that I didn't want to sign."[28]

Removed from the room, Nugent was put into a jeep and driven to the radio station in Seoul. He was shoved into a recording booth, a speech was put in front of him, and he was ordered to read. The major, however, had second thoughts and refused. The North Koreans had no intention of

---

* Nugent's signature on the paper was later affixed to surrender leaflets and dropped over UN lines.

being denied their broadcast and began to beat him with their fists and the butt of a tommy gun. A guard pulled out his pistol, palmed it, and broke all the teeth on the left side of Nugent's face. Because he was still not cooperating, a North Korean officer entered with a pair of pliers, and, while the guards held Nugent's right hand, the officer grasped the center finger and began to lift its nail with the pliers. Blood flowed, and shortly thereafter so did words.[29]

At a U.S. monitoring station on Okinawa, although the reception was weak and static and other distortions interrupted the words, James Kashiwahara still could not believe what he was hearing and recording:

> It is really most generous of the North Koreans to forgive us and give us kind consideration for our health, for food, clothing, and habitation. . . .
> We realize we were sent here for the benefit of the monopolistic merchants. . . .
> The armed intervention in Korean internal affairs is quite barbaristic; aggressive action to protect the benefit of the capital monopolists of the U.S. . . .
> Dear friends in Korea: Come over to the People's Army of Korea or turn your guns back to the capital monopolists and peoples who are the real enemies of us—us the toiling peoples.[30]

On his fifth day of captivity, Maj. Ambrose Nugent, no matter how unwillingly, had cooperated with the enemy. Directly to the south, across the East China Sea, James Kashiwahara would be kept very busy for the next three years, recording and transcribing more than 250 similar propaganda broadcasts made by American soldiers from Radio P'yŏngyang and Radio Peking.[31]

>«

The war was going badly for the South Koreans and their American allies. By July 15, the fluid front was centered around the city of Taejon, about fifty miles south of where Task Force Smith fought the first battle of the war and where the first GIs had been captured. Although units of the 24th Infantry Division were flowing onto the beleaguered peninsula, Maj. Gen. William Dean was totally frustrated. Communication among units was nonexistent, and, Dean recalled, "I could not even be certain we still held a solid line northwest of Taejon, and very few important command decisions were made at that time."[32]

Away from his headquarters on the evening of July 19, General Dean and some aides entered an abandoned house in Taejon and fell into a restless sleep. Just before dawn Dean was rudely awakened by the sound of nearby rifle fire. The city was a war zone and about to fall, and Dean, lacking communication with his various commands, decided to do a little fighting himself. Leaving the house with an aide and Korean interpreter, he stopped a truck that had a mounted 75–mm recoiless rifle. "Perhaps," he thought "we could do something about a couple of tanks."

From dawn until late afternoon, General Dean and his party of two hunted tanks in the streets of Taejon. In the first encounter, they met two T-34s at an intersection, fired four or five rounds, and missed. They later met another tank and, from a range of a hundred yards, missed again. In the third encounter, a direct hit destroyed a T-34.

By late afternoon, Dean had returned to headquarters. The decision was made to withdraw what was left of the 34th Regiment from Taejon in two columns, with Dean in the last group. When the lead column reached the southern part of the city, it was ambushed by North Koreans firing down from windows and rooftops of the taller buildings. The column was stalled, and Dean's driver, attempting to get the jeep up to the battle, missed a turn. The general found himself on strange streets in the war-torn city. Whenever he found wounded GIs, he instructed the driver to pick them up. Soon, however, the vehicle was so cramped that Dean got out and ordered the driver to continue south with the wounded.

The tide of American soldiers retreating southward seemed endless, and Dean soon caught a ride on an overcrowded half-track. It wasn't long, however, before they were once again ambushed and forced to continue on foot. That night, walking on loose soil, General Dean thought he heard running water and moved toward the sound. Because of the darkness, he didn't realize he was on a ridge. Suddenly, he found himself falling, unable to stop, down a steep slope. The general was knocked unconscious. When he awoke, he discovered that his shoulder was broken, blood was running down his face from a deep cut on his head, and "my abdomen where I'd had an operation a year before hurt fearfully." He was alone.

In terrible pain, for thirty-five days General Dean wandered around South Korea, begging or stealing food and constantly on the lookout for North Korean patrols. He escaped capture at least six times. On August 25, however, two civilians offered to lead him to the American positions but instead reported him to the North Koreans, who went to his hiding place and captured him. The two men who made the report received $5 each, and the enemy had in their possession a division commander and the highest-ranking American officer to become a POW during the Korean War.

>«

Maj. Ambrose Nugent, together with all the other American POWs imprisoned in the South Korean capitol building, were herded out in mid-July and formed into a column of twos. Then they were paraded through the city and occasionally spat upon by South Korean students but safely reached the main Seoul railway station around 7:30 P.M. There they met other captured men. Within an hour, several hundred American soldiers had been squeezed into cattle cars. Their destination was P'yŏngyang, capital of communist North Korea.[33]

It was the height of the Korean summer, and temperatures were often above 90 degrees. For the two days it took to travel north the men were given neither food nor water. Once they reached P'yŏngyang station, they were unloaded and forced to kneel in rows. A small bowl of fish heads was given to each of them, in addition to some water. While the famished Americans greedily ate the fish, photographers recorded the scene.

The next morning, the GIs were once again formed into a double column and paraded through P'yŏngyang. The victorious North Korean army marched the humiliated soldiers of the supposedly invincible United States through streets crowded with civilians, North Korean officers, Soviet officers and women, and many other representatives of various communist-bloc countries. The long line of fatigued Americans was paced by a slow-moving jeep, and their flanks were guarded by armed soldiers and cavalry. They were spat upon, cursed, and occasionally stoned. As the march wore on, Capt. Herb Marlatt "saw a gray-haired gentleman almost collapse to the rear of me. Someone yelled, 'Help me carry this man!' and I started to drop back. The guard ran the bayonet in the seat of my pants but anyway, we dropped back." The man who needed help was Major Nugent. Marlatt and others helped carry the totally exhausted officer the rest of the way. The march, which took about two hours, ended in a temporary camp on the northern outskirts of the city.[34]

During the last week of July 1950, while General Dean was busy evading the enemy in his attempt to reach American lines, captured U.S. soldiers from all over South Korea were herded to the collection point just north of P'yŏngyang. Within three days after Nugent's arrival, 715 enlisted men and thirty-five officers had joined him. They remained in the camp for about six weeks.[35]

Although the enemy fed them enough to survive, there were other problems. Capt. Alexander Boysen, M.D., a surgeon with the 3d Battalion, 21st Regiment, 24th Division, had been captured a week after Nugent, when his unit was overrun. The men, he noted, were "bitter, depressed, and because of their present predicament, fearful of the future. The general atmosphere of terror further contributed to demoralizing the men. There were constant threats of being shot if you did not concur with the North Korean requests." Beatings were common, and Maj. Marlin Green recalled, "It didn't take much to get a Korean to beat you up; it didn't take anything, just get close to one is all it took."[36]

Medical facilities were practically nonexistent. Doctor Boysen "had merthiolate; we had some iodine; we had some sulfadiazine; then we had some aspirin. We had some diarrhea powders that contained ipeucate, or an opium derivative; we had a few bandages. I believe that was the extent of it."[37]

Captives were warned that they were not prisoners of war but political prisoners and would be treated as such. "As long as we served their usefulness we may [have] remain[ed] alive," Captain Marlatt remembered. "But if they felt that their reasons were sufficient to do away with us, they felt they could do so at any time; and they kept us constantly reminded of that during our period at P'yŏngyang."[38]

On September 5, all prisoners in P'yŏngyang were taken to the railhead and shipped to Manp'o, North Korea. The journey took a week, and when they reached the town on the Yalu River in central North Korea they were quartered there for only a few days before being moved again. For the next month and a half, approximately 750 dirty, unshaven prisoners were shuffled from one dingy village to another, although they usually remained within a ten-mile radius of Manp'o.[39]

October 1950 was, said Captain Boysen, "a period of general confusion for the Koreans as well as the Americans," who trudged up and down the southern bank of the Yalu River and back and forth through tiny villages. It had been only a month before, on September 15, 1950, when American soldiers and marines swarmed ashore at Inchon, twenty-two miles west of Seoul. These troops drove inland and liberated the South Korean capital on September 26. Then they prepared to cut across the waist of Korea to isolate the enemy in the south, after which the Allies would attack north. A few short weeks after the historic landing, the Pusan perimeter had been relieved, the North Korean army shattered, and approximately 125,000 prisoners had fallen into UN hands. On October 20, P'yŏngyang was taken, and UN and ROK forces were rushing headlong toward the Yalu.[40]

During the last week of October, Major Nugent and the others stayed in a cornfield. They dug holes, lined them with grass and cornstalks, and lived in them. The cold was coming on. Food was poor, and, Doctor Boysen noticed, it was almost a daily occurrence for a prisoner to die from the effects of hunger and prolonged exposure.[41]

On the last day of October 1950 (Halloween), the North Korean army guards and officers were relieved of their prisoners in the cornfield by the North Korean security police, the "Red Gestapo." It was the eve of All Saints' Day. Enter the Tiger.[42]

>«

The Tiger had no name that any American ever discovered, and he seemed to have only one function: to move the Manp'o cornfield prisoners very rapidly to the northeast. The only things anyone knew about the Security Police officer-in-charge of the march was that he was short, stocky, did not speak English, and was nicknamed "the Tiger." They also soon discovered that he had an absolute disregard for human life.

On the morning of November 1, the cornfield prisoners were gathered together and formed into fourteen sections of fifty each for an eighty-mile hike. The American officer who commanded each section was ordered to keep it together and at a distance from the section ahead of it. In the last section were fifty-nine civilians, captured when the invaders entered Seoul. These noncombatants included Catholic priests, missionaries, diplomats, women (including a number of nuns), and seven children, the youngest being two.[43]

Before they left, the Tiger, with seeming goodwill, announced that the sick and lame, if they didn't think they could make the march, should step out and lie down in the cornfield. A number of thankful people accepted his invitation.* The sections of fifty then began to march toward the desolate, northeastern reaches of Korea. After the column had disappeared into the barren mountains, those in the cornfield were shot. Although there were no witnesses to the incident, gunfire was clearly heard and the victims were never seen again.[44]

The Tiger halted the column a few hours after it set out. He had noticed that the sections were starting to get too close to each other and men were flowing from one to another. Prisoners had also begun to fall out of the line of march. The Tiger walked over to a little knoll on the right and ordered the officers in charge of each group to join him. There he berated them for their lack of control. Commissioner Herbert Lord of the London Salvation Army, a staunch anticommunist who had been in Korea for forty years and spoke the language fluently, interpreted for him. The Tiger sent nine officers back to their sections and kept five. The men who waited, listless and exhausted in crowds beside the trail, could see the commissioner begging him to keep only one. Finally, the Tiger agreed. The man chosen was a Lieutenant Thornton.

The young man was a remarkable soldier and liked by all his compatriots. He constantly attempted to keep up the spirits of those around him. One of the guards tied Thornton's hands behind his back, and then the Tiger took a dirty rag, blindfolded the lieutenant, and ordered the entire column to turn their backs and not look. Some of the marchers, however, peeked and watched the Tiger pull his pistol. Standing one pace in front of Lieutenant Thornton, he put a bullet into his skull. Two GIs were ordered to dig a grave and bury him.[45]

The march resumed. It lasted eight days. The prisoners marched all day and stopped at night. Doctor Boysen estimated that they were each given about ten ounces of some sort of grain to eat per day. The strong got weak, and the weak died.[46]

Fr. William Booth, an American Catholic priest and secretary to Bishop Patrick Byrne, had been in Korea for twenty years, was a prisoner of the Japanese during World War II for six months, and now was a captive again. He was in the last section and remembers that on November 2, it started "snowing and was quite cold. The first member of the civilian group fell

---

* The exact number is unknown, but estimates suggest that it may have been as high as fifty.

out at that point, a Sister; she was a little woman of seventy years old." The guards flanking the section would not allow anyone to fall out to help, and the prisoners soon heard a shot.[47]

Anyone who fell out was killed. Some prisoners who were carrying others eventually collapsed themselves and were shot. Everyone tried to help, including Major Nugent (who had a serious lung-congestion problem) and Doctor Boysen. Fr. Paul Villemont, an eighty-two-year-old French priest, marched with Monsignor Quinlan, holding him up on one side while another priest held him on the other.[48]

Father Booth passed a young American soldier sitting by the roadside, and the youth said to him, "Please, Father, please give me a gun. Do you have a gun?" Booth saw that the boy was broken and terrified and asked him, "What do you want a gun for?" "I want to shoot myself," the soldier replied, and the priest walked sadly on. He knew the North Koreans could be relied upon for that.[49]

As for the children, the Tiger allowed the two-year-old to be carried on her father's back, but the rest walked. A six-year-old made the complete march, holding her father's hand the entire time.[50]

The call of nature took place while walking. As the men began to enter the initial stages of dysentery, brown liquid soiled their summer combat uniforms.[51]

On the third night, a stopover was made at a small schoolhouse in an unknown village. The Tiger tried to jam all the prisoners into the building but could fit only about three hundred. The next day they left behind four dead men who had been smothered during the night.[52]

On the fourth day, the Tiger ordered that no prisoner was to help another prisoner. If a man couldn't make it on his own, he had to fall out. M. Sgt. Austin Flack remembers that anyone who stopped that day, even to relieve himself, was shot. "There was a man that developed himself a name of 'Burp-gun Charley,'" said Flack. "He done a lot of shooting that day."[53]

"Balli, balli (quickly, quickly)," screamed the guards, and Father Booth kept hearing shots behind him. That day, November 4, 1950, twenty-eight U.S. soldiers were executed on the march.[54]

Several Carmelite nuns who had worn out their sandals walked barefoot over jagged rocks and through the first light snow of winter.[55]

The next day, twenty-two more Americans were executed.[56]

The death march was over on November 8. In eight days, nearly a hundred people had been killed. The march was a taste of things to come. After they reached their isolated destination in northeastern Korea on the Yalu River that formed the border with Manchuria, the Tiger didn't go away. He remained their master, and their killer, for another three months.[57]

>«

After reaching the town of Chunggang-jin, the final destination of the death march, the prisoners were put into the yard of a schoolhouse and searched. The Tiger then decided that they needed exercise and prescribed an hour of physical training for everyone, young and old, military and civilian, men, women, and children.[58]

The day after the march, Anglican Sr. Mary Claire died. So did Father Villemot, Father Gombert (who was seventy), and another priest who was seventy-five. Shortly thereafter, Bishop Byrne, the apostolic delegate in Korea, died.[59]

The group remained at the schoolhouse for a little over a week, and on November 19 was moved six miles westward to a small village. When the prisoners entered the village, the North Korean civilians occupying the scattered houses were either evicted or relegated to a single room in their homes, and the captives were billeted in the empty rooms. The area, where they were to remain until the middle of March 1951, became known as "the shacks." Each house had two rooms and a kitchen, and each room was about ten feet square. The only furnishing was a straw mat on the floor.[60]

Father Booth was quartered with Major Nugent, who was very ill and refused to eat. The men practically force-fed him to help him survive. The cold was intense, and the Yalu was so frozen that, Father Booth remembered, "They used to draw bull carts across the river, loaded bull carts, and the snow was frozen on top of the river, and there were nine people in this cart and the wheels made no dents in the snow."[61]

The conditions were appalling. Not only did the exhausted prisoners suffer from the cold, but they also found that food was practically nonexistent. They were at the mercy of the Tiger's generosity. As one survivor put it, "A head of cabbage and a pint of beans would make five hundred gallons of soup without a bit of trouble."[62]

The room that Maj. Marlin Green occupied was so crowded that when guards wouldn't let people go to the latrine, their defecation would splatter those near them. There was no water with which to wash. When a prisoner was allowed to go to the building that housed two latrines for about six hundred, there would always be long lines of soldiers, swaying side by side, awaiting their turn. Dysentery was a serious problem, and men began to evacuate where they stood. The guards beat those whom they saw doing this and often smeared the captives' faces with excrement.[63]

At the shacks, the Tiger's men proved that they could fully live up to the brutal standards he had established. Each guard was, in his own right, an apprentice Tiger. Physical torture was common. One method was to have a man kneel on the ground and then kick him in the chin. Another was to make a soldier kneel next to a building then grab him by the hair and butt his head against the wall until he fell over. A more spectacular torture, of which the guards were fond, was to strip a GI naked, make him kneel in the snow, and pour cold water over him. Such incidents were neither isolated nor uncommon, and they created terror among the prisoners.[64]

The captives had only one goal during the winter of 1950–51: Survival. Death was very close. The men knew when it was coming or when they were in its presence. Major Green recalls people getting sick, "Then they would get what we would call the death stare. They would get a look in their eyes . . . , they would be looking way off in the distance sometime, and you could usually tell that they wasn't going to last long. . . . I have seen men sit around when they would get their meal, maybe they would take one bite out of their millet ball, and when you would look around again they would be sitting there, dead, with the millet ball in their hand."[65]

Death was becoming acceptable. When Father Booth woke in the morning and saw dead men next to him, men with whom he had talked just a few hours before, it did not affect him as one might expect. "Normally," he said, "you would feel sorry and feel—make something of it, but actually it didn't impress you that way; it didn't, it just didn't register. I mean, it didn't seem to make any difference. I mean, your senses, your emotions, your whole mental outlook was sort of numb."[66]

≫≪

In mid-March 1951, all the prisoners, both civilian and military, were moved again to an old Japanese army barrack about six miles west. The

Tiger was relieved, and regular North Korean army personnel took over. The barrack and surrounding area was officially designated Camp 7.[67]*

Camp 7 consisted of one frame building containing very large rooms, with Russian-built stoves (that hardly ever worked) in each room. The civilians were quartered with the officers until May 1951, when they were moved across the Yalu into Manchuria. Although men continued to die, with the establishment of this camp the worst was over.[68]

Of the approximately 750 men, women, and children who left the cornfield in Manp'o for northeastern Korea, thirty-eight civilians out of fifty-nine survived the death march and the shacks. Only 280 of 650 enlisted men lived, as did twelve officers, including Major Nugent, out of thirty-five. Father Booth observed:

> I don't believe, personally, that anyone can understand these things unless they have experienced them. I mean, you cannot get the feeling; that's all there is to it, of having dirt on your body, and lice, and not being able to sleep, and being hungry all the time, and the cold, the surroundings. Not having any news, either in or out, not having anything to read, to have to lie on a hard floor twelve to fourteen hours at night, and to have dysentery, diarrhea all the time.
>
> The mental torture of being under communism is so great. The thing is so hideous in itself, to have to live that way. Well, of course you would but if it was a question of going on indefinitely, you would much rather die. I mean, there is no decency about it. I mean, there is a repugnance about it, a repulsiveness that you cannot, that has an effect on the mind. I mean, the mental attitude that is just so contrary to everything that we hold so dear. By that, of course, I mean truth and decency, and goodness, and there is none of it there.[69]

Notes

1. Background information can be found throughout volume 14 of the Maj. Ambrose Nugent, USA, Transcripts; see also Nugent Transcripts, 12:3271 and 12:3275–79.
2. Ibid., 12:3279.
3. Ibid.; Goulden, *Korea,* 116.
4. Nugent Transcripts, 1:44, 12:3279.
5. Ibid., 12:3280.
6. Ibid., 12:3281–82.

---

* Camp 7 existed from March to October 1951, when it was disbanded and all POWs were moved to Camp 3.

7. Ibid.

8. Ibid., 12:3282; Goulden, *Korea,* 116.

9. Nugent Transcripts, 12:3283.

10. Ibid.

11. Ibid., 12:3283–84.

12. Ibid., 12:3284.

13. Ibid., 12:3285.

14. Ibid., 12:3286–87.

15. Ibid., 12:3287.

16. Ibid., 12:3288; Goulden, *Korea,* 123.

17. Nugent Transcripts, 12:3288–89.

18. Ibid., 12:3288–90.

19. Ibid., 2:198–201.

20. The entire scenario in the shack can be found in the Nugent Transcripts, 1:44, 2:205–13, 12:3271, 12:3290–94, and 12:3515.

21. Ibid., 12:3301.

22. Ibid., 12:3305–6.

23. Ibid., 12:3312.

24. Ibid., 12:3322.

25. Ibid., 12:3313.

26. Ibid., 12:3316–17, 12:3322.

27. Ibid., 3:338, 3:462–63, 3:488, 12:3314, 12:3345.

28. Nugent Transcripts, 3:375, 3:495, 12:3328–39, see also 3:397, 12:3356, and 3:358.

29. Ibid., 12:3330–39.

30. Ibid., 3:572–76.

31. Ibid., 3:539.

32. General Dean's evasion and subsequent capture can be found in Goulden, *Korea,* 147–50; see also Dean, *General Dean's Story,* passim.

33. Nugent Transcripts, 4:877–78, 12:3347.

34. Ibid., 4:877–78.

35. Ibid., 1:146.

36. Ibid., 1:111, 4:633, 8:2012.

37. Ibid., 4:630.

38. Ibid., 4:879.

39. Ibid., 1:112, 8:2020, 8:2136.

40. Ibid., 1:112.

41. Ibid., see also 4:750.

42. Ibid., 4:750.

43. Ibid., 8:1964–65, 8:1969, 12:3439.

44. Ibid., 4:752–55, 8:2043.

45. Ibid., 1:112, 4:752–55, 8:1967, 9:2185.

46. Ibid., 1:112.

47. Ibid., 8:1961, see also 8:1994.

48. Ibid., 8:1965, 8:1968, 8:2042, 12:3348.

49. Ibid., 8:1966.

50. Ibid., 8:1969.

51. Ibid., 8:2040.
52. Ibid., 8:2041.
53. Ibid., 4:756–57.
54. Ibid., 8:1965–66.
55. Ibid., 8:1969.
56. Ibid., 8:2042.
57. Ibid., 4:758, 8:1970, 8:2043.
58. Ibid., 4:693–94, 5:966–68, 8:1975, 8:2044.
59. Ibid., 8:1975, 8:1983.
60. Ibid., 4:692–93, 5:966–68, 8:1976.
61. Ibid., 8:1977, see also 8:1985.
62. Ibid., 4:750.
63. Ibid., 8:2046.
64. Ibid., 8:1980, 8:2044, 8:2054, 8:2137.
65. Ibid., 8:2044, see also 8:1990 and 8:2052.
66. Ibid., 8:1989–90.
67. Ibid., 4:692–93.
68. Ibid., see also 5:966–68, 8:1985, and 8:1992.
69. Ibid., 8:1996–97, see also 1:146 and 8:1993.

TWO

Into the Valley
of Death

That day—it is the Lord Yahweh who speaks—
I will make the sun go down at noon,
and darken the earth in broad daylight.
I am going to turn your feasts into funerals,
all your singing into lamentation;
I will have your loins all in sackcloth,
your heads all shaved.
I will make it a mourning like the
mourning for an only son,
as long as it lasts it will be like
a day of bitterness.

—Amos VIII:9–10

During the last week of October 1950, while Maj. Ambrose Nugent and his group camped out in the cornfield near Manp'o, the Chinese army intervened in the war on the side of the North Koreans.

The first (and only) UN unit ever to reach the Yalu was the 7th Regiment of the 6th ROK Division, accompanied by their American advisor, forty-three-year-old Lt. Col. Harry Fleming. Commissioned a second lieutenant in 1943, Fleming, who was married, had attended St. Petersburg Junior College, where he lettered in baseball, football, and boxing. He had arrived in Korea only a month earlier from duty in Wisconsin. On October 26, 1950, Fleming was the first American of the Korean conflict to stare down at the Yalu River and into Manchuria from the bluff of a hill in the river town of Ch'osan. He didn't know it at the time, but along the same river and only thirty-five miles to the northeast were Major Nugent and the other prisoners. He also didn't know that he would be the last free American during the war years to look into Manchuria from North Korea.[1]

Infantry officer Harry Fleming and the 7th ROK Regiment thought that reaching the Yalu had ended the war. "We put out our defenses and actually thought that we were there on occupation duty," he remembered. "I listened to the radio from Seoul and I heard speeches that were being made as to the tremendous victory by the United Nations in Korea, and our morale was pretty good." At that very moment, however, Colonel Fleming and his entire regiment were being outflanked and encircled by the Chinese. His support unit, the 2d Regiment of the 6th ROK Division, located to his rear and accompanied by their senior American advisor, Lt. Col. Paul Liles, was fighting for its life.[2]

Born in 1916 in Savannah, Georgia, Paul Liles was the eldest of four boys. When he was a few years old, his father, an employee of the Bell System, moved the family to Bloomington, Alabama, where he grew up. After high school, he entered Birmingham Southern College, where he remained for three years, majoring in English and history. The military was in his blood, however, and in 1937 he jumped at a chance to go to the U.S. Military Academy. His father died while Liles was in his plebe year, but he stuck it out and graduated from West Point in 1941 as a second lieutenant.

During World War II, Liles saw action in the Pacific. After the war, he participated in the occupation of Japan, served on the general staff of the Intelligence Division at the War Department in Washington, and finally was an instructor at the Infantry School at Fort Benning, Georgia. He was married in 1944 and became the father of two boys, of whom he said, "I'd like to send the eldest one to either West Point or Annapolis. The youngest is a little bit too quiet. He might be a doctor." In September 1950, while at Fort Benning, Paul Liles received orders for Korea. He arrived at Pusan on October 12 and was immediately assigned as senior advisor to the 2d Regiment.[3]

On October 24, 1950, Colonel Liles reported to division headquarters, where he met Harry Fleming. Colonel Fleming was ordered to move with his unit and, according to Liles, when the 7th actually reached Ch'osan it was "the only unit to reach its official objective in the Korean War." The 2d Regiment had orders to back up Fleming. "At that time," said Liles, "the division was pursuing the broken remnants of the North Korean Army."[4]

Before he was permitted to join his regiment, though, he was given a heartbreaking job: burying the dead. Thirty-one American soldiers had been executed in a railroad tunnel by fleeing North Koreans, and Colonel Liles was in charge of the South Korean soldiers who had the ghastly job of putting them into their graves. The sight of the slain GIs shook him: "Each prisoner had some dog tags in his pocket, anywhere from one to four and, of course, some of them had none. I was impressed by the emaciated condition of these men. They were Caucasian, all of them had long beards, wearing American uniforms of the summer issue, barefooted, had been shot in the head and face and neck by small-caliber bullets. They were obviously starved and a few of them had shriveled turnips in their pockets."[5]

The following day, October 25, Liles reached the 2d Regiment. The unit was in a heavy firefight north of Onjong with what he later claimed to be a Chinese division. The Chinese were blocking the northward movement of the regiment, and they fought all day and into the night. By "the next morning," recalled Liles, "it became obvious that we were cut off by a road block in the rear." When the ROKs discovered that they were virtually surrounded, they panicked. The regiment began falling apart, "obviously due to ill training among the South Korean troops at that time."[6]

On the morning of October 26, with Colonel Fleming and the 7th Regiment in the town of Ch'osan thinking the war was over, Colonel Liles and the broken 2d Regiment were trapped to the south. Wanting to save as many vehicles and howitzers as possible, Liles formed a truck column and put the ROK wounded into the vehicles. "I did not think the enemy could possibly have enough strength in our rear to stop us," he said. "I was sadly mistaken." The colonel sat in the lead truck, but the column didn't get very far in the attempt to pierce the block to the south; heavy and accurate fire stopped it. Everyone jumped from the trucks and ran up the side of a mountain. "The South Koreans quickly outdistanced me," Liles said, "and after a while, I was alone."[7] Taking a rest, the thirty-four-year-old officer looked down on the abandoned column and saw that "the Chinese were searching around for survivors. I watched them bayonet some wounded—they pulled the wounded off the trucks and bayoneted them. They seemed especially skilled in it."[8]

For two days he evaded the Chinese, but "near noon on the 28th of October, I was attempting to bypass some enemy whom I saw entrenched. I saw them and turned around to sneak away when a sentinel whom I had not seen had his rifle leveled at me. I acted as if I had not seen him and moved on, but he called out to the Chinese platoon and in a twinkling of an eye, I was looking down the bores of about forty rifles."[9]

≫≪

On the southern bank of the Yalu on October 26, Lt. Col. Harry Fleming admitted that "we had extended our supplies and communications to the point where we . . . just had no contact with the rear whatsoever except through radio." On that morning, Radio Seoul was broadcasting victory. In early afternoon, Fleming received a radio message from division: He'd been outflanked, and the supporting regiment to the rear "had been completely decimated in battle, with great loss." He was ordered to pull the 7th out and retreat to Unsan about sixty miles to the south.[10] Within a few hours, the 7th Regiment was in a fight. "Actually," Fleming reported, "we were attacking to the south at that time." When asked the location of his headquarters, the colonel replied, "There was no regimental headquarters. I was regimental headquarters."[11]

For four days they fought and marched south. On the morning of October 30, they were fired upon near a rice paddy by what Fleming took to be a Chinese patrol of about twenty-five men. He set up a firing line of approximately fifty ROK troops at the edge of the paddy. When firing began, most of the South Koreans ran. Fleming called over the interpreter and "told him to go in the direction in which I had seen the Korean officers go, and to contact them and tell them to deploy the men that were with them around the flank and bring fire on the enemy. In the meantime, we would hold them off."[12] Within a few minutes,

> there was an explosion which, . . was from a mortar of the approximate size of a 60 millimeter . . . [which] exploded to my left rear, and the concussion . . . rendered me unconscious. . . . The first recollection I [had] is some-

thing was hitting me in the head. I was in a prone position, and I turned around to look up to see what it was, and it was this Chinaman standing there with a burp gun right on me. . . . He was tapping me in the head with his foot. Apparently they were going down the line and anybody that could not get up, they were shooting them. . . . When I looked at him I started to get up, and he reached down, grabbed a hold of me, and dragged me to my feet.[13]

Fleming was bleeding in a few places but not badly hurt. A few feet away, however, he saw his assistant, Capt. Alfred Roesch, severely wounded and lying in the paddy. Fleming started over to help him but was pushed back by a soldier with a rifle with fixed bayonet. "And while he was holding me," said Colonel Fleming, "I was at bayonet point, the same one, I believe, that actually got me first, stood over Capt. Roesch with this burp gun and opened it up into him—killed him."[14]

Harry Fleming was the only one of the fifty men on the firing line to survive and the only surviving American of the four-thousand-man ROK 7th Regiment. Of the South Koreans, only twenty-five officers and five hundred enlisted personnel survived the Chinese attack.[15]

≫≪

Claude Batchelor was born on December 14, 1931, in Goldthwaite, Texas, a small town near Waco. He was the second of eight children from a poor family. Batchelor was nine when his father, who held various jobs during the depression and then found work in the oil fields, moved them to Kermit. There young Claude, who grew up to be of medium build and height, became a Boy Scout, went to school, and played the trumpet in the school band.[16]

He was a restless boy and at fifteen ran away from home for a few weeks. In the sixth week of his junior year, he quit high school and decided to join the navy. The recruiter wasn't available at the enlistment center, so Batchelor joined the army instead. He was only sixteen, but he persuaded his mother to sign a statement saying he was eighteen. On November 16, 1948, only four months after joining the army and still a month shy of his seventeenth birthday, Claude Batchelor was on a ship bound for Yokohama, Japan.[17]

Being a good trumpet player, Batchelor was assigned to the 1st Cavalry Division band. A month after reaching Japan he met a Japanese woman, and six months later, in a Shinto ceremony, they were married. He was seventeen and a half.[18]

After the war broke out, young Batchelor's trumpet was taken away, and he was handed a rifle. Assigned to the 8th Cavalry Regiment, 1st Cavalry Division, he, together with thousands of other young men, was shipped to Korea in the middle of July 1950. For more than three months he fought the North Korean army, and by the end of October he and his regiment had advanced to about sixty miles above P'yŏngyang.[19]

On the evening of October 31, 1950, three days after Colonel Liles surrendered, a day after Colonel Fleming submitted, and the same day that the Tiger took command of Major Nugent's group in the cornfield, Cpl. Claude Batchelor and fourteen other men were sent on patrol. Their mission was to make contact with an outpost on a high, steep hill north of the company's defensive perimeter.

After cautiously making their way up that hill, they heard explosions behind them; turning, they saw the night sky illuminated with flares. They were unable to communicate with their headquarters. Around midnight, fifteen other GIs joined the group and reported that the company had been overrun. The thirty cut-off men were commanded by a lieutenant, the only officer among them.[20]

They spent a restless night on the side of the hill and moved south the following morning, hoping to encounter friendly troops. They hiked in the barren mountains but then stumbled onto a road and for the first time saw Chinese soldiers. According to Batchelor, "We saw them about the same time they spotted us, so we opened fire." As the enemy ran for cover, the thirty isolated Americans also retreated. They continued to march south, but at dusk the exhausted men decided to spend the night in a small valley.[21]

Early the next morning, November 2, they packed their gear and continued south. They saw more enemy troops during the day but stayed away from them. They spent the second night of their journey in another valley but couldn't sleep. Directly on the ridge above them, they heard Chinese soldiers talking, and they remained awake all night, listening and watching.[22]

As dawn broke on November 3, the voices above them stilled, and it was time to move again. But which way? They knew that thousands of Chinese blocked southward movement, so they determined to hike back north. They spent the night in the same valley in which they were the evening before.[23]

No one in the small band of lost GIs had eaten since being cut off, and the following morning they decided that they must find food. Shortly after they started out, they saw two of the enemy with an ROK prisoner. They killed the two Chinese, but the South Korean informed them that the situation was hopeless. They were surrounded, and there was no way out. Across the valley, however, was a small village where possibly they could beg or steal food. They decided to try for it.[24] After crossing the valley and a small river, they entered the village. Corporal Batchelor remembered:

> At the first house we passed—about fifty yards from us—we saw some Chinese soldiers outside looking curiously at us. The word was passed around to keep on walking and not try anything, although we should be extremely alert. We walked on by, both groups looking but not attempting anything. Halfway through this village, we stopped at a Korean house and asked for food. They were extremely scared and said they had no food, so we moved on. On approaching the last house, we saw more Chinese soldiers looking at us. When we got closer, they started running back into the compound. We immediately circled the place, covering it with rifle and grenade fire.

As fast as they could run, they crossed the valley, machine gun bullets flying by their heads. It was a close call, but they safely made it across and set up a night defense on a ridge. Throughout the night, they saw flashlights blinking all around them.[25]

On the morning of November 5, it was all over for the hungry, tired, frightened, and lost patrol on a ridge near the town of Unsan. Around 8 in the morning:

> Someone said, "Here they come," and as I looked up I saw one right above me. The group made a mad scramble for a little hill just below. There we met more of them, so we stopped and attempted to fight it out. We fought for almost two hours; two of our men were killed and several wounded. The situation looked hopeless but we were all afraid of capture so we kept firing. Eventually the lieutenant said that the situation was hopeless and we might be better off to surrender. That threw the men into chaos. Some of them were waving yellow scarves shouting surrender and some kept on firing, yelling "no we don't." Eventually, everything got straightened out and we all decided to surrender.[26]

The Chinese stood and motioned for everyone to throw down his rifle and put his hands in the air. Then, Corporal Batchelor said, they "lined us up before a ditch where a soldier came in front of us with a British-made Bern gun. I remember I thought we were going to be shot and I was wondering what it would feel or be like. I thought of the possibility of falling when they fired and playing dead, wondering at the same time what the others were thinking. I turned to the left—I was on the extreme right—and saw a Chinese officer coming down the line, taking our hands off our heads and shaking them in a 'gesture of friendship.'" They were taken to a house and given food and cigarettes.* That night many more captured men from the regiment were brought into the area.[27]

Batchelor's unit, the 8th Cavalry, which occupied a position near Unsan, was a wreck. While he and his group were running and hiding, a short distance to the south the regiment had been taking an terrible beating. The night attack of October 31 and November 1 shattered the unit.

Sgt. James Gallagher was only nineteen when he was captured. Born and raised in Brooklyn, the eighth-grade graduate had delivered telegrams for Western Union before joining the army and becoming a prisoner of the Chinese. His outfit, the 3d Battalion, 8th Cavalry, was pinned down near Unsan. For two nights there was desperate fighting, but word finally came that they were on their own. Gallagher and three hundred other men were to try to punch their way south to the newly established front lines. The Chinese trap, however, was much too tight, and the men surrendered in droves. Gallagher laid down his arms on November 5.[28]

Cpl. Edward Dickenson, twenty, had completed the sixth grade.** He had been in the army only seven months when he surrendered. Born in Big Stone Gap, Virginia, he was one of thirteen children whose father was a carpenter and farmer. While with the 8th Cavalry, he became separated from his unit, K Company, and on November 5 the enemy found him hiding under brush at the foot of a small mountain. "At the time of my

---

* This "gesture of friendship" was not at all uncommon, and many former POWs tell a similar story.

** The U.S. Army of the 1950s cannot be compared to the army of today. Five years after World War II ended, the army was taking anyone who wanted to join, as were the other services. Many of the men were high school dropouts, some had criminal records, and some were essentially illiterate.

capture," said Dickenson, "it seemed that the Chinese soldiers outnumbered the United Nations soldiers about seven or eight to one." He wasn't far off.[29]

Cpl. Harold Dunn was born in Fulton, New York, and had completed the ninth grade. As a youth he had been a maverick and had run away from home three times before joining the army in 1947, a month after his seventeenth birthday. The tall, heavily built Dunn was assigned as a scout with the Intelligence and Reconnaissance Section of Headquarters Company, 3d Battalion, 8th Cavalry. On the night of November 1, he was sent on patrol with his section, and they ran into the Chinese. Dunn was wounded in both legs, and the patrol retreated, leaving behind five wounded men, including him. The following morning, the Chinese came upon them and made them prisoners of war.[30]

>«

The Chinese were in the war with thirty divisions, amounting to 180,000 men. After the first massive blow, they withdrew into the mountains, and the front lay quiet. The last three weeks of November 1950 were the quietest of the war. Then all hell broke loose.

Short but muscular, M. Sgt. William Olson was from Jamestown, New York, and a professional boxer before he joined the army in January 1934. The tough combat veteran of World War II was thirty-six when he was captured at Koto-ri, a small town about ten miles south of the lower tip of the Chosin Reservoir. At 5 P.M. on November 29, the Chinese attacked Olson's heavy weapons company of the 1st Battalion, 31st Infantry Regiment, 7th Infantry Division. For twelve hours they battled the numerically superior enemy, but by 5 A.M. they had been surrounded. The choice was either surrender or die, and the officers decided to surrender the 130 survivors (many of them wounded) to the enemy.[31]

Lt. Jefferson Erwin from Blanchard, Oklahoma, quit high school in his first year and in July 1936 joined the army. By 1941 he made first sergeant and in 1943 was promoted to warrant officer. During World War II he fought in the South Pacific and in July 1950 left for Korea with the 2d Division artillery. In the middle of October 1950, he was meritoriously awarded a battlefield commission as a second lieutenant.[32] Erwin was captured on December 1:

At the end of November, all the division artillery was cut off near Kunu-ri—about eighty miles southwest of the Chosin Reservoir. We had all these long columns of vehicles there in the road—the Chinese were shooting at us from hills, dropping mortars in on us for two days—and on the night of 30 November, the decision was finally made by the senior officers to destroy and abandon the equipment and take to the hills. I had one truck loaded with gasoline in the middle of the convoy of the service battery, so I had a couple of sergeants chop a couple of holes into the gas tanks. We tossed a match in there where all the trucks were bunched; all of them loaded up with ammunition. There was no question of all of them being destroyed. Then we took to the hills and all through the night I could hear these ammunitions going off in the road block there.

During the night there was one continuous skirmish with the Chinese patrols and Korean patrols—everything we came in contact with. Early the next morning, after daylight, we were finally surrounded and I had about fifteen men and myself in a bomb crater by the side of the road near Kunu-ri. The Chinese were attacking across an open field and while they were coming across the field, as long as we had ammunition it was just like shooting fish in a barrel. We ran out of ammunition so there was nothing to do except to be captured or killed, so the Chinese lieutenant came on up and captured us.[33]

In just two days the United Nations command lost eleven thousand men, either killed, wounded, or captured. Most of the action took place in the vicinity of the Chosin Reservoir and on the sixty-four-mile-long dirt road (and escape route) connecting the small town of Hagaru on the southern tip of the reservoir with the port city of Hungnam. It is difficult to know precisely how many men were captured, but the number was between four and five thousand.

As Maj. Ambrose Nugent's wanderings demonstrate, the North Koreans (and then the Chinese) were unprepared for a vast influx of prisoners and therefore didn't immediately establish permanent POW camps in which to place them. Doing the next best thing, they set up numerous collection points behind their advance, and men captured during battle were marched to the temporary camp in that area. These holding pens remained in existence for up to three months, and then the POWs were funneled north to permanent sites on the Yalu. Three temporary collection points—Death Valley, the Valley Camp, and Bean Camp—were typical of what also went on elsewhere.

During World War II, the Japanese, who had occupied the Korean peninsula since 1905, established a number of mining camps throughout the northern half of the country. After the war, many of those camps were abandoned, and some of the deserted shanty towns were used as collection points for prisoners. Because Americans tend to nickname everything, one camp was appropriately given the sobriquet "Death Valley."

It was located about twenty-five miles above P'yŏngyang, near the western town of Unsan close to the narrow waist of North Korea. The camp was situated in a deep, north-south ravine flanked by two high mountains. It was rare indeed when sunlight touched the floor of the chasm. A narrow dirt road ran through the middle of the camp, and at the southern half of the ravine were three rows of long, barracks-type buildings on each side of the dirt street, four buildings per row. A few hundred yards to the north was the upper compound, which had two rows, three buildings to a side. It was a typical mining camp of Japanese architecture, common throughout Korea. The long, narrow buildings contained a number of rooms as well as an end room that housed the kitchen. Each separated living compartment in the building was ten feet square, and there were between six and eight rooms in each barrack. No windows broke the sides; occasionally, Japanese-style sliding doors divided the rooms. Most important, the rooms were unheated. All winters in Korea are extremely severe, but during the last month of 1950 and the early months of the following year North Korea suffered the harshest winter in twenty-five years.[34]

Death Valley housed approximately three thousand men. Until they were moved in late January 1951, the only clothing they had was what they wore when captured. Nearly fifty were without trousers or jackets. Meanwhile, the temperature often plummeted to thirty degrees below zero.[35]

No matter how uncomfortable the crowding, the extremely cramped conditions at Death Valley saved many because they could share the only heat available—each others' bodies. The average living space, about the size of a small dining room, held thirty men. During the day, a man would sit grasping his spread knees tightly to his chest, then another man would slide backward between the first man's knees and grab his own. This would be repeated twenty-eight more times until all were tightly squeezed into the same position. At night in some rooms, sleeping was carried out in shifts, with a third standing, a third sitting, and the final third lying down.[36]

Occupants of each room developed their own system of how to sleep. Lt. Jeff Erwin slept next to Capt. Robert Wise, and the captain woke the lieutenant about six times a night for two months so Erwin would turn over and allow him to do the same. Another prisoner from Portsmouth, Ohio, Joel Adams, had a similar problem and remembers, "We laid on the floor and there would be so many men on each side of the room and the room was so small and crowded that we were forced to sleep on our sides; if you wanted to change from your right to your left side you had to wake up all the men in the room and change over from the right side to the left side or vice-versa."[37]

The foulest sanitary conditions imaginable prevailed at Death Valley. Only a few half-full latrines were available for thousands of men. No shovels were available to dig new holes. Even if they had been, the ground was so frozen that a weak man with a spade wouldn't have been able to dent it. The call of nature was absolute, and Dr. (Capt.) William Shadish described the situation: "The men defecated on the ground at will, a lot of them because they couldn't help it. Diarrhea was very severe at that time, and explosive, so it was a very marked picture of not being able to find a square yard of ground without material on it. This was all frozen, of course, but it was a very potentially dangerous situation and I am sure the men walked in this material and took it into the rooms, and it was bad. Some of the men with severe diarrhea never made it out of the room."[38]

Prisoners tried to stay in the crowded rooms at all times. If they did go out into the frigid daylight, they returned as quickly as possible. Boredom was not a problem, however, because men were busy watching for, picking, and killing lice. This parasite survived the dreadful winter by clinging to the grubby bodies of the men. There were thousands upon thousands of them, and, Doctor Shadish recalled, "You could see [a man's] collar just walking away with lice." In Lieutenant Erwin's room, POWs removed their clothing twice a day, according to the lieutenant, "to pick the lice off to keep them from eating you up. They would take blood out of you which we all knew and realized could not be replaced on the diet that we were on."[39]

The food given to the three thousand confined Americans was cracked corn and only cracked corn, the same thing put into bird feeders or fed to chickens. Every man received about ten ounces a day. At the end of each building was a small sunken kitchen, where the corn was prepared for the several hundred people in that building. Jeff Erwin, the volunteer cook for his barrack, would awaken about 3:30 every morning to get started. A couple of GIs helped, but no one was really anxious to assist. It seemed to Erwin that "everyone had the idea that they had to husband their strength in order to survive."[40]

In the kitchen was an iron pot, and the first thing that had to be done was to fill that rusted receptacle with water. About a hundred yards away from the building was a very small, polluted stream, and they would take two old gourds from the kitchen and walk to the water. The frozen stream was used by many prisoners as a latrine. A space would be cleared of the waste, and with whatever was available they would pick through the ice, fill the gourds, and return to the kitchen. Brush would be gathered from around the barracks area and used to build a smoky fire under the pot. When the water eventually came to a boil, the corn was tossed in and cooked for about four hours or until it became soft enough to chew and digest.[41]

The mush was served by Erwin, and he made certain that everyone received exactly the same amount. In that abandoned mining camp, there was nothing to eat from and nothing to eat with. Men used whatever they could find to contain their food—often their caps—and they picked at it with their fingers. Those without any head covering cupped their hands, brought the soft pulp to their bearded faces, and slurped.

Ten ounces of corn mush daily was starvation fare, and every particle was precious. As captives ate, they guarded themselves and their food. "The men were more or less down to an animal stage," Erwin remembered. "They would sit and watch with a wolfish look and if a man was unable to eat—or anything like that, they would always grab it away from him."[42] As many as twenty Americans died daily. Death Valley, North Korea, is the graveyard of perhaps five hundred young U.S. soldiers.[43]

As for health care, the camp had two captured doctors, although, according to Erwin, "there is nothing in God's world they could do for anyone except give them a little sympathy." Doctor Shadish had a few rolls of bandages that he washed and used again and again, a hundred aspirin, a hundred sulfaguanidine tablets for diarrhea, and 150 sulfadiazine tablets. That was it.[44] The camp also had a nominal hospital, but prisoners sent there were as good as dead (the POWs called it the "death house"). The long, mud-covered former cowshed had paper-draped windows and no heat.

One morning, Lieutenant Erwin was at the so-called hospital, and some of his men inside begged him to come over. A few steps later, a Chinese guard pressed a bayonet into his stomach, and Erwin went no further, but he could see the men who called for him; some were kneeling in prayer on the cold mud floor. Outside were two English-speaking Chinese and a British correspondent named Shapiro from the *London Daily Worker,* the same man who had interviewed Major Nugent six months earlier in Seoul. One of the Chinese looked at those kneeling in the death house and said, "God can't help you now. Only the Chinese volunteers can help you." He began to laugh, and the other two joined in.[45]

Bodies were stacked in the camp like cordwood, and all were naked. The moment someone died, the corpse would be stripped of everything. As Erwin pointed out, "We were facing reality."[46] There was no point in leaving dead men with any item of clothing that the living could use to remain alive. Death Valley not only stripped men of their clothing but also of their civilization and, finally, their lives. Death Valley was not unique, however. The same thing was occurring at numerous collection points throughout North Korea during the winter of 1950 and 1951.

≫≪

Ten miles south of the Manchurian border, in a four-and-a-half-mile long, east-west valley, was a collection point suitably named the Valley Camp. The floor of the valley was dotted with typical Korean mud-walled, tile-roofed houses. Each hut averaged three rooms, eight feet square, with its own little sunken kitchen, and each housed sixty POWs, twenty per room. The population of the camp during December and January was 750 Americans, including forty officers. Officers were housed at the east end of the valley and enlisted men at the west. Although armed guards patrolled the area, there was no barbed wire or any other physical restraint. Escape was impossible in the freezing winter over high surrounding mountains deep in enemy territory.[47]

Like every place else in North Korea, conditions were intolerable. Water was practically unavailable, wood was difficult to obtain for cooking, food was scarce, rooms were crowded, sanitation was sloppy, bodies were eaten with lice, and morale was low. But Valley Camp was different from any other collection point in Korea in that practically all the men there survived thanks to the American officers who exercised authority. Of the 750 men in the camp, only twenty-four died. Twelve of those deaths resulted from wounds received in combat and twelve from pneumonia. It was a startlingly high survival rate compared to that of the rest of northern Korea during the winter of 1950.[48]

On November 23, Lt. Col. Harry Fleming was taken into the valley.* This was the same officer who, only a month before, had been standing on a bluff overlooking the Yalu River, thinking that the war was over and occupation duty was at hand. He was forty-three and a gray-haired grandfather, not a big man physically but tough. As a career infantry officer, he had earned one of his nation's higher military decorations, the Legion of Merit. After making a quick check of the camp, Fleming asked to be directed to the senior American officer present. He was pointed toward a three-room Korean house. Upon entering the frigid hut, unfurnished except for straw on the floor, he saw Lt. Col. Paul Liles.[49]

Liles was the exact opposite of Fleming. Only thirty-four, tall, blond, and boyish, he had been described as having "the typical calm of the West Pointer." Although the officers had known each other before being captured, they had been unaware of who had more time in grade and was therefore senior. Now that was important. They immediately compared dates of rank and discovered that Liles had been promoted a little more than two years before Fleming and was thus the ranking officer in the camp.[50]

There was a serious discipline problem at Valley Camp, not only among the enlisted men but also among the officers. They had, for all intent and purposes, been reduced to the level of animals. As Capt. Clifford Allen recalled, "When a man [was] sick and all he needed was a helping hand, or someone with a little sympathy to kind of help him along in an effort to get him back on his feet, we, the prisoners of war were inclined—and we did—kick the man off to the side and let him fend for

---

* Many officers and enlisted men were promoted during their three years in captivity. For example, Harry Fleming was a major when captured and upon release in 1953 was a lieutenant colonel. Because their testimony was obtained after release, the final grade they held while a POW is used throughout this history.

himself because he was stinking, or he was in the way and he was making life for the rest of us a little bit too uncomfortable. That is my idea of savages, reduction to a savage state as a prisoner of war."[51]

On the overnight march to Valley Camp in the middle of November, Paul Liles saw the swift deterioration of the American soldiers' sense of discipline. Seventeen of the 450 men who made the ten-hour hike were litter cases. Dr. Clarence Anderson, however, could find very few who would carry the improvised stretchers. At one point, four GIs became tired, put a wounded man down at the side of a dirt road, and walked on. Because the guards were very strict, it was likely that they would shoot the abandoned men, so Doctor Anderson carried the stretcher himself with the help of three volunteers.

The 433 soldiers considered their seventeen wounded comrades to be a terrible burden, and when Liles ordered reliefs to take over the litters, a typical response was, "You are just a POW—you go to hell; you are just like the rest of us." Several times during the march he asked Doctor Anderson, "What is the American soldier coming to?" If his rank carried no weight, his two years on the West Point boxing team did. "I had to use physical force, actually pull the men out physically," Liles remembered. "I booted them in the rear and made them go back and carry the stretchers. And after an hour or two, I was aware I was actually hitting them with my fists." Just before entering the valley, the North Korean lieutenant in charge of their progress said to Liles, "So this is how your army is. We thought you had a pretty good army until now. Your men won't even carry the wounded and you, the senior officer, can't even make them."[52]

The guards didn't care how much chaos was around them at Valley Camp, but Liles and Fleming did. Later, even in their own compound, Liles noticed that "all the officers were strictly out for themselves, more like a group of beasts." He was ill with fever, diarrhea, and, worst of all, scabies, but he said to Fleming, "We've got to organize something here." Because he was physically unable to take command, however, Liles instructed Fleming to "take over, organize this place and get it operating on a military basis." That was easier said than done, but, Fleming remembers, "I then started discharging my responsibilities."[53]

The Valley Camp was jointly administered by the Chinese and North Koreans. Colonel Yuen of the Chinese army handled day-to-day camp operations through an English-speaking interpreter, a Madam Chow. He was rather easy-going compared to his counterpart, "Col." Kim Dong Suk of the North Korean army, who was responsible for security.* Kim was a former professor of English at Seoul University and could speak the language as well as—if not better than—most of his prisoners. Liles thought that "he was very, very intelligent; very acute in his observation of men. As a matter of fact, I thought he could almost read a person's mind."[54]

During the early stage of captivity at the various collection points, the Chinese and Koreans showed no desire to preach communism to the POWs. They did, however, make preliminary moves that had psychological portent, and separating the officers from the enlisted men was one. Soldiers who lose leadership frequently also lose their sense of identity with their military units. The resulting loss of discipline allows a group of soldiers to degenerate into a collection of self-serving individuals. Their captors decreed that American officers had lost their rank; it was forbidden for a colonel to approach a private and give him an order. Officers were required to remove their insignia of rank. "You are all equal," Colonel Kim said, and quite a few enlisted men accepted that dictate.[55]

After Colonel Fleming had taken over for Liles, he had to secure the enemy's permission to be in charge because "the Chinese and North Koreans did not like the POW compounds to be organized with regard to the rank of its members. They preferred to deal with elected POW leaders." When the election was held, word was passed that everyone should vote for Harry Fleming, who won by a landslide. The enemy would now deal with him.[56]

The first thing Colonel Fleming needed to do was gain entry to the enlisted men's compound, which was off-limits to officers. Fleming knew "they had absolutely no organization whatsoever. They were making very little, if any, attempt to take care of themselves." He went to Madam Chow and asked her to try to obtain Colonel Yuen's permission for him to see the men. After a few days, it was given.[57]

"Good morning, Sergeant," Fleming said on his first visit. "How are things going?"

"Just about the same as usual," was the response.

"Do you have any special problems I can help you with?" asked the colonel.

---

* Kim, a major, insisted that everyone address him as colonel.

"No, I don't think so," the sergeant said.

"Well," said Fleming, "if anything comes up, let me know."

Then, almost as an afterthought, the sergeant volunteered, "I got one man here that won't sleep inside."

"Why not?"

"He just can't stand the crowded conditions and the stench. He just wouldn't sleep inside last night. We tried to get him in but he wouldn't do it."

"Where is he?" asked the colonel.

"Lying on the porch," replied the sergeant.

They walked over to the porch, and Fleming saw a young man, about seventeen, with a light growth of peach-fuzz on his chin. The colonel put his arm around the youth and said, "Come on now, you got to buck up here. Everything is going to be all right."

"Why don't they—why doesn't the Red Cross send us supplies?" asked the boy.

"Well, they probably will but until they do, we've got to get along with what we've got."

"Why doesn't the Air Force drop us supplies?"

The colonel could only lie, "We might be able to work that out. Now you just buck up."

With the older man's arms around his bony shoulders, the boy began to cry. With small, gentle tears running down his cheeks, he looked at the colonel and said, "Oh, if I only had some of Mom's cookies."

"That stopped me. I walked away," Fleming remembered. From that moment on, he became hard-nosed—and hated.[58] There would be no more sympathy, no self-pity. Fleming's attitude was that the men had to stop feeling sorry for themselves, and "as time went on, I found the system worked."[59]

The colonel felt that "the most futile thing in the world was a dead prisoner of war in North Korea. I had determined that I was going to do everything in my power to keep those people alive." Colonel Liles had the same philosophy as his deputy, in that "I was more concerned with keeping myself and my men alive than in preserving my own honor and reputation." Therefore, Fleming's "general policies during all the time he was leader, when I was present with him, had my approval."[60]

One of the first things Harry Fleming did was set up an executive council of officers, including a mess officer, detail officer, and medical and religious advisors. Each officer was responsible for his own area, and if he didn't perform as expected for the benefit of the men he would be subject to the full force of the colonel's wrath. "At that time," recalls Capt. George Deakin, "we needed a firm guiding hand as well as a representative since we were cold, hungry, disappointed at being captured and dubious about our ultimate fate."[61]

It was impossible to dig latrines into the frozen valley floor. About thirty yards behind one of the buildings in the officers' compound was a ledge that had a table-top-high drop; it was at the lip of this ledge that the officers squatted to relieve themselves. Some were too lazy to use the improvised latrine, and when Fleming caught them defecating anywhere else in the compound he forced them to clean up their mess—and he didn't care how they did that.[62]

Colonel Fleming even gave orders to pick lice, and when he gave an order, even though many resented it, that order was obeyed. The colonel forced the men "to make a game out of it. We used to keep score, and par for half-a-day's picking used to run anywhere from 100 to 150 lice."[63]

Each man in the Valley Camp received thirteen ounces of food every day. It was indescribably bad, tasteless and with just enough protein to sustain life. There were two kinds of food, and Fleming described them as "millet . . . that very small grain that we call birdseed" and "sorghum . . . slightly larger than a wheat seed . . . but it was tremendously gooey." Unpalatable as it was, "Food was so scarce that some POWs couldn't get it off their minds and they talked themselves into despondency and hurt the morale of others. I, therefore, issued an order that food was not to be discussed except immediately prior to the evening meal. The order caused many of the loose-tongued POWs to dislike me. The order, however, was strictly enforced."[64]

Fleming's position was frustrating because he was required to deal with two sides of a very difficult situation. He had to keep his often-resentful men alive and also negotiate with Colonel Kim, whose "language and attitude towards me and the other POWs was insulting." Another problem concerned some of the men, who "wanted to individually complain and talk with Colonels Kim and Yuen, thereby angering them and making my job more difficult." Capt. Clifford Allen could understand Fleming's problems: "I have nothing but sympathy for the man who finds himself in the position of a leader when he is a captive among captives. . . . He comes in for criticism from his own people, and interrogation and pressure from the enemy."[65]

To do his job properly, it was necessary for Colonel Fleming to be in constant contact with Kim and Yuen for the betterment of conditions in the camp. It was only through them that prisoners' treatment could even be marginally improved. Because of his firmness, however, he was becoming more and more disliked by many of his own officers and men. As prisoners in a far-off land, they felt the colonel should give up requiring strict military discipline. Then, in early January 1951, according to Capt. George Deakin, "Someone started a whispering campaign against Fleming and imaginations ran rampant as to what he might be getting for himself during contacts with the Chinese. It was definitely contagious. An anti-Fleming group developed."[66]

The colonel lived with everything, however, and continued to do the best he could for American troops at Valley Camp during the winter of 1950. Even before the prisoners in the valley were moved to their permanent site of incarceration, evidence was emerging that only 3 percent of the men had died. Ultimately, that amazing statistic would not be bettered or duplicated at any other collection point in North Korea.

≫≪

The collection point called Bean Camp (map 1) was thirty-five miles southeast of P'yŏngyang, "just a little outside of the town [of Suan] and to the south." The compound was originally constructed by the Japanese as living quarters for Korean civilians who worked in a nearby mine. A long line of wooden buildings ran along each side of a dirt road that bisected the camp; each building was sixty feet long by eighteen feet wide. The barracks were compartmentalized into a number of very small rooms, each one of which housed about fifteen prisoners.[67]

In the middle of the dirt road were three separated wells, but only the center one was used; the other two were nearly dry. A number of the bearded, shaggy prisoners would defecate in their trousers, and because there was no water with which to bathe or do laundry throughout the entire camp, prisoners would toss feces-ridden clothing into the well to clean them. This only source of drinking water quickly became infested with worms, but the men, without attempting to boil the water, drank it anyway.[68]

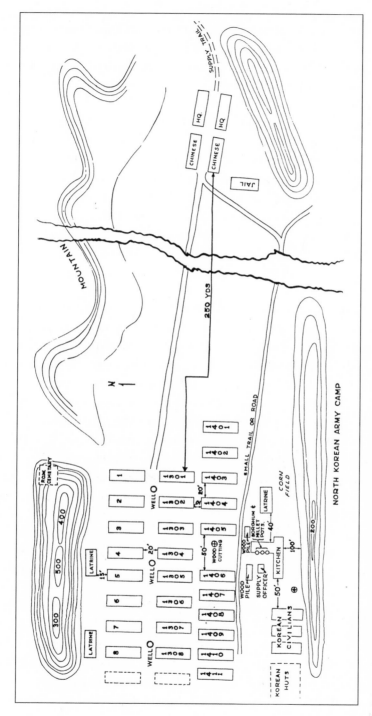

Map 1. Bean Camp. (Pfc. Rothwell Floyd, USA, Transcripts, 5b:5311)

Like Valley Camp, Bean Camp was jointly administered by the Chinese and North Koreans. Surrounding the camp were high mountains, and therefore barbed wire was deemed unnecessary. Armed North Korean soldiers were stationed at each end of the dirt street, however, and patrols walked the periphery of the camp.[69]

Bean Camp had a total population of nearly nine hundred prisoners, most of them American, along with some British (whom the GIs called "blokes"), Canadians, Turks, and Australians. The population also included about fifty officers; 20 percent of the inhabitants were African Americans. No serious racial problems occurred in any of the camps during the Korean War, even though it was widely perceived that the Chinese, in the words of Pfc. Lewis Hillis, "favored the colored race more than they did the white."[70] Even the isolated incidents that did occur were more often than not instigated by the captors to pit white against black.

Bean Camp was set up only for collection purposes, and during its short existence 32 percent of its prisoners died. There are 287 Allied troops, both white and black, buried there. Capt. Millard Allen, who tried to keep records of the men who perished, noted, "If it was the normal cause of death as we saw it, it was malnutrition. Take a man that had dried up to nothing and he died; I don't see how that can be anything else under the circumstances when he had good health three months before." Alfonzo Johnson remembered burial detail: "They were bringing the dead in and lining them up on the street . . . before they put them on the hill to bury them."[71] If the men at Bean Camp had little to eat, other creatures who shared their quarters had no shortage of food. Roosevelt Lunn reported that "the lice was eating the men up. As fast as you could pick them, they would come right back."[72]

The Chinese constituted another difficulty. "One day," according to Millard Allen, "they [would] let you do something and the next day . . . shoot you for it. I mean, that is one of their peculiarities. As to why, I have no idea."[73]

The greatest problem at Bean Camp, however, was a gross lack of discipline. Somehow, officers and NCOs completely lost control, and the soldiers became a mob. Officers were required to remove their insignia of rank, and camp administrators commanded captured enlisted men to neither talk with the officers nor take orders from them. To further undermine organization and morale, a Corporal Shamwell, who was quite young, was made company commander of the officers' company, and the officers had to report to him. Maj. Robert Copeland, a senior African American officer at Bean Camp, said, "It was a matter of survival . . . under . . . almost inhuman conditions."[74]

The magnitude of Colonel Fleming's achievement in enforcing discipline, keeping the men from becoming a mob, and stemming what could have become a tide of unnecessary deaths is evident in a statement from Capt. Millard Allen: "We had no . . . way of enforcing discipline or anything like that because in the beginning . . . the Chinese . . . more or less, kept harping on the fact that there was no rank; 'Now that you are a prisoner, there is no rank,' and all that. And, you couldn't be open with it. You had to keep it more or less under cover. You couldn't exercise your rank or authority there at all, in any way."[75]

During the early morning hours of a day in late February 1951 a new prisoner sauntered into this confusion. In many respects he was like any other, although J. D. Britton remembered him as "a lousy, no-good character." M. Sgt. Ray Langfitt said, "He was a man that cared nothing for anybody else's feelings. In other words, he was just a bully." "He always impressed me and most of the other men I talked with as being only interested in his own well-being at the expense of his fellow men," added Warren Henderson. "It is my opinion that he tried to better his own means of living in camp," recalled Alfred Simpson, "but he abided by no rules and did not care who he hurt or how much he hurt them for the betterment of himself. I would not care to have him for a personal friend." In the opinion of army psychiatrist William Dixon, "His main themes are the tremendous power of money and the idea that human survival is on a primitive animal level."[76]

At six feet, three inches and 250 pounds, the twenty-five-year-old African American from southeastern Kentucky was noticeable. Because nicknames such as the Shadow, Michigan, the Falcon, Alabama, and Half-Track were common in camp, it was only natural that Pfc. Rothwell B. Floyd be labeled "Tiny." Even the Chinese, who did not care what anyone was called, dubbed him "Taegusa" (Big Fellow).[77]

Floyd, who had a sixth-grade education, was large in mouth as well as body. If his voice wasn't recognized, his manner of speaking was. "What you going to do about it?" was his favorite question, and "motherfucker" was a cherished vulgarity. "Anytime he was talking to somebody he was using that one bad word," Private Hillis said, "the motherfucker, and that's hard for anybody to take."[78]

On his fourth day in camp, Floyd was part of a long, slow-moving line waiting for their first tobacco ration since being captured. After a short while, he left his position and began to walk toward the front. When he passed Lt. Col. John Keith, a five-foot, six-inch, 140–pound, soft-spoken officer from Alabama, Keith stepped out of line, grabbed Floyd's arm, and said, "I'm Colonel Keith. Get back in line, soldier." The command had no impact on Private Floyd, who later said, "You didn't find any officers giving orders to the men. And we mostly had to take orders from the Chinese at that time." Floyd peered down and claimed, "Well, the Chinese called me up here, Colonel." Keith, who was without insignia by order of the captors, firmly stated, "I am an officer in the United States Army." The simple retort was, "I don't care, Colonel, we are both prisoners of war." "I will take care of you when I get back," the colonel then warned the private. Apparently having second thoughts, Tiny Floyd returned to his former spot. Keith had won—this time.[79]

That food was of paramount importance to the POWs is reflected in the name they gave the camp; for two months, the unvarying daily menu consisted solely of bean balls. Each was just smaller than a tennis ball and made from millet and soy beans. The two ingredients were cooked in separate pots then mixed and formed into globs, with the gooey millet holding the soy beans together. "The food was very unpalatable," Major Copeland remembered. It "had no seasoning, and it was . . . not fully cooked."[80]

Because the diet was so poor and unsupplemented, men began to look like zombies. Most had sunken cheeks, suffered from night blindness, and were in an advanced state of malnutrition. "There certainly wasn't enough," recalled Capt. Luther Jones, "to give the muscles tone. I saw the prisoners on many occasions carry wood from a wood pile that was a mile or so from the camp, and at the very most a man could carry was a log maybe ten inches in diameter and about four feet long. By the time an individual got back to the camp with a piece of wood that large, he was completely 'done in.'"[81]

The food was so unappetizing that quite a few men refused to eat. At that point, Richard Davis said, a "buddy would usually . . . stay around and he would try to poke down most of it . . . all he could; he would try to force it down to keep him going, encourage him to eat."[82] Each prisoner received one bean ball in the morning and another at night. Because food was extremely scarce, cooks would go to each room daily to make an exact head count, write that number down, and then go back to the kitchen and put that precise number of bean balls on a wooden tray. The occupants of one crowded room kept a corpse with them for three weeks in order to receive an additional bean ball per meal.[83]

A POW from each space was delegated to go to the kitchen and get that room's tray. This was normally done on rotation, but Tiny Floyd more or less held the job full-time in his area. On his way back to the room, a number of men saw him eating the bean balls; once he attempted to sell one to Hillis for $20. While those in his area and throughout the camp lost an average of eighty pounds each, Tiny Floyd maintained close to his normal weight.[84]

Currency was abundant at Bean Camp, but "money didn't mean too much to the guys," said Pfc. Roosevelt Lunn, "because they would wipe themselves on it and smoke cigarettes made out of money."[85] That attitude was hardly universal, however. What did have a great deal of value to virtually everyone were wallets as well as watches, rings, and any other sort of jewelry. POWs had to keep an eye on their property; theft was all too common.

Tiny Floyd specialized in "helping" the sick. The camp had a so-called sick room (which the POWs named the "Death House"), but those who went in alive often didn't come out in the same condition. One day, he was helping an extremely ill black soldier to the sick room. The young man stumbled across the doorway and was unable to get up. Floyd reportedly kicked him in the hip and ribs, bent over, and took the wallet from the soldier's pocket. He then dragged the semiconscious, limp body into the sick room.[86]

Floyd also spent a great deal of time around the sick. In one case, he demanded that a man covered with lice clean himself, although the man was too weak to do so. Floyd then reputedly pummeled him with his fists. The battered young African American apparently believed he would die and asked Cpl. Alfonzo Johnson, who acted as a camp minister (although he was not ordained), to pray for him. Johnson had formed a small singing group. "I was a member of this quartet," George McGowan recalled. "The man that Tiny beat asked us to come into his room and pray for him and sing some hymns. We done this for him. The next morning this man was dead."[87]

One of Jack Simmons's buddies had severe dysentery, and Simmons, who had been captured on February 12, 1951, and was from Greenwood, South Carolina, had stopped by to visit him one day. A few minutes later, Tiny Floyd arrived with some black, charcoal-based powder that the Chinese sometimes dispensed for the treatment of dysentery. Floyd asked whether anyone wanted the medicine, and Simmons's friend said he did. "Well, I'll give you some for $15," was the reply. "I don't have any money," the patient responded. Turning his back and on his way elsewhere, Floyd then reportedly remarked, "Well, I can't give you any medicine then." The deprived man died the next day.[88]

One day George Walden, a cook for the sick room, was sitting in the doorway between the kitchen and the room, taking a short break. Tiny Floyd walked in, looking for the usual dead bodies, and found one lying on its back. He frisked it, reputedly took out the wallet, and left. A week later he rambled in again, found another corpse, and did the same thing. When Walden asked what he was doing, "he more or less told me that it was none of my darn business."[89]

Joe Labatto was very lucky. Although "most prisoners left the death house only for burial," he survived. One day, Floyd came through the door. "He's coming for my watch," Labatto immediately thought. Floyd walked right by him, however, and into an adjoining room. Labatto watched through the doorway as Tiny Floyd looked around and finally settled on someone. He asked a dying prisoner whether he wanted candy, and, of course, the reply was yes. Next came a question about money, and the man told Floyd to take out his wallet. Floyd did that, counted the money, put back the wallet, and left. Two days later he returned with a large chunk of candy, broke off a small piece, and put it between the weakened POW's teeth. He then took out the man's wallet and stuffed it into his pocket. A few minutes later, Floyd glanced at the POW and saw the candy still between his teeth. Apparently assuming that the young man was dead, he pried out the candy, went to another prisoner, and sold him the same piece.[90]

The most difficult thing to obtain at Bean Camp was "sick chow." It contained sorghum (rather than beans) combined with millet and was cooked much longer than bean balls, which made it soupy and easier to digest. This food was served in small c-ration cans that held about six ounces. Three soldiers who were very ill were sitting outside the building. Floyd, Ray Langfitt remembered, "had gone down and picked up this chow for these three men. He had also his own chow and when he came back with their chow . . . he sat down in front of them and proceeded to eat both his chow and theirs. Two of the soldiers that were sick didn't say a word but the other soldier turned to Tiny and said, 'Tiny, please give me my chow.' Tiny turned to him and said, 'You son of a bitch, you don't need it; you are going to die anyway and I am going to live.'" All three men were black, but Tiny Floyd was colorblind. To be a victim, the only qualification a fellow prisoner need have was to be weak.[91]

Trading between the POWs and civilians (most of them women) in the area of Bean Camp was quite common, and Floyd was an active trader. "I'm not the only one who did things like that," he later commented. "That went on all through the camp. From the day you were captured till the day you were released, that went on." Civilians would only accept jewelry in barter. In return they passed on food, especially a taffylike candy made from sorghum molasses. Floyd clearly wanted money. Although there was nothing he could do with it inside North Korea, accumulating it became an obsession. He would trade jewelry for taffy and then sell each half-dollar-size piece of taffy for $10 to $20, depending on the market. What Hillis found despicable was that "some of the prisoners would purchase the candy from him if they had the money, but the ones who could not afford Tiny's outrageous prices, he would tease with the candy and laugh at them. Some of the prisoners he would tease with the candy were those dying of starvation, who craved food to the extent that being tormented by the sight of even a piece of candy almost drove them insane. Those were the kind of prisoners that Tiny usually teased and tormented."[92]

The chaos at Bean Camp may or may not have been the fault of the officers. Colonel Keith, for example, was watched very closely by the Chinese to "try to find out what he [did] to see if he [tried] to exercise his rank in the camp," according to Millard Allen.[93] Because the Chinese had stated that officers had no rank, many POWs fell for that line of reasoning, including Tiny Floyd. Consequently, there was nothing to keep him, a private, from confronting a colonel if he imagined the colonel to be doing something wrong.

One early afternoon, about three weeks before the prisoners were moved to a permanent site on the Yalu, Tiny Floyd saw Keith standing outside a building. Pfc. Rothwell B. Floyd marched right up to Lt. Col. John Keith and demanded to know why officers were receiving more food than enlisted men. Oddly, Floyd was assuming the role of the men's protector. The huge private first class and the small colonel stood barely two feet apart as Keith calmly attempted to reason with Floyd and deny the charge. Floyd was reminded that he was talking to an officer. An eavesdropper heard him reply that "he didn't have to take orders from no United States officer," and "'I am in the Chinese Army now and I'll take their orders.'" The colonel warned Floyd to watch his step, which immediately triggered a response: "You're a motherfucking liar." There were a few more words, and then, swiftly and powerfully, Tiny Floyd backhanded Colonel Keith across the face, at the same time screaming, "You're a motherfucking son of a bitch." The smaller, older man staggered backward but somehow managed to maintain his feet. All he did was stare at Floyd, who turned and walked away.[94]*

Not all the violence Americans did to other Americans was intentional. The enemy refused to mark most of their POW camps, and when Colonel Keith asked the Chinese to label Bean Camp so it could be identified from the air, a GI who overheard the conversation reported that "they just more or less brushed it off and told him if we marked it, they would bomb it anyway." Bean Camp was just seventeen miles from P'yŏngyang, which was under constant air bombardment, and not far from the compound was a North Korean army bivouac area—tempting for any pilot searching for targets of opportunity.[95]

It was not unusual for prisoners to be strafed by American pilots, and the Chinese should have allowed the camps to be marked. There also should have been better intelligence from the U.S. Army and Air Force in locating the camps. Bean Camp had been attacked twice by U.S. aircraft; fortunately, only a few men were slightly wounded. The attack on a Sunday afternoon in mid-April 1951 was different, however.[96]

Two P-51s dropped from the clouds, and before the captives knew it, they had become targets. The aircraft made two passes, swooping low over the camp to fire guns and rockets. One bomb hit a frame building dead

---

* About two weeks after this incident, Lieutenant Colonel Keith was transferred from Bean Camp to an interrogation center in P'yŏngyang, where he died.

center, and it immediately collapsed, burying a group of Americans. Pvt. Roosevelt Lunn was in another barrack with eight men when "the rocket hit the side of the wall and the rocket burst came into the room and hit a POW's leg and took it off and that knocked me out the door. Another guy . . . was going out the door in front of me; a rocket hit exactly in front of him and that tore him up. That saved me."[97]

The entire camp was in a state of panic. Wounded men ran helter-skelter, seeking help, and friends who had been more severely shot-up lay moaning, crying, and bleeding to death on the ground. The captors were too busy with their own wounded to worry about the prisoners, but Sgt. Roosevelt Williams saw how one badly wounded American was treated: "The Chinese had amputated his leg, cut it off, and they didn't even bandage it up; nothing."[98]

About ten minutes after the attack, Cpl. Boyd Allred was inside one of the bombed barracks. With him were four dismembered bodies: An arm would be in one place, a leg in another, and a head somewhere else. They'd been "all torn to pieces," yet Tiny Floyd walked in and spent perhaps three minutes going through pockets and "getting billfolds; they looked like billfolds to me from where I was at," Allred reported.[99]

The number of wounded is unknown, but well-trained American pilots, in a five-minute strafing and rocket attack, killed eighteen prisoners, including eight officers. Two days later, the Chinese and North Koreans evacuated Bean Camp, and the prisoners were forced on a long death march.[100]

>«

The men of Bean Camp were marched in a northwesterly direction, passing the outskirts of P'yŏngyang and continuing on into Sinanju, where they boarded a train for Sinŭiju, the most northwestern city in Korea. From that bustling, wartime town at the mouth of the Yalu River, they detrained and hiked northeast along the river until they reached their destination, Camp 1 at Ch'ŏngsong, overlooking Manchuria. As the crow flies, the distance between Bean Camp and Camp 1 is about 160 miles. A decent car on a good road can cover that distance in three hours. For the prisoners, the trip took twenty-one days.

Approximately six hundred American soldiers began the march; fewer than three hundred men entered Camp 1. The remainder died. The largest concentration of African American POWs had been at Bean Camp; only forty-six of the ninety-six who began the march survived. Death marches in North Korea were not rare, but perhaps the two most infamous were Major Nugent's from the cornfield to Camp 7 under the auspices of the Tiger and the march from Bean Camp to Camp 1, controlled by a Chinese officer named Wong.[101]

Wong, nearly five feet, nine inches, was in his early thirties, had a very long nose, spoke excellent English, and carried himself like a soldier. As soon as the long, double file of weakened POWs was formed but before they had taken one step out of Bean Camp, he announced in a very deep voice, "I will march you American sons of bitches until you all die." Half of that vow was fulfilled.[102]

They began on a cold, starry night. Thirty POWs were designated as a "carrying party." Their announced job was to help the sick along the way, but fifteen were forced to carry ammunition and TNT for the Chinese. Fifty guards, each armed with a rifle with fixed bayonet, walked along the flanks of the column. Because American air power generally controlled the skies, the column marched at night and hid during the day.[103]

They hiked on roads, paths, and long-forgotten trails sometimes only two feet wide. Cpl. Laurence McShan has provided an account of the topography: "There is quite a few hills in Korea. I mean, you covered quite a few hills, I mean, when you were going over Korea, you covered quite a few hills. And most all your roads wound around hills, up and down, over and around." The march column crossed numerous small streams that afforded the captives their only drinking water. Escape was not an option. As Master Sergeant Langfitt recalled, "You didn't only have the guards to contend with, you had the whole country of Korea to contend with. To get away from the Chinese column wasn't hard; to get back to our own lines was impossible."[104]

In every ten-man squad, three men were designated to each carry a sack of beans. When the squad had consumed the food in these sacks, there was no more. "We had to get what we could to eat out of," Rothwell Floyd remembered. "Some of us would eat out of our hats and some of us would eat out of our hands." Three sacks of beans for ten young men over a three-week period wasn't enough; the prisoners were starving. One member of the carrying party snuck his hand into a bag he was hauling for the Chinese, pulled out a glob of something, and munched the whole thing down. His screams and agony were so terrible that witnesses fought even their memory; death came as a blessing. The ravenous boy had chewed, swallowed, and attempted to digest a block of TNT.[105]

The lack of discipline became more pronounced. Sgt. Jim Hodges said, "If someone would say something to you, you was ready to fight; everyone was that way." Among the officers, Major Copeland felt he could do nothing because of the belligerent attitude of the troops. "In order to enforce any type of order in that set-up would have necessitated physical force," he said. "I didn't assume any authority because I had nothing to back it up with other than physical force, and I didn't have too much of that."[106]

The march was not a leisurely stroll, and the guards' constant refrain, "Hubba, hubba," forced the men to move quickly. Many seemed to be among the walking dead. Capt. Luther Jones said, "Generally, a man in the condition we were in marched with his head down and more or less drug himself along. He attempted to think of everything except the step that you had to take." Master Sergeant Langfitt often saw those who had come to the end of the road. "I've seen men walk along that looked like they were drunk. You knew they weren't. It was either walking like a drunk man or a man walking in his sleep. You knew the minute you seen them walking like that that eventually they were going to be falling out of the column. In fact, we usually give them up when they got to be that case."[107]

The way to survive was to do everything in your power to move, then force the feet forward, drag yourself along, move the hands, think of something else, push your body, hurt yourself to follow the back in front of you, and stare at it and do whatever it does. It was vital not to fall out of line. Doing so would sign your death warrant. George Walden recalled:

> We was marching, I, Eugene Hall and Marvin E. Thompson. And Marvin E. Thompson accumulated hernias and he couldn't keep up. We stayed back with him. And Ho come up. And the guard was kicking Thompson at the time and he blacked out. And we was staying there with him. And then Ho come up and he told us to go ahead and that he would take care of him. And we went on. We walked aways right around the curve there—there was kind of a mountain—and we walked around the curve. And we heard a shot. And then Ho come up and said he wanted to give us his personal belongings. And he gave me his personal belongings. And that is the last I ever seen of him.[108]

A well-placed bullet in the head is swift, sure, and possibly painless, but many Americans on the march suffered beatings and deaths that were slow and agonizing. Wong carried a club similar to a baseball bat, as did one of his sadistic subordinates, a Lieutenant Yuan. Yuan's club was four feet long and an inch and a half thick, and a number of men suffered painful blows as a consequence of his rage. A field artillery lieutenant named Hayney was beaten so badly by the young Chinese officer that he died two days later. In order to determine whether a POW was too sick to continue, Wong would smack him across his upper lip, just below the nose, with the bat. If the man passed out and fell, he was considered too ill to travel and left by the side of the path for the waiting guards. Wong would work himself into a powerful anger each time he beat someone. The prisoners all knew what was happening, although they sometimes couldn't see the incident directly. They could, however, hear a deep voice resounding from the hills: "You son of a bitch American. You son of a bitch American."[109]

When a GI was not walking, it was often difficult to tell whether the man was alive or dead, because they had all deteriorated physically. At one point, Major Copeland was helping carry a sick man when the line of march took a short break for the benefit of the guards. After a few minutes, it was time to move on again. "At this point," Copeland remembered, "the prisoner that we were carrying didn't show any sign of life so when we got ready to pick him up the second time, we called the Chinese over and the Chinese rolled the man over and struck him once or twice with the butt of his gun and the man didn't show any signs, so he lit a cigarette and after smoking on it several minutes, he touched the cigarette to his nose and the man didn't make any movement so he just pushed us forward."[110]

After eleven days and sixty miles, the battered column of captives reached the town of Sinanju, where they were jammed on a ten-car train for a trip to the far northwestern corner of Korea. The gondola cars were filthy and crowded, but anything was better than what the prisoners had just been through—or so they thought.

The train traveled only at night because of the ever-present danger of Allied aircraft, and on the morning of the second day it was necessary to go into hiding. Somewhere near the western shore of upper North Korea were two tunnels, side by side. The train slid into one of them, stopping when the engine and first five cars emerged from the other end. The last five cars were left in the dark but safe enclosure. The exposed portion of the train was then uncoupled, and the engine and first five cars moved onto a siding and was backed into the other tunnel. The second tunnel was blocked at the back end because of a recent bombing. Sgt. John Tyler, who was in one of the cars in the blocked passage, recalled, "We were sleeping on a train in a tunnel which was sealed shut at one end. When I awoke, the fumes and smoke were so thick in the train that it was difficult to breath." The Chinese had left the engine running, and smoke was lazily drifting back into the tunnel, with no place to go. Soldiers were being gassed. By the time the guards had organized themselves and moved the men to the other tunnel, thirty-three Americans had died from carbon-monoxide poisoning.[111]

Once the line of cars reached Sinŭiju, the men were detrained and marched to the northeast. They arrived at Camp 1 in early May 1951.*

The occupants of Bean Camp were the last from a temporary collection area to be moved north to a permanent site. All of the other permanent camps along the Yalu had been set up and were operating for more than two months. Perhaps some of the prisoners entertained the notion that conditions would now be better. They would have ample time to find out differently.

Notes

1. Lt. Col. Harry Fleming, USA, Transcripts, 1:223–24, 1:251, 2:4, 3:217, 3:287.
2. Ibid., 11:1477, see also 5:8, 5:15–16, and 5:19.
3. Lt. Col. Paul Liles, USA, Transcripts, 1:68, see also 1:218–19 and 4b:1816–17.
4. Fleming Transcripts, 10:1207, 10:1206; see also Liles Transcripts, 4b:1816–17.
5. Liles Transcripts, 4b:1817–18; see also Fleming Transcripts, 10:1206.
6. Liles Transcripts, 4b:1818; see also Fleming Transcripts, 10:1207.
7. Liles Transcripts, 4b:1819.
8. Ibid., 1819–20.
9. Ibid.
10. Fleming Transcripts, 11:1477.
11. Ibid., 1478.
12. Ibid., 1480–82, see also 12:1741.
13. Ibid., 11:1476, 12:1737.
14. Ibid., 11:1483, see also 12:1743–44.

---

* That the discussion of the three-week march, train ride, and march makes scant mention of Tiny Floyd is deliberate, because although a number of witnesses accused him of terrible crimes during this period—including the premeditated murder of other prisoners—the weight of evidence was not strong enough to prove those things.

15. Ibid., 5:8, 5:15–16, 5:19, 11:1475, 11:1477, 12:1743–44.

16. Cpl. Claude Batchelor, USA, Transcripts, 3:1, 3:4, 3:13, 8:163.

17. Ibid., 3:1–2, 3:4, 3:14, 8:6, 8:163.

18. Ibid., 3:4, 3:14.

19. Ibid., 8:4.

20. Ibid.

21. Ibid.

22. Ibid.

23. Ibid., 8:5.

24. Ibid.

25. Ibid.

26. Ibid., 8:4–5, see also 3:5 and 8:164.

27. Ibid., 8:5.

28. Sgt. James Gallagher, USA, Transcripts, 1:43–44, 5:826–29.

29. Cpl. Edward Dickenson, USA, Transcripts, 4:215, see also 2:Brief, 4:23, and 4:214.

30. Cpl. Harold Dunn, USA, Transcripts, 1:78, 1:89, 1:111, 1:124, 1:127, 1:145, 1:303, 1:329.

31. M. Sgt. William Olson, USA, Transcripts, 2:27, 2:29, 2:47, 4:747–48, 5:5, 5:42, 5:44.

32. Lt. Jefferson Erwin, USA, Transcripts, 1:31, 5:1244–46.

33. Ibid., 5:1246.

34. Ibid., 2:511, 3:758, 5:1247; see also Liles Transcripts, 3:897–98 and Fleming Transcripts, 6:55–58.

35. Erwin Transcripts, 1:50a, 3:691, 3:760–61; Liles Transcripts, 3b:1190; Fleming Transcripts, 6:55–58.

36. Fleming Transcripts, 6:55–58.

37. Batchelor Transcripts, 7:1253–55, 7:1258; see also Erwin Transcripts, 4:1056–57.

38. Erwin Transcripts, 3:761.

39. Ibid.; 5:1251.

40. Ibid., 5:1247–48.

41. Ibid., 3:759; Fleming Transcripts, 6:55–58.

42. Erwin Transcripts, 4:1146, see also 1:179a, 1:180a, and 5:1251.

43. Ibid., 1:68a, 1:183a; Liles Transcripts, 3:898, 3:1039.

44. Erwin Transcripts, 5:1249, see also 3:760.

45. Ibid., 5:1249–50.

46. Ibid., 5:1249, see also 2:425, and Fleming Transcripts, 6:55–58.

47. Fleming Transcripts, 5:35, 5:56, 5:58, 5:278, 11:1497, 11:1503; Liles Transcripts, 2:83–84, 2:225, 4b:1842.

48. Fleming Transcripts, 5:56; Liles Transcripts, 2:82, 2b:428.

49. Fleming Transcripts, 1:223–24, 3:200, 3:217, 3:286–87, 3:316; Liles Transcripts, 2:256.

50. Liles Transcripts, 1:56, see also 1:15, 1:66, and 6:148–49.

51. Maj. Ambrose Nugent, USA, Transcripts, 10:2616.

52. Liles Transcripts, 3:792, 2:390–94, 4b:1832, 4b:1834–35, see also 1:53 and Fleming Transcripts, 10:1213.

53. Fleming Transcripts, 5:56, 10:1213–15; Liles Transcripts, 4b:1838; see also Fleming Transcripts, 5:278, 11:1495, 11:1497, 11:1499; Liles Transcripts, 2:75–76 and 2:256.

54. Fleming Transcripts, 10:1219, see also 5:35, 5:57–58, 5:144, and 10:1216.

55. Ibid., 10:1216.

56. Ibid., 5:58; see also Liles Transcripts, 3:836 and 4b:1836.

57. Fleming Transcripts, 11:1510, see also 10:1222 and 11:1508.

58. Ibid., 11:1559–60.

59. Ibid., 11:1561.

60. Ibid., 11:1690, 5:278; Liles Transcripts, 1:144;

61. Fleming Transcripts, 5:217, see also 5:57.

62. Ibid., 11:1525.

63. Ibid., 11:1501.

64. Ibid., 12:1772–73, 5:58–59, see also 8:875 and Liles Transcripts, 2b:433.

65. Fleming Transcripts, 5:57–59, 5:253.

66. Ibid., 5:346.

67. Sgt. John Tyler, USA, Transcripts, 1:53, 1:76; Pfc. Rothwell B. Floyd, USA, Transcripts, 1a:84, 1a:98, 1a:176, 1b:170, 1b:446, 3:1719, 3b:2326, 3b:2436.

68. Floyd Transcripts, 1b:467, 2a:1472, 3:1537, 3:1622, 5b:5068.

69. Ibid., 1b:191, 1b:221, 1b:315, 2:212.

70. Ibid., 1b:219, see also 1a:84, 1b:218, 2a:1351, 3:1717, 3b:2320, 3b:2523, and 4:3268.

71. Ibid., 3b:2394, 4:3200–201, see also 1b:198, 3:1544, and 3b:2490.

72. Ibid., 3a:2140.

73. Ibid., 3b:2432, see also 2a:1474, 3:1672, and 4:3202.

74. Ibid., 5b:5277

75. Ibid., 3b:2275, see also 1b:223, 1b:426, 1b:497, 3b:2424, and 3c:2667.

76. Ibid., 2:677, 1b:413, 1a:123, 1a:188, 1a:244.

77. Ibid., 1:10, 1a:84–85, 1a:243, 1b:299, 1b:594, 4:3181, 4:3187, 4:3194, 4a:3580, 4a:3593, 4a:3741, 4b:400.

78. Ibid., 1b:252, 1b:418, see also 1a:243 and 1b:210.

79. Ibid., 2:761, 4a:3572–73, 5:4802, 5:4780, 5:4797, see also 1a:176, 1b:190, 1b:402, 1b:410, 1b:589–90, 2:749, 2a:1346, 5:4809, and 5c:8.

80. Ibid., 3:1673, see also 1a:109, 1a:176, 1b:194–95, and 2:791.

81. Ibid., 2a:1473, see also 2:656, 2:661, and 2:730.

82. Ibid., 2:836.

83. Ibid., 1a:176, 1b:238–40, 2a:1369, 3:1698, 3a:2027, 3b:2478.

84. Ibid., 1a:176, 1b:197, 1b:440.

85. Ibid., 3b:2201, see also 1a:177 and 2:609.

86. Ibid., 1b:594, 2:616.

87. Ibid., 1a:135, see also 3c:3067.

88. Ibid., 2:692, see also 2:702.

89. Ibid., 2:975–78, see also 2:991.

90. Ibid., 1a:164.

91. Ibid., 1b:408–9, see also 1a:93, 1b:458, 2:632–33, and 2:971–72.

92. Ibid., 5c:12; 1a:177, see also 1a:115, 1a:168, 1b:384, and 3a:2120.

93. Ibid., 3b:2310–11.

94. Ibid., 1b:237, 1b:251–52, 1b:245, see also 1a:136, 1a:177, 1a:208, 1b:179–83, 1b:190, 1b:192, 1b:243, 1b:380–81, 2a:1164, and 4a:3579.

95. Ibid., 3b:2289.

96. Ibid., 1a:302, 1b:162, 2:611, 3a:2134, 3c:3026, 4:3134–35; Tyler Transcripts, 1:53.

97. Floyd Transcripts, 3a:2135, see also 1a:172, 2:757, and 3b:2609.

98. Ibid., 3:1536, see also 2:785.

99. Ibid., 2:775–76, see also 1a:172.

100. Ibid., 1a:168, 2:776, 3b:2307.

101. Ibid., 1a:84, 1b:414, 1b:419, 1b:452, 2a:1159, 2a:1180, 2a:1401–2, 3:1688, 3a:2163, 3b:2305, 3b:2323, 3b:2333, 3c:2723, 4:3109, 4:3112, 4c:4305; Tyler Transcripts, 1:36.

102. Tyler Transcripts, 1:226a; see also Floyd Transcripts, 1a:121.

103. Floyd Transcripts, 1b:346, 1b:448, 2a:1322, 3a:1808, 3b:2346, 4:3160, 4a:3545, 4a:3787.

104. Ibid., 2a:1162, 4c:4300, see also 2:1081, 4a:3338, and 4b:unnumbered ("Walden, Court").

105. Ibid., 5c:18, see also 1b:452, 2:789, 2a:1419–20 and Tyler Transcripts, 1:226a.

106. Floyd Transcripts, 2:1102, 3:1751.

107. Ibid., 2a:1455, 4c:4323, see also 3a:1799.

108. Ibid., 2:1003, see also 1a:132, 3a:1813, and 4c:4316.

109. Ibid., 2:642; Tyler Transcripts, 1:226a; see also Floyd Transcripts, 1a:121, 4:3191, 4c:4302, and 5a:4953.

110. Floyd Transcripts, 3:1682.

111. Tyler Transcripts, 1:226a; see also Floyd Transcripts, 1b:414–16, 2:856, 2a:1400, 2a:1403, 3:1676, 3a:1808, 4:3343, and 4b:unnumbered ("Direct, McCraw").

THREE
Death and New Life

Life is an island surrounded by the tides of death, and man has not known life until he has seen death.

—from an episode of *The Naked City*

By April 1951, the southern bank of the Yalu River was dotted with POW stockades, practically all of which were operated by the Chinese army.* The largest was Camp 5, which had been set up in January; the other camps were to the east and west of it.

Camp 5 was situated on a small, barren peninsula jutting into the deep, swift-flowing waters of the Yalu. The land side was enclosed by double-apron barbed wire. Guards patrolled the grounds, but water patrols were unnecessary because the river was a mile wide at that point. If a POW did make the swim, he would find himself in Manchuria. Less than a mile from the wire was the town of Pyoktong, boxed in by mountains to the east, west, and south. With nowhere to flee, for three years the majority of POWs remained cooped up on a finger of land a mile and a half square.[1]

---

* For the most part, the North Koreans were left out of prison administration and operated only an interrogation center (Pak's Palace), an indoctrination-propaganda camp (Traitors Row, No. 12), and Camp 9 (the Caves), all three being near P'yŏngyang. They also ran Camp 7 until October 1951, when it was disbanded.

Inside Camp 5 (map 2) were four separate areas: an officers' compound (upper and lower); a sergeants' compound; and two enlisted men's compounds, one for white soldiers and one for African Americans. Men were not allowed to visit among compounds, and giving or taking orders, saluting, or addressing any American by rank was forbidden. The policy had devastating effect on morale because enlisted men had no one to follow and officers and NCOs had no one to lead.

Discipline had been a problem at some collection points, especially Death Valley and Bean Camp. In Camp 5 and the other permanent POW enclosures on the Yalu, very little functioned properly because of the lack of discipline. Without a chain of command, without an organization they could call their own, the groups of Americans degenerated into rabble. Each man felt himself alone and isolated, unprotected by his fellows and fair game for anything the Chinese might choose to do to him.

The Chinese prisoner-of-war camp system was a peculiar one. In most past wars, the desire of camp commandants had been that POWs should, as much as practical, be allowed to govern themselves. The Germans took that attitude toward British and American prisoners and vice versa. Even the Japanese realized that soldiers from another culture could be most effectively used if given some share in deciding how to function among themselves. The Korean War was unusual, however. The Chinese could easily afford troops to guard and administer the prisoners because the most populous nation on earth had no manpower shortage. Neither were the Chinese interested in turning prisoners into an efficient work force, for their goals lay elsewhere.

The Chinese had forbidden officers to give orders and had separated the men by rank and by race. In place of the now-defunct American military hierarchy, they established their own organization. Although there were differences among various camps, the system in place at Camp 5 is representative of all camps. There the Chinese set up a regimental headquarters and various company headquarters. These were commanded by Chinese soldiers. Further down, POWs were platoon and squad leaders, the highest level at which Americans exercised authority. There was no discernible consistency in the selection procedure. In some cases, these leaders were elected by the men; in others, the Chinese appointed them. In this as in all other things, prisoners knew they were subject to the arbitrary authority and impulses of their Chinese captors.

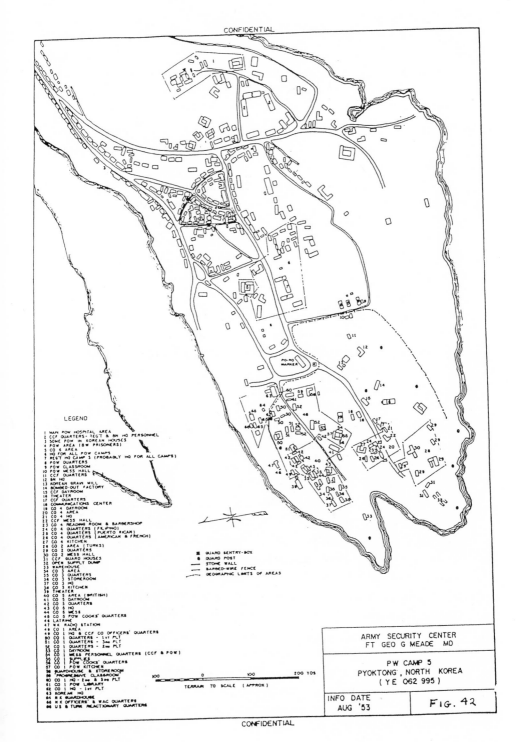

Map 2. Camp 5

The largest of all the camps was also the site of the headquarters for all prisoner of war camps in the country. A general named Wang, in charge of the entire countrywide operation, established himself at Camp 5.[2]

>«

In January 1951, three thousand emaciated men arrived at Camp 5 from all over Korea, including Lt. Jeff Erwin from Death Valley and Colonels Fleming and Liles from the Valley Camp.

The long lines of weakened Americans waiting to enter the camp were channeled through one small gate. As soon as each man entered, Chinese guards would lead him off to the compound designated for those of his rank and race. Fleming and Liles arrived a few days before the men from Death Valley, and Liles thought these later arrivals were "the most weakened and bedraggled and sick and dying prisoners that I had ever seen in all my experience." Fleming, too, noticed that although those from his valley were in bad shape, men from Death Valley were much worse. "Within a day or two, people were dying rapidly," he said. "You would go past these compounds and it wasn't unusual at all to see bodies laying out on the street or in front of the houses." The bodies were usually left in the road until a Korean bullock cart would trundle slowly by and collect them. The ghastly scene reminded Liles of stories of the Great Plague in London.[3]

The morning after his arrival from Death Valley, Lieutenant Erwin was permitted to enter the enlisted compound to obtain water from the only spigot in the camp at the time. Two soldiers, one white and the other black, were lying in a ditch by the spigot. Possibly they had been kicked off one of the cow-drawn sleds that the Chinese used to bring in POWs too sick or injured to walk; nevertheless, they were still lying there the next morning. When Colonel Liles saw the bodies, a dog was trying to drag them away. He threw stones at the beast until it fled.[4]

Camp 5 was not a former Japanese mining town as so many collection points further south had been. Instead of barracks, prisoners were kept in unfurnished Korean houses made of mud. The men slept on the floor, as was the case in all POW camps throughout the three years of the war. The rooms were so overcrowded that prisoners could not sleep in an extended position. The only clothing they had was what they were wearing when captured. Generally, twenty-five men were packed into a space about fourteen feet long and nine feet wide.[5]

The filth was almost indescribable. The men's hair and beards were long and matted and lice prospered over clothing and in body hair, including that under men's arms and on their genitals. Many GIs had no opportunity to wash themselves until eight months after capture.[6]

The soldiers soon nicknamed the various rooms in the one-story Korean houses. One—although no worse than all the others—was called the "death room." Like the rest, it was polluted with human feces. As Felix McCool, a marine warrant officer, recalled, "We lay in there like rows of corn. We were expected to cogitate."[7] Most rooms had dirt floors, occasionally covered by old straw mats. Because the houses were unheated, in February there was ice indoors. Body heat and breathing kept it melted about half-way up the walls, but ceilings were frost-covered. With desperate wit, one tiny cubicle was named the "Alaska room"; six of the eight people in it were soon dead.[8]

For many, God became very close. A well-educated medical doctor, Capt. William Shadish, remarked, "How many of us survived, I don't know, but I thank God for it." Lieutenant Erwin also became religious and later said, "I don't believe anyone could have lived through that mess without God's help. On the two occasions that I was in the hospital, I made a solemn vow to God that I would go to church regularly when I came out and I have kept that promise."[9]

Among its amenities, Camp 5 boasted a "hospital" to which the men gave a variety of nicknames, including "the morgue," "the elephant yard," "the charnal house," "the death house," and "the springboard." It was a shack made of mud and cornstalks, with a mud and rock floor; the doors were covered with dirty paper punched with holes. Just as in the living quarters, ice formed on interior walls and the place was filthy and littered with fecal matter. Jeff Erwin was there for two weeks because of pneumonia and was one of the few who survived. In the hospital as elsewhere in camp, the dead lay on the cold floor beside the living until, eventually, someone carted them away. "At night," Erwin remembered, "we would all huddle together—those of us that were living—to try to get as much body heat as we could." In that part of the world, the winter temperature could, and occasionally did, fall at night to 40 degrees below zero. Many of the sick froze to death in the unheated hospital hut. One day, a Korean doctor stopped by, looked in, and prescribed that the paper-covered door to the shack be left open to admit fresh air and allow the smell to escape.[10]

The few American physicians had virtually nothing to work with. Clarence Anderson, who had graduated from the University of Tennessee Medical School only eighteen months before being captured, pleaded with the Chinese for medication. An officer told him he would get all the medicine he could use. "All" consisted of one bottle of sulfa diazine, one bottle of sulfa diazole, and ten injections of penicillin.[11] Anderson sometimes had to perform surgery to repair old battle wounds, and he vividly remembered the only surgical equipment he had: "On one leg amputation we used one rather dull knife, we had two clamps or hemostats, we used ordinary cotton thread and ordinary needles for the sutures, we used a wooden rasp for a bone file and there was one small sort of meat saw which was used for a bone saw. Knives were improvised from the metal portion of the combat boot."[12]

The primary cause of death, however, was starvation, which was the reason for so many mortalities that Doctor Anderson considered "the extermination of the camp [to be] entirely possible."[13] During the first six months of 1951, soldiers at Camp 5 looked like the survivors of Nazi concentration camps. Lieutenant Erwin, who had a ruddy complexion, freckled face, and light hair, appeared to be a Norman Rockwell–like, small-town boy. At the time of his capture, he was 212 pounds of muscle; by the time he left the hospital, however, he weighed merely 125 pounds. The POWs at Camp 5 lost, on average, 40 percent of their normal body weight in early 1951.[14]

Some soldiers found existence unbearable and developed what one doctor termed "giveupitis." They would refuse to eat and then die. Most men, however, struggled for every speck of food they could find. A GI typically would receive ten ounces of birdseed daily and, as a treat, sometimes beans and boiled seaweed would be added. Of the seven thousand POWs in North Korea, three thousand died. Half of the total inmate population of Camp 5 died within the first twenty weeks of the camp's opening.[15]

Edward Smith, specialist second class, saw and felt starvation at Camp 5. He remembered, for example, that when a man would crouch to pass whatever little he had eaten, others would kneel around him and stare. The moment the less-than-solid waste was on the ground, fingers would rummage through the material to seek a lone, solitary bean that hadn't been digested. If one was found, the fortunate finder would wash it and eat it.[16]

Eli Cohen, a renowned Freudian psychologist and a former inmate at

Auschwitz, has observed, "In my opinion, food is the most important single thing in a concentration camp and it would seem to me to be the same in a prisoner of war camp. It is my experience that hunger largely controls the behavior of men in such camps. This may be hard to believe unless you experience it yourself." Capt. Charles Howard, who survived Camp 5, recalled, "You don't think as clearly as you would under normal conditions. You are confused . . . a man's primary instinct goes back to self-preservation and I know my own personal thoughts were devoted mostly to food. I didn't think too much about home or my wife, family, because I was primarily interested in eating at that time."[17]

Men would sit together and discuss recipes they remembered or ones they would wistfully invent in anticipation of returning home. Mouths would hang open and saliva would flow as someone described covering a juicy piece of ham with peanut butter. One GI recalled speculations about the flavor of bean curry prepared in twenty different ways.[18]

Talk, however, never filled an empty belly. Food was a deadly serious business to those young American men who still hoped to survive. "You see grown men sit down and cry because one person thinks he got shorted a quarter inch in his bowl or he didn't get his rightful share of crust out of the pot, that stuck to the pot," said Captain Howard. "I have seen a field-grade officer getting chow for a sick man who was unable to go get it and on the way back from the mess hall pour a little bit out of the sick man's bowl into his own. That man is a very fine person today. The man who was on the receiving end is dead but certainly I wouldn't consider the man who took the food a thief. Instances like that did happen and I honestly don't believe that the man was fully aware of what he was doing."[19]

Those whose bodies could not support them on such a diet, or who had ceased to care, went downhill rapidly. Starvation could produce hallucinations and in the end, pangs of hunger were no longer felt. As Colonel Liles described that last stage, "It is all very pleasant and it is the easiest thing in the world just to lie down and die."[20]

Lack of discipline was a serious problem at Camp 5. Senior officers had no control over their juniors and NCOs had none over their men. The system was survival of the fittest. There was no organization, a situation the Chinese intentionally created by "abolishing" individual rank and segregating officers, NCOs, and enlisted men. Within the compounds—even within the officers' compound, where discipline might have been expected—there was general disregard for authority. Comdr. Ralph Bagwell thought much of the problem was created by "the impertinence of junior officers in failing to realize that a unified front in carrying out the decisions of the senior officers was for the good of the camp." What Bagwell, a career naval officer, called "impertinence" others in the naval service might have termed mutiny. In Valley Camp, for example, Colonels Liles and Fleming had managed to maintain a significant measure of military discipline, and 97 percent of their people survived.[21]

Torture was not uncommon in Camp 5.* The POWs could never predict what the enemy would do and therefore were constantly off-balance. Lt. Sheldon Foss said, "They threw people into dungeons and wrapped their wrists in wire where they lost the use of their hands. Some people had frozen feet. You just did not know what they were going to do." Chinese reactions to escape attempts, of which there were an unsuccessful number, were especially unpredictable. Two enlisted men named Pritchard and Allen were caught after having run away. Both were taken to company headquarters, and after a short time Allen alone was released. "During the night," recalled Sgt. William Banghart, "screams and moans were heard coming from the general direction of the company headquarters." The next day, the Chinese detailed a group of four POWs to bury Pritchard's body.[22]

A deep concrete vault approximately six feet square in a bombed-out building at Camp 5 was known as "the hole." Water would leak in, turning to ice in winter. Those being punished violating camp rules were put there for a few days or weeks. A few were imprisoned in the hole for up to a year. It is not known how many died there, but surely some did.[23]

Prisoners who did not cooperate with the Chinese could suffer terrifying ordeals. A Major Hume, who refused to go for military interrogation, was marched off to a small hill within the camp and forced to stand at attention hour upon hour. When he eventually collapsed, the Chinese guards beat him with their rifle butts until he stood again. After falling several more times and suffering additional beatings, the major was finally unable to get up. He was carried back to his squad, where a few days later he died.[24]

---

* American troops were either captives of China or North Korea. Virtually all the returned men said they would rather be in a Chinese camp than a North Korean one, because the Chinese (after the six-month famine) worked on the mind, whereas the Koreans worked on the body (of course, a simplification). Both captors applied themselves against their prisoners' minds and bodies. The only thing that differed was how they did so.

The predictable futility of his effort not withstanding, one officer was discovered planning an escape. His wrists were tied, and he was hung from a rafter, feet off the floor, for eight hours. The pain was excruciating, and for months afterward he could not use his hands and had to be fed and cared for like a baby. From that moment, Lt. Col. George Hansen remembered, "He was deadly afraid of the Chinese. In fact, he obeyed every order they gave him after that because they told him they would hang him up again if he didn't."[25]

The purposeful extermination of American prisoners of war ended suddenly in the early summer of 1951. The Chinese admitted that the death rate was very high but claimed that the fault was not theirs but that of the American government. They argued that the interdiction of their supply lines by U.S. air power prevented medicine and food from reaching the camps. That argument, however, was nonsense. All the camps (with the minor exceptions of Camps 10 and 12) were situated along the Yalu River, and the average length of the supply line from Manchuria was no more than three miles—in the case of Camp 5, one mile. Because American aircraft were not permitted to cross the Yalu and enter Chinese territory, the logistics problem was essentially nonexistent.

Air Force Lt. Jack Henderson observed, "People stopped dying, not really because of anything the Koreans and Chinese did but because the weaker ones died off and the stronger ones were still around." Such Darwinian reasoning, however, is only partly valid. People stopped dying because the Chinese felt that the captives were now in a receptive state for a new phase of treatment. The prisoners' bodies were broken, their leadership lost, and their minds sorely stressed and at the breaking point. Many hardly identified themselves any longer as soldiers, and that meant they were now ready to become students of the Chinese government. Lt. Col. John Dunn, a survivor, said, "Mass starvation is a state policy employed by the Communists to control people politically. By the use of harsh treatment, starvation, cold, accusations, and almost never-ending interrogations, they eventually break their prisoners down to the point where they come to the decision that the only way to survive is to show some outward form of collaboration."[26] Just as Pavlov trained his dogs step by step, so, too, did the Chinese train their American captives. An important difference was that the great majority of Pavlov's dogs survived the course of instruction.

As if the prisoners hadn't enough problems trying to survive the winter under the Chinese, into Camp 5 burst Sgt. James Gallagher of Brooklyn, New York. The six-foot-tall, nineteen-year-old blond, whose accent was appropriate to his hometown, had an eighth-grade education and was extremely handsome. Somehow, although so many were dying around him, he had maintained his health. "I was in fairly good shape. I admit that," he later testified. People stayed away from Sergeant Gallagher, however, because of his attitude. "I would say from the time we were taken prisoner until the time we were transferred to another camp, it was a case of dog eat dog," he said. "Everybody was out for themselves." Even in a society of men who had become callous and self-involved, the sergeant's isolation was noteworthy: "I did not have too many friends in the camp. The men just didn't like me."[27]

It was the morning of February 17, 1951, when Sergeant Gallagher walked into his icy squad room and spotted Corporals John Jones and Donald Baxter lying in their own filth. Both were dreadfully ill from dysentery and too weak to leave the hut in order to soothe the painful ache in their bowels. "It did stink like hell," the sergeant recalled. If he had to live in that cesspool of waste, the least his roommates could do, he felt, was clean themselves.[28]

Unable to abide their lack of sanitation, the disgusted Gallagher hovered over both prisoners and ordered them to go outside, but Jones and Baxter could only moan in response. Impatient, the big man reportedly slapped them, apparently hoping to persuade the corporals to move. When that failed, Gallagher grabbed Jones, dragged him to the door, and flung him outside. He did the same to Baxter, "like a bartender bouncing a drunk," according to Sgt. Donnell Adams, who was only a few feet away. Then Gallagher cleaned the space where the two men had been and went about his business.[29]

Some who saw the eviction taking place made a few weak protests but then stopped. There was no effort, joint or individual, to help. Bobby Holcomb, a good friend of both Jones and Baxter since 1949, watched but would not come to their aid. "I was afraid to say anything," he admitted. "I was afraid I might be thrown out. Gallagher was very healthy and I was weak."[30]

Sgt. Donnell Adams wouldn't help either. "Hell, I was scared," he confessed. "There were two men out already. He could very easily come and throw me out. With the temperature outside, I wouldn't have lasted long." "I was scared, too," said Edward Smith. "I was afraid for my life. I didn't want to be thrown out in the cold and die. It was forty below. I didn't want to freeze to death." These same men had fought with rifles, bayonets, and even fists, but only ten weeks later their disintegrating physical condition presaged a disintegration of spirit. They knew what "dog eat dog" meant.[31]

Meanwhile, John Jones and Donald Baxter lay crying on the front porch of the house. They were almost two feet outside the door but lacked the strength to crawl back inside. Those who left the hut for any reason had to step over them, going and coming, yet not one person made the slightest effort to pull them back in. Soon the crying subsided into barely audible whimpering and then ceased altogether. Corporals Jones and Baxter had died.[32]

The bodies were left on the porch for twenty-four hours. The following morning, Billy Evans, in passing, walked over to the house and saw that "they were dead; froze stiff as a board." About fifty feet away was a room of another shack, where corpses were placed until burial. Evans called on another POW, and they carried the bodies to the hut. "They was just stiff. It was like picking up ice. That's what I thought when I picked him up."[33]

As he did almost every day, William Stevenson, the Camp 5 undertaker, entered the makeshift morgue that afternoon. Looking at Jones, he knew the man had frozen to death: "You could tell by the color—kind of grayish-looking—the way they turned." The funeral director and his team of eight men carried the bodies from the room; across the Yalu River, which had a covering of ice eight feet thick; and up a small hill. There, they moved aside some snow and buried them as best they could. Corporals Jones and Baxter are not the only Americans who repose on a small hill in Manchuria overlooking Camp 5.[34]

Exactly one month after this episode, Sgt. Lloyd Pate was standing near the end of a mud and stick, thatched-roof building with four other men. They were "just shooting the bull" and trying to absorb whatever warmth they could from the occasional sun. At the other end of the house, they heard a door squeak open and someone with a Brooklyn accent shout, "Get the hell out of the way." At first, Pate's group paid little attention, but then, according to the sergeant, there was another outburst: "God damn it, when I tell you to move, that's what the hell I mean." Soon they heard punching and crying. "I've been in too many barroom brawls and I know what flesh on flesh sounds like," Pate testified. "It sounded more like body blows to me."[35]

Through a chest-high window, Pate saw Gallagher pick up a prisoner named Dunn. The GI was light-complected and had fair hair; his 110 pounds hung loosely on a scrawny, five-foot-eight-inch frame. His beard and haggard appearance made him look much older than his eighteen years. Sergeant Gallagher easily slung Dunn onto his shoulder, and the victim emitted a low, weak moan. Then, Gallagher walked toward a corner of the room, apparently unaware of Pate's presence. A steel peg protruded from the mud wall about eighteen inches from one corner, and Sergeant Gallagher hung Dunn from that peg. Pate wasn't certain whether the boy dangled there, six inches from the floor, by his clothing or by his skin but reported that he was left there for nearly three minutes. During this period, Gallagher stepped back and laughingly said, "God damn it, whenever I tell you to move, that's exactly what I mean."[36]

Sergeant Pate was one of the few real heroes of the Korean camps, but in this instance he did nothing to help. When asked why, he replied, "I've asked myself that question, that same question a thousand times. It was such a shock to me, I was temporarily paralyzed." Looking at Dunn hanging on the peg, "I got sick on the stomach. I honestly got sick."[37] Within a short time Pate realized that Dunn was dead: "His eyes, the set of his face, the way his jaw sagged, his cheeks were sunk in." With the dying soldier still suspended, Gallagher kept himself busy doing other things in the hut. Then, according to Lloyd Pate, "He went back to the man and just snapped his head up, looked at him, took him down off the wall and took him to the door and threw him out."[38]

The five soldiers walked to the front of the building, "and there lay the kid on the ground in the snow. . . . He was not on his face, he wasn't on his back, just all twisted up there in one big ball." Pate straightened the hands and legs of the dead GI, and then they carried him to the makeshift morgue.[39]

During the afternoon, the Chinese came around looking for a burial detail to take accumulated American bodies out to "boot hill," as the prisoners called it. Sergeant Pate was part of the detail:

We went in there and there was eight of us, I believe, on this one stretcher. We had regular rice sacks stretched over two poles and we put six or eight men on this one stretcher and we worked as a relay team more or less; four carrying, four resting. It was about a mile and a half or two miles to boot hill, that was crossing the river, and so this kid was the last one that we put on the stretcher. I'd seen the man killed and, I don't know, I didn't know him. I'd seen him one time and that was that day but, I don't know, just something on the inside, I had respect for him or, I don't know, just something that was in there, and we put him on the stretcher and took him over to boot hill. We pulled the snow back because we had no tools to dig a hole. The ground was froze about four feet deep. None of us was in any condition to dig a hole. All we could do was scrape the snow back, the loose rock on top, lay the bodies down and cover them back up. We made one mass grave. It's in that one we put about fourteen men, I believe.[40]

While he carried, Sergeant Pate quietly resolved that he would see to it that Sgt. Jim Gallagher paid for what he had done.

≫≪

Ringed by mountains, Camp 1 (map 3), established in the spring of 1951, was located a little more than twenty miles south of the Yalu River near the town of Ch'ŏngsong. The camp's population in May 1951 was 1,452, including those who had made the death march from Bean Camp as well as other captives sent from minor collection points in the south.

Warmer weather was coming, and living conditions were not as desperate as they were at Camp 5. Food was scarce, however, and consisted of four or five tablespoons of rice each day along with a limited amount of beans and turnips. Men were not dying in large numbers from starvation, but night blindness was common because the food was deficient in Vitamin A. Capt. Millard Allen, who normally weighed 210 pounds and settled in at 115 in Camp 1, recalled that people would walk into posts or buildings after sundown, even on moonlit nights.[41]

The guards were brutal. One very ill man, for example, was placed in the "hospital," and the Chinese decided to remove his testicle, which they did. They "wanted to remove the other one," Sgt. John Tyler recalled, "but he would not let them. He went out of his head from the pain and finally got in a fight with the Chinese. He knocked a Chinese over a twenty-foot wall. After this he was tied by his hands and feet to a rafter of a building.

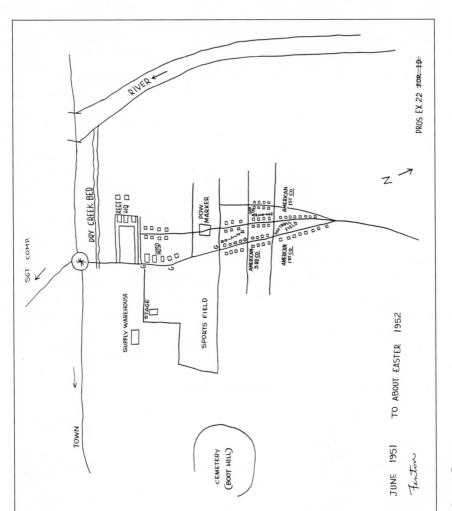

Map 3. Camp I

A Chinese boy medic stuffed his mouth with dirt to keep him from screaming." He died. In another instance, a young GI went insane and decided to leave. As Robert Shepard watched, "He picked up his clothes and said he was going home and started across the street at the end of the company, and the guard told him to stop and he kept going, and they shot him down."[42]

The captors were brutal to the GIs, but Americans could also be brutal to other Americans. Tiny Floyd was at Camp 1. As in most camps, the kitchen was run by prisoners or by North Korean civilians. Several POWs testified that they had seen Floyd steal food from the kitchen and try to sell what he could not eat. Cpl. Melvin Taylor described one typical scene: "He came by the room that we were staying in, me and several other guys; he came up and was asking us a few questions such as how long we had been captured, what outfit we was in, stuff like that. He then pulled a small bag of sugar out of his pocket and wanted to know if anybody wanted to buy any sugar; he said he would take twenty dollars." On another occasion, he reportedly approached a group that included Corporal Taylor and pulled two wallets from his pocket, asking whether anyone wanted to buy one. No one did, and Floyd moved on. When Tiny Floyd was captured, he had $15 in his pocket, but at Camp 1, when Pfc. Lewis Hillis asked how much he had, Floyd replied that he was worth about $3,000. "I am going to buy a car off dead men's money," Pvt. Richard Drennan heard him say.[43]

Many prisoners at Camp 1 carried crude knives made by removing the metal arch support from a combat boot and then fashioning and sharpening it into a small blade. There were plenty of personal animosities in the camp, but Stanley Furnish, a fellow enlisted man and prisoner, noticed that "everyone had trouble getting along with Tiny. He seemed to be always looking for a fight. Tiny not only had trouble with the white fellows, the colored boys found it hard to get along with him, too, and had frequent fights with him. Tiny always had some kind of homemade weapon at hand."[44]

Against the sick, weapons were unnecessary, and Cpl. James Green had heard of Tiny Floyd dragging sick men from their huts and leaving them in the cold to die. When asked whether that was true, according to Green, Floyd replied, "Hell, yes, I did it and if you get sick, I'll drag you out, too."[45]

A typical incident took place between Floyd and Cpl. Ellas Preece, a tough young man from Texas. As the latter told the story, he had arrived early for what was a long chow line and was second in the queue. In front of him, a small, sickly soldier was waiting patiently. When the Chinese blew the whistle, each man would fill his bowl from the hot trough and trudge on. Just then, Tiny Floyd walked out of his room and went to the front of the line. The sick man said something, but Floyd silenced him with a look. Preece, however, was another matter. Stepping up to Floyd, he said, "I ain't sick." The huge man smirked down at Preece and replied, "I thought I taught you better than that when my daddy was fucking your mother." Preece immediately punched Floyd in the mouth. They grappled and fell into a ditch, but the guards broke up the fight by hitting Preece in the back with clubs and dragging the men apart.[46] They were both taken to headquarters, where an interpreter lectured them by saying, "You Americans are always speaking of peace and you're always fighting among yourselves." "There'll never be peace as long as there's a Yankee nigger and a southern white," Floyd retorted. The captors found Preece to be at fault. "So," he recalled, "I had to write a criticism and supposed to salute [Tiny], and more or less kiss his ass, and everything else, and said I's prejudice, and first one thing and another."[47]

Tiny Floyd was a special case, of course, but, in general, the Chinese seemed to enjoy pitting black men against white. They knew about the difficulties and racial tensions in American society at the time and frequently tried to exploit that situation to divide their captives. They often told black soldiers that the white POWs were against them, held them in low regard, and, for the most part, let it be known that the Chinese favored black soldiers over white. Nevertheless, racial animosities never became a truly serious problem in the POW camps.

Tiny Floyd kept on in the same manner in which he had begun. He was warned, however, to think about what would happen to him once the war was over. Others, like Cpl. Lawrence McShan, spoke to him in language he could understand. McShan told Floyd with satisfaction, "You motherfucker, when you struck Colonel Keith, you are going to be court-martialed when you get back."[48]

Meanwhile, throughout all the camps in North Korea, the summer of 1951 brought a change in policy by the Chinese. They concentrated less on their prisoners' bodies and began a massive attack on their minds.

>«

Whomever in Peking first formulated the concept of altering the minds of the POWs was employing a brilliant although brutal idea. That Chinese officer undoubtedly realized that a challenging and unusual task lay before him. The material at hand—ordinary American GIs—had been reared in an environment entirely different than his and brought up on ideas and ideals that were generally opposed to communism. A captive would not be likely to change his mindset for just anyone who asked him to do so; steps would have to be taken to break down his resistance. The circumstances of imprisonment were an initial advantage for the Chinese. The thousands of American POWs in the Yalu River camps were isolated from everything familiar. Their disorientation and discouragement increased when the Chinese abolished all military rank in the camps. But something more was needed to make the GIs malleable: terror and death. The extinction of thousands of their fellows gave most Americans little doubt that survival meant appeasing their captors. By the summer of 1951 the lesson had been thoroughly taught. The Chinese were ready to set to work on a large scale.

In order to understand what was about to happen in the camps on the Yalu, it is helpful to back-track to the fall of 1950 and a place named Kanggye. It was there that the first Chinese experiments in political indoctrination ("brainwashing" as the American press would later melodramatically dub it) took place.

The city of Kanggye is located in central Korea, about twenty miles south of the Yalu River. North of the city is a valley six miles long and a half-mile wide. Scattered throughout this valley were a number of small houses, each of which was the focus of a tiny farm. This glen was labeled Camp 10 and became the first indoctrination center of the Political Department of the Chinese army.

The usual relationship between the Chinese and North Koreans during the war was toleration; neither side much cared for the other. As happened throughout Korea, when the Chinese wanted something they took it. In December 1950, they entered the valley above Kanggye, evicted all the Korean farmers from their homes, and replaced them with about 250 American prisoners captured at the Chosin Reservoir and force-marched for two weeks to Kanggye. There was no barbed wire or any other enclosure around the valley, but each house was individually guarded by an armed Chinese soldier.

The soldiers and marines were organized into two companies of 125 men each, which were further divided into ten-man squads. There was also a fifteen-man officer squad. Each squad was required to remain in its own unheated room and not permitted to mingle with others except during work details and company meetings. The two company commanders at Camp 10 were Lieutenants Pan and Wong.[49]

The captives were fed boiled sorghum twice a day—enough to keep them alive. The temperature, as elsewhere, was below zero, and one man remembered that a comrade's toes were so frozen that he just "pulled them off." The camp did afford some medical care of a sort, however. When one POW was very ill, the Chinese slit open his armpit, put a chicken gizzard inside, and sewed it up. It wasn't Western medicine, but the Chinese seemed to believe it an effective treatment—at least it was commonly employed at Camp 10 as well as other POW facilities. Only twelve men died at the camp.[50]

When captured soldiers entered the valley, their army uniforms were taken from them, and they were issued a blue shirt, trousers, and a cap, the garb that students wore in China. On December 22, 1950, a few days after all the men had arrived, Lieutenant Wong lectured his company on the rules of the camp—what was expected of them, the merits of communism, and the failure of capitalism. It was the beginning of their training.[51]

Two days later, on Christmas Eve, the captors announced that they had a big surprise and gave everyone a shave and haircut. The next day, the Chinese called the camp together in a large barn. As the men entered, they couldn't believe their eyes—they were going to have a Christmas party. The inside of the barn was decorated with pine trees, and a large printed sign read "Merry Christmas." Cigarettes and candy were passed out, and the GIs began to enjoy themselves. Soon, however, several Chinese began a series of political speeches in fluent English. In speeches peppered with Marxist clichés, they claimed that the United States was fighting an unjust war, spoke of killing innocent civilians by indiscriminate bombing, and asserted that the American government was an imperialist warmonger. After the Chinese had finished, the time came for some of the captives to talk.[52]

M. Sgt. William "Pop" Olson had been in the army for seventeen years and at thirty-six was one of the older, more mature NCOs in camp. Although he was only five feet four, the brown-haired father of three had hazel eyes and was a very tough individual. He had been a professional boxer and had acquired a broken nose in one of a score of street fights. Before the celebration began, Lieutenant Pan had pulled the veteran of Omaha Beach out of his squad room and informed him that he would speak at the party.[53]

Olson refused, but Pan suggested that it would be better for his health if he cooperated. The Chinese officer gave the American an outline to memorize and told him to get up and deliver the speech when given the signal. And so, on Christmas Day 1950, the master sergeant found himself telling the assembled POWs that they were to receive warm clothing, food, tobacco, and medicine from the lenient Chinese. He told them, too, how fortunate they were to have been captured by people from Peking rather than suffer, as others had, while prisoners of the Japanese and Germans during World War II. The speech lasted about five minutes.[54] A few other Americans were also brought forward to speak assigned pieces.

The men listened quietly, but marine M. Sgt. Chester Mathis remembered being shocked at such talk after only a short period as a POW in Camp 10. "We hadn't received any indoctrinations or lectures to speak of," he said, "and I was really amazed."[55] Too, no more than a veiled threat seemed to have been addressed to any who spoke. Olson's explanation for doing so concerned how the Chinese treated their own personnel, sending human wave after wave to be mown down by machine guns. "If they had as little regard for human life in all instances as they had for their own men, then I was justified in believing that I might be tortured or killed."[56]

A few days after Christmas, a study program began at Camp 10. The Chinese did not imagine that effective indoctrination would be a swift process. Study, and a good deal of it, would be required to alter the ideas of men who had no background in communism and no reason to believe in it. Soldiers were given reading material, and they were to study it and then write a review. A prisoner squad leader was responsible for work details, and another POW, a study leader, "took care of . . . the cultural aspects of POW life." The prisoners studied because "the Chinese were there listening to us," according to marine Pfc. Theron Hilburn. "If we hadn't went along with them, why we didn't know what would happen." Fear of the unknown played a major role in the American soldiers' decision to learn about communism.[57]

Initially, the indoctrination program was simple but direct. The Chinese would bring in the *Shanghai News,* the *Peking Daily Release,* or some other communist periodical published in English. Articles to be presented were circled in red. Each man in a squad would read one of the indicated articles aloud, and then the squad's educational (study) leader would ask for impressions or opinions. Responses were to be written in small notebooks. The two company commanders, Pan and Wong, would collect the notebooks from squad study leaders every two or three days and review them.[58]

The men were strongly tempted to cooperate with the system, and generally did, not only because of fear but also because of the prospect of an early release. Many had performed well in combat, but how to fight indoctrination techniques was not part of basic training. For example, although Charles Kaylor of the marine corps held the coveted Silver Star for exceptional bravery in battle, he, like many Americans in prison, soon adopted Chinese terminology. He believed that "the most progressive students* would possibly be released before the war was over. I was interested in only one thing and that was getting home. And I thought that if by cooperating I could get home, I'll do it."[59]

Pvt. Joseph Hammond remembered delighting the Chinese with a minor display of artistic talent. Noticing the star the Chinese wore on their caps, "A couple of us drew stars on our caps in the same position as the Chinese had theirs." Hammond—and who can say whether he was placating or secretly mocking the enemy—went one step further and printed under his star the letters USSA, which, he told them, meant "United Soviet Socialists of America."[60]

The Chinese instructors were leading American citizens at Camp 10 toward a new life, and it was only appropriate therefore that the prison's newspaper be named *New Life.* The first two-sheet rice paper tabloid came out on New Year's Day 1951 and was published weekly thereafter, with two-to-three-paragraph articles written by prisoners. For example, *New Life* of January 19, 1951, "published by 10th POW Camp, Chinese People's

---

* He refers to the men not as American soldiers or prisoners of war but as "students."

Volunteer Forces," featured such articles as "Capitalism and Its Aim," "Truman a Swindler," "Truth about Marshall Plan," "We Were 'Paid Killers,'" "Freedom," "Why Do We Have Slums," "What a Shame," "England for the Workers," and "A Workers' Wage."*

Both fear of the unknown and the hope of early release played some part in motivating prisoners to write. From the testimony of the men themselves, however, it seems that the overriding reason for smearing the United States in a communist publication was tobacco. While prisoners all over North Korea were dying of starvation, the men at Camp 10 were "dying" for tobacco.[61]

Each author of an article printed in *New Life* received four to six cigarettes. Marine S.Sgt. Leonard Maffioli, who wrote two pieces for the newspaper and received tobacco, later acknowledged, "That's why I was writing." Another marine, Charles Kaylor, said, "The Chinese brought out this *New Life* and if we would write an article and get this article published, we would get six cigarettes for it. Well, right there, we all of a sudden got an awful lot of journalists in our outfit because they were hurting for cigarettes." Competition over who could best slander the American way of life became keen.[62]

Lt. Charles Harrison of the marines reported that some wrote because of the badgering they received:

> The Chinese interpreter in our particular area was a Chinaman made known to us as Pan and he was the one who would come around and sit in on these squad indoctrination periods. He would pick out different people in the squad and tell them that they were going to write an article for this paper.
>
> And they were very persuasive—they would keep up until finally—at first we refused and then within the squad, we got together and decided that if we used discretion about the thing and tried to outwit the people, then we would go ahead with it; and we did. Within the squad, we wrote articles just to keep them off our backs. He was making a general nuisance of himself. He wouldn't leave until somebody agreed to do it.[63]

On March 1, 1951, a little more than two months after the indoctrination camp was established, it was disbanded. The experiment had gone

---

* For a typical "appeal" in the January 19 issue, allegedly written by M. Sgt. William Olson, see Appendix A.

well, and there was no need to continue on such a small scale. It was time to expand. The two companies of American POWs were put on a train, and for forty-eight hours the boxcars clanked southwest. When they reached the city of Anju, which was 110 miles from Kanggye, sixty men were taken off. The remaining 190 soldiers and marines were shipped back north to Camp 5, which was undergoing the period of starvation. It seems possible that the Chinese did consider releasing all of Camp 10's prisoners, as they sometimes suggested they might, and had moved the camp to Anju for that reason. They knew the effect that releasing 250 men would have on the malleability of the thousands who remained. Somewhere along the way, however, plans changed; perhaps only sixty would be freed.[64]

For twelve days they marched the detrained men—now down to fifty-nine after the death of a man named Roebuck—from one nondescript North Korean village to another, until finally the GIs found themselves in a place they dubbed "Peaceful Valley." It was not far from the front lines, and here a party was held, all fifty-nine prisoners attending. Photographers snapped pictures, and there was "quite a shindig." But the Chinese made a further selection; nineteen would be let go.* As Staff Sergeant Maffioli recalled, "They had filled our pockets with surrender leaflets and told us that when we got to the lines we could distribute these surrender leaflets to the front-line troops."[65]

In mid-May 1951, the nineteen Americans were taken near the front line and abandoned by their escort of eight guards. That night they slept in the hills. The following morning, they were spotted by an aircraft that made radio contact with three tanks of a reconnaissance company of the 7th Armored Division. When the tanks picked up the overjoyed men, a number threw away the propaganda bundles, although some "were thoughtful enough to hang on to it and turn it over to the G-2 Section."[66] The forty left behind were promised that their releases would soon follow, but in the meantime the Chinese had use for them.

---

* Eighteen marines and one army corporal were let go. One soldier heard that the Chinese expected to capture a large number of marines from the 1st Marine Division at Ch'ŭnch'ŏn, and so apparently felt they could spare these marines. Even though the Chinese wanted to release only marines, however, Cpl. Sam Shimameru, an interpreter, was released as well "because he was attached to the 1st Marine Division, the Chinese couldn't get it in their heads that he was a soldier—if he was in the 1st Marine Division, he must be a Marine" (Olson Transcripts, 3:194).

By May 1951, the big influx of prisoners was over, but battles continued and men were captured. The Chinese decided to have the remaining men act as liaison to new POWs. Their primary function would be to explain the "lenient policy" of the Chinese government toward prisoners of war. Of course, that leniency lay in the Chinese decision to no longer kill, beat, or starve their captives. They would, however, educate them. If education was accepted, a man would be considered a liberated soldier. If he resisted education, however, the Chinese felt entitled to treat him as a war criminal and thereby deprive him of the benefits normally accorded POWs.[67]

Lieutenant Pan approached Master Sergeant Olson and asked him to help orient newly captured men. He refused. Pan argued that somebody was going to do it, and an American POW could explain the lenient policy better than the Chinese themselves could. Olson felt an implied threat directed toward him and the others, so "I told him if it was just a matter of going down toward the front line and explaining the lenient policy to the men that I would do it." Olson became a *gong-so-yen* (worker for the staff).[68]

There were about thirty gong-so-yen, whom the Chinese also called "pioneers" and "peace fighters." They worked in pairs, traveling up and down the front line accompanied by a guard and interpreter. They were assigned to meet with groups of newly captured Americans before the POWs were shipped to a permanent camp in the north. What made the gong-so-yen unique was that although they were U.S. troops they wore yellow-brown Chinese army uniforms. On the left breast pocket was a white patch carrying the Chinese characters for "gong-so-yen." Master Sergeant Olson excused the garb by saying, "My uniform that I had at capture, portions of it had been stolen, it was worn out and it had been lost for various reasons and in order to be properly covered, the slopeheads gave us the uniforms."[69]

About forty miles north of the 38th Parallel, on June 2, 1951, Sfc. Raymond Frazier remembered that it was late afternoon when "the Chinese had driven us from the hills and assembled us. At this time, Sergeant Olson was introduced to us as a special comrade who had special education in learning the true way of life, one who has realized the glories of communism and the rights of the Politarion [*sic*] and denounced the capitalistic way of life. Sergeant Olson [had] eighteen years of service in the imperialistic army. His mind was contaminated by the imperialistic way of life but now he [was] fighting for the peaceful way of life."[70]

There was nothing Olson could do about how he was introduced, but he could control what he said. Nevertheless, Cpl. Reynaldo Acosta was with a group that had to listen to Olson for a half-hour and remembers that he praised the Chinese government and made derogatory statements about his own. According to Corporal Acosta, Olson concluded by telling the men that they were being used as cannon fodder by "the capitalistic American warmongers."[71]

Olson and the other gong-so-yen traveled for a few months and reached hundreds. Richard Reese heard Sergeant Olson say, "Some of you men joined the army to travel and get an education. Well, you've traveled and now you're going to get an education. But don't worry fellows, you'll be well taken care of when you get further north." For many younger GIs, Pop Olson's speeches were reassuring; others became angry at the sight of an American who wore a new Chinese uniform, smoked cigarettes, and chatted amiably with the enemy. Whatever their feelings about Olson personally, however, soldiers generally went away from his talks more relaxed about the future. That may or may not have been a good thing.[72]

≫≪

The GIs of Camp 10 had proved so pliable that one wonders whether the winter of terror and starvation that most other POWs endured was necessary. The weight of evidence, however, leads to the conclusion that what happened in Camp 10 from January to March 1, 1951 played a major part in the decision to indoctrinate all prisoners in North Korea. Camp 5 at Pyoktong was the largest of prisons, and orders were issued that lessons were to begin there on April 1.

Notes

1. Cpl. Edward Dickenson, USA, Transcripts, 4:294, 4:281, 4:296–97; Maj. Ambrose Nugent, USA, Transcripts, 6:1507; Maj. Ronald Alley, USA, Transcripts, 4:144, 5:21, 6:418, 7:588; Lt. Jefferson Erwin, USA, Transcripts, 3:693.

2. Alley Transcripts, 4:144, 4:213, 4:218, 6:340–41, 6:361–63, 6:375, 6:393–94, 6:432; Erwin Transcripts, 1:51a, 1:52, 2:538, 2:563, 3:736, 4:1079; Pfc. Rothwell B. Floyd, USA, Transcripts, 2a:1492, 3:1693, 3a:1995, 5b:5091; Cpl. Harold Dunn, USA, Transcripts, 1:152; Dickenson Transcripts, 4:263; Cpl. Claude Batchelor, USA, Transcripts, 5:280.

3. Lt. Col. Harry Fleming, USA, Transcripts, 10:1247–48, 11:1543–44; see also Lt. Col. Paul Liles, USA, Transcripts, 4b:1851–52, and 5:appendix, exhibit X:2.

4. Fleming Transcripts, 10:1247–48; Erwin Transcripts, 5:1252; Liles Transcripts, 4b:1851–52.

5. Alley Transcripts, 6:454, 7:791, 8:955.

6. Ibid., 7:768, 8:955; Erwin Transcripts, 5:1254.

7. Alley Transcripts, 4:133.

8. Erwin Transcripts, 2:428, 5:1254, 5:1261.

9. Dickenson Transcripts, 6:551; Erwin Transcripts, 5:1291.

10. Erwin Transcripts, 5:1258, see also 1:87, 2:565, 3:699, 4:143, 4:968, 4:1027–29, 5:1256, 5:1259 and Fleming Transcripts, 5:347.

11. Liles Transcripts, 2:388–89, 2b:437.

12. Cpl. Thomas Bayes, USA, Transcripts, 4:1097.

13. Liles Transcripts, 2b:436; see also Bayes Transcripts, 4:1105.

14. Alley Transcripts, 8:926; Erwin Transcripts, 3:699, 5:1287, 6:18, 6:75; Bayes Transcripts, 4:1098.

15. Alley Transcripts, 8:854, 8:963–64, 9:1177, 9:1201; Liles Transcripts, 2b:434.

16. Sgt. James Gallagher, USA, Transcripts, 6:1045.

17. Bayes Transcripts, 6:170–71; Erwin Transcripts, 3:815.

18. Alley Transcripts, 9:1154.

19. Erwin Transcripts, 3:815–16.

20. Fleming Transcripts, 10:1237.

21. Erwin Transcripts, 4:926, see also 1:49; Fleming Transcripts, 6:244.

22. Alley Transcripts, 4:206; Sgt. William Banghart, USA, Transcripts, 1:194.

23. Erwin Transcripts, 2:535, 2:540, 4:1098.

24. Ibid., 3:811; Alley Transcripts, 8:909.

25. Erwin Transcripts, 5:1423, see also 1:98, 1:100a, 2:330 and Alley Transcripts, 8:1058.

26. Nugent Transcripts, 1:291; Erwin Transcripts, 5:1223, see also Erwin Transcripts, 2:580 and Alley Transcripts, 4:143, 6:362.

27. Gallagher Transcripts, 6:933, 6:979, 7:10, see also 1:43, 1:90–92, 2:2, 4:338, 4:495, 4:592, 5:826–27, 6:1174, and 7:38.

28. Ibid., 6:936, see also 4:512, 4:522, 4:565, 4:569–70, 4:611–12, 4:618, 4:628, and 5:832–33.

29. Ibid., 4:512, see also 4:514, 4:521, 4:528–29, 4:536, 4:571, 4:626, and 5:716.

30. Ibid., 4:574.

31. Ibid., 4:514, 4:539, see also 4:525 and 4:566–69.

32. Ibid., 4:572, 4:584.

33. Ibid., 4:407–10.

34. Ibid., 5:640, see also 4:538, 4:550, 4:615, and 5:643.

35. Ibid., 4:219–23.

36. Ibid.

37. Ibid., 4:219–23, 4:472, see also 4:424–25, 4:432, 4:499, 4:501, 4:504, 5:746, 5:838, and 5:892.

38. Ibid., 4:219–23, see also 5:739.

39. Ibid., 4:424.

40. Ibid., 4:426.

41. Sgt. John Tyler, USA, Transcripts, 1:53, 1:160a; Bayes Transcripts, 2:73, 3:302; Floyd Transcripts, 2:803, 2:1044, 3:1688, 3b:2365, 3b:2403.

42. Tyler Transcripts, 1:227a, 1:186a.

43. Floyd Transcripts, 1a:106, 2:1046–47, see also 1a:123, 1b:255, 2:801–2, and 5c:12.

44. Ibid., 1a:105; see also Tyler Transcripts, 1:156a.

45. Floyd Transcripts, 1a:102.

46. Ibid., 2:726–29, see also 2:733.

47. Ibid., 2:726–29.

48. Ibid., 2:811, see also 2:1015.

49. Alley Transcripts, 4:141; M. Sgt. William Olson, USA, Transcripts, 3:126, 3:128, 3:168, 3:197, 3:315, 4:534, 4:564, 4:614, 4:749–50, 4:776.

50. Olson Transcripts, 5:44, see also 3:161, 3:323, and 4:776.

51. Ibid., 2:394, 4:750.

52. Ibid., 3:136.

53. Ibid., 1:4–5, 2:27, 2:267, 3:26, 4:747, 5:13, 5:46.

54. Ibid., 3:39, 3:176, 4:752–54.

55. Ibid., 3:213.

56. Ibid., 4:752.

57. Ibid., 3:166, 3:243, see also 3:175.

58. Ibid., 3:178.

59. Ibid., 4:535, see also 4:660.

60. Ibid., 3:306, see also 3:291 and 3:322.

61. Ibid., 2:92, 3:164, 3:180, 3:209, 4:803, 5:126–27; Alley Transcripts, 4:146.

62. Olson Transcripts, 3:183, 4:536, see also 3:283.

63. Ibid., 3:96.

64. Ibid., 3:189, 3:191, 3:320, 3:326, 4:755–56, 5:136.

65. Ibid., 3:194–95, 4:757, see also 3:151, 3:191–92, 4:755–56, and 4:758–59.

66. Ibid., 3:115, see also 3:114 and 3:194.

67. Ibid., 3:323.

68. Ibid., 4:763–64.

69. Ibid., 4:764, see also 2:381, 2:394, 2:484, 2:495, 3:193, 3:220, 3:288, 4:424, 4:760, and 4:762.

70. Ibid., 2:279.

71. Ibid., 2:73.

72. Ibid., 2:284–85, see also 2:381, 4:457, 4:633, and 4:793.

FOUR

Toward Truth
and Peace

*Had Achilles any thought of death and danger? For whatever a man's
place is, whether the place which he has chosen or that which he has
been placed by a commander, there he ought to remain in the hour of
danger; he should not think of death or of anything but of disgrace.
And this, o'men of Athens, is a true saying.*

—"Apology," *Dialogues of Plato*

On a crisp day in April, sunlight streamed over the mountains and fell at the feet of Lt. Jeff Erwin, who stood at attention outside one of the hundreds of small Korean houses that sheltered POWs at Camp 5. The men in the officers' compound knew why he was there, but most gave him only a glance as an armed Chinese guard stood nearby. Occasionally, the sentry would walk away, and sometimes he would circle Erwin, like a cat playing with a mouse. Every now and then he would pound the lieutenant's legs with his rifle butt if he saw that Erwin's feet were not together. The American was still shaky from his bout with pneumonia, and his back and legs throbbed with pain. Once or twice, when the guard walked away, Erwin sat and tried to regain some strength. The guard would always return, however, and, shouting indignantly, kick him back into a position of attention.

Although such physical abuse was not in keeping with the policy the captors seemed to have adopted, word had apparently not filtered down to everyone. Erwin had refused to be a monitor in the camp's indoctrination program, and the Chinese were helping him "reconsider."[1]

>«

The Chinese tutors sent to North Korea to initiate a new stage in the POW experience were extremely intelligent and spoke fluent English (with an easy command of slang); most had been educated in the United States. The minds of most of the self-confident, determined indoctrinators had been sharpened at the University of California and the University of Chicago. At Camp 5, according to navy helicopter pilot Lt. John Thornton, a man named Sun "ran the whole educational program." His command of the English language was good, "not the King's perfect English," said Thornton, "but very understandable and legible and probably as well as I do without the accent." Sun usually stayed in the background, but he brought with him on April 1, 1951, a large group of instructors, including "Dirty Pictures" Wong and "Snake Eye" Ding, as the GIs dubbed them. There were even a few female lecturers. A considerable band of indoctrinators was necessary because Camp 5 was by far the largest POW camp, eventually containing almost three-quarters of the American POWs in North Korea. It was here that the Chinese would make their most determined effort to influence and "educate" their captive audience.[2]

Wong, who received his nickname once the Americans learned he collected lewd photographs, gathered virtually all the prisoners of Camp 5 into a large barn that first day of April 1951. He lectured them on what they could expect, and gain, from conscientious study. The soldiers fidgeted and called back and forth to each other. Very few paid attention to Wong, who then burst out:

> You are the aggressors and if you don't accept the lenient policy and change your views, we have dug a hole which we are going to throw you in. You capitalist warmongers do stink. We are quite right in burying you. A person who does not accept our doctrine is not a human being because he is not for the masses and a man that is not for the masses does not deserve treatment any better than you give an animal. As an animal, we have

a right to eliminate you. You will learn the truth and we don't care if it takes one year, two years, ten years, twenty years; we don't care if you die here because we will bury you and bury you deep so that you won't stink.

The prisoners, both artillery captain Frederick Smith and marine warrant officer Felix McCool remembered, shut up. They knew he was serious, as was his government.[3]

Wong and his compatriots soon showed their "students" how serious a business study could be. The school day, often as long as ten hours, usually consisted of mass indoctrination lectures by Chinese instructors, followed by small classes conducted in the squad rooms. Lectures, reading, and writing went on day after day, month after month. A POW, no matter how ignorant or illiterate, could not help but learn something.[4]

The most common term used to describe what went on is *brainwashing*,* although the communists did not wash any brains. Rather, they were intent on filling them. "From daybreak in the morning until approximately two hours after darkness," recalled Maj. Milford Stanley, "we were subjected to continuous indoctrination, reading and discussing Marxism and other communist propaganda defacing the United States and the United Nations." All men were furnished pencils and three-and-a-half-inch-thick, red and blue rice paper notebooks. In the notebooks they were to write what they learned and thought about a particular lecture or reading.[5]

The average company-size lecture of approximately two hundred men would go on for many hours. A young Chinese would get up and talk, and prisoners were required to sit still and listen. No questions were permitted, and when the speaker finished he would walk away. The men were then ordered back to their squad rooms to discuss the lesson.[6] They frequently heard that the economic organization of the United States was capitalistic and unjust, that the country was being run by a group of Wall Street warmongers, that the United States was the aggressor in Korea, and that China had been liberated by the communists and was prospering under that recent liberation. America's leaders—Truman and MacArthur in particular—were also denounced.[7]

In any school, the course of study includes homework as well as class attendance. The indoctrinators were well aware that the men's attention

---

* The POWs never heard the word *brainwash* until the survivors returned to the United States.

wandered during lectures, but to remedy that they assigned homework. Required reading for all was *The Twilight of Capitalism* by William Z. Foster, chair of the Communist Party of the United States. Other readings included *A Political History of the Americas, The Decline and Fall of American Capitalism,* the Communist Manifesto, *The Life of Karl Marx,* and *High Treason.* Ideologically correct magazines and newspapers were shipped to North Korean POW camps from all over the world. Prisoners had access to *Cross Roads* from India; the *China Monthly Review,* published in Shanghai by a U.S. citizen; *People's China; Shanghai News;* and the London and New York editions of the *Daily Worker.* Even those who did not respond to the propaganda in the *Daily Worker* were glad to receive it, because it provided some news of what was happening back home.[8]

The GIs did their reading in the squad rooms—or rather they were read to. The Chinese did not believe their charges would truly study the assigned readings, and therefore a reader was appointed from among the men. Lack of trust was not the only reason for appointing readers; quite a few prisoners were barely literate. Joseph Goulden has pointed out that "with the postwar economy booming the army had been forced to take whatever recruits it could find, relying on shorter enlistment terms and lower mental and physical standards. When the Korean War began, 43 percent of the army enlisted men in the Far Eastern Command were rated Class IV and V, lowest on the Army General Qualification Tests—the stumbling dullards drill sergeants called yo-yos or bolos."[9]

A great many POWs in North Korea could not fight Chinese indoctrination because they were generally ignorant of how democracy functions, as well as the workings of the economic system and the contents of the Constitution and Bill of Rights—virtually everything that would have explained their country to them. Lt. Col. Paul Liles said, "I was very much surprised to find out that the American soldier knew practically nothing about the United States Government and didn't even know there were two senators from each state."[10] In many instances, the Chinese had captured men who were effectively children. They were not so much reeducating them as educating them for the first time.

The POW readers did not volunteer, and after the mandatory daily lecture "whichever Chinese was in charge would have the book in his hands and he would just designate somebody and hand him the book and tell him what he wanted for him to read," said Maj. John Kahaniak. Some who claimed illiteracy or poor eyesight were excused, but the Chinese were not easy to fool. As a rule, when prisoners were ordered to read, they read. Anyone who took a strict view of a soldier's duty would consider reading communist propaganda to comrades as a criminal act because the texts defamed the United States.[11]

Lack of enough trained indoctrinators precluded an English-speaking captor from personally supervising each squad, so the Chinese appointed squad monitors. Those GIs had the unenviable task of carrying out the reading and study program. Early each morning, every monitor would appear at company headquarters and pick up a newspaper, magazine, book, or occasionally a typewritten sheet with questions on it. "Today, this will be your topic of discussion," he would be told. "You are to conduct it for a period of six hours and then obtain answers from each member of the squad." At these briefings, the Chinese would also berate any squad monitor whose squad was not showing sufficient "progress."[12]

Upon returning to the men, each monitor would read and then initiate and lead discussions on the prescribed subject. Once the discussion was over, a "cognition" (the Chinese were very fond of that word) was written up—either by the monitor for the entire squad or by the individual members themselves—and turned in later that day, along with the study material that had been picked up that morning.

The daily routine, then, usually began with a mass lecture, the reading of the study material that the monitors had collected, and then a squad discussion of it. It concluded with the writing down of the squad's interpretation of that material and the handing back of these so-called cognitions to the captors. And this indoctrination went on daily—for months on end. Repetition was the central element of Chinese indoctrination theory; it was difficult to hear something hundreds of times without coming to believe that it was, at least in part, true.[13]

Most felt that resistance was futile. They would give the answers the enemy wanted, and if a Chinese was present during a discussion period they would discuss the world in the anti-American, pro-communist terms desired of them. Americans did not argue with the Chinese. They had just been through the winter of 1950–51 and had seen thousands die. No one was certain that a wrong answer would not mean the death of the individual who rendered it. It is not surprising that, as Air Force major David Little recalled, "It was more or less customary to give a school solution, so to speak, to a question."[14] Old camp practices did not completely give way to new. Camp 5 had been in the famine period when the studies began, and men who feared for their lives cooperated. As one officer said, "I don't think an American is alive who defied them. I know some who defied them and are dead."[15]

Whether officers and men could have resisted had they stood together and refused to participate is uncertain. Some who defied the Chinese did live. Nothing happened to navy helicopter pilot John Thornton, for example, who refused to cooperate. "I did not write," he recalled. "I would not answer the questions. I would hand in a blank paper. I would say I am not a diplomat and I don't know these things. If we had a united front and refused to do it, collectively, we could have stopped all this." The British were somewhat successful—indeed, enthusiastic—in fighting Chinese indoctrination. According to Lt. Sheldon Foss, their "discipline was better than ours and they were, for the most part, a unit. I know some British officers who are still alive and to my knowledge never went along with them. Colonel Carne, commanding officer of the Gloucestershire Regiment; Major Joseph Ryan, who was with the Royal Ulster Rifles; and Major Sam Weller of the Gloucestershire Regiment."[16]

The monitor system worked well for the Chinese. Every day, approximately one hundred captives conducted classes as ordered. Those who refused to do the job when selected were beaten. Lieutenant Erwin, after the day spent standing at attention, had gone back to Dirty Pictures Wong and agreed to monitor a squad. Options were, after all, very limited.

A monitor's fellow prisoners often could easily discern whether he was a "collaborator" by the manner in which he conducted classes. Some men were willing tools of the Chinese. In many cases, however, a class's antipathy and resentment were merely reflections of a monitor's insistence on some measure of discipline during instructional periods. When Lieutenant Erwin found that a number of his men were ripping pages from the *China Monthly Review* to use as toilet paper or rolling paper for cigarettes, he insisted they stop the practice. He had little choice. Each monitor was responsible for the material he took to the squad room and would be in trouble if he did not return it in the proper order that evening. The men— in this case some of Erwin's fellow officers—resented having to practice even that small measure of self-control. Erwin, like many another unwilling monitor, was labeled a communist by some members of the squad. Once the rumor mill began, word would be passed from squad to squad. In a very short time a POW monitor could find he was known throughout the camp as a communist sympathizer.[17]

To be a monitor was to court bad feeling from fellow GIs. The situation of Maj. Ronald Alley was typical. One of his squad members considered the major a garrulous individual who loved the sound of his own voice. It was even intimated that his fondness for talking was the reason he supposedly cooperated with the Chinese. But the squad could give him their written cognitions only after he had read the lesson to them, and without the cognitions Major Alley would have been the first to bear the weight of Chinese displeasure.[18] Perhaps what rankled most men was the major's degree of literacy. Lieutenant Thornton remembered that "he read chapter after chapter, hour after hour. He read very legibly, audibly, and understandably. He read better than the Chinese . . . in my opinion, and you did not have to do that."[19] On such grounds was the approval or disapproval of one's fellows often bestowed.

In Alley's case, somewhat more substantial reasons for questioning his loyalty were provided by Dr. Gene Lam, who said that he "discredited the United States while building up China and Russia. I recall hearing him support the Communist point of view that the United Nations was the aggressor in Korea and that our country was ruled by a small number of big money families that wanted war so that they could increase their profits."[20]

It may have been true that Alley argued in such a manner, but the fact that he was eventually brought to court-martial after the war does not necessarily indicate that he was guiltier than many—or perhaps most—other monitors in POW camps along the Yalu. A monitor, after all, had to prepare his squad to make cognitions that would vigorously denounce the United States. Monitors who spent time defending the United States and denouncing China placed themselves in grave danger. The Chinese response to such opposition would have involved violence, even death. To be a monitor was to be in a particularly tight spot. The very duties that a man was assigned to perform involved collaboration of an unpleasant kind, and POWs were so conditioned to obedience that it took extraordinary courage to refuse.

The indoctrination program had twelve phases, and each prisoner was required to study them all. The syllabus required discussion of:

1. The Cause of the Korean War
   a. Why the Chinese entered the war
   b. Why the United Nations entered the war
2. The Large Ruling Rich Families in the United States
   a. DuPont
   b. Morgan
   c. Ford
   d. Vanderbilt
   e. Lodge
   f. Rockefeller
3. The Organization of the United Nations
4. The Admission of China to the United Nations
5. Profits of Big Business and Wall Street—How They Are Derived
6. [The] Illegality of President Truman Sending Troops to Korea
7. Capitalism
8. Imperialism
9. The Decline of Capitalism
10. The Construction of New China
11. The Re-Division of the World after World War II
    a. The role the Soviet Union played in World War II
12. General Discussions on Communism

Each phase of the twelve-step program was worked through with great intensity; in the absence of counterarguments, many soldiers admitted to being impressed. Some even began to call their guards and instructors "comrade."[21] Even the most educated and patriotic of men became disconcerted. Maj. (Dr.) Clarence Anderson said:

> For several months, the indoctrination program had harped on a few basic ideas: That the Americans were the aggressors in Korea; that the South Koreans crossed the 38th Parallel first; that it was South Korean aggression; that the United States was unjustly keeping Formosa away from its historical connection with the mainland of China; and that the United States

was controlled by the Wall Street warmongers, and so forth. The persistent harassment of this indoctrination program did not lead me to believe what was told me; however, it did create a confusion. I did not know the answers to many of these questions and a considerable confusion was created in my mind insofar as the solidity of our stand on these issues.[22]

The lectures, readings, and studying were just the foundation. The next step was to have prisoners "voluntarily" write articles about what they had learned. Pieces judged good enough were posted on the bulletin board and constituted what the men called their "wallpaper." The board measured six by eight feet and displayed about twenty articles daily. "On articles of that type that were published on the bulletin board," Capt. Tommy Trexler said, "to the best of my knowledge all of them definitely were written in such fashion that they were certainly following the communist line." The best wallpaper articles appeared in the mimeographed Camp 5 newspaper, *Toward Truth and Peace.* Authors were rewarded with candy and cigarettes.[23]

The initial and basic indoctrination program spanned approximately three months and took place within the confines of the camp. But the Chinese aspired to a wider audience. The world should know what American soldiers thought of their country, that American citizens believed they were the aggressors in Korea and fought for Wall Street warmongers, rich capitalists, and imperialists. The world would know, because the next step was about to be taken.

>«

In early June 1951, the Chinese called out all the Allied officers in Camp 5 (about 150 men) and told them it would be a good idea if they'd sign a document proclaiming the United States to be the aggressor in Korea and stating that the only thing the soldiers wanted was peace. This "Peace Appeal" would be sent to the United Nations and to Stockholm, Sweden, where a communist-sponsored peace conference was taking place. The officers were asked their opinion of signing and then separated into three groups: those who favored the appeal, those who opposed it, and those who maintained a prudent neutrality and refused to commit themselves either way. Many stepped to the side in favor of signing, about the same number were on the fence, and only a few brave men said at the outset that they would not sign. The Chinese, therefore, insisted upon a debate between the groups favoring and against signing. Middle-of-the-roaders were ignored because it was assumed that they would swing with the majority.[24]

Lt. Col. John McLaughlin of the marines wasn't signing anything and forcefully argued against officers allowing their names to be used on a communist propaganda document. Other officers remembered McLaughlin as being a staunch anticommunist who argued aggressively against the Chinese.[25]

Debate went on for three days, and hour by hour more and more people switched from the "no" and "fence" groups to the "yes" group. Quite a few men in the assembly that favored signing argued heatedly; Capt. Tommy Trexler later testified that they "made statements that I felt were detrimental to the United States. Practically every word that came out of their mouth in my opinion was not what was expected of an officer." As membership in the yes group began to swell, more and more officers would stand up and argue, and Capt. Hamilton B. Shaw, USAF, agreed that it was "because the Russian member of the Security Council was absent from the meeting at which troops were authorized for Korea, the action of the United Nations and United States in sending troops to Korea was illegal."[26]

By the third day of the debate, only eight holdouts were left, including Lt. Col. John McLaughlin and Lt. Joseph Magnant. The Chinese wanted unanimity but were not going to allow the controversy to go on indefinitely. If the few objectors had not yet learned the truth after months of indoctrination, then other methods would have to be employed. Lieutenant Magnant was made to stand at attention in the sun all day and then brought inside and reminded of what had happened to Major Hume. Driven nearly out of his mind by numerous beatings, that officer had died a few months earlier. Magnant changed his mind about the Peace Appeal.[27]

Finally, the principal holdout, John McLaughlin, USMC, was hauled to company headquarters "and," he reported, "eventually they laid it on the line and told me that either I would sign this document or I would never see my family again, that I would be tried by the Korean People's Court and get at least a twenty-five year sentence. Frankly, prior to that I saw that we were getting nowhere; we had no unity in opposition to this Peace Appeal and I just thought it was useless, futile to oppose this thing, and stated that I would sign it."[28] When Colonel McLaughlin returned to the yard, he instructed the remaining holdouts to switch their votes. Realizing that the men were disappointed in him and nervous about the commission of this act, McLaughlin, as senior officer, informed them that he would assume responsibility for the deed. At the end of the third day, resistance was over.[29]

Before the assembled men were dismissed from the yard, Snake Eye Ding stood on a small platform and applauded. Then he said, "By accepting our viewpoint, you have joined the camp of peace. We will no longer treat you as war criminals but as liberated officers." Most of the tired men loudly cheered him. Finally, Ding announced, "Since you have joined the camp of peace, you must now translate your thoughts into deeds."[30] Then, the Chinese supplied paper, paint, ink, sticks, and everything else required to make banners. For two days, the POWs drew. All five companies were assembled within the camp, and each organized into platoons. The American POWs were to hold a parade; more than 1,600 officers and men would be put on display. At the head of each company, two men were to carry a large white banner saying "we want peace" or a similar slogan in red. Behind them, each prisoner carried a three-foot-long stick with either a yellow or blue pennant stenciled with the word *peace*.[31]

On a hot June day, the men were marched through the camp gate "in celebration of the happy prisoners of war coming from the imperialist camp into the camp of peace." Guards walked along the flanks of the long column, and other "cheerleading" prisoners also flanked the marchers. Their job was to shout slogans that the main body would repeat in loud voices. To chants of "end the Korean War," "down with American warmongers," "we want peace," "we have seen the light," and "long live Mao Tse-tung," the parade moved down the dirt road toward the town of Pyoktong.[32]

The dirt road wound up a hill in town and led to a large schoolyard where a Chinese band was playing. As Lt. William Boswell described the scene, "After the parade arrived at the schoolhouse or in the schoolyard area, there was a kind of reviewing stand at one end which was gaily decorated with banners flying around. There was quite a bit of motion-picture taking and still photography. There were some speeches made on this stand by certain prisoners." In addition, the Chinese general in charge of all POW camps in Korea gave a talk. It was a momentous occasion.[33] After the celebration, the parade was turned around and doubled back to prison. The Chinese had a debate, they had a parade, and now it was time to have signatures.[34]

When the marchers reentered the compound, there were three tables, each containing a copy of the Peace Appeal, which was to be sent to the United Nations. Bound to the appeal was blank, lined paper. Officers were also required to sign a certificate of aggression that read: "We, the liberated officers of North Korea, through study, realize that South Korea invaded North Korea with the backing of the United States, and that the United States is an aggressor in coming to Korea and we, therefore, leave the camp of aggression and join the camp of the Peace Loving Peoples of the World." The lines of men waiting to sign were long, and to entertain the POWs the Chinese brought out a phonograph and played music while photographers continually snapped pictures. Halfway through the ritual, the hot, sunny day suddenly darkened and rain fell. The men returned to their squads, and the remainder of the signatures were obtained indoors. The last was that of Dr. William Shadish, who was number 1,671.[35]

Many men were ashamed of what they had done, but all participated, whether from weakness or fear.* Every prisoner had his own reason for signing. Young, enlisted troops followed their officers, reasoning that if an officer signed it must be permissible for them to do so, too. Cpl. Claude Batchelor said, "In the camp where I was prisoner, I found out that many of the officers were as bad, or worse, than some of the enlisted prisoners in their support of communism."[36] In most cases, the officers did not support communism, but it is not surprising that a young and uneducated corporal saw things that way.

Batchelor and his peers were also affected by the simplest kinds of propaganda. The Chinese were adept at exploiting the magic power of words. Using the word *peace* to describe their new policy would, they realized, be sufficient. It was the word itself that counted. "The Chinese and Koreans started telling us about peace, peace, peace," said Batchelor, "and I felt, like most of the men, that it was not a crime to fight for peace and talk about peace."[37] In the end, however, most signed the peace petition for commonsense, practical reasons best expressed in their own words:

---

* Some men later testified that there were a few holdouts, but if there were, they were very few.

Lt. Paul Roach: Everybody else was signing it and I realized that if I did not sign it that it would make myself conspicuous to the Chinese and I preferred to remain with the majority of the group.[38]

Capt. Robert Wise: During that particular period, the Chinese had unquestionably set out to starve us into submission, to force us to come to their terms or to believe in their ways and to accept the ideology. Death had become a commonplace thing rather than something unusual and having an officer die in our room, almost daily, certainly had some effect on a man's reasoning power.[39]

Air Force officer John Gaston: I can't give you a definite reason why I signed it, sir. It was just one of those things that everyone signed.[40]

Maj. Harold Kaschko: I mean, let's be honest about this whole thing. I signed the thing because I was scared of the Chinese and that's the reason the rest of them signed it.[41]

Major Kaschko, who had a way with words, also remarked, "When I've lost about seventy-five pounds, I don't roar very loud."[42]

None admitted to signing the petition, or doing anything else, because of Chinese indoctrination. It is as if those under extreme circumstances are willing to admit fear yet ashamed to allow it thought that someone controlled their thinking. Given the conditions the POWs endured, it is not surprising that a sizable percentage of prisoners did indeed succumb to the ideology of their captors.

≫≪

Captured Americans in North Korea were prisoners of the Chinese army. Indoctrination was conducted by the political department of that army, but quite apart from indoctrination the army itself conducted military interrogations. Every army in the world, upon capturing an enemy soldier, attempts to glean military data, and the Chinese were no different.

Interrogations at Camp 5 took place about a mile away, in Pyoktong proper. In general, only officers were interrogated. Many dreaded the questioning, not necessarily because they feared the Chinese but because of the aspersions that other POWs would cast upon them. "Everyone who was taken out was under suspicion by the other men," Comdr. Ralph Bagwell said, "particularly those who were taken out more frequently than others." Rumormongers in POW camps liked to suggest that those taken to Pyoktong were going for advanced indoctrination, presumably because they had already indicated, to the Chinese, their basic acceptance of communist doctrine. Evidence to support that assumption, however, is rare.[43]

Maj. Ronald Alley was a career field artillery officer. Because the Chinese appeared to concentrate interrogations in the area of artillery, he and others in the artillery branch of the army were subjected to constant questioning. Capt. Ralph Nardella noticed that Major Alley "on frequent occasions was called down by the Chinese—for what purpose I don't know—and he was placed in a cloud of suspicion by these activities by some members of the compound."[44]

Military interrogations came into full swing by the late summer of 1951. At the interrogation center in Pyoktong, Chinese army officers grilled and grilled until getting what they wanted. Capt. Frederick Smith recalled being put into a room where a Chinese officer, through an interpreter, examined him. The interrogator then went back and forth over the same things for a week or ten days. "While they were interrogating they were using intimidations such as, if you ever want to see your family . . . you . . . have to cooperate. There was never anyone standing there holding a gun up to my head or anything like that." Smith later said he was convinced that he gave them only information he was positive they already had.[45]

The enemy not only wanted artillery information orally but also in writing. One day, Major Alley was sitting at a desk, and Lt. Sheldon Foss was about twenty-five feet away. When Foss got up to go to the latrine, he glanced at what was on Alley's desk and "quickly leafed through his manuscript. All I could see of it pertained to artillery, artillery gunnery, the use of the target-grid system, and artillery fire control."[46] The prisoners in Korea had broken the rule of furnishing the enemy with only name, rank, and service number.

Unfortunately, the rule of name, rank, and service number is even more difficult to interpret than to carry out. A dogtag contains additional information—blood type and religion—and most newly captured prisoners carry wallets that contain personal papers. More important is the fact that the name, rank, service number regulation imposes a rule of silence that cannot be reasonably borne, especially under the conditions that prevailed in North Korea. A POW often must deal with the enemy for years and can be interrogated for weeks and months on end. To expect the same ritual response to every question is to expect too much. Those who have sensitive information should, of course, be willing to undergo extensive hardship rather than divulge it. But that situation differs significantly from the norm, in which a POW has no knowledge of classified material yet still is supposed to answer only three questions.*

The intent of those who had devised the rule is clear enough—a technical solution to a difficult problem. Even steadfastly loyal soldiers will inevitably make mistakes if allowed to answer questions as they see fit (just as long as, in their opinion, they are not providing the enemy with information of military usefulness). Some of what they say will be found useful. At minimum, the combination of the small bits of novel information the enemy obtains through interrogation will, when collated, serve some useful purpose. Undoubtedly that is true, and it may be a price worth paying.

The name, rank, and service number regulation has two difficulties. One revolves around its practicality, and the other concerns its ultimate influence on justice. First, it is a fact that the regulation does not work and never has worked. Few soldiers have maintained, after days of interrogation, a blanket refusal to discuss anything but the three permitted facts. If most break the rule, then in a practical organization such as an army that rule is wrong. One cannot impose a technical solution on a human question such as what to say to the enemy. It is demeaning to expect soldiers to behave like machines—and it fails in its purpose.

It would be far more beneficial to teach soldiers to do their best not to reveal militarily useful information than to impose an impossible rule upon them. As things now stand, prisoners who violate the name, rank, and service number regulation are technically "communicating with the enemy." Should military law be strictly enforced when they return home, they will be liable to the penalties that such an act involves. It may be that soldiers say to themselves, "Well, since I'm already a collaborator, it doesn't matter what I tell them now." People under stress do not reason well. Those who know they must do their best will likely do it. Those who know they must comply with an impossibly difficult rule, and that transgressing the rule is dangerous, will despair and give up.

---

* Shortly after the Korean War, the Code of Conduct (Appendix B) was drafted. The code permits POWs to give the enemy their date of birth in addition to name, rank, and service number.

The rule also gives the military justice system an arbitrary authority difficult to reconcile with a sense of fair and impartial justice. Because almost every prisoner of war eventually violates the name, rank, and service number rule, and many shatter it into a thousand pieces well before imprisonment is over, the rule allows the armed forces to prosecute those whom they wish—for whatever reason they wish. If a thousand people violated a rule, for example, and the army chose to court-martial twenty, the arbitrariness of that procedure is a compelling indictment of those who wield power.

In any event, soldiers in Korea had to make do with the rules as they were written. In general, and at whatever cost in guilt to themselves, they compromised with the Chinese. Many POWs felt there was no reason not to answer Chinese questions about the U.S. military because they believed the Chinese already knew the answers. And they did.

When Ronald Alley wrote about the field artillery and attempted to mislead the Chinese in doing so, his interrogator immediately screamed, "You lie, Alley, you lie." He then took a new U.S. Army field artillery manual and threw it in front of him. An enlisted man being interrogated also lied, and his Chinese interrogator "threw a perfectly new NCO Guide down on the floor in front of me." Just a few years before the Korean War began, many officers in the Chinese Nationalist Army had received basic infantry training at Fort Bragg, North Carolina, and artillery training at Fort Sill, Oklahoma.[47]

In 1949, only a year before the Korean War, the communist Chinese under Mao Tse-tung booted the corrupt Nationalist government of Chiang Kai-shek off the mainland. Just before defeat, many of Chiang's officers and men had defected to the communist forces. They brought with them not only equipment but also all types of U.S. Army technical manuals. In some cases, the army "had the kindness to translate [the manuals] into Chinese for the use of the Chinese Nationalist Army," pointed out Col. George Shank, a senior American advisor to the Nationalist forces.[48]

Presumably, therefore, interrogations went on not because the Chinese were deriving much useful information from them but because the interrogators had a job to do, and, like anyone else, they did it. It is difficult to expect American soldiers to hold back information about what was essentially common knowledge when doing so may cost their lives. The rule of name, rank, and service number was ignored.

>«

The lectures, forced study, writing, debate, peace parade, and the signing of the Peace Appeal and certificate of aggression were only the beginnings. A short while after the Peace Appeal had been signed, the Chinese came up with the idea of "peace committees." In June 1951, each squad in Camp 5 elected one man to a company peace committee and then the companies elected men to the camp peace committee. The same thing took place in every other POW camp in North Korea. By the summer of 1951, every camp had a peace committee. Next, each camp elected a certain number of men to a central peace committee, and those POWs were transferred from their various camps to P'yŏngyang, the capital of North Korea.[49]

The men elected to the committees were put there because their fellow prisoners trusted them. As Capt. Robert Wise said, "After the Chinese had announced that a committee would be elected by us it was a matter of determining who are the most likely suckers. The most likely suckers in this case happened to be the individuals who we were certain were the types that were not going to do us any harm and could not particularly do the Chinese any good." No one wanted the job, but as Maj. Mike Lorenzo pointed out, "Someone had to be on the darn thing."[50]

Jeff Erwin was one of those elected for the camp peace committee from the officers' compound; 127 of the 136 surviving officers at Camp 5 in June 1951 voted for him. In addition to being trusted, "Lieutenant Erwin happened to be junior of the whole blooming shooting match and naturally was going to get elected first."[51]

In the sergeants' compound, according to one POW, the Chinese told them "what we were going to do was just fight for peace and that sort of trivial stuff, and that we had no worries, that there would be no court martials, our government would not punish us when we got back, that the people of the world would not allow it." The enlisted compound was even more confused. There had been no training for this sort of thing, and there was no one to whom the men could turn for guidance. At this point, the Chinese allowed officers a short visit to the enlisted area. "In 1951, when they first started to form these peace committees," said Claude Batchelor, "the officers came around and told us the thing was all right, that it was okay to do this; that they didn't think anything would happen about it." Obviously, that was going far beyond name, rank, and service number. Confusion reigned and was coupled with a great deal of emotional stress.[52]

The sergeants, too, according to M. Sgt. Richard Artesani, "tried to pick out the men we could trust and that we thought that would best represent us and still not sell us out." Sgt. Leroy Carter was elected and later said, "I felt that I had been done—I had been done a very mean injustice." M. Sgt. John Porter, a leader of one of the platoons in the black company at Camp 5, said, "It wasn't no honor throwed up on me. I did not want to be elected. We was already told that we do nothing against this committee; we'd be considered a mess to human society and we'd be destroyed."[53]

The peace committees were a front for propaganda. According to Major Lorenzo, "Through my experience as a member of that committee, that committee was set up by the communists to destroy our way of life. There is no question of it." But how was a young, uneducated enlisted man to answer the Chinese when they asked, "Don't you want peace? Are you truly a warmonger?" Whichever way he answered, he was wrong. If the POW replied, "Yes, I want peace," the next step was, "Well, if that's the case, you must fight for peace." If he answered no, he was a warmonger. It was a classic Catch-22 situation.[54]

The North Koreans wanted a say in the conduct of the indoctrination and propaganda effort, and because the war was taking place in their country it was decided that the Central Peace Committee—to which all camp committees reported—should be based in P'yŏngyang. The idea had been well thought out before its inception. Even before the various camp committees were formed, however, a small nucleus of POWs had been transferred to P'yŏngyang. Although the group was associated only indirectly with the Central Peace Committee when it came down to the capital, it was a way for the North Koreans to monitor the indoctrination and propaganda process.

Notes

1. Lt. Jefferson Erwin, USA, Transcripts, 5:1262, 5:1266.
2. Maj. Ronald Alley, USA, Transcripts, 7:725, see also 4:177–78, 4:180, 4:189,

6:397, 6:444–45; Erwin Transcripts, 1:142a; and Cpl. Claude Batchelor, USA, Transcripts, 8:1879.

3. Alley Transcripts, 4:135–36, 8:854, see also 8:923 and Erwin Transcripts, 6:19.

4. Alley Transcripts, 7:764.

5. Lt. Col. Paul Liles, USA, Transcripts, 3:860; see also Alley Transcripts, 7:820, 8:922, 8:953 and Fleming Transcripts, 11:1695.

6. Erwin Transcripts, 4:1115.

7. Alley Transcripts, 6:343.

8. Ibid., 4:181, 4:212, 4:239, 4:264, 5:28, 6:343–44, 6:349, 6:369.

9. Goulden, *Korea,* 141.

10. Liles Transcripts, 4b:1928.

11. Alley Transcripts, 7:790, see also 4:110, 4:225, and 8:1124.

12. Erwin Transcripts, 3:805; see also Alley Transcripts, 4:202 and 4:218.

13. Erwin Transcripts, 5:1375; Alley Transcripts, 5:59, 5:103, 7:544, 7:567, 7:844.

14. Alley Transcripts, 7:844.

15. Ibid., 4:205.

16. Ibid., 4:179, 4:205, see also 4:125 and Erwin Transcripts, 5:1263.

17. Alley Transcripts, 6:386, 8:983; Erwin Transcripts, 1:244a, 1:278a, 1:287a, 3:807, 5:1262, 5:1264.

18. Alley Transcripts, 5:103.

19. Ibid., 4:168.

20. Ibid., 5:33, see also 4:240.

21. Ibid., 9:1410; Batchelor Transcripts, 1:34–35, 13:45.

22. Cpl. Thomas Bayes, USA, Transcripts, 4:1099–100.

23. Alley Transcripts, 4:185, see also 4:160, 4:179, 4:185, 4:199, 4:208, 8:887, 8:915, 8:1055, and Cpl. Harold Dunn, USA, Transcripts, 1:301.

24. Alley Transcripts, 4:113, 7:816; Erwin Transcripts, 2:338.

25. Alley Transcripts, 4:215–16.

26. Ibid., 4:193; 6:365, see also 4:113, 6:375, 6:420, 7:765, and Erwin Transcripts, 1:113a.

27. Alley Transcripts, 6:372; Erwin Transcripts, 1:83–84, 1:95–96, 1:110, 1:115a, 2:378, 5:1265–66.

28. Erwin Transcripts, 2:573; see also Alley Transcripts, 4:114.

29. Alley Transcripts, 4:84–85, 4:114, 5:61; Erwin Transcripts, 1:97.

30. Alley Transcripts, 8:990, 8:993.

31. Ibid., 6:480–81, 7:591, 8:906, 8:994.

32. Ibid., 6:467, see also 6:345–46, 6:481, 6:521, 7:587, 7:686, and 8:886.

33. Ibid., 6:515; see also Erwin Transcripts, 3:813.

34. Alley Transcripts, 8:994–95.

35. Erwin Transcripts, 4:979, see also 2:572, 4:996, 4:1035, Alley Transcripts, 4:113, 6:366, 8:870, 8:902, 8:996–97, 8:1122, and Liles Transcripts, 2:280–81.

36. Batchelor Transcripts, 13:17.

37. Ibid., 13:9.

38. Erwin Transcripts, 2:301.

39. Ibid., 4:1037.

40. Ibid., 1:226a.

41. Ibid., 1:46.

42. Ibid., 1:50.

43. Ibid., 4:931; see also Alley Transcripts, 4:144–45, 4:175, 5:11, and 5:33.

44. Alley Transcripts, 4:213.

45. Ibid., 8:857–58.

46. Ibid., 7:616–17, see also 7:560–61 and 7:670.

47. Ibid., 9:1384; Erwin Transcripts, 1:251a; see also Alley Transcripts, 4:131 and 4:224.

48. Alley Transcripts, 5:288, see also 10:34 and 10:40–41.

49. Erwin Transcripts, 1:52, 2:325–27; Alley Transcripts, 7:632–33, 8:995.

50. Erwin Transcripts, 4:1050–51; Alley Transcripts, 7:696; see also Erwin Transcripts, 3:834.

51. Erwin Transcripts, 4:1051, see also 5:1273.

52. Ibid., 3:833; Batchelor Transcripts, 8:1702.

53. Erwin Transcripts, 2:549, 3:882; Maj. Ambrose Nugent, USA, Transcripts, 6:1342; see also Erwin Transcripts, 3:744.

54. Alley Transcripts, 7:697.

FIVE

Traitors Row?

Son: What is a traitor?
Lady MacDuff: Why one who swears and lies.
  —*Macbeth,* act IV, scene II, line 47

P'yŏngyang is the oldest city in Korea, and in 1950 it had a population of five hundred thousand. After the invasion of Inchon, American troops pushed north and captured the enemy capital on October 20. At the same time, however, the Chinese were entering the war, and P'yŏngyang was only held for six weeks and then abandoned by 8th Army on December 5.

P'yŏngyang is split by the Taedong River; on the north side is the old city and seat of government and on the south is a large, sprawling industrial area. In 1950 the two sections were connected by a highway bridge and two railway bridges. Due to prolonged, intensive bombing by the Air Force and street fighting by ground troops, P'yŏngyang had been devastated by the end of the year.

In late January 1951, Col. Kim Dong Suk, second in command of the Political Bureau of the North Korean army, drove into the squalor of Camp 5 and told the Chinese that he needed twenty prisoners to take south with him to P'yŏngyang. This was the same Colonel Kim who had made life so miserable for Colonels Liles and Fleming at the Valley Camp collection point; who had a "brilliant, keen mind" and would quote passages from the Bible that seemed to contradict each other so as to unnerve and confuse Christian POWs; and who always wore a small Italian pistol and, according to Capt. Clifford Allen, "had a good command of English and knew the facts of life."[1]

The Chinese permitted Captain Allen to choose the men he wanted. Kim obviously had in mind some of the officers from Valley Camp but spent some days interviewing other men as well. It was not likely difficult to persuade POWs to leave the death trap of Camp 5, especially because Kim cunningly concealed that he intended to establish a major North Korean army propaganda center in the capital city.

The men were notified, either individually or in small groups, that the North Koreans needed them for only about ten days. The reasons given were remote. Capt. Bernard Galing was questioned about whether he would care to go to P'yŏngyang and broadcast a list of all POWs in Camp 5. If he did as he was told, he would also be permitted to broadcast a letter to his wife. All POWs were aware that the North Korean government had only one major radio station, and so the offer to speak from P'yŏngyang made sense. They also knew that the enemy had not released the names to the Red Cross; they were all listed as missing in action. Getting names out would mean that the U.S. government would change their designation from MIA to POW. That would be important for their families' peace of mind and would also be a kind of life insurance. The Americans had seen how casually their captors killed POWs. Nothing seemed better calculated to restrain them than a record of the living, a list that would cause the Chinese and North Koreans some embarrassment before the tribunal of world opinion if too many on it were dead when the war was over. Captain Galing may have been thinking of all those things when he said to Kim, "All right, I'll do it."[2]

Kim told Capt. Clifford Allen, "You will gather and identify dead men that were on the battlefields and collect their names and bring them back to us." Lt. Alvin Anderson was notified that he had been picked to join the group of twenty because he was to go on a body recovery detail in the area of Sinŭiju. Some men were more reluctant than others to leave. M. Sgt. Roy Gordon said, "I was called to the Chinese headquarters and asked by Colonel Kim if I wanted to write a letter home or to broadcast a letter home.

There were other prisoners there, as well as myself, and I indicated that I did not want to go along with anything of that nature. The following day I was called out of the place where I was living and told that I was going to leave anyway."[3]

Lt. Col. Harry Fleming could not argue when instructed that he would be one of two senior officers in the group to leave Camp 5. He was told that arrangements had been made for him to make a broadcast to his wife. Fleming—now weak, tired, and thin—was also severely depressed. "I might best sum it up by saying I was very confused," he recalled. "I believe that I was still in a partial state of shock. At that time, I don't believe I had yet resigned myself to the fact that I was a prisoner of the communists. I didn't have very much hope. In fact, I had very little hope; that is hope of survival because of what I had seen. I had the firm realization in my mind that if they didn't shoot me today, they were going to tomorrow. I was figuring every day that the next day was it."[4]

As ranking officer, Kim chose Lt. Col. Paul Liles. Just before leaving Camp 5 with the POWs, Kim asked him, "Are you ready to go to P'yŏng-yang?" "Yes," the colonel replied. "Do you remember the discussion we had? I will go if you allow me to appeal for food." Exuding confidence, Kim firmly stated, "The government seat is there; I am certain that the government will approve your request because they have a humanitarian view."[5]

The twenty men whom Colonel Kim chose to be the nucleus of the propaganda center constituted a cross-section of America. There were ten officers and ten enlisted men: lieutenant colonels and lieutenants, master sergeants and privates, the educated and uneducated, a forty-eight-year-old and an eighteen-year-old, and blacks as well as whites.* All were taken into town and given a shave and haircut, their first in two months. At dusk on January 30, 1951, they were sent off on the 110-mile ride to P'yŏngyang.[6]

The Soviet-made truck traveled throughout the night. Colonel Kim sat

---

* The officers were Lt. Col. Paul Liles, Lt. Col. Harry Fleming, Maj. David MacGhee, Maj. Robert Copeland (black), Capt. Clifford Allen (black), Capt. Bernard Galing, Lt. Louis Wilson (black), Lt. Alvin Anderson (black); Lt. John Crockett, and CWO Dwight Coxe. The enlisted men were M. Sgt. Clarence Covington (black), M. Sgt. Roy Gordon, M. Sgt. Gilbert Christie, Sgt. Clifford Neel, Sgt. Joseph Gardiner, Sgt. Jose Mares, Cpl. Robert Gorr, Cpl. Henry Gambacourta, Pfc. John Ward, and a Private First Class Muse. It is possible that there were more black enlisted personnel than Covington, but that is difficult to ascertain from the documents available.

up front in the cab with two drivers, and the men were crowded in the rear along with three North Korean guards and two fifty-five-gallon drums of gasoline. The truck bed had eighteen-inch wooden sideboards and no canopy. The ride was very, very cold, and fear of the unknown put everyone in the pitch-black Korean night on edge. Sgt. Clifford Neel said, "All of us in the truck were under a mental and physical strain. You might say we were mentally unbalanced at the time." The driver pushed on as fast as the truck could go—along the rough, winding mountainous roads, through snow, and around hairpin turns. The swaying of the truck threw the POWs back and forth against each other, and fights and arguments broke out. The night passed slowly. Sleep was impossible, and the cold bit into the men. At dawn on January 31 they reached the bombed-out town of T'aech'on, where they disembarked and were fed.[7]

It didn't take long for word to get around the small town that POWs had arrived. People gathered to inspect the foreign soldiers and comment on them, and one young woman claimed to have been raped by a U.S. soldier. It was full daylight, and, as other villagers watched, she recounted her story, eventually becoming so agitated that she began to spit at the POWs. Suddenly, an old man began to speak, too. He pointed to an abandoned U.S. 7th Cavalry Regiment tank and began to describe, haltingly and slightly incoherently, how he had lost a family member. The crowd was becoming angry. Many went to their homes and returned with sticks, picks, hoes, and axes. The POWs were surrounded by a shouting mob of more than a hundred.[8]

The only protection they had was Colonel Kim, his two drivers, and three guards. One of the men asked Kim what the people wanted, and he replied, "They want you shot." Lt. Alvin Anderson stood in the middle of the street, the mob all around him: "I was afraid of being struck down or possibly killed and most of the time I just turned in a circle to watch the people in the crowd, to see that no one would get a chance to hit me without me attempting to protect myself in some way." Colonel Kim and the guards slowly moved their charges toward a large building that contained a meeting hall where the GIs would temporarily be held.[9]

In an effort to placate the angry townspeople, Kim agreed to allow them to question the Americans. Just before reaching the hall, he pulled Liles and Fleming aside and said:

This is a town meeting and the people are here to accuse you. If you want to be saved, you must convince them that you were not the ones who destroyed their houses and burned their town. You must convince them that it is the Americans back home. We here, the communists, are trying to educate the people that they must not harm prisoners of war. Every time an American pilot comes down, they kill him. We want to educate them. If it weren't for the communist education of these people, you would all be dead. We are trying to teach them that you, yourselves, are under orders from others and are not personally responsible. That is the only way that any prisoners will survive.[10]

The POWs were put at one end of the hall and ordered to sit on the floor. On the other side, nearly seventy civilians jammed in. Kim and the guards stood between the irate Koreans and worried Americans. For more than an hour, with Kim acting as translator, villagers flung questions at the American soldiers. Fleming and Liles acted as spokesmen and answered such questions as, "Why is the U.S. in Korea?" "Why did you bomb our town?" and "Why did you attack us?" The two colonels did their best to give the most prudent and conciliatory responses possible. Liles, for example, when asked why an American soldier had raped the Korean woman, replied, "In the American Army, such things were punishable by death; . . . we could not explain it but were very, very sorry if it had happened." When told that the crowd charged him with being a warmonger, criminal, and butcher, Fleming replied:

Well, war is something where people get hurt and it is a very unfortunate thing but when two armies are fighting—and this has been true throughout history—people get hurt and homes are destroyed. Frankly, I feel very sorry about it. It is too bad that that has to happen but if it does happen, and you people happen to be those that were in the way of combat, and if these things happen to you—your homes destroyed and other things—I personally feel bad about it. I am sure that there is nobody that does not. The people of the United States feel bad about it.[11]

Somehow the GIs talked themselves out of their predicament. The crowd eventually dispersed, and the soldiers were fed for a second time and allowed to rest. At dusk they boarded the truck once again and continued their southward journey. At 4 on the cold morning of February 1, 1951, the twenty men destined to become the core of all propaganda streaming out of North Korea for the remainder of the year (although they did not know that at the time) entered the northern outskirts of P'yŏng-yang.[12]

During the first half of 1951 the POWs were moved around the eastern and southern environs of the capital seven times. They were not situated permanently on the northern bank of the Taedong River until the second half of the year, when they were officially designated as Camp 12. In the early months, however, they were not in a traditional POW camp. Wherever they moved, they lived in small Korean houses, and the "Peace Camp"—so designated by Colonel Kim—had the smallest collection of prisoners in North Korea. Two weeks after the first group of twenty had arrived from the north, another party of fifteen was shipped in and led by Lt. Chester Van Orman, holder of the Distinguished Service Cross. Sometime during the summer the population increased to seventy-nine, the largest it ever became.[13]

In the area of P'yŏngyang were two other Korean-controlled POW compounds. One, known as "Pak's Palace" after its commanding officer, was the main interrogation center of North Korea; the other was Camp 9, commonly called "the Caves." Pak's Palace, a short distance north of the city, was a small compound surrounded by barbed wire and guarded by Korean soldiers. A great many downed pilots were shipped there for interrogation by North Korean and Soviet officers. Torture was common, and Capt. Lawrence Miller, an F-84 fighter pilot, said, "I don't know of anyone that stayed there more than six months and survived."[14] The Caves were even grimmer.

As soon as the twenty original GIs arrived in P'yŏngyang from Camp 5, Kim demanded that a leader be elected. As he had been in the Valley Camp, Colonel Fleming was again elected. "The man who is compound leader under the communists," Colonel Liles pointed out, "is in truly a terrible position, for no man can serve two masters; he must remain loyal to his government yet someone must emerge from the prisoners to be a go-between between them and the enemy." It did not take long for the stress of being leader to show. Before spring, Fleming's partially gray hair turned completely white. In order for his men to get what they needed for survival, Lieutenant Anderson reported, "I am sure Colonel Fleming had to prostitute his dignity." "I felt that Col. Fleming went as far with Kim as he could," Captain Allen commented, "since Col. Fleming was obviously at a disadvantage, both in being a prisoner and Kim's being armed. I sometimes shook my head a bit and questioned whether or not he was being as prudent as he should have been, but he showed a great deal of spunk."[15]

With Fleming in charge at Camp 12, prisoners had to toe the line, for he would take no nonsense from anyone, officer or enlisted. "We had a perfect military organization in a sense," Captain Allen said. "We had more discipline there than any other camp that I was in. Colonel Fleming was responsible for it." Still, the men were suspicious of each other and showed very little interest in the welfare of fellow prisoners. Pvt. John Narvin, a member of the second group of fifteen POWs who arrived at Camp 12, remembered, "I didn't trust anybody."[16]

Harry Fleming didn't care how much he was resented. He intended to keep his men alive by organizing them and then fighting for them. At Valley Camp, his ability to keep men alive was demonstrated by that camp's far lower death rate than any other collection points in Korea. Fleming worked on one principle: "I will give my soul in hell to get every man out of here alive."[17]

≫≪

The only reason for the existence of Camp 12 was propaganda, and on the third day after the men arrived Colonel Kim gave Fleming blank pieces of paper and ordered him to have all the prisoners write about their experiences in Korea. Each was to sign his manuscript. Fleming was told that not forcing the men to write and sign would cost his life. The threat was not all that influenced Fleming. He was still swayed by the same reasoning that had caused many of the men to come willingly to P'yŏngyang: "We felt, either right or wrong at the time, that any name that we could get out to our own government, to our own army, that the name would go back to their folks at home and they would know that they were alive. Also, the chances of survival would probably be greater for those individuals because the communists, we felt, wouldn't be quite as apt to murder somebody if our people knew that they were alive behind the lines." The compositions, of course, were written within the arrangements desired by Kim and were returned to him in a few days.[18]

In addition to writing about their experiences and signing that document, signing blank pieces of paper to be laid beneath various "appeals" was also a common practice at Camp 12 during 1951. Fleming accepted that procedure, because "whether you placed your signature on a blank piece of paper that was under one of the appeals that you would not sign, or whether it was under some other one, all it meant was that papers could be shifted very easily so actually, strictly speaking, it didn't mean anything to refuse to sign one and sign another one, the way the communists operate."[19]

When word of Camp 12 filtered into the POW camps along the Yalu, the area around the capital became known as "Traitors Row." In spite of the fact that Camp 12 had been created specifically to produce propaganda, that name seems harsh; each camp, after all, was producing propaganda in one form or another.[20]

Colonel Liles managed to take a positive view of the work done at his camp and said, "Camp 12 exposes to all the people in the United States, and it should expose all over the world, the techniques the communists used to obtain these things from the prisoners; by extreme duress, starvation, and absence of medical care for the prisoners, and the degradation to which they subjected us. This, in the long run, should convince free people all over the world the true nature of communism." Perhaps. Liles was on more debatable ground, however, when he added, "Therefore, I consider that we dealt communism a very severe blow at Camp 12 and at no time did we ever give any real aid or comfort to the enemy."[21]

≫≪

Classes were held during the day, and readings occurred nightly. If Camp 12 was to be the propaganda center of the war, then prisoners expected to spout the gospel of communism were also expected to know about it. During the deliberative periods after the readings, Clifford Allen said, "We discussed speeches by Vihinsky at the United Nations, speeches by Molotov at the meetings of the United Nations in San Francisco in 1945—the charter meetings. We discussed the history of the Communist Party. We discussed the proceedings of the Second World Peace Congress, which was a communist organization, which held a meeting in Warsaw, Poland, in 1950. We discussed that type of thing—all of it communist literature and the like." The discussions went on every day from the moment the men formed the camp in early February 1951.[22]

POWs interned at Camp 12 reported that during the first three weeks of indoctrination many classes were conducted by a Mr. and Mrs. Suh, employees of Radio P'yŏngyang. Mrs. Suh was the former Ann Wallis, who had been born in Arkansas, moved to Oklahoma, and gone to Korea as a missionary. There she met and married her husband and returned to the United States for the last time in 1939 for a brief visit. She was alleged to have been the counterpart of World War II propagandists Axis Sally and Tokyo Rose. The forty-year-old American was commonly known throughout the Korean War as "Seoul City Sue." She reportedly took on the soldiers of Camp 12 with a vengeance. During her three-week stay, the Americans would sit on the floor and be read to from various magazines and then asked for comments. Mrs. Suh had gone to Korea to spread Christianity but instead attempted to indoctrinate U.S. citizens into the virtues of atheistic communism. When she left Camp 12 to continue broadcasting English-language information to American front-line troops, Colonel Kim took over the studies. After Kim, the prisoners themselves were forced to lead classes.[23]

In addition to readings, the men at Camp 12 were required to study the history of the Communist Party and concentrate on learning everything in a work entitled *The State and Social Structure of the USSR*. Colonel Fleming did much of the instruction and recalled, "I was very pleased to handle that subject; there are in [that book] wide open loopholes of the soviet government and it gives anyone who wants to read it, and study it, an idea of exactly what is wrong with communism." Whenever possible, he tried to downplay propaganda. "In the classes that I attended," Lieutenant Van Orman noted, "Colonel Fleming's comments were favorable to the United States at all times." Although it is difficult to do while under supervision, Fleming did attempt to teach. "I learned considerable about the United States from Col. Fleming," remarked Dan Oldwage. "He would compare our system of free enterprise to their system and I know he opened my eyes. I knew nothing about communism when I went there and he opened my eyes to a lot of things that were detrimental to communism."[24]

Communist newspapers and periodicals flowed into the tiny group at Camp 12 all during the summer and fall of 1951. The men received, read, and debated articles from the *China Monthly Review*, the *Shanghai News*, *Voks*, *Soviet Union*, the New York and London editions of the *Daily Worker*, the *People's Guardian*, *New Korea*, and a Bulgarian publication entitled *For an Everlasting Peace*. As in Chinese-administered camps to the far north, what was required at Camp 12 was to read, study, and learn. Yet from all accounts it seems the teaching was ineffective. The small band of officers and men were tightly organized and well led. The most intense communist instruction seemed neither to convince them nor alter their loyalty to the United States. It did, however, impress them.[25] There was no way to oppose the North Koreans openly and live. The men had to appear to believe what they were being told, and doing so lowered their already low morale.[26]

>«

Every man received two meals a day, each consisting of one small cup of a poor grade of millet. Because the prisoners were moved around so much during the first half of the year, Korean women were pressed into cooking service by Colonel Kim in whatever area the prisoners happened to be. To supplement their subsistence diet, whenever the men could they picked grass, dandelions, and other weeds to boil and eat. Until mid-summer, all the men were in horrible physical condition. M. Sgt. Roy Gordon remembered, "I was passing worms almost daily, as well as blood—both [in] fecal matter, urine and also vomiting blood at the same time." "You know what I dreamed of mostly, my continuous thought?" Fleming said. "I would like to tell you what it was. It was a cool, clear, cold glass of water."[27]

Food was used in Camp 12—as elsewhere—as a tool. Liles remembered that "whenever you would oppose them, down would go the rations," although the captors would never admit to such a cause-and-effect relationship. When Fleming asked for more food, Kim replied, "You are always demanding more. Can't you see the poor starving Koreans? We have nothing. You have bombed it all. The brutal American Air Force, those barbarians, have bombed it all. There is nothing left." Fleming developed a deep-seated hatred for Kim and "spent many sleepless nights in figuring out fantastic plans where some day we would meet again, under slightly different circumstances."[28]

While Seoul City Sue was instructing one day, Colonel Fleming approached her and pleaded for food. Apparently, his petition touched her, for she spoke on their behalf, and, as Colonel Liles related, "Kim finally agreed to give us a meal of dog." The first dog they were to receive disappeared, to be eaten by the guards. Another was provided, and the prisoners ate that even though it was small and served in a soup. In Liles's opinion, it was very tasty.[29]

Men at Camp 12 underwent the most extreme indoctrinational pressure endured by POWs in North Korea. That was because of the strictly propagandistic purpose of the camp and the small group involved. It was easy for the Koreans to watch each man and, if he wasn't learning "the truth," place him under duress. Normally, however, the enemy took collective rather than individual action. According to Captain Allen, they treated the Americans like animals:

> They used the wild animal treatment on us. You know, when you want to tame a wild animal you starve him out first, then give him a little morsel of food. And the plan is that when you give it that little morsel of food, it loses some of its wildness and becomes a little more tame and related to you; and then you give it a little more and it begins to dance a little to your tune. That is the same technique they were using with us. Our objective, in the final analysis, was survival—as long as we did not have to prostitute our patriotism or our country.[30]

It was becoming increasingly hard to be sure what constituted such a prostitution. The prisoners had nothing to give but themselves, which was all the communists wanted. Colonel Fleming, the sternly demanding, old-fashioned army officer that he was, had said he would go to hell to get his men out alive. The compromises that such a noble attitude required, however, were going to become severe. Only the first of the compromises was covered by a statement from Fleming: "I was in no mood or position to argue with them—so if the communists wanted to say that the North was attacked by the South, or the South was attacked by the North, that was perfectly all right with me and the rest of the prisoners. Nobody was going to get hurt by it."[31]

Four weeks after arriving at Camp 12 and a mere few days after Seoul City Sue had completed her preliminary indoctrination, Colonel Kim announced that some would be required to make voice recordings for broadcast. Colonels Fleming and Liles protested vigorously, but Kim replied, "I will march you back north to Pyoktong [Camp 5] on foot. The winter is very, very cold. Do you think you could make it?" Fleming did not think it an idle threat, and Liles said, "In our weakened condition, it was tantamount to a death sentence."[32]

The POWs had to write their own broadcasts. Colonel Fleming wrote a letter home, as had been suggested by Kim as the reason for being at P'yŏngyang in the first place. "One of the most important things that I had in my mind was to let my wife know I was alive," he said. When he showed his letter to Kim, he was told that it should be longer. The colonel replied that he had included everything he intended to say.[33]

Colonel Kim gave way to an exceptionally intense outburst of anger and told Fleming to make the letter long enough to fill fifteen minutes of air time. When Fleming brought back the result of his second effort, Kim found that too personal. What was desired, of course, was that Fleming, after greeting his wife, should give the communist version of his experiences in North Korea. When he retorted, "Well, I can't do that," Kim reminded him of the realities of the long return march north, mentioned further cuts in rations, and sent the emaciated but still stubborn American officer back to work. Fleming rewrote the script twenty-five times before it was accepted.[34]

Fleming and Liles were two of the five men chosen in early March 1951 to make the short trip to P'yŏngyang and record their scripts. "Fleming was one of those who made a broadcast but he did not do it voluntarily," Liles said. "It was made quite clear by the Koreans that if he wanted to eat, we would have to comply and all the rest of the men ate the food that was obtained by these broadcasts. The broadcast was cleverly written by Fleming and was purposely very vague and nebulous."[35]

Colonel Fleming had resisted saying many of the more extreme things that Kim desired of him. He did not say, for example, that South Korea had attacked the north, as the communists liked to claim, but evasively remarked, "As we all know, a civil war broke out." Nor did he declare that communism was the answer to world problems or call upon UN soldiers to throw down their arms and surrender. Nevertheless, the broadcast was replete with propaganda and lies, including the extraordinary statement that from the day of his capture until the present Fleming had "received treatment that [was] in strict accordance with the principles of humanity and democracy." The broadcast sharply criticized the U.S. bombing of North Korea and compared it to the Nazi destruction of Coventry. "I have seen many Coventries here in Korea," Fleming added. He also described U.S. support for its ally as interference in Korea's internal affairs. "If the United States and other foreign armies will leave this county at once, peace will be immediately restored," he concluded. The phrase "other foreign armies" was not intended to include the Chinese, whom Fleming never once mentioned in the broadcast.[36]

Liles made a recording at the same time as Fleming and tried in every way possible to insert intelligence information into his script. Although the recordings were made at the main radio station, they did not air until a few weeks after they were made. Capt. Clifford Allen, who also read a script, later said, "I was ashamed of the whole recording. I was pointedly—very, very pointedly ashamed of any portion of the recording that referred to the Korean War."[37]

Kim still was not satisfied. He now had thirty-five POWs in the camp.* Therefore, he had thirty-five voices with which to preach the "truth." Kim called Fleming to his quarters and shocked him by saying, "You and the rest of the prisoners have shown, by your attitude and what you have been doing, that you are insincere. Everyone must make a broadcast. Many of these people do not have an education or intelligence enough to write, so I am going to start roundtable discussions where many people can be on the same recording."[38] It must by now have been clear to all in Camp 12 that their purpose at P'yŏngyang was to make propaganda for the enemy.

At the outbreak of the war, Radio P'yŏngyang and Radio Peking (many tapes were shipped to China for broadcast) received saturation coverage by the Foreign Broadcast Information Service. The National Security Council had charged that agency of the U.S. government with monitoring all foreign broadcasts. Their receiving station on Bolo Point, Okinawa ("Zampa-Misaki" in Japanese) was a busy place for three years. Its receivers were capable of intercepting long-, medium-, and short-wave transmissions, which were then recorded on dictabelts, slowed, transcribed, and forwarded to Washington. Messages out of China were clear because Peking's station was powerful and had many bands. Radio P'yŏngyang was a problem, however, because it was a low-power station and broadcast over a band commonly used by morse code stations. Nevertheless, during the first eighteen months of the war, Bolo Point intercepted (from either Peking or P'yŏngyang), transcribed, and sent to Washington approximately 215 broadcasts by American POWs.[39]

---

* The original twenty were in camp, as well as fifteen men who arrived with Van Orman a few weeks later.

Camp 12 was constantly covered by a cloud of fear, "a fear of the food being cut out from under us, fear of going to the Caves, and just a fear of not knowing what was going on, no news from home or anything like that," said Van Orman. Harry Fleming took a heavy share of the mental punishment. As camp leader, he acted as a buffer between the men and Colonel Kim, who did not hesitate to threaten, berate, or embarrass Fleming on a regular basis.[40]

The men at Camp 12 knew of nothing that frightened them more than the place known as "the Caves."* The site was located northeast of the capital, near the small town of Kangdong. There were nine caves, each between seventy-five and a hundred feet long, and entrances were between ten and fifteen feet wide. Sgt. Jose Mares said, "The Caves were something like what the Koreans built for air raid shelters, just big holes in the ground with trees over the top and logs—built right over the hillside. You can't even tell they are there." Outwardly, the purpose of the facility was to hold South Korean POWs and unruly American prisoners and serve as a collection point for captured GIs before their move north to a permanent camp. Those at Camp 12, however, regarded the Caves as a place of horror.[41]

In order to obtain their meager rations from the main distribution center, the soldiers of Camp 12 were required to pass the Caves regularly. "The Caves were a dreadful place," Captain Allen recalled. "I saw scores of United Nations prisoners lying there just dying. They were skeletons—living skeletons or walking corpses, with their eyes bulging just like a bullfrogs. They would look at you and they didn't know who you were and you didn't know who they were. I estimate at the time I passed through there that there must have been three hundred graves." Other POWs saw frozen South Korean bodies piled on the ground above the Caves and their entrances. One officer who tried counting the bodies guessed there might have been as many as a hundred.[42]

One day, after Colonel Kim had remarked to Colonel Fleming on the "insincerity" the Americans had exhibited toward the North Korean propaganda program, he suddenly turned to Fleming and said, "There are

---

* The Caves were known officially as Camp 9.

some American prisoners over in the Caves. Would you like to go over and talk to them?" "Yes, I would," was the reply. "All right, we will go."

They walked about a half-mile to the entrance of one of the holes, and Fleming saw fourteen recently captured GIs from the 2d Infantry Division inside. Kim walked away, leaving the colonel alone with the men. Their morale was gone, and they all had dysentery and were using the front of the cave as a latrine. There was no water except for a slimy pool of accumulated brown, muddy liquid inside the hole. Fleming told them where Camp 12 was and then said, "We are caught in this propaganda thing. We are fighting against it with everything we can do but if you come there, you are going to get caught in it. But I think that it would be much better than here." The GIs begged him to get them out, and the colonel asked Kim to transfer them to Camp 12. The request was refused. A few days later, Kim once again brought Fleming to the Caves. Now there were fewer people, and he saw bodies of some who had died.[43]

Within the week, Kim walked Harry Fleming to the Caves yet again. One man remained. He was crying. "He could barely talk," Fleming recalled. "He couldn't stand. I knelt down beside him and talked with him and he knew that he was going to die—and I knew he was going to die." And soon enough, he did. Fourteen young American soldiers had died to demonstrate to Colonel Fleming and the men of Camp 12 that Colonel Kim did not make idle threats.[44]

Some Americans did survive the Caves, however. When Airman First Class Marvin King entered the Caves on Mother's Day in 1951, seventy-six American and British POWs were there with him. Six weeks later he was transferred to Camp 12, together with eleven others. The remaining sixty-five were dead. King remembered lying on the mud floor to go to sleep on one of his first nights in the Caves. The man on his right said to the man on his left, "Hey, Joe, I think I'll die tonight." The other man replied, "All right, if you will, I will, too." The next morning, Airman King awoke and found them both dead.[45]

After his capture in April 1951, Air Force S. Sgt. George Millward had been shipped to China for interrogation, but two weeks later he was sent south to the Caves. A severe wound in his left leg received no attention and "was torn completely to the bone to the extent that you could run your finger underneath the bone and out the other side." Gangrene set in, and, Millward remembered, "I probably would have lost my life if I had not let the flies into the wound and blow it to cause maggots to get into it." He was one of the lucky few who survived, but, he recalled, "When we would go outside for our morning sunlight, we could see the burial details, as we called them, leaving the other caves and carrying the stretchers, heading toward the mountains."[46]

Twice during the year of Camp 12's existence, two groups of four men each were, as Kim put it, "purged." Included in the first group was Capt. Bernard Galing, who had taken strenuous exception to things Kim said. Also purged was Air Force Maj. David MacGhee, who had a habit of looking up at B-29s on bombing missions and laughing. "He was always waving to them with a happy expression on his face and saying, 'There goes my boys; I wish I was up there with them,'" Fleming said. One day Kim caught him, and MacGhee's next three weeks were spent among the dying. The first four men from Camp 12 joined twenty-three other U.S. prisoners who had been there for some time, and everyone died during that three-week period except the four. MacGhee said, "I know of no one surviving from the original group [of twenty-three]. Of the four of us who went to the place, the only way I can think of it is that the good lord intervened and we were taken away before it was too late." Fortunately, the second group of four also survived.[47]

≫≪

In April 1951, Colonel Kim set up four different panels with five POWs on each. Each panel, or "roundtable," was given a separate topic for discussion, and Colonel Fleming moderated a panel on the subject of the Second World Peace Conference. If some of the prisoners could not write, at least they could talk, and Fleming's recorded discussion was aired over Radio P'yŏngyang on May 4, 1951.[48]

It had taken about a month to work on their thirty-minute broadcast, and, Fleming said, "We were all trying to use the brains of all of us to stall, sabotage, change words, change ideas." Yet there was also a temptation to hurry the thing along. Kim, after all, had told Harry Fleming, "If you would quit stalling and get this thing done, I will do what I can to get these people out of the Caves." The strain showed on everyone. At one point, Fleming recalled, "Colonel Kim had been harassing me for so long and our living conditions were so terrible at that time that I must have gone almost berserk. I told Kim to 'go fuck himself,' that I quit as compound leader. I told him to shoot me, send me to the Caves—I couldn't take anymore." Kim then said, "You go back." Nothing resulted from the incident.[49]

During the month-long preparation for the panel discussion, Kim brought in a captured South Korean soldier to act as translator for Fleming. He stuck to the colonel like glue and even slept beside him. Sgt. Clifford Neel pointed out, "It was strange that anything you said about the North Koreans got back to them. You could not even trust your buddy who sat next to you." That became easier to understand after the recordings, when Fleming saw his South Korean interpreter in the uniform of the North Korean army.[50]

Immediately after the rather stiff and unspontaneous panel discussions were recorded, two "appeals" were read into a microphone. The prisoners were ordered to voice-sign them and did. One appeal was to Truman and MacArthur and the other to the "Five Great Powers."* CWO Dwight Coxe said, "The statement was read by a member of the camp and the rest of the camp then filed through in order of rank and announced their name, rank, serial number, and organization on the two." M. Sgt. Gilbert Christie volunteered to read the second appeal "because to me there was nothing wrong with it; it was just an appeal to the Five Great Powers. It didn't mean anything, for or against any form of government. It merely asked for a peaceful solution to the Korean War. Another reason I read it was because if you didn't take an active part in this group, or cooperate as Colonel Kim called it, then you were due to be sent to the Caves." One of those who voice-signed both appeals was M. Sgt. Roy Gordon because "initially, they didn't look to me as though by a soldier they would be considered treasonous; and then it was another way of notifying my family that I was still alive, inasmuch as there was no opportunity for any letters to go home." Unless something was done, some action taken, and some of these things recorded, serious harm might come to the group for failure to cooperate.[51]

The third recorded appeal called for capitulation and included in its script the words "lay down your arms and surrender." Fleming stood to the side of the room, frustrated and confused. Liles was also there but not listening because he had been seized with severe stomach cramps and was

---

*The Five Great Powers included the United States, the Soviet Union, Great Britain, France, and China.

kneeling and writhing in pain. Fleming, who later insisted that he had no intention of signing a surrender appeal, was called up to voice-sign the third recording and did so. Liles staggered to his feet and did the same. At that point, something resembling a riot broke out.[52]

Lt. Bonnie Bowling, who had heard the recording, looked over at Wilson and Van Orman and told them he would not sign. Lt. Louis Wilson agreed because he felt that "the idea of announcing my name to that was quite a bit more serious than to the one to the Five Great Powers which, in my opinion, was innocuous." Men were protesting to each other all around the room, and Bowling stood and motioned Wilson and Van Orman to leave the building with him. They did, and everyone left with them. Colonel Kim, upon seeing this, lost control and screamed "come back, come back." "Make them come back and sign their names," he yelled at Fleming. "You will be shot to death." It was, however, out of Fleming's hands.[53]

A tape was in existence asking for the surrender of United Nations troops in Korea, and two field-grade officers of the U.S. Army had signed it. "I was determined that something had to be done right there," Liles recalled. "It was in the moment of confusion that this happened." While everyone was milling around in the courtyard, Paul Liles was watching the attendant wind the tape, take it off the machine, and place it on the lid. When the operator left, he "eased back into the room, picked up the tape, put it in my field jacket pocket and put another tape in its place." He then slipped out the door and mingled with the crowd. About sixty yards away was a well of circular stone construction three feet high. Liles walked over to it, removed the tape from his pocket, and placed his hand on the edge of the well. No one was watching. He released the tape and heard it hit the water thirty feet down. After the war, a pleased Paul Liles announced, "To my knowledge, that tape is there this day."[54]

The most important (and damaging) of the recordings was that concerning surrender, and Kim no doubt knew he'd hit a brick wall. The POWs stuck together and won, and Colonel Kim never followed up in the execution of another surrender recording. In Colonel Fleming's opinion, "We lost a battle but Kim lost the war because that was the turning point for Kim and he did not last very much longer. I am certain in my own mind that he fell into disfavor with his higher commanders because he did not get what he thought he was going to get. I think in the short while he stayed with us afterwards, he was retaliating against us for the uprising that had happened on that particular day."[55]

About three weeks after the recordings, Camp 12 was required, as were all Chinese-controlled camps along the Yalu, to form a camp peace committee.* At the formation meeting in Kim's quarters, he told the POWs that they could now write letters home and even send a delegate back to the American lines. When Liles heard they could send someone back to the lines, he began to plan an escape. First, he would try to place a few of his men on the committee. Liles wanted Coxe, Neel, and Van Orman and tried to convince Kim, even telling him that Sgt. Clifford Neel was an American peasant and would make "a fine fighter for the cause of peace." Kim agreed to Coxe and Neel but refused Van Orman, whom he called a hardened reactionary. The final composition of Camp 12's peace committee was Colonel Liles, chair; M. Sgt. Clarence Covington, vice chair; Cpl. James Taylor of the British army, secretary; and Chief Warrant Officer Coxe and Sergeant Neel as members.[56]

The peace committee had only two meetings, one on May 12 to form itself and another on May 23 to pass a resolution to send two POWs out of Korea, one to be a representative to the United Nations and the other to the World Peace Conference. Nothing was done immediately, however, because Kim pointed out that the Central Peace Committee (CPC), which consisted of representatives of all POW camp peace committees, would be coming into Camp 12 within the next week or so. Liles was happy about the delay, for it gave him more time to make preparations.[57]

Before men started to flow in from other camps, a major change took place at Camp 12. Col. Harry Fleming, who had led the camp for four months, was replaced by Capt. Clifford Allen, a black infantry company commander. A new election had been ordered, likely by Kim; as senior officer, Liles could have ordered the men to reelect Fleming but chose not to do so. In his opinion, Fleming had become "an old broken man" after being dismissed by those he had led.[58]

Fleming's reputation as a severe and sometimes cranky disciplinarian was, in the opinion of many, well earned. Evidently, the POWs no longer thought of themselves as being in a military environment and so replaced

---

* The North Korean administration officially labeled the propaganda area around P'yŏngyang as Camp 12 on May 19, 1951.

Fleming with an officer whom they felt would not be as hard on them. Judged by normal military standards it was an astonishing act. Even more astonishing, given the era in which the events occurred, was that Allen was black. He was also an extremely capable leader in the opinion of Paul Liles, and clearly that must have been so.[59]

»«

In mid-June 1951, the Central Peace Committee members elected from Camps 5 and 7 arrived in the outskirts of P'yŏngyang. At Camp 7, Maj. Ambrose Nugent, who had survived the Tiger's death march, had been elected by the camp peace committee to be part of the central committee. Also elected from Camp 7 was Cpl. Robert Ghyers, who was essentially illiterate. Neither wanted the transfer.[60]

Before leaving Camp 7, Nugent, down to 125 pounds from his normal 215, was in a casual conversation with Capt. Herb Marlatt and "mentioned the fact . . . that he was deeply concerned with the survival of the camp." By going to P'yŏngyang, "he would certainly see what he could do to save some of the lives in that group and he felt that maybe, in that way, he could improve our chances of survival." On the day of departure Major Nugent also reported to his superior, Lt. Col. John Dunn. "I don't know how far I am getting into this thing," he said, "but at least I will be two hundred miles closer to the 38th. When I get down there, I will try to get some information back to you. I don't know how I'm going to do it, but I will try to work out some system."[61]

Six delegates were sent from Camp 5, including Lt. Jeff Erwin, who did not want to go. When he made his resistance known to the Chinese, "We went through this haranguing again. It was 'You are either going to do it or you are going to die—you are going to move.' The first ultimatum they gave me was going into China that night and face eternal non-repatriation." On the morning of June 13, 1951, the group from Camp 5, Erwin among them, headed south.[62]*

When the men from Camps 5 and 7 arrived, Camp 12 was assigned its permanent location on the north bank of the Taedong River (map 4). Until that time, the original thirty-five men had been moved about on the

---

* The group from Camp 5 was composed of Capt. Harold Kaschko, Lt. Jefferson Erwin, M. Sgt. John Porter, Sgt. Leroy Carter, Rifleman Ted Spencer (British), and Sgt. Hatta Ozturk (Turkish).

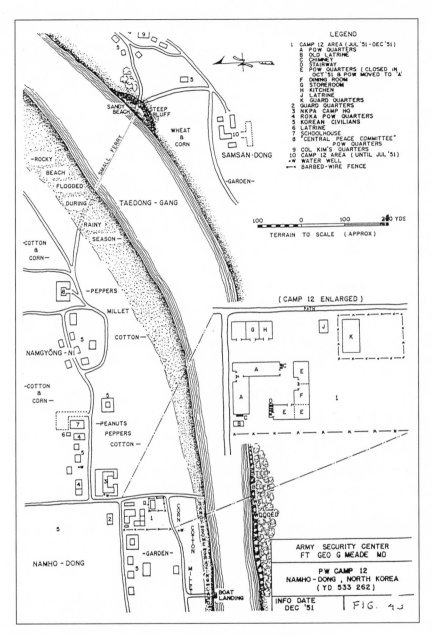

Map 4. Camp 12. (Lt. Col. Paul Liles, USA, Transcripts, 6:147)

southern side of the river. Also at this time, Colonel Kim was relegated to a subordinate position and a new North Korean administration took over. Although Camp 12 and the CPC were not formally affiliated, they were about five hundred yards from each other and under the same Korean control. There was much interaction between the two groups. A Major Kwon became the officer in charge of political indoctrination, a Major Pak acted as commanding officer, and a Major Sul was also involved. Sul had two years at Columbia University and then transferred to Ohio State University, where he received an undergraduate degree. Because the CPC was moving in, an additional thirty guards arrived. The total POW population in the area reached approximately seventy men.[63]

The soldiers of Camp 12 did not trust the new men from Camps 5 and 7. "We suspected them of having turned communist and they suspected us," noted Colonel Liles. "For days we talked the 'party line' to each other, wondering how to break the ice."[64]

When Major Nugent arrived from Camp 7, everyone immediately took notice of him. At first he would not eat and handed his food away, yet he talked incessantly about different recipes. At night he would awaken and sit in the compound, his head in his hands. Upon first seeing Nugent, Lieutenant Van Orman said, "It appeared to me that the man seemed to have an uncontrollable fear of the Koreans. Perhaps the best way that I can describe it is if you can envision children that are scared of a drunken father who beats them when he comes in drunk and are afraid, or willing to do anything that they might be able to do to please him to keep him from beating them." Paul Liles felt that Nugent had reached the thin line separating sanity from insanity:

He was extremely emaciated, legs swollen from beri-beri, faltering gait, hand trembling, eyes looking around all the time, behind him; that was his condition physically—gaunt, his head or his face looked like a skull, something like the Buchenwald pictures. His mental condition; extreme terror, incoherence, hardly able to carry a decent conversation; talked incessantly about the Tiger and atrocities and killings; about how the Koreans were—you just couldn't do anything with them—they were maddening. I thought that he was on the verge of a nervous breakdown. I don't believe he was insane; I have very little experience with psychopathic cases, I don't know. I have seen only a very few insane people in my whole life but I would just say that from a layman's point of view he was in a very, very critical mental state.[65]

A more serious problem concerned Trooper Ronald Cocks of the 8th Hussars, 29th British Brigade. Cocks, many believed and testified to, was a member of the British Communist Party. Sometime before the CPC came in, this British soldier was transferred to Camp 12 proper and became the only representative from Camp 12 to the Central Peace Committee.[66]

Cocks was a thorn in everyone's side. When he was around, the men were extremely careful about what they said. One day Liles cornered the Englishman and said, "At least you don't have to work hard like you are doing. Look at everyone else." "Yes," Cocks replied. "They are insincere; they are not really behind the people's cause. I am in this all the way I tell you, all the way." A short time later, Van Orman and Allen were standing in the compound when Cocks walked in with a Korean. Both were laughing. Cocks was waving a surrender leaflet he was acknowledging to have just written and said, "This one will really hang me." Van Orman, a steely, cold expression on his face, turned to Allen and said, "I think I'll kill that son of a bitch."[67]

A plan to eliminate Trooper Cocks was formulated, and it was agreed that Lieutenant Van Orman and Sergeant Neel would perform the murder. They planned to entice Cocks down toward the river, only a short distance away, and drown him. Somehow Cocks got wind of the plot, however, and began walking down a trail toward headquarters to ask for protection. On the dirt path he met Lieutenant Erwin, who asked what was wrong. Cocks complained that a plan was in effect to kill him. Erwin knew that and told Cocks that informing would surely make him a dead man. He also tried to persuade Cocks that he was imagining the event. Finally, "I convinced him that actually there was no plot to kill him and he relaxed." For some reason, possibly because of Erwin's intervention, the plan to kill Cocks was dropped.[68]

When all representatives from Camps 5 and 7 eventually arrived, Paul Liles let it be known to everyone that they must obey his orders even though the other groups of prisoners were separate and distinct from Camp 12. The colonel had an ingenious plan, but if his commands were not carried out—to the letter—it would fail (map 5). Liles went up to Nugent and talked to him about the strict cooperation that would be needed. He also spoke with Erwin, informing him that he was accepting full responsibility for any commands given and subsequently carried out. Erwin replied that any orders given would be obeyed without question. Liles

To: Commanding General Eighth U.S. Army

Seventy American POWs at Camp No. 12 in Village "X" (Honan-Ri, Chizung Pyongyang Namdo)
in latitude 39.1 N, longitude 125.9 E on bank of Taedong River 12 miles east of Pyongyang. No enemy troops within 5 miles except guard detachment of 35 North Korean boys armament 16 rifles, 7 tommy guns, 3 pistols. Enemy anti-aircraft artillery weak 2 heavy AA at
Pyongyang & AAAW guns along road southward. POWs 50% able bodied others sick.

    1. Plan Able—rescue 70 POWs at Camp 12 by helicopters under cover of heavy air strike
on village.
        a. Signals. At noon forty-eight hours prior to day of rescue two U.S. fighter air-
craft strafe west along Taedong River past village, then strafe east. At midnight, five
hours prior to rescue, fly over village and drop four white flares. POWs will then flash code
letters Able Zebra from the ground by lamp signifying they will be ready for rescue.
        b. At zero five hundred hours on day of rescue bomb and strafe village then land he-
licopters on LZ (stoney beach). POWs will be lying on the beach in a "Tee" formation
wearing white shirts. Helicopters land at extremities of TEE and embark POWs. First helicopter bring in six BARS with ammo. Helicopters approach Camp 12 from north flying low
along river, as bluffs provide defilade against AAAW along road south of Pyongyang.

    2. Plan Baker—drop arms and equipment at Camp 12 and rescue 40 able bodied POWs any-
where within 20 miles.
        a. Signals. At noon thirty-six hours prior to airdrop two U.S. fighter aircraft
strafe east along Taedong River past village, then strafe west. At midnight just prior to
airdrop, fly over village and drop four green flares. POWs will then flash code letters Able
Zebra from the ground by lamp signifying they will receive airdrop. Twenty minutes later
drop arms and equipment into DZ.
        b. List of Arms and equipment in bundles w/luminous markers.

    38 Rifles (M1) w/2 bandoliers each
    1 Carbine w/4 loaded clips
    2 bayonet, knife
    2 launcher, grenade, rifle
    40 grenades, hand, frag.
    12 grenade rifle, smoke, signal, violet
    2 pots, smoke
    40 Ration "C"
    2 Flashlight
    2 Radio, SCR 300
    1 Set signal panels
    2 Compass, lensatic
    1 Binocular
    1 Map, annotated
    1 First Aid Kit

    c. POWs will recover equipment, organize one rifle platoon and move out to location
marked on map. This rendezvous should be within 20 miles of Camp 12 and on high ground
suitable for organizing a defensive perimeter. Thirty hours after making airdrop send
aircraft over rendezvous with radio open. Upon sighting friendly aircraft POWs will display panels, fire violet smoke signals and contact aircraft by radio for helicopter pick-
up.

    3. Plan Charlie—Rescue five POWs from a rendezvous somewhere on the west coast.
        a. Signals—same as for Plan B. except drop four amber flares.
        b. Twenty minutes after dropping flares, drop equipment with annotated map and in-
structions for five POWs to use in marching to rendezvous on west coast.

    4. If none of these three plans are acceptable follow signal plan B except drop four
red flares, indicating no rescue will be attempted.

                                                  Paul V. Liles
                                                    Major, Inf.

Map 5. Liles's Escape Plan. (Lt. Col. Paul Liles, USA, Transcripts, 7:3–4)

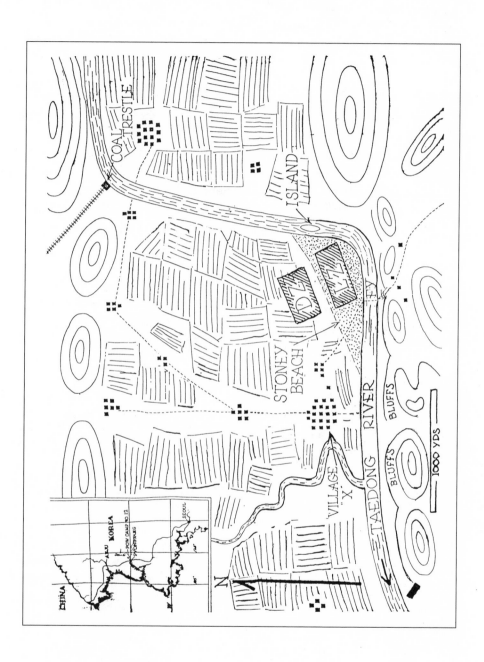

later remarked, "Lieutenant Erwin never failed me; never disappointed me."[69] Colonel Liles was planning what could have been the greatest propaganda coup of the Korean war: the mass escape of Camp 12.

≫≪

After the war, an army law officer, instructing the court on various points of law before they went into deliberation, told them, "Although it is a custom of the service to escape, such custom does not place upon a prisoner of war a legal duty to escape." Each individual captive must decide whether or not to escape. No man in three years—not one single person— ever escaped from a permanent POW camp in North Korea. Those who attempted to escape were either recaptured or killed. Others (generally pilots) evaded capture behind the lines. No single soldier, however, ran away and made it. CWO Dwight Coxe said, "The simplest thing of all was getting out and the hard part was survival after you got out."[70] Geography was the major drawback in any escape attempt. To the north was Manchuria; to the east, the Sea of Japan; to the west, the Yellow Sea; and to the south was two hundred miles of enemy-held territory. The odds were against anyone who attempted escape, but Colonel Liles was going to try.

Near dusk on a day in late June, Paul Liles pulled his insignia of rank from his pocket, pinned it to his cap, and walked down to the river bank on the pretext of getting water. Joining him were four men from Camp 12 and three from the CPC.* Each man made his way to the river separately and had an excuse ready, if stopped, for heading in that direction. The eight men, with the colonel as their leader, were going to plan the escape of Camp 12.[71]

The first order of business was to have their own men appointed to positions of responsibility in the CPC. It was common knowledge that the Koreans wanted Trooper Cocks elected president. "We had to make some move," said Liles, "we had to penetrate the Central Committee to get in there to control it." They needed that control not to sabotage whatever propaganda was disseminated, for that was difficult to do, but to control which two men from the CPC were to be elected as POW emissaries to the

---

* In the group from Camp 12 were Capt. Clifford Allen, CWO Dwight Coxe, Lt. Chester Van Orman, and Sgt. Clifford Neel. Members of the Central Peace Committee group were Capt. Harold Kaschko, Lt. Jefferson Erwin, and M. Sgt. John Porter.

United Nations and the World Peace Conference. The two men had to be soldiers whom Liles could trust implicitly, for only through them could the escape plan be implemented.[72]

The key factor concerned who would be elected president of the Central Peace Committee. Colonel Liles had considered them all and said, "There is a very dangerous situation here in that we have Trooper Ronald Cocks, who is favorably disposed toward the enemy, and we must devote all efforts to preventing the Koreans from having him president. They want him. To circumvent this desire, it is my desire that the president be an American and it should be an officer. Now, there are only three officers in the CPC: Kaschko, Erwin, and Nugent. I will leave it up to you but under no circumstances allow Trooper Cocks to become president." Neither Kaschko or Erwin wanted the job, and, Van Orman recalled, "Colonel Liles suggested facetiously, perhaps, that Major Nugent might be a good man to put in as the president as he was, at that time, about half blind and not too coherent; he wasn't too stable mentally—or we thought he wasn't—and suggested that he might be a good man to put in as president of the Peace Committee. We knew that he was loyal at least, at that we could trust him." The deed was done. "We figured a man who couldn't write and couldn't walk would make a good president," Liles later remarked. "It proved an excellent decision."[73]

Next, the colonel instructed his men on what they could and could not do. "These Koreans believe that we are interested in bringing about peace in Korea. In order to convince them and lead them into selecting someone to go home, we will have to lead them to believe that we believe some of the propaganda. Do that." Liles cautioned them, however, about not addressing U.S. troops in their propaganda statements, much less calling on them to surrender in battle.[74]

Liles used the CPC as an instrument for three different escape plans: ABLE called for the rescue, by helicopter, of the entire camp; BAKER was somewhat similar, but only forty men would be rescued; and CHARLIE, a scaled-back final alternative, asked that weapons be dropped for five men, who would then attempt to go overland.

The main rescue attempt—Plan ABLE—called for aircraft to come in during an afternoon to strafe the eastern width of the Taedong River from the camp and then do the same to the western width. That would signal the POWs that something was happening. That same night, they would watch for other planes. If they arrived at midnight and dropped four flares, the men would know that Plan ABLE would go into action. The next morning, the air force was to come in at daylight and strafe the north side of the village, where the POWs lived. While the planes worked over the village, the men would already be out for calisthenics. In the confusion, they would move in formation to the river. Helicopters would then come in under cover of the jets strafing the village. Prisoners would board the helicopters and be taken away from camp before the Koreans knew what was going on. Anti-aircraft shelling would be no problem. The guns were up on the hills surrounding the river and could not depress deeply enough to fire on helicopters that came in low.[75]*

After the war, it was the opinion of army, navy, and marine experts that Plan ABLE would have worked. The men who knew of the plan were behind Liles 100 percent. Lieutenant Van Orman remembered telling him, "That's the most logical thing I have ever seen. You can't help but succeed."[76] Chief Warrant Officer Coxe and Sergeant Neel had been chosen to take the plan back to the world: Coxe because he was forty-eight and had five children and Neel because he was from a farm and Liles had convinced Kim that this young American "peasant" was a stouthearted Progressive.[77]

Dwight Coxe, who could write very small, printed the escape plan on a five-inch-square piece of paper that had a map of the area drawn on its reverse. The paper was then sewed into a slit made in Sergeant Neel's belt. If, by some chance, the Central Peace Committee did not choose Neel as a POW peace delegate to the outside world, the belt would be exchanged with whomever was chosen. The only thing that remained was for the CPC to recommend that the two "peace fighters" be immediately repatriated.[78]

If Plans ABLE or BAKER could not be effected, Plan CHARLIE was left— dropping arms and ammunition for five men, who would attempt an overland escape south to the front lines. Because the men had no idea of the location of the front lines they attempted to glean that information from North Korean civilians in and around camp. When they encountered one who appeared friendly, they would draw a crude map of Korea in the dirt, a line slashed through it representing the 38th Parallel, and try by sign language to inquire about the position of the lines.

---

* Maj. Henry Segal, a noted army psychiatrist, has said that during capitivity Paul Liles had "an exquisite contact with reality."

Lt. Col. Monroe Hargood of Army Intelligence said later that agents of the United States and its allies had penetrated fairly deeply into North Korea. The spies were North Koreans, and, Hargood added, were seldom very trustworthy, but some may have been around Camp 12.[79] As Liles recalled, "There were some occurrences taking place which indicated that friendly agents were trying to contact us. There were Koreans sneaking into camp at night, being fired on, and civilians—Korean civilians on the beach—meeting prisoners, saying, 'Quickly, tell me your name; tell me how many Americans in this camp, I am your friend,' and things like that. I could see no better way to devastate the communist propaganda than by having an armed rebellion breaking out in the Peace Committee."[80] He was absolutely right.

Sadly, in view of the difficulties that awaited him after the war, Colonel Liles said, "I dreamed of being the hero of the war, of leading the helicopter rescue of all POWs in Camp 12. I was always trained that when it came time to make a decision, for gosh sake, do something; don't sit down and do nothing. That is what I did. I was an officer in the United States Army, I was in hostile territory, I made a decision, and that's it."[81]

Because Camp 12 had no electricity, the first meeting of the CPC took place in a small town twelve miles east of P'yŏngyang on June 30, 1951. Delegates were put into a white schoolhouse decorated with white doves of peace. The Koreans managed to get POW work details out of camp and gather pine boughs to further enhance the decor. Paper was furnished for slogans, and the schoolhouse's decorations even included a white cloth over the top of the table. "They tried to make it look like a big celebration," Nugent said. All of Camp 12 was present. Liles saw that "newsmen and cameramen were there as well as a North Korean brigadier general, many lesser North Korean officers of the Political Department of the Korean People's Army, as well as North Korean government officials, Chinese visitors, etc. Little Korean children spoke, telling how their mothers had been killed by bombs. Everybody denounced the American aggressors and the capitalistic warmongers."[82]

After the speeches, the communist press was permitted to speak with the POWs. Major Nugent, as senior officer of the Central Peace Committee, acted as spokesman. At one point, Sgt. Leroy Carter became nervous, for "during the course of the interview, the question was asked whether what Major Nugent and the rest of us was doing was forced on us. Major

Nugent hesitated to answer. . . . I was standing between him and Major Pak, who began to draw his automatic pistol. . . . I thought he was going to shoot so I was very pleased when Maj. Nugent answered 'No, sir.'"[83]

The next order of business was an election, and, as instructed by Liles, Ambrose Nugent became president of the Central Peace Committee. The other members were:

Tpr. Ronald Cocks	Camp 12	Vice President
Sgt. Leroy Carter	Camp 5	Secretary
Capt. Harold Kaschko	Camp 5	Member
Lt. Jeff Erwin	Camp 5	Member
M. Sgt. John Porter	Camp 5	Member
Pvt. Ted Spencer	Camp 5	Member
Sgt. Hatta Ozturk	Camp 5	Member
Cpl. Robert Ghyers	Camp 7	Member

Nugent never suspected that he was going to be designated president because he was never let in on the escape plan that would make use of the CPC. Nonetheless, he would obey orders.[84]

Speeches were given, recorded, and broadcast that day. In one of them describing the function of the Central Peace Committee, it was said to the world: "The Central Committee shall encourage and lead a campaign for the writing of letters by the prisoners of war to their families and friends urging them to fight for peace. The Central Committee shall elect certain prisoners of war, instruct them, and with the permission of the Supreme Commander of the Korean People's Army, send them as peace emissaries to the World Peace Council and the United Nations Organization's General Assembly, . . . to speak for peace by every means at their disposal."[85]

Liles's apparent success was short-lived. On that same day, a North Korean officer deleted from the speeches the part resolving to dispatch the two representatives. The rug had been pulled out from under the colonel and his cohorts at the last minute. If they could not get the escape plan out, they could not get the helicopters in.[86]

The CPC was active for about four months longer and then slowly ceased to exist. During this time a number of propaganda broadcasts were made by various members of the CPC, and writing from POWs in all the camps along the Yalu flowed into the committee. Lieutenant Erwin said that many writings were burned: "We figured that we were already on the Peace Committee and there was no use in getting a lot of other people involved in this propaganda effort if we could keep them out of it."[87] All in all, it was a banner year for the communist propaganda machine.

The purpose of the North Korean and Chinese propaganda broadcasts should be kept in mind. Americans who listened to the radio and heard anti-American propaganda from U.S. soldiers would have been saddened but otherwise unaffected. In all probability, they would have correctly concluded that the POWs were acting under duress. But the average American in 1951 never heard these broadcasts and was never intended to. The broadcasts were directed toward the noncommunist, developing nations. China, with the support of the Soviet Union, had its sights on those countries and was looking to convert them. Proclamations of American soldiers denouncing their own country were perfect tools to begin shaping the minds of people in developing nations of the Far East in preparation for further communist expansion. Camp 12 and the satellite Central Peace Committee served that purpose.

Colonel Liles tried to escape three times after the major plan was aborted. On the night of August 16, he crept to the river, looking for a boat in order to float downstream and into the Yellow Sea, but fishermen were using them. Twelve nights later he tried again, but the boats were guarded by soldiers. His third attempt was on the night of September 7. This time, the boats had been shifted to the opposite bank, and the current was too swift for him to swim across.[88]

On December 10, 1951, Camp 12 and the Central Peace Committee were disbanded, and the men loaded on trucks and shipped north to Camp 5 on the Yalu. Many were troubled by what they had done. As Erwin testified, "I believe that every POW has a mental block against admitting that he was brainwashed by a bunch of apes with tennis shoes on but unfortunately, I believe we were brainwashed to some degree." Other soldiers, for example Capt. Harold Kaschko, were ashamed: "I was sick along with everybody else; probably lost seventy or seventy-five pounds of weight, had diarrhea, suffered from beri-beri, and the will to resist just wasn't there." The young captain's final comment was, "I'm sorry"—a fitting conclusion to the short, sad existence of Camp 12.[89]

Notes

1. Lt. Col. Harry Fleming, USA, Transcripts, 9:941, see also 5:8, 5:40, 5:61, 5:272, 12:1857, 12:1860, Lt. Jefferson Erwin, USA, Transcripts, 5:1320, and Lt. Col. Paul Liles, USA, Transcripts, 2b:491.

2. Liles Transcripts, 2b:461; see also Fleming Transcripts, 11:1547.

3. Liles Transcripts, 3:1041, see also 3:900; Fleming Transcripts, 7:493.

4. Fleming Transcripts, 11:1539, see also 11:1547.

5. Maj. Ambrose Nugent, USA, Transcripts, 11:3044.

6. Ibid., 11:3043; Fleming Transcripts, 5:171, 5:174, 5:287, 5:364, 6:69.

7. Fleming Transcripts, 5:300, see also 5:60, 5:171, 5:174, 5:265, 5:288, 5:361, and 7:516.

8. Ibid., 5:279, 9:939–41, 9:1111–12; Liles Transcripts, 3:923.

9. Fleming Transcripts, 9:1111–12, see also 7:520 and 9:939–41.

10. Ibid., 10:1264.

11. Ibid., 7:519, 9:943, 10:1265, 11:1565.

12. Ibid., 5:171, 5:174, 6:71–72; Liles Transcripts, 4b:1858.

13. Fleming Transcripts, 5:66, 7:440, 7:464–65, 9:1074, 9:1086, 10:1269, 10:1327, 10:1361, 12:1871; Liles Transcripts, 3:942–43.

14. Liles Transcripts, 2b:724; see also Erwin Transcripts, 4:1137, Fleming Transcripts, 5:343, and Col. Frank Schwable, USMC, Transcripts, 3:1277, 3:1285.

15. Fleming Transcripts, 5:285, 9:951, 9:1121–22, see also 5:60, 7:434, and 10:1266.

16. Ibid., 8:702, 9:977–78, see also 11:1442.

17. Ibid., 9:965, see also 12:1718 and Nugent Transcripts, 9:2226.

18. Nugent Transcripts, 9:2282; see also Fleming Transcripts, 8:663, 10:1342, and 11:1575.

19. Fleming Transcripts, 11:1616–17.

20. Nugent Transcripts, 1:267.

21. Fleming Transcripts, 11:1438.

22. Ibid., 9:1016, see also 7:321.

23. Ibid., 5:40, 5:334–35, 6:80, 10:1267, 10:1285–87, 11:1394; Liles Transcripts, 2b:522, 5:appendix, exhibit X:2.

24. Fleming Transcripts, 7:431, 9:1103, 11:1174, see also 7:344 and 7:426–28.

25. Ibid., 3:108, 10:1333.

26. Ibid., 10:1278.

27. Erwin Transcripts, 3:634–35; Fleming Transcripts, 12:1828, see also 6:78, 9:994, 9:997, and 11:1645.

28. Fleming Transcripts, 10:1379, 10:1382, 12:1877; see also Liles Transcripts, 4c:2038.

29. Fleming Transcripts, 10:1277, see also 10:1384.

30. Ibid., 9:971, 9:1013, see also 5:281 and Nugent Transcripts, 1:197.

31. Fleming Transcripts, 12:1824.

32. Ibid., 5:279, 10:1273, see also 11:1583–84.

33. Ibid., 11:1514.

34. Ibid., 11:1575–78.

35. Ibid., 5:279–80.

36. Ibid., 5:104–12, see also 11:1579.

37. Ibid., 9:1061, see also 12:1865.

38. Ibid., 11:1596.

39. Liles Transcripts, 2:298, 2:300–301, 2:304, 2:309, 2:311, 2:334; Nugent Transcripts, 3:539, 5:1088, 5:1090; Fleming Transcripts, 3:213–15; Schwable Transcripts, 1:375.

40. Nugent Transcripts, 11:3004; see also Fleming Transcripts, 9:998.

41. Fleming Transcripts, 5:231–32, see also 5:289, 5:297, 5:309, 7:328, 7:394, Nugent Transcripts, 10:2830, and Liles Transcripts, 2b:477, 3:1053.

42. Liles Transcripts, 3:1053, see also 3:944 and Nugent Transcripts, 9:2558.

43. Fleming Transcripts, 11:1600–602.

44. Ibid., 12:1753–55.

45. Nugent Transcripts, 10:2830, see also 1:312.

46. Liles Transcripts, 4a:1576; Fleming Transcripts, 9:1077–81, see also 9:1088–89.

47. Fleming Transcripts, 5:280, 6:97–101, see also 5:331, 6:228, 6:240, 10:1285, Liles Transcripts, 2b:477, and Erwin Transcripts, 4:1173.

48. Fleming Transcripts, 6:220, 7:333, 11:1597–98; Liles Transcripts, 2b:566.

49. Fleming Transcripts, 5:61, 11:1607, 11:1614, see also 11:1604 and 11:1612–13.

50. Ibid., 5:301–2, see also 11:1686.

51. Ibid., 7:557, 7:590–91, 7:607, see also 7:412, 7:414, and 11:1634.

52. Ibid., 11:1635–36, 11:1641, 12:1851; Liles Transcripts, 4b:1877–78.

53. Fleming Transcripts, 7:290, 13:1901–2, see also 11:1635–36, 12:1848, and Liles Transcripts, 2b:555, 4b:1877–78.

54. Liles Transcripts, 4b:1877–78; Fleming Transcripts, 13:1901, see also 11:1646 and Liles Transcripts, 4c:2050–51.

55. Fleming Transcripts, 11:1646.

56. Nugent Transcripts, 11:3068, see also 11:2981, Fleming Transcripts, 11:1447–48, and Liles Transcripts, 1:147, 2:386, 3:929, 3b:1241, 4b:1993, 5:appellate exhibit X:5.

57. Liles Transcripts, 1:147.

58. Fleming Transcripts, 10:1319, see also 5:284–85, 12:1779–80, and Nugent Transcripts, 10:2677.

59. Fleming Transcripts, 5:284, 5:293; Liles Transcripts, 1:148, 5:appellate exhibit X:6.

60. Nugent Transcripts, 5:977, 5:1139, 5:1143, 5:1148, 5:1151, 12:3376.

61. Ibid., 4:874, 5:994.

62. Erwin Transcripts, 5:1275–77, see also 2:515, 2:547, and Maj. Ronald Alley, USA, Transcripts, 4:114.

63. Erwin Transcripts, 1:61, 1:86, 1:91, 2:518, 4:1126, 4:1131, 5:1277; Nugent Transcripts, 11:3077, 11:3083, 12:3384–85; Fleming Transcripts, 11:1646, 11:1662, 12:1757; Liles Transcripts, 1:148, 3:1067.

64. Liles Transcripts, 5:appellate exhibit X:6, 1:148.

65. Nugent Transcripts, 11:2967, 11:3079–80, see also 11:2969.

66. Ibid., 9:2340; Liles Transcripts, 1:43, 4b:1935; Erwin Transcripts, 4:1189.

67. Nugent Transcripts, 11:3241; Liles Transcripts, 3:1027.

68. Erwin Transcripts, 5:1289.

69. Ibid., 1:62; see also Nugent Transcripts, 12:3259, 12:3504, and 13:3579.

70. Nugent Transcripts, 13:3779; Erwin Transcripts, 4:1157; see also Liles Transcripts, secret volume, 171.

71. Erwin Transcripts, 4:1164; Nugent Transcripts, 11:3086; Liles Transcripts, 1:148–49.

72. Nugent Transcripts, 11:3086.

73. Ibid., 11:3088–89; Erwin Transcripts, 4:1165–66; Liles Transcripts, 1:148–49, see also 3:971.

74. Nugent Transcripts, 11:3088.

75. Erwin Transcripts, 4:1129–30, 5:1278; Liles Transcripts, 3:1019–23, 3:1099–100, 5: appellate exhibit V:40.

76. Nugent Transcripts, 11:3061; see also Liles Transcripts, 3b:1336.

77. Liles Transcripts, 3:965–66, 3b:1318; Erwin Transcripts, 4:1133, 4:1162.

78. Liles Transcripts, 3:961–62; Erwin Transcripts, 4:1163.

79. Liles Transcripts, secret volume, 168–70.

80. Nugent Transcripts, 11:3097. During the Erwin trial, Liles testified, "I reasoned that that there could be nothing more devastating to the communist propaganda than for an armed revolt in the peace committee itself." Erwin Transcripts, 1:61–62.

81. Liles Transcripts, 1:148; 5:appellate exhibit X:6; Nugent Transcripts, 4c:2040a, 11:3198. Liles was also quoted as saying, "I was always taught that when the time comes to act, do something, even if it's wrong, it's better than nothing. So I did it." Liles Transcripts, 1:167.

82. Nugent Transcripts, 12:3390–91; Liles Transcripts, 5:appellate exhibit X:7, see also Nugent Transcripts, 9:2425, 12:3386 and Erwin Transcripts, 5:1279.

83. Erwin Transcripts, 2:536.

84. Ibid., 1:91, 2:516–17; Nugent Transcripts, 12:3388–89; Liles Transcripts, 2:385–86, 5:appellate exhibit X:6.

85. Liles Transcripts, 3:1136.

86. Liles Transcripts, 1:149.

87. Erwin Transcripts, 5:1283, see also 4:1193.

88. Liles Transcripts, 1:150–52; Fleming Transcripts, 11:1462.

89. Nugent Transcripts, 5:1295, 9:2455; see also Erwin Transcripts, 4:1138.

Maj. Gen. William Dean holding a press conference at Freedom Village immediately after release. (National Archives A84356AC)

Cpl. Claude Batchelor and wife Kyoko Araki two months before his arrest. (National Archives SC442474)

Capt. Alexander Boysen (left) and Capt. William Shandish at Tokyo Army Hospital exhibit surgical equipment used in the camps. Doctor Boysen shows a scalpel made from the arch of a combat boot, and Doctor Shadish a stethoscope cut out of a piece of wood. (National Archives SC436824)

Col. Frank Schwable, USMC, shortly after repatriation. (National Archives SC446884)

Upon repatriation, Ronald Alley receives notice from Lt. Col. Charles Taylor that he had been promoted to major while a POW. (National Archives SC433003)

Bodies of American POWs shot in a prison yard in October 1950 by retreating North Korean soldiers. (National Archives SC349104)

CWO Dwight Coxe and his family holding a television interview on the pier shortly after his ship had tied up. (National Archives SC425777)

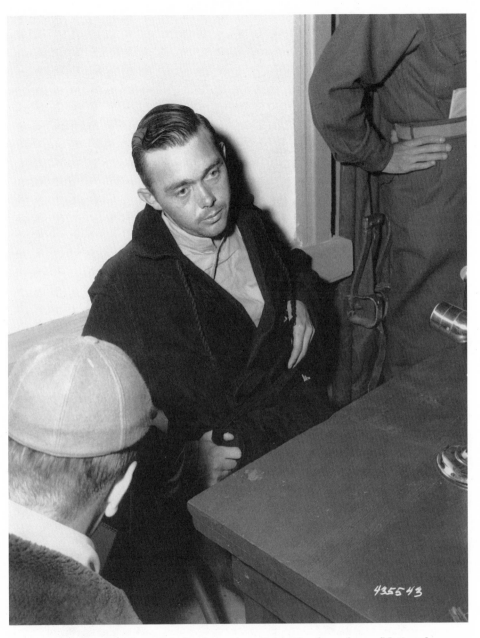

Cpl. Edward Dickenson being interviewed shortly after release. (National Archives SC435543)

Opposite page: Lt. Col. John McLaughlin speaks with Sen. William Knowland during repatriation. (National Archives SC432618)

Maj. Ambrose Nugent at Fort Sill, Oklahoma, in January 1955. (National Archives SC491730)

SIX

Limbo

Toward nine o'clock in the morning, when the troops were already moving through Moscow, nobody came to the court any more for instructions. Those who were able to get away were going of their own accord; those who remained behind decided for themselves what they must do.

Leo Tolstoy, *War and Peace*, Book II

If 1951 can be seen as an all-encompassing blackness, a constant dark night, then 1952, the second year of captivity for most of the men, can be looked at as a dawn. The first rays of light began to peek over the mountainous Korean horizon. The light remained feeble, for there was still cooperation with the enemy, still a shortage of food, still forms of brutality, and still indoctrination. But now there was some hope, and the prisoners' will to live was returning.

That will to live became more realistic when the Chinese stopped killing men by starvation. They realized, of course, that in 1951 three thousand American POWs had died in their camps; now only four thousand were left. It seems likely that if the captors continued as they had in late 1950 and the first half of 1951, few prisoners would survive. Only after the exchange of "name lists" in 1951 during cease-fire negotiations did conditions begin to improve measurably. At Camp 5, the principal camp along the Yalu River, Sgt. John Wells recalled, "If there were any who died after August, '51, it was very seldom, very seldom."[1]

Food was the key. Men did not become fat on the new diet supplied, but at least they no longer were emaciated. With the new year came sugar, pork, flour, onions, garlic, and eggs. They were also given fish, which frequently was maggoty but was eaten nonetheless. Some camps began receiving an issue of cigarettes; in others, on occasion, a shot of saki was distributed. The changed diet gave some of the GIs the strength to resist; it gave others the strength to collaborate more effectively.[2] In many instances, collaboration became deeper as conditions became better. The only explanation seems to be that, for these men, the Chinese indoctrination programs of 1951 had worked. As a rule, by 1952 anyone who was going to be "brainwashed" was, in fact, brainwashed.

≫≪

All the men from the disbanded Camp 12 and Central Peace Committee were moved to Camp 5. Many changes had taken place while they were away. The bedraggled newcomers noticed that everyone wore warm, comfortable Chinese uniforms, which consisted of cotton-padded trousers and jackets that were approximately an inch thick and caps with earflaps. Each man had also been issued a cotton quilt and woolen blanket. The population had decreased somewhat, for in October 1951 officers had been transferred to a new site designated Camp 2, about ten miles northeast of Pyoktong and near the small town of P'anjung-ni. When the men from Camp 12 arrived, the enlisted were kept at Camp 5, but within a few days of arrival the officers were marched five hours northeast to the two-month-old officers' camp.[3] Camp 2 was nothing more than a large schoolhouse, a yard in front and several additional small buildings on the grounds. It was completely enclosed by barbed wire, and the 350 officers who constituted the camp population were guarded by a large Chinese company of two hundred soldiers.[4]

It was late in December 1951 when the officers from Camp 12 arrived at Camp 2. Another cold, bitter North Korean winter was underway, and daylight was fading when the men were marched in through the wire. The Chinese processed them efficiently and with a certain indifference. One newcomer, Maj. David MacGhee, went up to a group of Americans standing in the yard, but something about the way they were watching him made him uneasy. As he got closer, one leaned toward him and said, "How is everything in Traitors Row?"[5]

It was the first inkling the men from Camp 12 and the Central Peace Committee had that they would be treated as pariahs. Maj. Ambrose Nugent, who had headed the CPC only upon the instructions of Lt. Col. Paul Liles, was referred to as "that fucking Nugent" and a "no good bastard." In testimony after the war, Capt. Waldron Berry, USAF, remembered that Nugent's reputation as a collaborator "effectively precluded any conversation with him so far as I was concerned." Another Air Force officer, Capt. Robert Burke, was of the opinion that Nugent and those who arrived from Camp 12 were unfit to be officers in the U.S. armed forces. That was the common view among the 350 prisoners at Camp 2, whose consciences seemed to be perfectly clear.[6]

Capt. Clifford Allen angrily remembered the ostracism and, upon entering Camp 2, saw that officers there lived better than anyone he had seen during captivity: "We were the worst off of the bunch and still we were the ones who had been traitors, which is a nasty name, something no one likes to be called."[7] The rumor had spread that Camp 12 was Traitors Row, however, and the mud was impossible to remove.

Lt. Jeff Erwin, a particularly friendly and sociable individual, slowly withdrew into himself, as did virtually all officers brought from P'yŏngyang. All realized they were being shunned. Even Colonel Liles, a strong person, became severely depressed and for a long time withdrew from a situation he found almost unendurable.[8]

Lt. Col. John Dunn, a senior officer at Camp 2, attempted to excuse the actions of subordinates by saying they were always on the lookout for informers. Newcomers had to undergo a testing period before being accepted. Others remembered that although senior officers showed a certain degree of tolerance and understanding, a sizable group of chronic critics and complainers was more than happy to have people at whom to point a finger. The stigma attached to the men of Camp 12 and the Central Peace Committee lasted for several months and was a very heavy burden for them to bear.[9]

From early 1952 onward, morale at the officers' camp gradually improved. As Lt. Alvin Anderson recalled, "The food was better, the medical care was better,* everything was good. In fact, if I'd had a gun, I would have started fighting again at Camp 2." Even Harry Fleming, disconsolate because of the treatment he was receiving from his peers, said, "I got my first letter from my wife the latter part of January, 1952, and from then on I could have made it standing on my head."[10]

If the Chinese and North Koreans thought the intense indoctrination programs of 1951 would succeed in teaching American prisoners about the workings of communism, they were absolutely correct. Yet not as many prisoners as the captors wished found the system attractive, at least not once they understood it. And then there were those whose dislike for communism grew even more intense, as Ambrose Nugent testified: "To paint a picture of the actual POW life is quite impossible. If a movie camera had been used to follow these various groups of prisoners and been projected in the U.S., people wouldn't believe it. It wasn't what appeared on the outside. Inwardly, within each individual prisoner, there was nothing but contempt and resentment and bitterness, and a desire to live and to seek revenge."[11]

Nugent was exaggerating when he claimed that "each individual prisoner" felt this way, but many did. When speaking with Nugent, Maj. Filmore McAbee noticed that "he appeared to have an intense, almost pathological, hatred for the communists." Commander Bagwell made the same observation and remembered that "on many occasions in private conversation with Fleming, we discussed the communist menace and he shared my feelings—an extreme dislike bordering on hatred for any part of that system."[12]

Whatever their personal feelings, men in all the camps that stretched along the southern bank of the Yalu River for nearly eighty miles lived by rules the Chinese laid down. Typical regulations were:

1. All captured officers and men must correctly understand the Lenient Policy of our [the Chinese] army, observe the directions, and strictly adhere to the disciplinary rules. . . .

---

* There were eight American doctors at Camp 2.

2. All captured officers and men shall continue to abide by the study regulations, attend classes at the fixed times, and pay full attention to study.

3. All squads should systematically read the issued reading materials. These materials must be registered and kept in good form. It is absolutely forbidden to lose or damage any of them without justifiable reasons. . . .

4. Every Sunday the squad should hold a daily-life criticism meeting to review [the] focal points, the carrying out of life and study disciplinary rules and regulations of the past week. . . .

5. Except the seriously sick men who have obtained the certificate of the doctor and permission from the platoon leader (or the instructor), all the rest must attend classes. No pretext should be used for absence. . . .

6. While attending classes everybody must be serious and in orderly manner; should line up to report the number of men present; pay full attention to lectures and taking notes; ask permission from the instructor before leaving for the latrine. The bad behaviors of disobedience, free action, making noises, joking and dozing are strictly forbidden.[13]

Nonetheless, the spirit of resistance was returning. In late December 1951, shortly after the men of Camp 12 and the CPC entered Camp 2, about thirty POWs were pulled out of the compound and called to the schoolhouse yard. Standing on the balcony of the school building was an unfamiliar North Korean officer. Looking down at the assembled captives, he told them he was in camp to conduct a military interrogation and then distributed a mimeographed form that contained nearly two hundred questions. Capt. Tommy Trexler looked over the paper and concluded that a general officer would be required to answer the questions. No one wrote, and, Trexler recalled, "I got pretty well mad at the whole thing and I stood up and told them my name, rank and service number and I said, 'That is all I intend to tell you.'"[14]

The North Korean, as can be imagined, was mightily displeased. Trexler was taken to another building and threatened, beaten, and kicked, but the captain wouldn't give in:

[They] continued to threaten me and made statements to the effect that Korea was a very beautiful country and would I want to remain in Korea forever. Another statement I remember was why did I believe in Jesus Christ, a man that was dead, a man that could not do anything for me when I had a great man like Stalin, a man who could show me and lead me and a man who was alive. For approximately two hours the North Korean officer walked around me with his pistol and he walked around and pulled the trigger. Each time he pulled the trigger, it was only a click.

Seeing that intimidation had not shaken Trexler, they sent him back to the compound and never bothered him again. Had the incident happened a year earlier, consequences would have been extremely severe. Times were changing.[15]

Eight weeks after the Trexler episode an even more dramatic event took place in the 4th Company of Camp 5, ten miles southwest of Camp 2. Approximately four hundred sergeants made up that company, and in early March 1952 they went on strike. Formations and classes were not attended, and any orders given by the Chinese were not obeyed. All the sergeants did was sit and not participate. The risk was great, but there was safety in the fact that on December 27, 1951, the names of all POWs had been exchanged at Panmunjom. According to Sgt. Joe Gardiner, "Everybody was reasonably sure that the Chinese weren't going to take anyone out and shoot them because they were going to have to account for prisoners at that time; before that time they didn't have to."[16]

The purpose of the sit-down strike was to force the Chinese to end, throughout Korea, all mandatory indoctrination classes, all peace committees, and all forced propaganda efforts. The revolt lasted two days, and then the Chinese relented. M. Sgt. Ralph Krieger recalled, "It was the first time since we had been captured that we acted like American soldiers."[17]

Compulsory classes were over, but in their place the Chinese introduced voluntary sessions in the instruction of communism, and a startling number of soldiers attended. In Camp 5 alone, an estimated 25 percent of prisoners went to "self-study" sessions or "group meetings for cooperatives." Many did so from boredom, some in order to placate the Chinese, and others because they had become genuinely convinced of the merits of communism. Whatever their reasons, those who attended the voluntary assemblies discovered that in doing so they were taking sides in a struggle that was just beginning. It would divide each camp into two groups: progressive and reactionary.[18]

Progressives were men who went along with the Chinese; they either accepted communist ideology or were willing to let it appear that they leaned that way. The most advanced progressives were sometimes derisively referred to as "red stars." The smaller group of reactionaries were

POWs who made it plain that they had no sympathy with the commu-nist worldview and did not intend to cooperate with their captors.[19]*

Many believed that the majority of progressives took that position in order to gain favors, because, in general, progressives ate better, were treat-ed with more consideration, and lived in a degree of communion with their captors. The last was a particularly important point because emo-tional deprivation can be intense in a POW camp. Claude Batchelor—the uneducated, twenty-year-old corporal from a small town near Waco, Texas—was impressed when the Chinese congratulated him on his work as a class monitor at Camp 5 and informed him he was a "Young Lenin." Still dazzled, he commented later, "I think the Chinese selected me be-cause of certain leadership abilities I possessed." Like many other young progressives, he later seemed unclear about what he had believed while in captivity. Batchelor denied being a communist and said he was merely struggling for world peace. At other times, he recalled his intention of re-turning to America and working for the many virtues of communism.[20]

Most of the young soldiers were not intellectuals, either before or af-ter captivity, and it is difficult to ascertain how much they understood. In remarks after the war, Cpl. Harold Dunn, who was in regular attendance at the voluntary lectures, said that neither the Soviet Union nor any oth-er country had communism. He commented, "You've got to have superi-or human beings before you can have it."[21] Political sophistication gen-erally did not extend much higher than that.

One example of the difficulty of discovering what made a progressive was provided by Sgt. William Banghart of Pennsylvania, a married man with two children, who recalled that he started "thinking in unison with the Chinese" around October 1952. One of his fellow POWs, Sgt. Waldo Cook, was of the opinion, however, that Banghart first began to collabo-

---

* The U.S. Army, in a legal stipulation after the war, defined progressive and reactionary as follows: "In the common parlance of United Nations prisoners of war, 'reactionaries' were those prisoners who actively resisted indoctrination by their captors, who actively resisted unnecessary cooperation with their captors and who, whenever possible, refused to sign anything which could be used for propaganda purposes. The term 'progressive' was applied to those prisoners who voluntarily associated with their captors more than was required, provided their captors more cooperation than was demanded by the exigencies of prison life, who voluntarily signed or provided their captors with writings or statements which might be used for publication or propaganda, who voluntarily studied and discussed political the-ory under direction of their captors, and who attempted to persuade other prisoners to act in the same or similar manner."

rate for extra cigarettes and rations, and eventually it was impossible for him to quit. Sergeant Banghart described his motive differently and revealed how, at a certain stage in his indoctrination, the company commander, Wong, took over training and showed him the greatest attentiveness and concern. "Flattery was one of Wong's prize weapons," said Banghart. "He worked on your vanity. Wong would tell me how much good I could do for the people of the world by advocating peace and praise me for my ability to read and learn."[22] The ordinary human desire to be accepted and appreciated was being exploited by the enemy.

Progressives at Camp 3 had their own "private clubhouse" where meetings and classes were held. The inside of the small building was decorated with pictures of Stalin, Mao, and William Z. Foster, as well as with the flags of the Soviet Union, China, and North Korea. Pinned to any blank spaces left on the walls were posters drawn by the POWs. One GI remembered that "one of the posters was a picture of Uncle Sam with a bayonet in his rectum." Camp 5 had its own library and reading room, which offered mostly communist literature. In addition to nearly five hundred magazines and pamphlets, there were, according to Harold Dunn, who was the librarian, "two hundred books of a good level to read by good authors."[23]

> Our company, with 349 men has 398 books. They cover a wide range of subjects and are the works of many authors. There are many classical novels such as *Don Quixote, Kenilworth, Les Miserables, The Man in the Iron Mask,* etc. It was surprising to see that among those works were those that were compulsory reading during my school days—*Tale of Two Cities, Silas Mariner* and others. We also have the favorite works of Mark Twain, also *Kidnapped, Doctor Jekyll and Mr. Hyde, The Invisible Man, Twenty Thousand Leagues Under The Sea, Great Expectations, Black Beauty, Arabian Nights* and Lew Wallace's *Ben Hur.* Besides, there are the works of modern Chinese and Soviet authors. And one cannot forget the great Marxist classics—*Capital,* Frederick Engles' *Origin of the Family,* and the outstanding political works of Lenin and Stalin. In popularity, judging by the books read, the favorite author is Howard Fast.[24]

It was a classic mixture of literature, but communist propaganda always formed the heart of camp libraries. Lt. Col. John Dunn once said, "By any methods they think necessary they exact concession after concession, increasing their demands until the victim's will and powers of resistance vanishes and he becomes a resigned, sullen bitter puppet, hating his tormentors but bowing to their every demand through a sense of helplessness and despair."[25]

That statement may have been somewhat true in 1951 but is inconsistent with most evidence for 1952 and 1953. The progressives did not hate their captors and in certain cases even seemed to have loved them. One POW cried like a baby when Stalin died in 1953. Indeed, the death of Joseph Stalin brought such apparent sorrow to the progressives of Camp 5 that a group of them drafted, signed, and sent a letter of condolence to Moscow. Contrarily, the reactionaries, called "backward students" by the Chinese, hated not only their captors but also the progressives.[26]

Both factions emerged in every Chinese camp along the Yalu River. M. Sgt. Joe Dutra, one of the organizers of the reactionaries at Camp 5, declared, "I believe that all of the members of the POW camp knew we were a tough core—if you want to put it that way—and that we always were giving the Chinese a hard time and the Chinese never did like this."[27]

At Camp 1, the reactionary organization consisted of nearly a hundred men in various subgroups. The main clique (or gang) of reactionaries were known as the "KKK," and some said that the initials had no special meaning. Others, however, reported that it stood for "Ku Klux Klan," which seems a reasonable assumption. Another grouping of reactionaries was the FHA (the Federated [or Faithful] Hearts of America). A third was known as the FFA (Future Fathers of America). It was also reported that a fourth group in Camp 1 was known as the "Cannibal Group" and sealed an oath of allegiance by drinking their own blood.[28]

Most men familiar with the KKK claimed it was not racist and that its only function was to harrass the progressive movement. One army lieutenant colonel, who was not a POW but studied the matter after the war, concluded, "The organization was . . . pro-American. . . . There was no question of color involved . . .; the whole purpose of the KKK was to combat communism among the prisoners of war." The KKK at Camp 1 delivered notes to progressives, for example, "wise up, you're doing wrong" or "don't forget about your buddies—they're friends and not enemies."[29] If that did not work, the reactionaries used force. Sgt. Lloyd Pate, who hated Sgt. James Gallagher, was also the leader of the reactionaries at Camp

3. They would first try speaking with progressives. If nothing came of that, Pate remarked, "Well, we would just beat the hell out of them. Maybe bust his mouth and give him a black eye, or something, so the Company would know. They'd see him walk around with that black eye and they would know—there he is."[30]

In each camp, the Chinese reacted differently to the mini-war between reactionaries and progressives. All reactionaries at Camp 3, led by Sergeant Pate, were separated from the progressives and put into Squad 11 in order, said the sergeant, to "give us intensified indoctrination, as they put it." Reactionaries could only use physical force against the "pros," but that was difficult because the progressives were protected by the enemy.[31]

Among the instructors at Camp 3 was Paul Ling, who, for reasons never clear to the men, sometimes helped the reactionaries. One day in February 1952, he walked into Sergeant Pate's squad, pulled him out, and ordered Pate to go with him. "We went up to headquarters and as we walked into the room, he motioned for me to be quiet. He didn't say anything. He just put his hand up to his mouth and pointed to me to sit down." Soon afterward the door to the next room opened, and because they were separated by only a thin, paper wall, Pate heard Wong, the instructor who occupied the adjoining space, say, "Sit down, Gallagher. How are you doing? Have you written home lately?" Sergeant Gallagher and Wong carried on a general conversation for a short period, and then Wong asked how his studies were going. "They're not going over very good," replied Gallagher. "Haven't you seen all these guys walking around here with black eyes?" Gallagher then told Wong about the abuse the progressives were taking from the reactionaries. When the instructor asked the sergeant what should be done about it, the reply was, "Well, hell, if I was in your position, I'd just shoot them all." When Pate later told Gallagher what he'd overheard, the handsome sergeant from Brooklyn said, "That's a damn lie."[32]

About a week later, the Chinese went to work on Squad 11. They were made to fall out by day and night—often up to six times in a twenty-four-hour period—and were personally searched while the squad hut was ripped apart. After some days of this, ten members of the squad, including Pate, were court-martialed. All members of the kangaroo court were Chinese, and sixty-seven charges were brought against Pate, including sabotaging studies, beating up progressives, and acting "against the peace loving people of the world." He was also sternly informed that for every word he said in his defense, six months would be added to his sentence. When the "trial" was over, Pate was put into the camp's jail to serve a year at hard labor.[33]

Meanwhile, life in the now somewhat normalized POW camps had other unpleasant aspects. In 1952 the adequately fed but terminally bored Americans began to carve away at each other. Informing was rife. Lt. Col. John McLaughlin remembered that prisoners frequently suspected each others' actions. Given the intense criticism that POWs often directed at men who had acted no differently than they, that isn't surprising. The hostility between progressives and reactionaries completed the mutual distrust. Although many have said it was the Chinese objective to divide prisoners, it is also true that prisoners did a good job of dividing themselves. Nothing, however, was worse for morale than the knowledge that informers were in camp. One sergeant recalled that everyone was suspect and that he would not have trusted anyone, even his own brother. Lt. Chester Van Orman found that disconcerting and after his release made a statement: "Throughout the thirty-two months that I was a prisoner, things we discussed or things we would plan would invariably get out to our captors. It resulted in people getting mighty suspicious of one another and they broke up into little groups, going around together with people they thought they could trust, and a lot of people came under suspicion and it turned into a pretty vicious thing, actually, before we got out of there."[34]

If a man was even suspected of being an informer, rumors would start flying and his name would be furnished to the senior officer in the compound or camp. McLaughlin took much of that with a grain of salt and said, "The prisoners were constantly coming to me and telling me about their suspicions of another person—so and so is an informer, and I knew that he had no evidence of that. And then, perhaps another day later, that individual would come and say that the one who originally had spoken to me about him was informing."[35]

Some accusations were true, but many were not; false indictments flourished in the rich soil of rumor. Dr. Philip Bloemsma, a general surgeon who had been a prisoner of war under the Japanese for five years, said, "Rumors are always believed and if a rumor hasn't been in a camp for a certain time, rumors are made up, and this is a typical thing of an advanced 'fence complex' patient." Capt. Claud Boren admitted that they "lived on rumors, yes. We had rumors every day. We lived for them. We got up every morning waiting for them." Of course, rumors can sometimes have a positive effect, although optimistic suppositions were few and far between in North Korea. Camp gossip tended to be negative and unsubstantiated. Sgt. Lyle Jacobson testified after the war, for example, that Cpl. Edward Dickenson was untrustworthy. When asked how—other than by rumor—he knew that, Jacobson could only say, "You know, inside you, you know. You just feel it; you get the feeling."[36]

Some POWs thought that the Chinese also planted rumors about individual prisoners, intending to keep the camp divided against itself.[37] Lieutenant Erwin believed that the people who spread rumors were only interested in protecting themselves. In the dark days of 1951, all POWs had taken part in forced communist indoctrination, and the vast majority had signed petitions. Now that conditions had improved, a number of prisoners became self-proclaimed heroes who brightened their reputations by spattering those of others.[38]

Although the worst was over for the POWs, their participation in communist propaganda was not at an end. According to Cpl. Claude Batchelor, "Signing petitions at Camp 5 during the latter part of 1951 [and through 1952] was routine and most prisoners signed them without any intimidation." In fact, young Batchelor boasted, "I was consulted [by the Chinese] on many petitions and helped in wording some of them." Recordings were continually made. Corporal Dickenson noted that "hundreds of American prisoners made recordings as a means of informing the outside world of our status in the camp."[39]

The various camp bulletin boards, or "wallpaper," were still being plastered with anti-American leaflets written by POWs. Articles continued to be submitted to the camp newspapers, the best known of which was *Toward Truth and Peace*. The Chinese held contests to see who could write the best party-line articles, and those who produced the winning pieces were rewarded with candy, cigarettes, apples, and money.[40]

Beginning in early 1952, the Chinese permitted men to write two censored letters home per month—the first communication POWs had with their families. The stationary supplied by the enemy bore a peace dove, and each man had the same return address:

POW CAMP (#)
DEMOCRATIC PEOPLE'S REPUBLIC OF KOREA
C/O CHINESE PEOPLE'S COMMITTEE FOR WORLD PEACE
PEKING, CHINA

Replies from families began to flow into camps, and that, together with better food, virtually no deaths, no forced studies, and familiarity with their environment, not only allowed men to think of survival but also of enjoyment, often in the form of marijuana or sex.[41]

Of the 7,190 soldiers captured, approximately four thousand remained alive early in 1952. Not all were progressives, neither did they all write articles, actively collaborate with the enemy, or smoke marijuana and have homosexual experiences. The intent in this overview of POW life in 1952 is to describe certain things that certain people did in a very closed society.

At Camp 1, marijuana grew wild by the side of the dirt road. In the summer of 1952, POWs sent out of camp for one reason or another would nearly always return with the weed stuffed in their pockets. Various prisoners reported that approximately 80 percent of those interned in Camp 1 smoked marijuana.[42] At Camp 5, in addition to picking the plant while on wood-cutting details, some men had small gardens and grew their own marijuana, hiding it among the overgrowth of other plants. The Chinese did not condone smoking and gave lectures on its ill-effects, but that did not stop its use. One prisoner said that he smoked it because "it gave you a good appetite"; others did it just to relax.[43]

Sex, too, relaxed the POWs, and it was inevitable that some engaged in homosexual acts during their years in the camps. In the enclosed conditions of camp life, sex became a marketable commodity and was sometimes performed in exchange for favors, food, or marijuana. There were noncommercial homosexual relationships as well. For the majority of men, however, the months and years passed in a state of acute sexual deprivation.[44]

Between November 14 and 26, 1952, Camp 5 sponsored an inter-camp "Olympics." Teams from every camp along the south bank of the Yalu

River entered Camp 5 to participate against each other in various sports, including track, volleyball, baseball, football, and tug-of-war. The purpose of the games was to entertain the men and create propaganda. Reporters and photographers attended, representing many communist newspapers and periodicals. Sidney Esensten and Clarence Anderson, two doctors from Camp 2, also attended. Esensten was there because "at this time, we had heard numerous rumors of homosexuality and excessive marijuana use among the enlisted personnel." He and Anderson spoke to many POWs, cautioning them about smoking marijuana and, in Anderson's words, "attempting to preserve sanitation."[45]

The year 1952 marked a period of lessening enemy pressure and improved conditions for the prisoners. The Chinese and North Koreans had not had a change of heart, however, only a change of strategy. The eyes of the enemy left the ground and turned skyward. They were looking for white nylon floating to earth with men harnessed beneath them. The time had come for the pilots.

>«

On May 4, 1952, Radio P'yŏngyang broadcast the startling announcement that two U.S. Air Force officers, former crewmen aboard a B-26, Lt. John Quinn (the pilot) and Lt. Kenneth Enoch (the navigator), had confessed to dropping germ-filled bombs on North Korea. From that day on, the POWs were vigorously propagandized on this subject.[46]

During one briefing, according to Harold Dunn, "down to the smallest detail they told us how U.S. flyers had been trained at home to drop germ bombs; the size of the bombs; the kinds of planes used; the speed and altitude when the bombs were dropped; even the types of screws used in the bombs. It was the detail like that—little details I wouldn't even have thought of—that made it so convincing. They read us reports of 'scientific commissions' and 'impartial investigations.'" The POWs were supplied statements to prove the use of "the B-bomb," as the men referred to it— the protests issued by the International Scientists Commission, the International Lawyers Commission, the Dean of Canterbury Cathedral, and many other organizations and individuals. The stupefied Americans were told that Camp Detrick had been established in Frederick, Maryland, for experimentation in germ warfare. "The Chinese appeared to be well informed on this subject," Banghart observed, "especially concerning the size, location, and layout of Camp Detrick—number of employees, cost of building and cost of maintenance." When asked how they knew so much, the Chinese always replied, "We have our own CIC.[47]*

Finally the Chinese brought captured pilots in to speak to the POWs, and they described dropping bacterial bombs. In October 1952, Lieutenant Quinn was taken to a classroom in Camp 5 and, before a number of prisoners, confessed that he had participated in germ warfare. Sgt. John Wells, who was present, said, "If I ever heard a confession by a person in any more detail—what I mean, that was a confession of all confessions." Quinn was crying as he apologized for his actions.[48]

A month later, during the Olympics, the PA system ("bitch box") constantly announced the use of germ bombs by the Air Force. As the games were going on, another pilot, Lt. Floyd O'Neil, USAF, was brought into camp. Eleven men were given a chance to hear him speak, and, one said, he "drew up a chair and started telling us of the orientation, instructions, and orders he had received in regards to handling, dropping and reporting germ missions, also of the top secret priority rating given this subject by the top 'Brass.' As Lt. O'Neil talked, he appeared normal with the exception of his hands and eyes. He didn't seem to know what to do with them. Lieutenant O'Neil spoke in a simple, direct, and what appeared to me to be a heartfelt way."[49]

After Quinn and O'Neil had finished speaking, prisoners were permitted to gather around the pilots and talk with them individually. The more they talked, the more the men began to believe them. Word spread, and within a short time the majority of American POWs in Korea firmly believed that the United States was practicing germ warfare. Upon hearing Quinn, Cpl. Johnnie Moore, a progressive, said, "After he, an American officer, told what he did . . . , there was no way I could keep from believing him." Another reported progressive, Corporal Dunn, recalled, "I was kind of peeved to believe that our country could go to the extreme of using bacteriological warfare."[50]

Many POWs were so incensed by the purported use of germs that they

---

* The reference is to the Counter Intelligence Corps.

wrote letters home and asked their families to intercede with the government and put a stop to it.* Gallagher received a letter from his mother and, having heard of germ warfare, she said, "I hope it hasn't come near you." Of course, the Chinese used that as propaganda, and her statement was soon all over camp.[51]

Quinn and O'Neil were not the only pilots who confessed to germ warfare. Altogether, thirty-six men admitted to either planning or participating in the program. The admissions stunned the world. If they were true, it was deplorable. If they were false, they constituted one of the greatest propaganda coups of the Korean or any other war.

Notes

1. Cpl. Claude Batchelor, USA, Transcripts, 7:1006; see also Lt. Col. Harry Fleming, USA, Transcripts, 5:285 and Pfc. Rothwell B. Floyd, USA, Transcripts, 2:1052.

2. Floyd Transcripts, 3a:2152; Sgt. John Tyler, USA, Transcripts, 1:114a; Maj. Ronald Alley, USA, Transcripts, 4:122–23.

3. Alley Transcripts, 4:109, 4:167, 4:174, 4:181, 4:217, 4:264, 5:16, 5:28, 5:111, 6:416; Fleming Transcripts, 6:104, 11:1423–24; Lt. Jefferson Erwin, USA, Transcripts, 1:80; Lt. Col. Paul Liles, USA, Transcripts, 3:983; Maj. Ambrose Nugent, USA, Transcripts, 1:268; Cpl. Edward Dickenson, USA, Transcripts, 4:290.

4. Alley Transcripts, 4:212, 4:232, 8:1030; Liles Transcripts, 3b:1409; Fleming Transcripts, 10:1362.

5. Fleming Transcripts, 10:1163.

6. Nugent Transcripts, 1:98, 1:137, see also 1:126 and Fleming Transcripts, 9:1150–51.

7. Fleming Transcripts, 9:1021.

8. Ibid., 5:330; Liles Transcripts, 2b:675–76; Erwin Transcripts, 4:1046, 5:1286.

9. Fleming Transcripts, 4:2; Erwin Transcripts, 4:932, 5:1219.

10. Fleming Transcripts, 5:66, 9:1137, 12:1794; Liles Transcripts, 2b:438.

11. Nugent Transcripts, 13:3561.

12. Ibid., 1:354; Fleming Transcripts, 4:3.

13. Alley Transcripts, 6:357–58.

14. Ibid., 4:191; see also Fleming Transcripts, 12:1790.

15. Alley Transcripts, 4:191.

16. Nugent Transcripts, 7:1762, see also 7:1730 and 7:1760.

17. Erwin Transcripts, 3:860, see also 5:1285–86.

18. Alley Transcripts, 5:4; Dickenson Transcripts, 4:263, 4:280; Sgt. James Gallagher, USA, Transcripts, 3:62–63, 3:116, 4:389; Cpl. Thomas Bayes, USA, Transcripts, secret volume, 37.

---

* Cpl. Claude Batchelor wrote one to the editor of his hometown newspaper, but it was never printed and forwarded to army intelligence. The letter later caused him much trouble.

19. Gallagher Transcripts, 5:683, 6:1074; Cpl. Harold Dunn, USA, Transcripts, 1:114.

20. Batchelor Transcripts, 13:8, see also 8:1731, 8:1785, and 13:167.

21. Dunn Transcripts, 1:181, see also 1:147–48 and 1:158.

22. Sgt. William Banghart, USA, Transcripts, 1:201, see also 1:56, 1:94, 1:177–78, and 1:196.

23. Ibid., 1:181; Dunn Transcripts, 1:164–66.

24. Article written by a POW for a Chinese propaganda booklet.

25. Nugent Transcripts, 1:197.

26. Batchelor Transcripts, 8:1649; see also Dunn transcripts, 1:286.

27. Nugent Transcripts, 7:1722; see also Gallagher Transcripts, 3:200.

28. Floyd Transcripts, 2:732; Tyler Transcripts, 1:37, 1:157a, 1:172a.

29. Floyd Transcripts, 5b:5233; Tyler Transcripts, 1:70a.

30. Gallagher Transcripts, 4:440.

31. Ibid., 4:436, see also 3:142–43, 3:201, and 4:324–27.

32. Ibid., 4:457–58, 7:54, see also 3:257, 4:378, 5:667, and 7:67.

33. Ibid., 3:220, 4:434–35, 4:463–64, 4:466.

34. Fleming Transcripts, 7:483; see also Erwin Transcripts, 2:577 and Batchelor Transcripts, 6:663.

35. Erwin Transcripts, 2:591–92.

36. Dickenson Transcripts, 5:386, 6:628; Erwin Transcripts, 1:263a.

37. Fleming Transcripts, 4:4.

38. Liles Transcripts, 1:211.

39. Batchelor Transcripts, 13:8; Dickenson Transcripts, 4:216.

40. Banghart Transcripts, 1:100; M. Sgt. William Olson, USA, Transcripts, 2:542; Dickenson Transcripts, 4:215, 4:251; Gallagher Transcripts, 3:130, 4:387.

41. Alley Transcripts, 5:120, 9:1399; Tyler Transcripts, 1:80, 1:112a.

42. Floyd Transcripts, 2:698, 2:731, 2:740; Tyler Transcripts, 1:45, 1:114a.

43. Floyd Transcripts, 2:740; see also Batchelor Transcripts, 8:1652, 8:1655, 8:1672 and Tyler Transcripts, 1:45.

44. Dickenson Transcripts, 4:224, 4:236; Gallagher Transcripts, 7:defense exhibit F.

45. Liles Transcripts, 2:106, 2b:439; see also Banghart Transcripts, 1:184 and 1:199.

46. Rees, *Korea,* 355–56; White, *Captives of Korea,* 148; Middleton, *Compact History of the Korean War,* 210; Goulden, *Korea,* 601–2.

47. Dunn Transcripts, 1:322; Banghart Transcripts, 1:199; see also Dickenson Transcripts, 5:253.

48. Batchelor Transcripts, 6:998; see also Dunn Transcripts, 1:181, 1:322 and Dickenson Transcripts, secret volume, 147.

49. Banghart Transcripts, 1:199–200; see also Liles Transcripts, 4b:1936–37.

50. Batchelor Transcripts, secret volume, 558; Dunn Transcripts, 1:154; see also Batchelor Transcripts, 8:1970 and 13:166.

51. Gallagher Transcripts, 6:18–19; see also Batchelor Transcripts, 8:1718.

SEVEN

"My Words, Their Thoughts"

To yield to force is an act of necessity, not of will—at the most, an act of prudence.

    —Jean-Jacques Rousseau, *The Social Contract*

Due to the breakdown of health services because of the war, typhus, smallpox, influenza, and other diseases were rampant throughout the civilian and military populations of North Korea and in parts of China from late 1951 into the following year. In February 1952 China launched a germ-warfare propaganda campaign in earnest. Their delegate to the World Peace Conference in Oslo denounced the United Nations and United States, alleging that the Allies were dropping bacteria-laden bombs on North Korea. At the same time, the Chinese stepped up the torture and interrogation of seventy-eight American flyers, for these men would substantiate the charges.[1]

Not every captured pilot was singled out for the special effort. Of the seventy-eight who were, thirty-eight capitulated and confessed to either planning the germ-warfare operation or actually performing it. Each man was treated differently. Some were physically maltreated, whereas others were subjected to mental torture. The flyers did not give in immediately, however. As Allen Dulles of the CIA observed, "There is a period of some six months between the date of capture and the alleged confession: Adequate time to allow for the elaborate planning by the communists of what the confession should contain—the drafting of the 'scenario' as it were."[2]

The commandant of the marine corps, Gen. Lemuel Shepherd, noted that pilots in particular have virtually no control over whether they will be captured "since it is the result of enemy action combined with the law of gravity." At some time and in some place, what goes up must come down. Shepherd continued, "Men who become prisoners of war must learn to accept the implications of their fate with the same fortitude with which they have learned in the past to steel themselves to accept the stark reality of death in battle. The prisoner-of-war stockade is only an extension of the battlefield where they must . . . carry on a unequal struggle with the only weapons remaining to them—faith and courage." General Shepherd was an unswerving advocate of providing only name, rank, and service number. Reality, however, intruded on that philosophy, and his own men were instructed that if captured they could give more than that.[3]

It has remained a little-known fact that during the Korean War many ground troops and airmen were told by their superiors to disregard the restriction of furnishing only name, rank, and service number in the event of capture. Doing so, they were told, did not work. Those who had sensitive information were not to just hand it over, but, as Maj. Ronald Alley said to protect the men in his command, POWs had to use "common horse sense" in addition to giving name, rank, and service number. Before Lt. Col. Harry Fleming arrived in Korea he had been present at a briefing given by the commanding officer of the Korean Military Advisory Group (KMAG), Brig. Gen. Francis W. Farrell, and one of Farrell's senior staff officers. Fleming had been instructed to "let discretion be the greater part of valor if you get yourself captured."[4]

In April 1952, Maj. William Harris, USMC, was part of the 20th Replacement Draft at the sprawling Marine Air Station at El Toro, California. Before he was shipped out, "Red Hot Fighter Pilot Harris" and the other members of his draft spent nearly a week learning escape and evasion tactics in addition to undergoing basic refresher courses. As training came to a close, a marine instructor told the assembled pilots, "This war is a little different from any you have been fighting. We have told you how to escape and evade. Now we are going to tell you what to do in case you cannot escape and evade and get captured. It is not a pleasant thought. Name, rank and serial number is out, gentlemen. They are going to find out anything they want to find out anyway. Go ahead and tell them the truth right off."[5] One can imagine that heads would have rolled had General Shepherd heard that advice.

Before a mission, Lt. Col. Gerald Brown, USAF, would be "briefed by his group intelligence officer in this respect: That they didn't believe the Chinese were taking prisoners anyway but in the event you were captured, [in order] to prevent torture or being killed, you could give information that was of an unclassified nature or of general knowledge." Such briefings were common throughout the air force and marine corps. David Little, a B-29 pilot, stated that he had been informed he could give out anything that was not officially secure, "for instance, performance characteristics of a B-29 were common knowledge and therefore, we used that as a point of truth to make other portions of our interrogation which were not true sound plausible." Capt. Laurence Miller, who flew an F-84, concurred: "We were instructed to tell them anything they wanted to know."[6]

These were not isolated briefings to only a select few pilots but rather standard procedure for the majority of aviators who flew combat missions over North Korea. As early as June 1951, Capt. James Wilkins, USMC, had attended a preflight briefing along with a Lt. Col. Shelley and Captains Degen and Cunningham. An intelligence officer from Marine Aircraft Group 33 was giving instructions, and Wilkins asked what to do in case of capture. The reply "was to the effect that if you did get captured to tell them what they wanted to know because they knew it anyway and if you had to go along with them, to go ahead. And I remember one statement the intelligence officer said, which was 'The Marine Corps wants you back and that is the important thing.'" When Captain Wilkins was questioned about what he thought upon hearing that drastic deviation from policy and tradition, he replied: "I accepted it as most of our people, I think, accepted it; that when you had to do something, that was the time to do it. In other words, you couldn't stick with just name, rank and serial number. They were going to get it out of you anyway and if you had to go further than that, then go ahead and do it."[7]

Many captured pilots were eventually deposited into the regular POW camps along the Yalu. For example, in July 1951 a group of twenty air force pilots were taken to Camp 5. When new men arrived, earlier captives would gather around and ask questions. Soon the ordinary ground soldiers learned that air force and marine pilots had been told what they could disclose if captured. The not-surprising reaction was, If it's good enough for them, then it's good enough for us. Captain Wilkins was brought into Camp 12 (Traitors Row) in August 1951, and Capt. Harold Kaschko heard him say marine corps officers had authorized that "if signing a peace petition—or something like that—would give you better treatment, why go ahead and sign it." Jeff Erwin also claimed to have heard Wilkins say the same thing, as well as Capt. Horace Cormin, USAF. Once they filtered down to common GIs, such abrogations of established policy could do nothing but create confusion among the ranks.[8]

The highest-ranking American officer captured during the war was Maj. Gen. William Dean, commander of the 24th Infantry Division. When asked after his release if name, rank, and service number were all that should be given to the enemy, he replied, "It is hard for me to judge others. I didn't have the intelligence or strength to stop there." Col. Frank Schwable, the most senior marine officer captured, observed that "the days of POWs being required to furnish only their names, ranks and serial numbers in accordance with the Geneva Convention . . . are gone forever, I am sure."[9]

>«

The U.S. Marines were proud of Col. Frank Schwable—and rightly so. The Naval Academy graduate, whose father had also been a career marine, had earned four Distinguished Flying Crosses, ten Air Medals, and two Legions of Merit with a gold star in lieu of a third. Frank Schwable was no one to fool with. The Japanese found that out at Bougainville when he shot down four of their aircraft.[10]

On April 10, 1952, Schwable arrived in Korea from the Pentagon, where he had completed a tour of duty as chief of staff at the Aviation Division, Headquarters, Marine Corps. He was glad to be back on active duty, although he was less than pleased with his new assignment. His orders were to report to the 1st Marine Aircraft Wing, where, on May 1, he would become chief of staff to Brig. Gen. Clayton C. Jerome, the commanding officer. The general was more than happy to have Schwable on board because he considered "him one of the brightest, finest, most conscientious, and, during the war, one of the bravest officers [he had] ever known." Because Schwable preferred flying and fighting to pushing paper, shortly after his arrival General Jerome promised that he would soon give him a group command.[11]

As chief of staff, Schwable's responsibilities were immense because the wing was large and complex. In addition to a headquarters squadron, the 1st Marine Aircraft Wing was composed of Marine Aircraft Group–12 (MAG-12), which had seven squadrons; MAG-33 of another seven squadrons; and MAG-2 of four squadrons. Although the marines are part of the Department of the Navy, during the Korean War the wing had only one squadron attached to an escort carrier at sea. The remainder of the wing took orders from—and were under the operational control of—5th U.S. Air Force, which, in turn, reported to the commanding general, Far East Air Force. That made sound organizational sense, and the Air Force assigned missions, furnished intelligence, and briefed the wing's pilots before missions. The air war in Korea was under the sole command of the U.S. Air Force.[12]

Colonel Schwable hoped he could take over MAG-12 some time in September. On the morning of July 8, 1952, he flew from wing headquarters to the MAG base at P'yongt'aek, which was below Seoul on the west coast of South Korea. After landing, he toured the complex, checked out operations, and in general did what a chief of staff would do on any inspection tour. After lunch he decided to return to wing headquarters, which was at P'ohang on the eastern coast and even further south than P'yongt'aek. All he need have done was fly across the friendly peninsula in a southeasterly direction. Because the colonel expected to assume command of the combat group within a few months, however, he requested and received permission to first go north and reconnoiter the front lines. His plan was to fly north and, upon reaching the main line of resistance, fly on the southerly side of the front lines from west to east and then go south to wing headquarters, having the Sea of Japan off his port wing.[13]

It was shortly after 2 on the hot summer afternoon of July 8 when the thin, graying colonel slid his five-foot-eight-inch body into the pilot's seat of a twin-engine Beechcraft (SNB). Taking the copilot's seat was Maj. Roy Bley, USMC, the wing staff ordnance officer who had made the trip to MAG-12 with Schwable. With engines at full power, the Beechcraft accelerated down the runway and was airborne. Heading straight north, Schwable climbed over Seoul, and when they reached the front he turned to the right and began a reconnaissance. Everything was going fine until Schwable and Bley were only thirty miles from the rugged east coast. Then, at an altitude of 5,500 feet, the colonel saw 40–mm tracer shells passing his right wing. Somehow either he or Bley had made a navigational error. They were behind enemy lines.[14]

Within seconds the tracers were directly in front of the men's faces and then there was a tremendous explosion on the right side of the cockpit. A 40–mm shell came up through Bley's seat and passed between his legs. Schwable made a steep ninety-degree turn south, applied full power to both propellers, and climbed. Major Bley couldn't help him because blood was spilling from holes in his right wrist, right foot, right thigh, and under his right arm. He also had shrapnel in his left leg and in the right side of his chest.[15]

They scrambled skyward for about fifteen seconds, and then suddenly both engines stalled at once. The colonel tried to restart them, but the fuel system had been shot out. There was nothing they could do but jump. "I didn't realize when the engines had stopped because I was hit in so many places and I didn't have my full wits about me," Bley recalled. The Beechcraft was losing altitude. If they didn't get out soon, they wouldn't get out at all. Schwable attempted to hold the powerless aircraft steady and at two thousand feet ordered Bley to jump. As soon as his copilot was clear, the colonel abandoned the destroyed airplane.[16]

Bley's parachute hit a large tree, and he was knocked unconscious. When he came to a few seconds later, he found himself hanging about ten feet off the ground. Jerking open his harness, he fell to earth and was knocked out again. Recovering, he painfully crawled an exhausting forty yards to the top of a small ridge. He was "lying there in a stupor" when Colonel Schwable, who had landed unhurt not far away, reached him. He took Bley's knife and said he would climb the tree and cut shrouds from the parachute to bind his wounds. Shortly after Schwable left, Bley heard shots aimed in his direction and immediately rolled down the opposite side of the ridge. He'd been seen, however, and was captured a few minutes later.[17] On the opposite side of the hill, Schwable was busy cutting up shrouds. The task didn't last long, however. Before he knew it, ten armed Chinese soldiers had surrounded him. He was taken prisoner.[18]

Frank Schwable was unarmed and wearing his regular uniform, silver eagles on the collar of his shirt and gold wings pinned above the left breast pocket. Schwable, who had been in the marine corps twenty-three years, was a prize for the Chinese because he was the highest-ranking marine captured during the war. Schwable remembered: "The minute I got my feet on the ground and had not broken my neck, there I was, a colonel, and I had some pretty good experience and pretty good background and there I was—in the Chinaman's hands." His problem was abetted by the fact that the enemy detested U.S. Marines. They had spelled it out in so many words to Major Harris, a captured marine pilot: "We do not like marines. They are professional fighters, professional killers. They do not fight because they have to, they fight because they love to."[19] Colonel Schwable, with his combat experience and courage, had never been in bigger trouble.

Schwable was searched and "caught flat-footed. Not having anticipated flying across the enemy lines," he recalled, "I had the works on me." The "works" included his wallet, which contained a driver's license, flight instrument ticket, cards to the officers' mess at Bethesda and Anacostia, and pictures of his wife and children in addition to various other papers. He also had a flight clearance ticket showing his home station, the base from which he had taken off, and the base to which he was heading. He didn't need to say a word; the Chinese knew much more about him than he or the Corps cared for them to know.[20]

For a week, Schwable and Bley were moved by jeep in a northwesterly direction. Then they were separated and didn't see each other until much later in the year. During his first two weeks of captivity, Schwable underwent some low-level military interrogation, and it appeared the Chinese questioners were more interested in what was happening on the front lines than in Schwable's identity. In answer to practically all of their questions, the colonel replied, "I was brand new in Korea, I had just come there; I was as yet unassigned, had no job, and that was the very thing I was doing that day; [i.e.,] taking my first look around Korea along the front lines. Therefore, I didn't know anything of the ground situation; I didn't know anything of the organization; I was just brand new; I didn't know anything."[21]

For fifteen days, between July 8 and July 23, Schwable was interrogated about the articles in his possession and the operations of ground forces in the immediate area. He stuck to his story (and lie), however: He knew nothing because of his recent transfer. On July 24 Frank Schwable was moved to an interrogation center named Pike's Peak somewhere at the thin waist of North Korea. There he remained for more than four months.[22]*

While Frank Schwable was playing dumb, the Defense Department in Washington was being stupid. Someone in the department, and it had to have been a high-level someone, decided to inform the public through a press release that Schwable had been captured. That itself wouldn't have been all that bad. The Chinese knew who they had—they just didn't know what they had. On July 12, 1952, four days after Schwable had been taken prisoner, major American newspapers, including the *New York Times,* published a sanctioned story that gave not only his name but also the information that he was chief of staff of the 1st Marine Aircraft Wing and had graduated from Annapolis in 1929. The story also furnished the names of his wife (Beverly) and two children (David, fourteen, and Susan, five) and his home address in Arlington, Virginia, as well as those of his mother. In addition, the Defense Department provided the name of Bley's wife (Margaret) and parents. The report ended by saying, "Both flyers went to Korea last April with Brig. Gen. Clayton C. Jerome, present commander of the 1st Wing." While Schwable was attempting to con his way out of a tricky situation, his biography had become public information across the United States.[23]

By the time Frank Schwable reached Pike's Peak, the Chinese, who were not as stupid as the Defense Department seemed to think they were, had done their homework. He was brought into a room and once again asked his name, unit, and function. Once again, he responded that he knew nothing due to his recent arrival in the area. At that moment, according to Schwable, "The Chinaman leaned back a little—he had a piece of paper in his hand—he said, 'You are the chief of staff of the 1st Marine Aircraft Wing. You came to Korea in April.'" Colonel Schwable gave a tiny smile and nodded his head.[24]

After the lie was uncovered, Schwable expected "to be tortured phys-

---

* Pike's Peak was also known as Pick-up Camp and Mountain Camp. It's difficult to determine the precise location of this center although available documents indicate that it was thirty-five miles east-north-east of Suchon and just southwest of Yongdok. However, these are phonetic spellings and although there is a town named Yongdok on a map of North Korea, there doesn't appear to be any town named Suchon thirty-five miles west-south-west of it. In addition, once or twice in the documents, this interrogation center is called Pak's Palace but it is doubtful that Schwable was in that camp.

ically by oriental methods," but in his case that was not to be. There was no hanging by the thumbs or no drops of water pounding relentlessly on his forehead for days. Shortly after the session in the room, however, he "encountered organized, methodical, high-level, preplanned interrogation, political indoctrination and torment [in order] to accomplish the foul propaganda objectives the Chinese had in store." As Schwable's commandant General Shepherd said, "It is to be noted that the chain of events leading to the collapse of Col. Schwable's moral resistance began when he was confronted with the falsity of his original account. From then on he was continually on the defensive and successfully deprived of any element of moral ascendancy which might otherwise have assisted him in resisting his captors."[25]

The Chinese did not immediately badger Schwable about germ warfare. They would take their time before deciding how to use their prize captive most effectively. Therefore, during the first two weeks of August he was placed in a very small room of a house and left alone. That time was called the "thinking period." "During these several weeks," Schwable recalled, "no particular pressure was put upon me [and] in fact, it was a period of just sitting stupidly like an animal in a cage to think and think—to reflect—to become bitter at my own misfortunes, to delve into the uncertainties of the future, to let my fears, worries and imagination run rampant."[26]

After the thinking period, the colonel was moved to a dark, damp tent and kept there for another three weeks. During this interval, two Chinese Air Force officers visited him from 7 A.M. to 6 P.M. daily to interrogate him about various military subjects. Schwable was tough, however, and for a long period would not provide any information. Because his interrogators had to go back to their superiors with something, and in order to pacify them, he did comply when ordered to describe his flight training at Pensacola. In view of the fact that the training had taken place twenty-one years earlier, he had no guilt in this regard and even wrote a paper on naval aviation training in 1931. After that the two officers left and Frank Schwable sat and waited. His time was coming.[27]

>«

In early September 1952, Schwable was moved from his tent to a stick and mud lean-to "on the outside of a Korean house tucked away back in a deep, obscure, isolated valley in the North Korean wilderness where [he] could easily be disposed of without attracting attention or notice." The shelter was three feet wide, six and a half feet long, and seven feet high—about as much flat surface as an average dining-room table. There he was to stay for three months.[28] In that claustrophobia-inducing space he was not permitted to lie down except during designated hours of sleep. Neither was he allowed to stand. He was required to sit at attention, hands in his lap. He had no chair. "I started my sitting," he remembered. "Sitting cross-legged on a mat-covered floor in a very confined space; sitting for hours on end, day after day, for months."[29]

When he wasn't being interrogated there was nothing for him to do but think, which is exactly what the enemy wanted. As General Dean confirmed, "One of the most difficult problems for a prisoner is maintaining his judgment. A thought grows in your mind until you are sure it must be exceptionally clever. And sober reflection, which might show it up as being foolish rather than clever, just isn't possible under prison conditions." That is all that Colonel Schwable did—sit at attention all day, every day, and think. His isolation was almost total during the fourteen months under Chinese control. He was guarded twenty-four hours a day, never permitted to communicate with another prisoner, and only rarely allowed to look at other Americans. His repetitive testimony of this solitary confinement provides a sense of his mental anguish: "I thought a great deal of my family and I worried about them no end." Even worse, according to Schwable, "You are sitting there all alone; you don't understand anybody. There is no distraction. You sit there and you just think. You reflect. You analyze. You grasp at anything that your mind can concoct—anything—and anything you flash back as you go along is exaggerated more and more. Your judgment becomes warped."[30]

Although Schwable was given winter clothing and a quilt, the unheated lean-to "was damn cold, awfully cold." One freezing morning he awoke about 4 and desperately needed to go to the latrine. When the guard refused, he was forced to urinate into a small tin can that he used for drinking. He then went back to his usual, restless sleep. When he was awakened two hours later, the urine in the can had formed a circular block of yellow ice. For two days he chipped away at the once-liquid waste with a sharp stone, and also for two days he had nothing to drink. "I can assure you at the end of two days when I got most of it out and we were able to put hot water in there, that drink of hot water and melted urine didn't taste very good but I was thirsty," he testified.[31]

The lean-to was attached to a cottage that housed a Korean family that included children. "Those little kids," said Schwable, "would go out and relieve themselves right in front of the place and the dog is there to eat it because that is all the dog eats." The first few times the colonel saw that, he was eating his daily ration of rice and vomited. Sanitation was poor, and on many occasions he was not permitted outside the lean-to to relieve himself. When that happened, he said, "Your place of confinement is just small enough so that you relieve yourself in a corner, you sleep in it. Your choices are awfully limited." Schwable was having bouts of diarrhea and during those episodes was permitted the use of a latrine. But "when you have diarrhea and you have to go an awful lot of times and you use leaves with a heavy coat of frost on top, you can imagine what that does. It is not pleasant. It is one more irritating—irritating physically but more irritating mentally. And I knew those monkeys had paper around there."[32]

Frank Schwable was a colonel in the U.S. Marine Corps and proud of it. His spirit was genuine and lasting, which the Chinese knew. They knew marines. As he remembered:

> A Marine officer among a bunch of Chinamen certainly has a feeling of superiority right off the bat—you can't help it; they broke that down. They did everything to just make you feel as little and as insignificant and use-less as they possibly could. . . . Every effort was made to degrade and hu-miliate me and to reduce me to the level of an animal wallowing around in dirt and filth, living practically the life of a beast in a cage. My inherent pride as a Marine officer was submerged and with it my moral and spiritu-al outlook was contaminated.[33]

For Frank Schwable, both days and nights were too long. He became so confused that he didn't know which he wanted: "I used to pray for night time to come and at least bring me unconsciousness. But as the evening time came along, then I used to dread it because I know that the minute the sun goes down it gets cold. And if I were cold all day long and chilled to the bone, I knew it was going to be that much colder that night. And the minute I would lie down, I would start praying for morning to come." During the dark Korean nights, his sleep, if it can be called that, was "an apprehensive, restless, rolling around, I guess, with your eyes closed. That is about the only way I know how to put it."[34]

If nights were lonely and apprehensive, days in the lean-to were spent trying to outwit interrogators. They came to the little hovel and "like the slow dripping water working on the nerves, the Chinese kept repeating that the only course of action . . . was to confess, confess, CONFESS!!" But confess to what? Schwable couldn't confess to dropping "germ bombs" from a small twin-engine Beechcraft flying along the front lines. No one would believe that. The Chinese wanted him to confess to participating, at a very high level, in the planning of bacteriological warfare against North Korea. They "had a chief of staff, they had a colonel, they had an aviator, all in one plane; and who would sit alongside of him but, among all people, the wing ordnance officer who knows all about bombs." Yet during the entire fourteen months under the Chinese, Schwable never gave away classified information. Even more remarkable, the Chinese never asked for any. Because of his recent duties and experiences, Schwable knew a great deal of highly sensitive information that one would think the enemy would want. Instead of military information, however, he "was constantly told that as a war criminal, [he] must fight for peace by 'confessing.'"[35]

The interrogators kept up the pace day after day, week after week, month after month. It was a "constant, constant nagging. They questioned here and they questioned there, and back to this, here, there, and back to that." When Schwable tried to reason with them that there was no such thing as germ warfare and denied participating in it at any time, they were not persuaded. According to Schwable, "They say black is white and you try in every way you can to show that black isn't white but there is no use because you end up—black is white." Interrogators became so proficient at producing anxiety that when the enemy did not arrive at the lean-to one day it "was the worst day that came along because all day long you are sitting there holding on, dreading that guy coming and you don't know when he is coming so you worry about it all day long."[36]

The Chinese were always telling him to "clear his problem." If he did not do so, he would "never leave [the] valley—not even after the peace [was] signed." Intimidation was the most effective weapon used against the colonel. General Shepherd's opinion aside, Schwable's resistance began to crumble not so much because he initially was caught in a lie but because his captors threatened to kill him. He was given "the choice of a false 'confession' or death."[37] It was simple and direct. There was absolutely no reason in the world why Frank Schwable should not have believed them.

Schwable was to do only one thing: write. With his life in the balance, he took up pen and paper and wrote anything that came to mind—except information about germ warfare. "All right," he thought, "here is a subject I can stall them off on for some time and it is not going to hurt anybody or anything." When he took that first step, however, he placed himself on a slippery slope. Whenever he wrote something—whatever it was—his captors would return it and order him to expand upon it. That continued, with each swap promising to be the last. "At each step in the entire process the Chinese lied to me," Schwable recalled, "always saying that, 'This is the last step which must be completed if you are to clear the problem,' upon completion of which they invariably found just one more step to take in order to clear the problem. It was explained to me with a perfectly straight face each time that I had misunderstood them."[38]

September turned to October and then November. The colonel said, "I can only portray this phase of the treatment by likening it to sitting for some ten uninterrupted weeks on the floor of a closet in a deserted house in winter." Although the Chinese did not touch him, he was undergoing physical torture nonetheless. "Of all the actual things I think I went through, I would say the thing that bothered me the most—the thing that hurt me the most—was a continuous, [un]relenting backache that got worse and worse as time went on. I was almost driven wild by a constant gnawing backache resulting from sitting on the floor, relatively immobile, for so long in a confined space."[39]

In October 1952 William Shockley was in a cell about thirty yards from Schwable and saw him every day. Shockley, an enlisted marine, said, "The first time I really noticed him, he looked something like a little mouse. I hate to say this about the colonel but his features were so drawn, he reminded me of a little mouse. That was the main thing. . . . His jowls were sunk in and his eyes seemed to be very droopy. He moved very slow, as if he was tired and drowsy." Schwable described himself as living "under such a cloud of fear, futility, and make-believe—yet bitter realism—that confusion reigned supreme and I existed in a world of fantasy that is beyond my power of description." Major Harris has noted that the Chinese "are masters at mental torture. They don't have to lay a hand on you to make you the most miserable person in the world. I would rather take a beating any day than be subjected to their type of questioning and treatment." As Schwable summed things up, "It was obvious to me during my desperately lonely and miserable months of solitary confinement, when I would have given my soul for advice and guidance, that we were totally unprepared to handle propaganda as it is being used by the Chinese Communists."[40]

By the time the crisp November winds blew through the valley, Schwable felt he had to make a choice: "I was convinced that at my age and condition, I would freeze to death in that exposed little hovel during the winter at that camp. When it was really getting cold, that snotty yellow interrogator would sit on the steps in front of me, watching me shiver to death, and say, 'You know, winter is just coming along. It is going to get a lot, lot colder around here.' I got his point." The point was, according to the colonel, that a "POW has his own decision to make and he makes it all by himself; it is a hard, dreadfully hard decision to make, but he must 'call 'em as he sees 'em.'"[41]

It was toward the end of November 1952, around 10 P.M., when Colonel Schwable was escorted to the camp commander's quarters. There he received "the most concentrated talking to that I had in my whole experience over there." For two hours the Chinese colonel berated him and kept repeating over and over, "You must confess; it is for the good of the world. It is the peace appeal. You must cleanse your soul; you know you did it. We have an international scientific commission report; we know your night fighters started this thing." The marine had reached a breaking point and "felt I was sitting there banging my head against the wall. I couldn't believe I was there." The next morning, his interrogator smiled and said, "The colonel is so happy that you have decided to cleanse your soul and to confess and thus help the peace movement. The night fighters were the first ones, weren't they?" Col. Frank Schwable, USMC, replied, "Yes."[42]

"Even in my torment and mental and physical anguish," he later said, "I could see I was of little value to the U.S. if I were six feet under the ground." Therefore, "I made my evaluation of my worth to the U.S.—dead or alive—and I then capitulated to the Chinese in utter desperation the end of November, 1952."[43]

Winfred Overholser, a psychiatrist who examined the colonel after his release, noted that "he was not a man who was competent, at that time, to exercise any substantial degree of judgment as to what he was about; that he was unable to judge the demands of the situation fully; that he was really, in essence, without a will." Schwable agreed: "When you have gotten to the point where you will make such a terrific concession to another man, as I did to that little Chinaman, then I did not have any resistance left. I did what that guy told me."[44]

After agreeing to write his "misstatement" (the "Fleas, Flies and Mosquito Confession" as he called it), Schwable was kept in the lean-to for almost another two weeks, along with pen and paper. It was so cold that the knuckles on his right hand became frostbitten. After every few words the ink in the pen would freeze, and he would have to unscrew the top and sit on the ink bottle to thaw it. Although he did not believe a word he put on paper, he stated:

> It was real to me, the conferences and how the planes would fly up there and how they would go about their missions—that was real. . . . It became habitual and easy to lie and as natural to write false . . . as it is to speak and honor the truth in a free land. . . . It was while writing these "confessions" that I felt most that I was living in a world of ungodly fantasy; it was impossible to believe that what was happening was real; that civilized human beings in this modern day and age could seriously plan, direct, and force such a diabolical swindle [as germ warfare] on their fellow human being— friend and foe alike.[45]

On December 6, 1952, Frank Schwable submitted a rough draft of his confession. Two days later, he and eighteen other POWs were put aboard two trucks for a fourteen-hour overnight trip to Camp 5. Most men who saw Schwable on the ride north thought him insane. Some said he would suddenly yell out, "I'm surrounded by oil," and in the freezing truck he would warm himself by removing his jacket. At a stop, a few men saw him shadowboxing. Once he reached Camp 5, the colonel was removed from the principal compound and again isolated. On the other side of Pyoktong, he was placed in a mud cell six feet wide, eight feet long, and seven feet high. The prisoners named these cells "dog houses."[46]

Between December 10 and the 21 his confession was revised, edited, and expanded. The cold made it very difficult for him to write, but his cell at Camp 5 happened to have a sixty-watt bulb in it. "When the light was on," he said, "I would stand there by hours just holding that little bulb, and that is when I began to get feeling back in my fingers again." During the third week in January 1953, he signed the final version of his "misstate-ment," which the Chinese predated to December 6, 1952. It was over. "They had edited the English, they threw in a few things of their own, but unfortunately, most of that was mine. My words, their thoughts."[47]*

As wing ordnance officer, Major Bley had it no easier than his superi-or; he, too, underwent very harsh treatment. About three weeks before Schwable was relocated to the outskirts of Camp 5, Bley was shipped there and underwent his thinking period. When he refused to cooperate, the major was placed in a cave. He was forced to sit at attention on the mud floor and sleep in the mud; his only companions were lice and rats. Dur-ing periods of questioning, Bley reported, his interrogator would "walk in eating an apple or smoking cigarettes, blow smoke in my face, but never offer me a cigarette. Occasionally he would, but if I reached for it he would hold it back and say, 'After you cooperate with us, you can have all the cigarettes you want.' Most of the time, when the interrogator was work-ing on me, I had to stand at attention. After a long period of time, if I fell over from exhaustion, he had the guards come in and get me up. If I re-fused to get up, or I couldn't get up, they kicked me or used rifle butts on me until I did get up."[48]

In January 1953 the Chinese pronounced Maj. Roy Bley, USMC, a war criminal and informed him that he was to be shipped to China and exe-cuted. For five full days after his sentence, Bley was forced to stand at at-tention in a cell whose walls and floor were plastered with chunks of ice. With no sleep for well over ninety-six hours and with frostbitten fingers and feet, Bley had virtually no more endurance. "At the end of about five nights," recalled the major, "I was pretty well mentally and physically broken." Being presented with Schwable's confession was the final straw. Shortly thereafter Bley signed.[49]

In late January 1953, for the first time since his capture, Colonel Schwa-ble was permitted to comb his hair. He had to look presentable for the audience about to receive him. Between February 1 and 20, he was forced to read his confession in front of recording machines and motion picture cameras. The statement was broadcast worldwide over powerful Radio Peking on February 22, 23, and 24. His confession also appeared in many communist bloc newspapers and in various POW publications. Further-

---

* See Appendix C for Colonel Schwable's confession.

more, the admission was introduced before the United Nations on March 12, 1953, by Soviet Foreign Minister Andrei Vishinsky.[50]

In mid-June, Schwable was transferred to the officers' camp (Camp 2), although the Chinese continued to keep him in solitary confinement. The haranguing and related mental torture were over, but his living conditions continued to be no better than those of an animal. He particularly recalled his visits to the latrine, which was situated atop a hog pen "and there is this hog—while you are squatting—waiting, and while you are squatting the flies go back and forth between you and the hog. To me, that is repulsive."[51]

On September 3, 1953, Frank Schwable was taken before a military board of four Chinese and one North Korean officer and convicted of being a war criminal. Three days later he was released from imprisonment and returned to his countrymen. For him, the terrifying ordeal with the Chinese was over, but another ordeal was about to begin. Colonel Schwable was to discover shortly that he would not be welcomed back to the Corps with open arms. The tough commandant was readying his arsenal of weapons against him and hoping to drum him out of the marines.[52]

>«

During the first week of captivity, Major General Dean had been interrogated about military matters but had furnished no useful information. After the questioning and just a few weeks before the Inchon invasion on September 15, 1950, the general was moved north to Seoul. He remained in the occupied South Korean capital only two days before being moved north again to P'yŏngyang, and from there sixteen miles further north to Sunan.

Upon reaching Sunan, Dean met a Colonel Kim, whom he almost immediately learned to hate.* On September 10, Kim brought to the general two documents that he wanted signed. One statement was to the effect that the United States was making a mistake fighting in Korea and the other was that Syngman Rhee, president of South Korea, "was no good, a rascal, a crook, a senile old man, a thief who looked after his own personal interests." Dean refused, but a few days later—after extensive pressure from Kim—he agreed to write a letter to his superior, Lt. Gen. Walton

---

* "I don't know that his name was Kim. There are many Kims in Korea," noted Dean.

Walker at 8th Army Headquarters. In the letter, Dean said to Walker, "I urge that you impress upon the Air [Force] the necessity to confine our attacks to military targets."[53]

On September 14 he was taken back to P'yŏngyang, where he remained briefly. It was likely that because of the Inchon invasion he was again moved north to Sunan. Once again Colonel Kim arrived, and for sixty-eight straight hours the fifty-one-year-old general was interrogated. "There was an almost pathological insistence on getting something signed," Dean remembered. "I would not broadcast on the radio, therefore I must sign a paper saying that I would not go on the radio." During these three sleepless days and nights, the general denied any and all of the propaganda arguments Kim put forward. It was a very confusing time, and Dean later recalled, "To this day, I don't know exactly why you go about refuting absolute absurdities or lies so bald. Once the lie or absurdity had transcended the whole realm of reasonableness, there simply is no reasonable answer."[54]

Because American troops were pushing north, Dean was eventually moved to Manp'o on the Yalu River in early October 1950.* During captivity he was always quartered in a Korean house and was never under the control of the Chinese. The North Koreans realized who they had and were going to keep him. "I was unhappy about being kept away from a regular camp," Dean said, "but after I came home and read about the things that happened in those camps, I realized that I should have thanked my lucky stars that I was not in one of them. I never lived as badly as the men in them lived most of the time."[55]

His one diversion at Manp'o was a game called *chong-gun,* which is similar to chess. He played it regularly with his guards and became good at it. "Generally these people treated me kindly," Dean said. "Most of the time I was treated, more or less, like a member of a big family. I ate what they ate, including the occasional treats someone brought in." Although he was not starved as men in the camps were, the diet was meager by American standards. "Over and over again, I planned a dinner," he recalled. "This would be served on my first night of freedom. It would include

---

* It's safe to assume that Major Nugent and his large group of prisoners were within a very few miles of General Dean when they began their death march under the Tiger.

prime ribs, an artichoke, a small baked potato with cheese on it and a good-sized hunk of butter, quick-frozed peas, a big helping of head lettuce with french dressing, ice cream, and a huge cup of black coffee."[56]

Dean was once again moved south to Sunan in mid-January 1951 and remained in the vicinity of that town for the next two years. The general remembered, "This was the beginning of my worst year—a year of two houses, two caves, many flies, malaria, a succession of odd guards, and terrific boredom—all within a three-mile radius. This was the year the North Koreans appeared to forget about Dean almost entirely and I had difficulty myself in remembering who or where I was and in maintaining any sort of sanity."[57]

On December 21, the general was introduced to Wilfred Burchett, an Australian correspondent for *Ce Soir,* the French left-wing newspaper. Believed by many to be a communist, Burchett was making the rounds of various POW camps in North Korea. Other than the progressives, prisoners who met him despised him. Dean, however, said that his time as a POW became more bearable after meeting with Burchett and credited the correspondent with the change. "I don't think it's surprising that I like Burchett and am grateful to him," Dean remarked and entitled a chapter of his book, *General Dean's Story,* "My Friend Wilfred Burchett."[58] Just after the journalist's visit, Dean began receiving mail and other correspondence, books, movies, and a great deal of communist literature.

The general read everything he could find because he "was interested in finding out what modern communism was all about." "I'd studied Marxism as a political-science course at the University of California," he recalled, "but their [the North Korean] interpretation of Leninism was all new to me. But I'm an authority now."[59]*

During the remainder of his captivity, liquor was readily available to him, including gin, U.S. bourbon, Canadian whiskey, "and almost endless gifts of sake, ginseng, and vodka." In February 1953, he was moved north to Kanggye, and "here we lived as comfortably as anyone in North Korea does during winter and early spring."[60]

When he left his guards to be shuttled to Kaesong for repatriation,

---

* Dean stated that an outline summary of his Korean War experience was "a chase and capture, the battle of ideas, attack by boredom, and attack by luxury. Of all these, the battle of ideas is the one that, to my mind, has the most importance."

Dean noted, "I felt as if I were parting from long time friends." But that feeling was hardly unalloyed:

> I hate the thought—and always will—that I was well treated while others suffered; and there is very little satisfaction in the fact that I didn't know about it and could not have done anything if I had. I should have been able to represent other prisoners and do something about their treatment but I was not able to and did not. So while the welcome I received when I finally got home was wonderful and heartwarming, in some other ways it was also a little hard to take. I wish those other soldiers, thousands of them, could have shared it much more than they did.[61]

Notes

Almost every one of the fourteen courts-martial transcripts contains classified information that the army had withheld from me. These classifications, in the majority of cases, pertained to testimony offered by U.S. Air Force pilots, more specifically to permission briefings about what pilots may or may not do—or say— if captured and to the large area of germ warfare. Over years of research, these documents were, at my request, declassified and incorporated into the missing pages of the various volumes. Therefore, all army courts-martial volumes are complete.

That is also true with the three-volume court of inquiry concerning Col. Frank Schwable. Approximately three-quarters of the testimony in the case was in open court, but when the doors were closed the marines labeled all that testimony "secret," a high-security classification. That is because the colonel signed what has been called the "confession of confessions" on how he organized and planned a germ warfare operation against North Korea and China. These secret portions of the transcript have also been declassified at my insistence and incorporated into the three volumes. This chapter contains the account of the torture that Schwable underwent and his final, degrading confession.

1. Middleton, *Compact History of the Korean War,* 209–11.

2. "Red 'Brain Washing,'" 80.

3. Col. Frank Schwable, USMC, Transcripts, 1:exhibit F, exhibit I.

4. Maj. Ronald Alley, USA, Transcripts, 1:229; Lt. Col. Harry Fleming, USA, Transcripts, 11:1474.

5. Schwable Transcripts, 1:331–32.

6. Alley Transcripts, 7:838; Lt. Col. Paul Liles, USA, Transcripts, 2b:730; see also Alley Transcripts, 10:146.

7. Liles Transcripts, 4b:1631; Maj. Ambrose Nugent, USA, Transcripts, 11:2908, see also 11:2890–96 and Schwable Transcripts, 2:608, 2:730–38, 3:1096–97.

8. Liles Transcripts, 1:208, see also 1:211 and Alley Transcripts, 7:847, 10:145.

9. Schwable Transcripts, 2:862, 2:1255.

10. Goulden, *Korea,* 603; "A Tough Task," 33; "Schwable Freed but Is Criticized," 1; "Text of Inquiry Findings on Marine Col. Schwable and Comments by Defense Officials," April 28, 1954, 16; Schwable Transcripts, 1:52, 3:927.

11. Schwable Transcripts, 1:43, see also 1:9, 1:42, 1:52, 3:1186, and 3:1209.

12. Ibid., 1:37, 2:727, 2:743, 2:785–86, 3:1191.

13. Ibid., 1:30, 1:87, 2:788, 3:1091, 3:1189, 3:1191, 3:1209.

14. Ibid., 1:92–95, 1:390, 3:978, 3:1076, 3:1171, 3:1209, 3:1232.

15. Ibid., 1:104, 3:1209.

16. Ibid., 1:92–95.

17. Ibid., 1:95–96.

18. Ibid., 3:1003, 3:1210.

19. Ibid., 3:1012; 1:334–35, see also 3:971, 3:1122, 3:1133, and 3:1210.

20. Ibid., 3:1004, see also 3:1007.

21. Ibid., 3:1006–7, see also 1:98.

22. Ibid., 3:975, 3:1111, 3:1124, 3:1172.

23. Ibid., 3:1297.

24. Ibid., 3:1010, see also 3:1173.

25. Ibid., 3:1211, 3:1213, 1:exhibit G.

26. Ibid., 3:1211.

27. Ibid.

28. Ibid., 3:1212, see also 3:977–78, 3:1013, 3:1173, and 3:1267.

29. Ibid., 3:1254, see also 1:120.

30. Fleming Transcripts, 3:300; Schwable Transcripts, 3:965, 3:1257, see also 3:1254.

31. Schwable Transcripts, 3:983; 3:991, see also 3:1268.

32. Ibid., 3:990; 3:992, 3:988.

33. Ibid., 3:1014, 3:1213.

34. Ibid., 3:996–97.

35. Ibid., 3:1038, 3:1213–14, see also 3:1013 and 3:1269.

36. Ibid., 3:978, 3:1051, 3:1054.

37. Ibid., 3:1211, 3:1256.

38. Ibid., 3:1051, 3:1212.

39. Ibid., 3:999, 3:1214.

40. Ibid., 1:133, 1:333, 3:1221, 3:1253.

41. Ibid., 3:1040, 3:1257, 3:1268.

42. Ibid., 3:1019–20.

43. Ibid., 3:1215, see also 3:1212 and 3:1256.

44. Ibid., 2:703, 3:1058

45. Ibid., 3:1081, 3:1213, 3:1216, see also 3:1024, 3:1062, 3:1212, 3:1233, and 3:1253.

46. Ibid., 1:267, see also 1:119, 1:207, 1:230, 1:236, 1:240, 1:270, 3:1056, 3:1067, and 3:1212.

47. Ibid., 3:985, 3:1025, see also 3:1024, 3:1115, 3:1131, and 3:1208.

48. Ibid., 1:119–21, see also 1:123.

49. Ibid., 1:124, see also 1:118, 1:123, 3:1033, and 3:1215.

50. Ibid., 1:233, 1:350, 1:376, 3:1034, 3:1115–16, 3:1212, 3:1224, and 3:1254.

51. Ibid., 3:991, see also 3:972.

52. Ibid., 1:exhibit Q, 3:1269.

53. Dean, *General Dean's Story,* 127; Fleming Transcripts, 3:300; Schwable Transcripts, 3:812, 3:825.

54. Dean, *General Dean's Story,* 108, 138–39; see also Schwable Transcripts, 3:815.

55. Dean, *General Dean's Story,* 168–69.

56. Ibid., 191–93.

57. Ibid., 207.

58. Ibid., 244.

59. Ibid., 107, 122–23; see also Fleming Transcripts, 3:299.

60. Dean, *General Dean's Story,* 256–57, 275; see also Fleming Transcripts, 3:294.

61. Dean, *General Dean's Story,* 246, 287. Dean stated, "It is possible for men to be enemies and friends at the same time, and we were" (292).

EIGHT
Pledge of Allegiance

He who betrays his country is like the insane sailor who bores a hole in the ship that carries him.

—Roman maxim

Between April 20 and May 3, 1953, 149 sick and wounded American prisoners of war were returned by the Chinese and North Koreans to United Nations lines under a program called Operation Little Switch. On July 27, 1953, the armistice ending the bloody Korean War was signed, and within the next five weeks nearly four thousand captive U.S. troops were transferred to UN control during Operation Big Switch at Freedom Village. Shortly after Little Switch, Lt. Jeff Erwin noted:

> The Chinks made a determined effort to fatten us up. By that time we had gotten rid of all of our lice, they had given us some cotton underwear, some blue clothing, and they improved conditions a great deal. We got two old scroungy pigs a week which we had to butcher ourselves. These pigs that we butchered were just loaded with a germ called trichinosis, a little white thing that looks like a louse, so we had to boil them—and boil them for hours in rice—before we figured it was safe to eat it. But all the prisoners had picked up weight there during these months.

Just before repatriation, Lt. Col. Harry Fleming remembered, "Then, and only then, were conditions prevailing that might be acceptable under the Geneva Convention. So I don't want to give the idea that Camp 2, or any of these Yalu River camps, were paradises."[1]

Officers at Camp 2 were busy memorizing the names of the dead, and Lt. Col. Paul Liles suggested that a written list of fallen comrades be compiled. Once it was complete, Liles took the top of a fountain pen, squeezed the list into its open end, sealed it with wax, and shoved it deep into his rectum. On August 20, 1953, with the dead secreted in the bowels of Paul Liles, Camp 2 was vacated and the men loaded aboard trucks and shipped south to Kaesong, about five miles above the 38th Parallel. The same process was taking place all along the northeast-to-southwest-oriented border separating North Korea from Manchuria. Convoys of trucks carrying weakened American soldiers headed south toward Kaesong.[2]

Many were happy to be going home, but others were apprehensive. For example, M. Sgt. William Olson mentioned in front of M. Sgt. Vincent Doyle that "he had written many articles and collaborated in many ways with the Chinese and that he was worried to death and would inform the military authorities of his activities when he was repatriated." Olson thought that he would "pull time" upon returning to the United States, a common attitude among returning survivors. During the final hours of their imprisonment, most soldiers who had collaborated began to realize the magnitude of what they had done. Their long truck ride south was guilt-ridden and filled with worry.[3]

≫≪

By the summer of 1953 the Chinese still could play a number of trump cards, even though the war was over. The shooting war may have ended in a draw, but that was not the case in the propaganda war, which the enemy won hands down. The final assault of the Chinese, and it was a massive one, had two objectives. One was to convince American citizen-soldiers to renounce their citizenship and voluntarily remain behind to make their new home in China. The other was to persuade those who were returning to America to continue their studies and proselytize for communism in hometowns throughout the country. Both objectives were frighteningly successful.

The captors spoke with as many GIs as they could and attempted to cajole them into "nonrepatriation." They worked on each man differently, attempting to discover his needs and satisfy them through deceit. American soldiers were promised the world if only they would remain behind. Sgt. William Banghart's talking-to began as early as July 8, 1953, and did not stop until he was loaded aboard a truck on August 23. The sergeant was promised an education and employment. When Banghart "asked them about whether I would be able to have whiskey and women should I decide to remain and not accept repatriation, I was assured that in China the communists have nothing against drinking and that there are many women there who still have backward ways. This apparently meant that I could have plenty of whiskey and women."[4]

Incredibly, the progressives at Camp 5 continued to carry on voluntary study-group meetings even while repatriation was occurring in August. The final conclave, according to Cpl. Harold Dunn, who was present, "was more or less a unity meeting of the Progressives [such as] getting organized among ourselves in the camp . . . and even when we returned to the Interior." Although they used the term *study groups,* what these men were planning was to establish communist cells throughout the United States. Back home, said Dunn, they would start small groups "to follow, more or less, the same type of study, same line of study, as we had in the camp."[5]

A Chinese instructor named Lim attended the unity meeting. Corporal Dunn testified that "more or less, [Lim] went [about] uniting ourselves, being more friendly, getting—you know—better knowing each other so that we could carry on our studies to their line of thinking, the communist line of thinking, back in our country, and forming groups within our neighborhood, things of that nature." When the GIs got home and were spread out across the country, their little cell was to contact friends, neighbors, and associations in the community and ask them to join the study group, "more or less starting it off gradually on current event studies," recalled Dunn, "and working it out into a higher category of Progressive studies."[6]

≫≪

The Chinese headquarters for all POW camps in North Korea was located at Pyoktong in a large brick school building. Inside was a room containing a long conference table, where in mid-summer 1953 a secret meeting took place that lasted for several days. Wang, the Chinese general in charge of all camps, attended, together with two members of his staff, Commander Chang and Commander Tien. One of the six American POWs there was Claude Batchelor, who said, "Chang was a very smooth talker who could sway anyone to his way of thinking if they were of a very low intellectual level and wanted to listen."[7]

Batchelor and a British marine, Andrew Condron, represented Camp 5 at the conference; Pfc. James Veneris and Cpl. Bohus Janda represented Camp 3; and Bobby DeGraw and Thomas Davis, Camp 1. It was no ordinary meeting. The three high-ranking Chinese officers did not attend the meeting until it had gone on for several days—until a useful purpose was to be served. The goals of the event were to establish a progressive (i.e., communist) club in the United States; have the members of that club fan out and infiltrate various organizations and governments, including the federal establishment; and eventually, with the help of other communist movements in America, overthrow the government of the United States. The plan was to implemented by certain former Korean prisoners of war who would be controlled by Peking.

General Wang began innocuously by telling the six men that their purpose for being there was to review their studies. Within a short time the GIs would be going home, and he and his staff merely wanted a critique of their accomplishments. The talk was friendly, and the men were asked to draw up individual reports on the progressive movement in the camps. They did so and then discussed the reports. After that, each wrote a "mass line," a synopsis of how the writer thought his followers (all six were considered progressive leaders) regarded him and how popular he was with them. Claude Batchelor proudly proclaimed, "My 'mass line' was appraised by the Chinese as superior. To be well liked by any group is something of a credit to a man and I am not ashamed of the respect the men had for me."[8] This was, of course, all sparring.

Finally, the real purpose of the conference surfaced. According to Batchelor, "The Chinese thought up an idea of sending secret agents into the United States for Communist work. This was to be a super secret organization, and I was called in to consult with the Chinese on how this organization should be operated."[9] Were there to be spies and cloak-and-dagger happenings? Nothing of the sort. What could be more perfect and up-front than a veterans' group?

General Wang approached the subject by explaining how the progressive and communist parties in the United States worked together. Corporal Janda recalled, "When they started telling us about the Communist Party in the United States, we could just about tell what they were up to. The first thing that hit our mind was for us to get back to the States and join the Party but further down, then they started going into that secret organization." The term *secret organization* is inappropriate. Once the captives returned home the organization was not to remain secret, only its purpose.[10]

The men at the meeting were ordered to go back to their respective camps and "work on the reliable Progressives," meaning that their studies and other progressive activities were to continue once they got home. They were also informed that when they reached the United States they were to be prepared to join a veterans' organization when contacted. General Wang suggested that the name of the group be "Ex-Prisoners of War for Peace." The names "Ex-Prisoners of War Welfare Association" and "POW Mutual Aid Club" were also suggested and discussed. Once again, the average progressive prisoner in North Korea did not know any of this. Each was just being prepared to be contacted after he was released.[11]

Ex-Prisoners of War for Peace was to aid members by contributing or lending money to them in times of unemployment or need. For all outward appearances, it was a mutual-aid society for men who had suffered during war and would stick together in peace. According to Bohus Janda, "If any man would get in trouble after such an organization would be formed in the U.S., they would back each other and automatically a Progressive Party [member] would contact this organization and [they] would support us."[12]

That cover story made the group appear noble. It would have not only progressives on its membership roster but also many other unsuspecting men who had virtually no leftist leanings. Beneath the public surface, however, "it would also serve as a contact for communist activities in the United States," said Batchelor, "and only a few would know the real meaning of its function." In fact, Batchelor continued, the Chinese "wanted me to secretly link this organization with the Communist Party of the United States. We could set a peace platform through our propaganda sheet and gradually turn it into a revolutionary organization. [Furthermore], the part of this mission which pertains to relationships with the communists in the United States was not to be known to the general membership of the organization."[13]*

After the purpose of Ex-Prisoners of War for Peace had been established, the group set up a preliminary organizational chart and command structure. Of course, only true progressives were placed at the top of the hierarchy. Before repatriation, "these people were given instructions to contact all Progressives in their area [upon their return home] and work in close contact with the leader," said Batchelor, who was to become head of the group once it became established in the United States. The names of those in the top layer were switched around frequently as people decided whether or not to be repatriated.[14] Batchelor, for example, and twenty-two others opted to remain in North Korea for eventual transfer to China.

≫≪

In mid-July 1953, shortly after the meeting with General Wang, Batchelor was called into Commander Chang's office. The Chinese officer told Batchelor that his mass line was the best and his natural leadership abilities had prompted Chang to ask the corporal to refuse repatriation and become dean of those who were not repatriated. Chang also said that "within five years or so the American people would wake up and elect a government with more peaceful intentions and then the American people would be able to receive me with open arms and would be very proud of me." The young soldier was enormously vain about his acknowledged leadership abilities. All Chang had to do was play on that ego, and before long, testified Batchelor, "I told him that I would stay."[15]

The enemy used differing methods to convince each of the twenty-three who eventually refused repatriation. With some they played on vanity; others were seduced by the prospect of whiskey and women; still others succumbed to threats. Cpl. Edward Dickenson said, "I actually joined the Progressive element about August 1952, and was never able to get out of the organization. I wanted to leave the Progressives on several occasions, but once you got in that group of Communist supporters, it was very difficult to get out." Dickenson was afraid, and the Chinese knew

---

* Selected British POWs were also planning their own secret organization upon return to the United Kingdom.

that. On July 20, 1953, Lim, the commanding officer of 3d Company at Camp 5, called Dickenson to his quarters and asked him to shelve his departure. The corporal declined. Two days later, Lim called him in again. Still the response was negative. Suddenly the company commander, Dickenson said, "became angry and told me that if I did not consider staying with the Communists, that he would send all of the articles and recordings I had written and made, to the United States Government, and that the United States Government would be forced to prosecute me for collaborating with an enemy. At that time I did not know that the United States Government would or would not prosecute me, and because of this threat, I agreed to refuse repatriation."[16]

Just before the cease-fire, the twenty-three Americans were collected at Camp 5 from the other camps along the Yalu.* Claude Batchelor was their leader, together with Pfc. James Veneris. "More Americans wanted to remain behind than the Chinese cared to have," Batchelor once claimed. "The Chinese did not want too many to remain back and refused to permit some to remain."[17] That statement, however, is difficult to accept at face value, because the Chinese tried to persuade many Americans to refuse release. The more who would stay behind, the greater would have been the propaganda coup for the enemy. More than a score of combat veterans of the Korean War, however, chose to renounce their citizenship and their nation.

At the first big meeting of the twenty-three in July 1953, Commander Chang gave the men an idea of what would happen to them and also informed them of their final goal. "You will be sent to China for the purpose of being trained to become communist agitators," he said, "and you will be smuggled back into the States or any place that they feel it would be necessary to send you at that time."[18] The GIs took that in without objection.

---

* Some of the documents reflect slightly different spellings of a few of the last names. Every effort has been made to obtain accuracy, but one or two of the following names may be misspelled. The initial twenty-three who remained behind were: Cpl. Clarence Adams, Sgt. Howard Adams, Cpl. Claude Batchelor, Cpl. Albert Belhonne, Cpl. Otho Bell, SFC Richard Corden, Cpl. William Cowart, Cpl. Edward Dickenson, Sgt. Rufus Douglas, Cpl. John Dunn, Sgt. Andrew Foruna, Cpl. Lewis Griggs, Pfc. Samuel Hawkins, Cpl. Arlie Pate, Sgt. Scott Rush, Cpl. Lowell Skinner, Sgt. Larence Sullivan, Pfc. Richard Tenneson, Pvt. James Veneris, Sgt. Harold Webb, Cpl. William White, Morris Wills, and Cpl. Aaron Wilson. In addition to the twenty-three Americans, it is believed that four British soldiers refused repatriation. That cannot be completely verified, however, because relevant documents have not been made available by that government. U.S. Army documents merely mention the fact in passing.

Before the twenty-three were shipped out of Camp 5, they still had unfinished business concerning Pfc. Wilbur Watson. When Watson was captured, he had in his possession papers identifying him as a deputy sheriff of Tishomingo County, Mississippi. The Chinese immediately concluded that he was associated with army intelligence and was a spy.* After being beaten to a bloody pulp, Watson said, "I signed a statement stating that I was an American spy—captured purposely—to come behind the communist lines and disrupt any activities that I could."[19] For the next three years his life was miserable. In addition to being beaten, Watson was kept in solitary confinement for the entire time. Now that the war was over, the Chinese seemed not to know what to do with him.

Near the end of July 1953, Wilbur Watson was hauled to company headquarters, kept overnight, and taken to another building on the following morning. In one of the rooms, five Chinese, including Commander Chang, were seated at a table. The twenty-three who were not being repatriated were arranged near the wall in a formation "kind of like a horseshoe deal." With Watson standing at attention, one of the Chinese announced, "The commander wants you men to know that we are gathered here to decide the fate of Watson." They were told of his confession, and then Chang said, "It is our policy, under circumstances like this, when we catch a spy, is to kill him. We feel like he should be killed." A number of Americans agreed that Watson should die.

Some considered death too harsh, and one said, "Well, due to the fact that you people have watched Watson all the time, he couldn't have done too much, he couldn't have learned anything that could help anyone. I feel like that since he has been kept in solitary confinement, since he has been placed in the hard-labor camp, since he couldn't have possibly done anything detrimental to the Chinese, I think he should be allowed to return home."

The fifth opinion to be solicited was Batchelor's, who had "a ready smile which, no doubt, some people might find charming and winning." Watson didn't think so. "In my opinion," Batchelor allegedly declared, "Watson is detrimental to the group. He may have information that G-2

---

* Throughout the three years they held Americans captive, the Chinese and North Koreans constantly looked for prisoners who had been, or were, members of the Counter Intelligence Corps of the U.S. Army. Those found were accused of spying, labeled war criminals, and brutalized if not executed.

or American intelligence would be very interested in. I feel, I go along with the commander's idea; I definitely think the man should be shot."

The moment he heard that sentence passed on him by a fellow American, Watson said, "I felt like I wanted to faint. I was worried for my life. It was just in the balance and I didn't know exactly what was going to happen. I mean, I didn't know what was going on. It just seemed like I wanted to pass out." Chang, however, made the final decision and concluded that Watson could go home. While he headed for freedom, the twenty-three were directed toward their captor's version of truth and peace.

On August 5 the nonrepatriates were moved to houses in the town of Pyoktong and for several weeks were given lectures by Chinese and North Korean officers.* During the talks, the enemy constantly reinforced the prisoners' decision: "You are not communists. You are peace fighters, only common GIs who want to fight for peace. The bulk of the American people are like that. You don't have anything to worry about."[20]

On August 25 the men were honored at general headquarters with a large dinner party hosted by General Wang. Dickenson recalled that "Wang gave an address to the nonrepatriates, welcomed them to the communist fold, and thanked each nonrepatriate for having the courage to give up his native country—and background—and join the communist movement and work as a revolutionist. Wang called the action of the nonrepatriates a victory over the United States and against Wall Street."[21]

Under the terms of the armistice, all nonrepatriates were to be shipped south to the Netural Zone, where they would be retained during a ninety-day grace period followed by an additional thirty-day holding phase. After January 22, 1954, the UN command would consent to their decision to remain with their captors.[22] On September 12, 1953, the twenty-three, under the command of Colonel Chong, were put aboard trucks for the ride south to the Neutral Zone about seven miles below Kaesong. There they were to renounce their country.[23]

In the Zone, Colonel Chong turned his charges over to the United Nations Repatriation Commission, and they were housed in a new building constructed especially for them. The UN, in turn, assigned Custodial Forces, India to keep watch over the twenty-three GIs. The Chinese had

---

* The lectures were given by a Colonel Chong, Lieutenant Commander Tim, Captain Lim, and Lieutenants Coo and Yung.

lost physical custody of their turncoats, but they continued to hold the psychological strings. They were permitted to speak with the men any time they wished as long as the soldiers were willing to listen, which they always were. An American "explainer group" was to have the same privilege of access if the prisoners were willing to listen, which they were not.

The Chinese talked and talked and talked. In the Neutral Zone they wheedled away at the twenty-three, beginning with fame and fortune and ending with power. Dickenson remembered that "the Chinese promised all nonrepatriates homes, jobs, income, women, a married life, travel to any country, including Russia. We were told we could have any woman in China for a wife and as soon as the ninety-day period of explanation was over, we would begin to receive everything that the Chinese promised. For the three colored nonrepatriates, the Chinese told them that they could have Chinese women for wives or the Chinese Communist Party would import some women from Africa for them."[24]

Nonrepatriates were informed that a revolution was already underway in the United States, triggered by the release of the POWs. An amplification of the previous plans was revealed to the men, according to Dickenson:

> Most of the Progressives who were repatriated, received some kind of mission which they were to perform after they reached their native lands. The Chinese designated certain nucleus groups among the Progressives, and gave them specific instructions as to what to do after they reached their native countries. They were told to keep in touch with each and every other Progressive. They were told to organize in their immediate communities, and carry on correspondence with Progressives in other communities. The stronger ones were told to keep an eye on the weaker ones, and not to let them deviate from their indoctrination which they had received while a prisoner. Following are some of the members of the various nucleus groups which have the above-mentioned instructions [seventeen names followed]. . . . The nucleus groups are scheduled to have a convention in Chicago on an undetermined date. Contact is to be made by telegram, and the place of meeting will be free of police interference.[25]

It is difficult to calculate accurately the proportion of progressives among the nearly four thousand prisoners who returned home and remained active in the movement for which they had studied for three long, hard years; 20 percent would be a cautious estimate. That being the case, by October 1953 hundreds of soldiers and former soldiers were back in the

United States with "missions" inspired and controlled by the Peking government. Corporal Dickenson expanded on the game plan as outlined by the Chinese:

> The revolution in the United States would follow an economic depression, which is predicted by the Chinese, and that the Communist Party in the United States would do all that it can to help bring on that depression, the means by which were not disclosed. Propaganda would be one of the big weapons the communists would use in fermenting a revolution in the United States and this would be done legally. The Chinese pointed out that the United States Constitution is broad and liberal in scope. The Constitution of the United States permits people to speak freely and without interference by police or any law enforcement officers. Freedom of speech in the United States is an important provision of the Constitution of the United States and communist agitation would be able to succeed without interference from the police. We were told by the Chinese we could do almost anything we wanted to do, for the communist cause, under the provisions of the United States Constitution and that would be done with propaganda and agitation among all elements of the population.[26]

In the Neutral Zone the Chinese elaborated on all their previous training of the twenty-three and emphasized their hopes for a new world. Because "most of the Progressives" who had been released were already on their way home and had "missions" in the United States, what was planned for nonrepatriates, the loyalest sympathizers? Their position in the global strategy of the Chinese had to be more responsible than those who had returned. The progressives who went back to the United States were the seeds, and the twenty-three GIs were the flowers—or so they thought.

As soon as the cooling-off period in the Neutral Zone was over, the people from Peking planned to take the dedicated Americans back to their capital city, where for five years they were to go to school and concentrate on the study of communism and "revolutionary tactics." During that period (1954–58), the revolution in America would have begun, instigated by labor organizations and directed by the American Communist Party. After graduation, each of the former soldiers would be assigned certain tasks in the United States. After the revolution, they all would hold important positions in the federal government. Dickenson said, "We were told that we would [have] no difficulty in getting back to the United States illegally for our missions" (likely via the Philippines). Furthermore, according to Dickenson, various Chinese peace organizations "would facilitate the infiltration to whatever country needed our services."[27]

What services? As young adults everywhere, many of the twenty-three had grandiose ideas about what they wanted to be, and the Chinese played upon those expectations. Although the Chinese did not expect twenty-three wayward GIs to subvert and overthrow the government of the United States, they played upon the men's egos, dreams, and aspirations. Each was to be fully trained and specialize in what he thought to be his field of expertise. Claude Batchelor was to participate in an intensive study program in military leadership. Arlie Pate was to learn espionage and return to the United States as a spy. Sam Hawkins liked flying and therefore was to become a specialist in MiG aircraft. Lowell Skinner was slated for military strategy and tactics. Harold Webb was to learn the tactics of agitation. Scott Rush was to become a professional "revolutionary photographer." Morris Wills took a liking to economics, so his field would be political economy. John R. Dunn, James Veneris, and Albert Belhonne were political science majors. Larence Sullivan, William White, and Clarence Adams, the three black nonrepatriates, were to be trained in the agitation of minorities.[28] A ridiculous exercise? These soldiers accepted the premise and were ready to take on the world, especially the United States.

They did so because they wanted peace. Some also wanted wine, women, and song, but peace was the foundation upon which everything else was to be built, including the eventual overthrow of their government. With that catchword as a catalyst for all other activities, how could anyone fault them? As Batchelor said, "One of the things that caused some to remain was the promises of travel, fame, and good living," but most important was "a leading place in the fight for peace throughout the world. At that time, I could think of nothing more honorable than working for peace. The idea we had that it was to fight for peace, which anyone would recognize as a worthy thing as long as you are doing it the right way. We thought we were doing the right thing. We thought we were making a great sacrifice in staying behind in order to fight for peace." As Corporal Batchelor explained, "a peace fighter is one who sincerely believes that the world should have peace and lends his services to that end. If I say I am a peace fighter, I do not want it understood that I am a revolutionist. I feel that a person can be for peace and not be playing in the hands of the communists." When asked if he were a communist, however, he replied, "I did have some degree of communist belief."[29]

>«

The twenty-three were a diverse group, and it did not take long for dissension—and then disunity—to occur. According to Batchelor, "I think that most of them stayed because of fear. Very few of them had any intellect to really understand that they were fighting for peace." Initially, Batchelor claimed, his comrades were for peace, loved their fellow man, and thought all would be right with the world if only their example of love and friendship were followed. After a few weeks in the Neutral Zone, however, Batchelor began to revise his opinion of the others. "Fights almost broke out three or four times among the Americans," he complained, "and the men did nothing but complain all the time. To me, this seemed to reflect the mixed-up state of mind they were in. I believe a lot of them were really sorry for the step they had taken."[30]

Claude Batchelor began grumbling to the enemy about the bad faith of his fellow nonrepatriates. One day, for example, he approached a Chinese officer and complained about Ed Dickenson, saying, "I didn't think that he should be allowed to stay because, I said, that he would regret it and that he was only staying because he was afraid and that he was not really serious in what he wants to do." He also began calling the other men materialists, adventurists, and opportunists.[31] It apparently did not occur to Batchelor that the Chinese did not care what he thought. He and the others were perceived only as simple-minded tools for a propaganda campaign.

Throughout the three years they held Americans captive, the Chinese were careful in their indoctrination program. In the Neutral Zone, however, they committed a colossal blunder. The twenty-three GIs, although intensely indoctrinated in the teachings of communism, still had been raised in a land of freedom. No matter how much instruction they received, there was no way the enemy could totally wash out of their brains the memory of that freedom. Even in the Neutral Zone, when the nonrepatriates were no longer in the custody of their former captors, the Chinese maintained a firm determination to curtail that freedom. To do so, they set up a network of spies. Each American was to spy on others—and be spied upon. That rubbed a few of the soldiers the wrong way.[32]

At first the Chinese set up a "secret" organization of eight informants, with Claude Batchelor in charge. It was essential that the remaining fifteen knew nothing of the organization initially, because the Chinese "did not have very much faith in some of the nonrepatriates and it was necessary to have some kind of organization inside that would keep an eye on certain people and their acts." The secret organization of eight spread its tentacles to the other fifteen by developing a program called "Brother's Keeper." As Batchelor explained it, "Veneris was charged with keeping an eye on Douglas, Wills, and Dickenson. However, Douglas was in our secret group and he kept an eye on Veneris. Belhonne was charged with the responsibility to keep an eye on Howard Adams and Aaron Wilson. But Adams was also to keep us informed on Belhonne's activities. Richard Corden had three nonrepatriates to look after and they were Lowell Skinner, Arlie Pate, and John Dunn. However, we had Corden covered by Skinner who was from the secret group, too."[33] It went on and on, until everyone was covered and double-covered.

Cpl. Edward Dickenson had had enough. At 10 P.M. on October 20, 1953, after four weeks in the Neutral Zone, he made sure that everyone was asleep and then got out of his bunk and walked from the building. Crossing the compound, he informed the guard at the gate that he had a toothache. The sentry took Dickenson to Indian headquarters, where he was introduced to an officer who asked the nature of the problem. Dickenson said that he wanted to go home. That night he slept over with the Indian troops, and the following morning he was passed to American military authorities. The army—especially the CIC—grabbed him.[34]

Now there were twenty-two nonrepatriates, and the army was very eager to persuade as many as possible to return home. The issue was a matter of prestige and propaganda value. The military was confident that a majority of the remaining twenty-two would renounce the Chinese and ask for repatriation. As October turned to November and then December, the confidence of the American authorities was dashed. The cold winds of Korea were nothing compared to the cold shoulders of the twenty-two recalcitrant GIs.[35]

Maj. John Bojus, a member of the army's explainer group, said it "was formed for the purpose of presenting an explanation to the twenty-three American nonrepatriates remaining in the hands of the communists." It became clear, however, that the explainer group ought more aptly to have been called the "persuader group."[36]

The Chinese knew the Americans had a right to speak with their own men, and therefore nonrepatriates had been schooled on what to do and how to behave when approached. The men learned eight principles:

1. Show the explainer that they were as tough as he.
2. Take a stand.
3. Make the explanation look ridiculous.
4. Show disinterest.
5. Display hostility.
6. Refuse to answer questions.
7. Denounce the explainer as an "imperialist lackey."
8. Show their true colors.

Dickenson recalled that they were told to do anything they possibly could to embarrass the explainer and make him look silly. They were even encouraged to hit him, because he could not retaliate. When asked questions, the men were to talk about the weather, look at the explainer with blank stares, act stupid, chant communist songs and slogans, and spit at the explainer. Dickenson further reported, "As a technique to further embarrass the Explainers, James Veneris has gathered garlic which he plans to spray in the face of the explainers when they begin to question him."[37]

But something was wrong with American tactics during the ninety-day grace period, for not until December 13 did the United States request that the twenty-two be delivered to them for an explanation. Did those in charge of the effort believe that after three years of indoctrination the hardened progressives would perform another about-face, or was it because they took confidence from Dickenson's change of heart? In any case, the Chinese had exclusive, almost daily, contact with the men. The twenty-two refused to attend any explanation sessions conducted by the American forces.[38]

Suddenly, the American command began to manifest growing concern. On December 22, 1953, each of the twenty-two GIs received a letter from Gen. Mark Clark, the United Nations commander in Tokyo. The long, wordy message was ignored by the nonrepatriates.[39] On the following day, December 23, a public address system was set up, and a loud announcement was made to the rebellious soldiers:

I am Major Edward Moorer of the United Nations Command Explainer Group. This is the final day of the ninety-day explanation period provided as a condition of the armistice in the Terms of Reference. Repeatedly through the Neutral Nations Repatriation Commission, we have offered you the opportunity to exercise your right to attend an explanation. You have not availed yourself of this opportunity and right which expires today.

We believe that there are some who desire to be repatriated—who want to return home but who are being forcibly prevented from expressing your free will by fear, threats and strong arm methods of certain of your fellow prisoners. It is clear that your so-called representatives are withholding information and restricting your freedom to speak and act as individuals.

We have taken these means in insure that your rights as individuals can be exercised. The Indian guards are present to assure your safety. We are personally here to receive any of you who desire to return home. Corporal Edward Dickenson returned home to his loved ones and enjoyed a combination thirty-day leave and honeymoon. This fact, explodes Communist charges that you and your family will be harmed if you return. I assure you nothing shall happen to your family at the hands of the United States government regardless of your decision—whether to remain or to return to the United States.[40]

As Moorer spoke, the army reported, "Corporal Batchelor and his colleagues shouted and danced and refused to listen to the broadcast."* It was too little, too late—except for one.[41]

Corporal Batchelor had become confused by the bitterness within the group. Coupled with the spying, he later testified, "I was getting more and more fed up with the whole mess and began to gather a hatred for communism." As the new year dawned, he walked up to the gate and informed the Indian guard that he was ill and needed medicine. Then he walked out, never to return.[42] The remaining twenty-one went to China but at last, after many years, Claude Batchelor seemed to be free.

Notes

1. Lt. Jefferson Erwin, USA, Transcripts, 5:1287; Lt. Col. Harry Fleming, USA, Transcripts, 12:1300.

2. Maj. Ronald Alley, USA, Transcripts, 5:38; Lt. Col. Paul Liles, USA, Transcripts, 1:161, secret volume, 125.

---

* Maj. Gen. John Klein, the army's adjutant general, informed Dickenson in November 1954 that "no actual plea to the anti-repatriates to come home was made in either the letter [from Clark] or broadcast [by Moorer]." Others interpretations of the letter and broadcast have differed.

3. M. Sgt. William Olson, USA, Transcripts, 2:220, see also 2:217 and 2:461.

4. Sgt. William Banghart, USA, Transcripts, 1:196.

5. Cpl. Claude Batchelor, USA, Transcripts, 5:293.

6. Ibid., 5:294, 5:299.

7. Ibid., 13:137.

8. Ibid., 13:11, see also 5:262–64 and 5:269.

9. Ibid., 13:10.

10. Ibid., 5:272, see also 5:262–63.

11. Ibid., 5:262–63, see also 5:266, 13:11–12, and 13:97.

12. Ibid., 5:262–63.

13. Ibid., 13:11–12, 13:97–98, see also 13:93.

14. Ibid., 13:11–12, see also 13:93 and 13:98.

15. Ibid., 13:101, see also 13:12 and 8:1902.

16. Cpl. Edward Dickenson, USA, Transcripts, 4: 216–17.

17. Batchelor Transcripts, 13:12, see also 13:13, 8:1645 and Dickenson Transcripts, 2:239, 4:220

18. Batchelor Transcripts, 7:1133.

19. See Batchelor Transcripts, 7:1133–37 for the following account of Wilbur Watson's experience. For the quotation about Batchelor, see 3:1. The observation was furnished in a report by 1st Lt. Arnold Rabin, a psychiatric social worker.

20. Ibid., 8:1694; Dickenson Transcripts, 4:220.

21. Dickenson Transcripts, 4:220.

22. Ibid., 6:797.

23. Ibid., 1:283, 4:220.

24. Ibid., 4:219.

25. Ibid., 4:221.

26. Ibid., 4:219. The statement was furnished by Dickenson to Capt. B. Cumby and 1st Lt. R. Cole, officers in the Counter Intelligence Corps, U.S. Army, in Tokyo shortly after his release. Interrogations of Dickenson lasted four weeks (see 2:13). Much of this information had heretofore been labeled secret.

27. Ibid., 4:218.

28. Ibid., 4:219.

29. Batchelor Transcripts, 8:1642–43, 13:12, 13:17.

30. Ibid., 13:132, 13:147.

31. Ibid., 8:1621, see also 8:1640–41 and 8:1643.

32. Ibid., 13:14.

33. Ibid.

34. Dickenson Transcripts, 1:85, 4:222.

35. Batchelor Transcripts, 12:20–21.

36. Dickenson Transcripts, 6:776.

37. Ibid., 4:221; see also Batchelor Transcripts, 13:118.

38. Dickenson Transcripts, 3:220.

39. Ibid.

40. Ibid., 1:284–85.

41. Ibid., 3:191, 3:220.

42. Batchelor Transcripts, 13:146, see also 13:160 and 1:146.

PART 2 Purgatory

> *General Ding, Chinese army: What do you intend to do when you go home? Do you intend to stay in the army?*
>
> *Lt. Col. Paul Liles, U.S. Army: I certainly do.*
>
> *Ding: Will you fight communists again?*
>
> *Liles: I am a soldier and I obey the orders I receive.*
>
> *Ding: Then you do not believe that our indoctrination program was successful?*
>
> *Liles: No. Until you build a better civilization which is much better than ours, you won't find any American that listens to you.*
>
> *Ding: We think our program has been very successful.*
>
> *Liles: Why?*
>
> *Ding: You will never be able to fight communists again, that is why. When you go home, they will not receive you there.*
>
> —Lt. Col. Harry Fleming, USA, Transcripts, 11:1407–8

NINE

Homeward Bound

If I did you great harm as an enemy, I could likewise do you good service as a friend, inasmuch as I know the plans of the Athenians while I only guessed yours.

—Thucydides, *The Peloponnesian War*

Maj. Ambrose Nugent, former president of the Central Peace Committee based at Camp 12, couldn't stop crying. When he crossed the line separating slave from free, his composure evaporated. He could barely talk. Tears streamed down his emaciated cheeks as he said, "When we were finally repatriated and reached the Americans, it was like coming out of a night—black." Silence prevailed as he choked up. After a few moments he valiantly continued: "Over the course of the—oh, maybe next month—like a dream—we might awaken."[1]

One member of the Big Switch team at Freedom Village was Lt. Gough Reinhart, who called it "a very satisfying job watching men come home alive and believe they're free again. A few almost break down. Others refuse to believe they are free at first. They've had so many disappointments they won't let themselves accept it. They think there must be a catch somewhere." When South Korean soldiers came over the line, they were ashamed at being former prisoners and begged for one last letter home before being shot. "When we'd convince them they are free and returning heroes," said Reinhart, "these impassive Orientals break down completely."[2]

The one-time American prisoners of the Korean War were to awaken, but it would be a rude awakening. They would not be greeted as returning heroes. Almost immediately upon repatriation, they would undergo psychiatric testing and intelligence interrogations and also receive legal advice.

From Freedom Village, returnees were moved west to the port of Inchon, where Henry Segal, M.D., was waiting for them. Segal was one of the army's preeminent psychiatrists, and at Inchon he was in charge of a mixed armed forces group of thirty-six psychiatrists, nine psychologists, and thirty-six enlisted technicians. Every POW sent to Inchon received a psychiatric evaluation from Segal's staff; 1,301 examinations were conducted there, with the remainder performed on the ships returning the men to the United States. The results were ultimately submitted to the surgeon general, and Segal published three scientific papers on the subject.[3]

What the military psychiatrists found was that the repatriated men did not know where they were or what they were doing there. Maj. Alphonse Smuda, M.D., a psychiatrist on Segal's staff, noted:

> Generally the returnees that came to our attention, we noticed a marked apathy at the very beginning during the first few days they were at the hospital at Inchon. By "apathy," we mean a lack of feeling; in other words, they didn't express the usual emotions that somebody would upon being released from some particularly unpleasant situation where they would be happy about it or something of that sort, and in these particular instances, most of the returnees . . . showed a lack of feeling . . . as though they cared little one way or the other what was transpiring. There was some confusion along with it.[4]

Segal labeled this apathy the "Zombie Reaction" and said, "I think the most striking thing in this connection was their apparent lack of concern with the environment. It was several days before the men took an active interest in what was going on about them and in their own personal appearance and in the personnel who were working on the ward."[5]

Segal examined ten of the repatriates personally. During the second and third days of September 1953 he spoke with Lt. Col. Paul Liles for five hours. Major Segal purposely chose Liles because he had heard that name mentioned several times by some of the 149 prisoners who returned during Little Switch. Segal found Liles to be very open. The colonel spoke freely, and the doctor considered him reasonably well adjusted and not a "Zombie." Col. Frank Schwable also appeared to understand everything going on about him. He worried, however, about whether he might be viewed as a traitor and be court-martialed when he got home.[6]

The men did not remain at Inchon very long—a week at most. Although many were airlifted to Tokyo and then home, the majority were put aboard ships. During the end of August and early September, large transports such as the USNS *General Walker, General Pope, General Brewster,* and *General Howze,* steamed into Inchon harbor to pick up the former captives. Before each vessel was loaded with its human cargo of approximately 350 men per ship, carpentry work had to be completed. Numerous booths, about four by four, were constructed in the innards of the ships. Each contained a small field desk and two chairs. If the former POWs believed that the questioning of the past three years was over, they were dead wrong. The ships became floating interrogation centers for the Counter Intelligence Corps (CIC) of the U.S. Army.[7]

In early 1945, when POWs in Manila were released by American forces after the Japanese had been routed, senior officers of the group held a meeting. After the conference, word had been passed down the line to the lowest private: "You must always remember that you are a hero of Bataan and Corregidor and you should always conduct yourself accordingly. It will be ill-becoming of you, as such, to ever repeat any of the gossip and loose talk which has been engaged in while you were a prisoner of war."[8] If only such advice had been planted into the minds of the Korean prisoners. But it wasn't, and the result was that the former POWs turned against each other. The ships became floating gossip factories, and virtually every man was interested in only one thing—covering himself.

"A great cargo of suspicion, conjecture, rumor and ill-will accompanied the repatriated prisoners of war to Freedom Village at Panmunjon," said Alfred LaFrance, a Wisconsin attorney. That suspicion carried itself aboard the ships for the long ocean voyage home. A psychiatrist who had been a prisoner of the Japanese during World War II remarked, "Criticisms of other people is the main trouble with prisoners of war." The ill-will was more than verbal. Aboard the USNS *General Pope,* for example, fistfights erupted between the progressives and other POWs. After the first few days at sea, progressives were segregated into a separate compartment of the vessel.[9]

Psychiatrists completed their examinations of the repatriates while at sea, and each ship also had one or more legal officers assigned to it from the Judge Advocate General's Office. The most relentless presence, however, was officers of the Counter Intelligence Corps. Their efforts perpetuated the "protect yourself" syndrome among the soldiers. These interrogators took every repatriate, locked him in a small cubicle, and grilled him for hours—sometimes days—about every aspect of prison life in North Korea. The agents had a prepared list of seventy questions, and each answer was written down and later reviewed. To some, the endeavor seemed to border on a witch hunt.[10]

Capt. Bert Cumby, an officer in the Counter Intelligence Corps, was aboard one of the ships. His orders, he noted, "directed us to obtain the maximum amount of counter-intelligence information regarding the returnee, to what extent he had been subjected to foreign ideology, to what extent he had accepted it, and to what extent he embraced it and supported it." Almost every POW answered that he had been subjected to indoctrination but had not accepted, embraced, or supported communist ideology. Yet almost every GI pointed an accusing finger at one comrade or another. The vast majority of these accusations were based on nothing more than hearsay, but CIC officers listened to everything and wrote it down. Much was extremely petty: "I saw Joe with a cigarette," "I saw Tom talking with a guard," or "I saw Al with more food than me." The questioning continued until CIC had statements from as many repatriated men as possible. As Lt. Col. Charles Fry acknowledged, "I gave lots of hearsay testimony aboard ship; it was encouraged."[11]*

Examples of the officially encouraged rumormongering (which continued when the returnees reached the United States) could fill volumes. A typical example concerned Cpl. Thomas Farrell, who said, "I saw [Sgt. John] Tyler kick and stomp a sick prisoner of war named Frederick Swartz [*sic*]. . . . The reason for this mistreatment is unknown to me unless it was because Tyler was big and strong and knew he had plenty of backing from the Chinese." Were that true, the act would be damning, and the sergeant would

---

* The U.S. Army has declassified the interrogation questionnaire used by the CIC aboard ship (Appendix D).

warrant severe punishment. The alleged victim in the case, however, Frederick Schwartz, said, "During approximately four weeks in August, 1951, I was sick and stayed in the same barracks with Tyler, who was a company medic at the time, and at no time did he mistreat me or any of my fellow prisoners."[12] Similar unsupported allegations were rampant for the next two years among the freed GIs. Mutual recriminations were ruthless.

The CIC knew what it was looking for because of early warnings it had received when 149 Americans were released during Little Switch. From their interrogations, the detectives developed and refined the questions they would ask later. Of course, a primary goal was to discover and break up the underground organizations to be established by the progressives in the United States. Interrogators had related concerns, however, and Captain Cumby, who interviewed approximately twenty-five GIs, was shocked at the degree of their indoctrination. Cumby, who was completing graduate studies in political science, said, "If you had talked to as many former POWs as I have, you would find the communists gave quite a number of our boys a classical education in [evaluating] many of our customs and institutions. Some of those fellows might not have gone any further than the fourth grade but they could tell you, in classical terms, more about communism and Karl Marx than I could." Interviewers also noticed that when a man was asked about communism, a typical reply would be, "It's no good for the United States but it's okay for China." The loss of unit identity was also clear. When asked about their unit, POWs would often reply "Camp 5" instead of "24th Infantry Division."[13]

Reams of sworn statements were generated as the transports crossed the Pacific. Lt. Jeff Erwin likely was correct when he talked to a psychiatrist aboard the USNS *General Brewster*. According to his psychiatric evaluation:

> On the way home, all repatriated soldiers were subjected to interrogations, and while Lt. Erwin takes no issue with the sound reason for these investigating procedures, he yet feels that the timing of holding them at that particular period—was a rather unfortunate one due to the fact that most of the soldiers, after several years of suffering under rather trying conditions, were not in the best shape to give unbiased opinions about what had been going on while others, with guilt feelings about their own participation in certain happenings, would look for scapegoats to shift the blame, exaggerate incidents or misinterpret them to fit their particular ideas and

purposes. Others saw an opportunity to give vent to grudges they had been carrying for one reason or another and probably maliciously blew up incidents that may have happened into exaggerated proportions. Everybody wanted to be a hero and in the urge to go home to his own loved ones, misinformation was probably promulgated freely and half-truths contorted in the hope of diverting the attention of the questioning body into the direction of somebody else.[14]

After returning to the United States, Lt. Col. George Hansen was given a command. He was tired, however, of the never-ending interrogation process that continued after the former POWs returned home: "I was a battalion commander. We were training reserves and national guard and also training our own battalion, and these CIC agents were continuously hounding me for statements like that, and at one time they tied me up for about three days when I was getting ready to move my battalion . . . to be honest with you I just wanted to get them out of my hair so I could perform my military duties." Another field-grade officer, Charles Fry, became so disgusted that he gave up his career. Lieutenant Colonel Fry recalled, "The tribulations and trials that all the ex-POWs have been through, the interrogations—I have spent more hours on interrogations than on duty since I've been back from Korea and in fact, it motivated my early retirement from the service to try to get away from it."[15]

Constant harassment by the CIC was the price the soldiers had to pay for freedom, but at least they were free. On the morning of September 23, 1953, the USNS *General Howze* sailed into San Francisco harbor. Col. Frank Schwable and twenty-two Air Force pilots who had signed germ warfare confessions walked down the gangway and set foot on American soil. Schwable—and others—immediately repudiated their "misstatements," and the pilots were warmly greeted by their comrades. The commandant of the marine corps, however, refused to see Schwable. Although *Time* magazine reported that the refusal was a "simple reaction" on the part of Gen. Lemuel Shepherd, Schwable, no doubt, had the sinking feeling that he was persona non grata and in deep trouble.[16]

When Lt. Col. Harry Fleming came home, he took a thirty-day leave and used that time to write a paper entitled "Overcoming Communist Indoctrination: Basic Survival, Escape and Evacuation." "I am not now and never have been a communist nor communist sympathizer," Fleming insisted. "I detest communism in all its phases and ramifications." He then took his paper to the Pentagon and roamed the cavernous halls of that building in an attempt to have someone of consequence read it. The colonel advocated that every recruit be taught a course on combating communist indoctrination if captured. Lt. Col. Rodham Routledge, who got to know Fleming well after he returned from Korea, pointed out: "He had known their technique and he was one of the foremost men in the United States who knew as much—or more—about the communists than any other person. His attitude when he reached the United States was that he was going to get sympathy and understanding and some consideration; that somebody would hear his story and help him go to war against the communists. He got no such sympathy, no such understanding." Fleming was unwelcome, and no one would receive him. Handshakes and smiles notwithstanding, almost every repatriated prisoner was in trouble and a suspect rather than a returned hero.[17]

Most men attempted to pick up their lives where they had left them as long as three years earlier, but things would never be the same. Ten days after repatriation, Maj. Ronald Alley was admitted to St. Alban's Naval Hospital with tuberculosis. His wife, who stayed with him for three weeks, said, "I was shocked when I first saw him. He would greet me like a stranger, greet me like somebody he maybe saw once or twice in his life, somebody who was not even related to him."[18]

Jeff Erwin went right back to work and in the middle of December 1953, was given command of Service Battery, 38th Field Artillery, 2d Infantry Division at Fort Lewis, Washington. On occasion, his bitterness would be evident, especially when he would say things like "I'm sorry that they got away so easy and that China was not bombed."[19] But the lieutenant carried on with his life—at least for the time being.

Cpl. Harold Dunn returned home and was, to all appearances, a hero. In September 1953 he was crowned king of the New York State Fair at Syracuse. On October 28, Rothwell "Tiny" Floyd was married. On that same day, Sgt. James Gallagher reenlisted in the army. It was one of the biggest mistakes Gallagher ever made.[20]

Everyone had readjustment problems. M. Sgt. William Olson, for example, would vomit his breakfast, cry whenever he talked about prison, and was given to suicidal tendencies. To calm his nerves he took to drinking—more heavily than he ought. Sgt. William Banghart also began to drink and at one point went AWOL for eighty-five days, spending fifteen of those in jail for driving while intoxicated. Heavy drinking was a common problem among the repatriates, and they could easily afford to do so because each had accrued as much as three years' back pay. Floyd, for example, received a check for $3,701, a good sum of money in 1953. Paul Liles collected $4,699.[21]

For the first few months of freedom everyone was left alone to handle his own personal problems. In Washington, meanwhile, the U.S. Army was planning a major assault on the former Korean War prisoners.

>«

When Cpl. Edward Dickenson walked out on the Chinese in the middle of October 1953, the vast majority of returnees were already back in the United States. He was immediately flown to Japan, where he was lodged in Room 2–D of the Tokyo Army Hospital. For the next three weeks, CIC officers Capt. Bert Cumby and Lt. Richard Cole interrogated him because he was the first of the twenty-three to return and could give the army an idea of what was going on in the Neutral Zone. Every morning at 9:30, a black 1952 Chevrolet sedan would pick up the corporal at the hospital and he would be driven to the Dai Iti Hotel. There, in Room 246, he was intensively questioned by Cumby and Cole.[22]

The room itself was pleasant. In addition to strong maple furniture, it contained two upright chairs and a cushioned arm chair. Because Dickenson was a special guest, he was always asked to make himself comfortable in the soft, pillowed lounger—nothing but the best for someone who had temporarily lost his senses but was now back in the fold and had information the army desperately needed.[23]

Cumby and Cole were smooth as silk. They both wore civilian clothes, and Dickenson never knew they were CIC agents or army officers. Everything was done on a casual, first-name basis.[24] "We were out to collect intelligence information," said Cumby, "and we weren't trying to build cases against anyone." That statement was true. Cumby and Cole were investigators not prosecutors, but the two agents were not privy to what was going on in the minds of their superiors in Washington. On November 6, Dickenson signed a nine-page statement concerning his activities as a progressive POW and gave some detail on Chinese plans to use former progressives in the United States.[25] The CIC was the hound chasing the fox.

After the questioning was complete, Dickenson returned to America and received a hero's welcome. He made a brief stopover in Honolulu and in a government car, escorted by an officer, was given a hundred-mile tour of the island of Oahu. In mid-November, when he reached the East Coast of the United States, a Combat Infantryman's Badge shining on his breast and nine battle stars pinned to his campaign ribbons, reporters proudly accompanied him on a tour of the nation's capital that included the White House. Reaching his home in Cracker's Neck, Virginia, he secured an enthusiastic reception from friends and relatives. On December 5 he married Lottie Kate Laney, and the couple went on a honeymoon. His leave and honeymoon ended on January 22, 1954, as did all else.[26]

But the army couldn't rush into things, because on January 1, 1954, Claude Batchelor had announced to the world that he was "very good and very happy." So was the army, especially Captain Cumby and Lieutenant Cole. Beginning on January 6, they followed exactly the same routine with Batchelor as they had with Dickenson. Every day for four weeks the car picked up the corporal at Tokyo Army Hospital and drove him to the Dai Iti Hotel. According to Cumby, "It was just a long series of interviews," but it also was "the newest and most important piece of intelligence information that we have ever received."[27]

The written statement that Corporal Batchelor gave Cumby and Cole was more like a book. Even Cumby was astonished: "The one-hundred-and-forty-eight-page [single-spaced and typewritten] statement was something completely new. It had never been done before. I had never suggested it; I did not suggest it then but since he prepared it, I submitted it just as he prepared it." When relating his story Batchelor displayed no guilt, although he did say that if the communists ever took control of the U.S. government they "would not hesitate to deal with me as a traitor to them."[28]*

After the interrogation, the impressionable young corporal applied for a job with army intelligence. In his application, he pointed out that "through actions of the communists, while I was a leader of the twenty-one Americans who stayed behind in Korea, I learned the two-face of the communists and have come to hate them for what they did to me. I have a personal score to settle with the communists and would like to get the

---

* Much of the material in this chapter was obtained from Dickenson's and Bachelor's statements to Cumby and Cole.

chance to make up for the wrong that I did while under the communists by trying to protect my country from them in the future."[29] Some, however, believed that the United States had a score to settle with Claude Batchelor.

>«

Before some of the men had even reached U.S. soil, Georgia's Senator Richard Russell said in a letter to Secretary of Defense Charles Wilson, "My views may be extreme but I believe that those who collaborated and the signers of the false 'confessions' should be immediately separated from the service under conditions other than honorable."[30] Because hundreds —even thousands—of men had signed something while a POW, quite a few of them could have received discharges that would punish them for the rest of their lives. But that was not to be the case. What the army did was to court-martial those whom it felt had provided sufficient cause; many trials carried the possibility of life in prison or even death. The majority of American servicemen who fought in Korea were army, and that service was going to clean its own house in determined and drastic fashion.

After World War II, the Nuremberg war crimes trials took place, and the Japanese leadership went on trial in Tokyo. After Korea, during 1954 and 1955, the trials of American soldiers who were former prisoners of war also made headlines. The army had a perfect right to court-martial soldiers whom it believed had collaborated. Less clear is whether the army had the right to hang those found guilty of collaboration or similar digressions while a POW. Article 104 of the Uniform Code of Military Justice (of May 5, 1950) provides for death or such other punishment as a court-martial may direct in the case of aiding the enemy. Article 105, however, dealing with misconduct as a prisoner, allows a court-martial to impose any statutory punishment other than death. Still, the army proceeded against some men under the previously applicable Articles of War. The following were court-martialed:

Lt. Col. Paul Liles
Lt. Col. Harry Fleming
Maj. Ronald Alley

Maj. Ambrose Nugent
Lt. Jeff Erwin
M. Sgt. William Olson
Sgt. William Banghart
Sgt. John Tyler
Sgt. James Gallagher
Cpl. Harold Dunn
Cpl. Thomas Bayes
Cpl. Edward Dickenson
Cpl. Claude Batchelor
Pfc. Rothwell Floyd

All except Floyd had the charge of collaboration with the enemy placed against them. If convicted, all could have been punished by either life imprisonment or death.

Fair-minded individuals likely would agree with the authorities' decision to try the men by court-martial and, in the extreme, even hang them if convicted. But fair-minded individuals might also note that the list contained only fourteen names. Was that because only fourteen men had collaborated—or performed other deeds—that warranted court-martial proceedings? Clearly, that was untrue. Were the men chosen as scapegoats? Yes and no. They bore the full force of military justice for all collaborators of the Korean War, but that was likely unintentional on the part of the army. What the army did do was handle the two-year affair unintelligently.

After the repatriates reached American soil, they were assigned to various posts in the United States. At the time, the continental U.S. was divided into various army areas, with headquarters as follows:

1st Army—Governors Island, New York
2d Army—Fort George G. Meade, Maryland
3d Army—Fort McPherson, Georgia
4th Army—Fort Sam Houston, Texas
5th Army—Chicago, Illinois
6th Army—Presidio of San Francisco
Military District of Washington, D.C.

Each army was commanded by a lieutenant general, who was the convening authority for such general courts-martial conducted in his jurisdiction.* Therefore, it was only with the blessing of the appropriate army commander that a court-martial of a former POW could take place.[31]

Washington passed down to the various Zone of the Interior armies the names of suspected collaborators obtained from the CIC interrogations. Each army was then ordered to further investigate those men in its territory and determine whether a court-martial was in order. Consequently, pretrial investigations took place across the United States within various army areas. Pretrial investigators would then recommend whether the generals should bring a case to trial. At that point it was the general's decision, which is where the problem arose. Two army commanders, for example, would receive comparable charges and evidence against two different former POWs. While one general would court-martial the man, the other general, possibly thousands of miles away, would make the opposite decision and turn his man loose. The army never should have decentralized the process in dealing with the issue.

Compounding the problem was the fact that each court-martial board consisted of an average of nine members. With fourteen courts-martial, therefore, there were approximately 126 people (as jurors) making decisions on largely identical charges. While one court would give a man life in prison, another would hand down ten years, and a third would let a similar defendant go. Every soldier knew the word *snafu,* and that term applied to these proceedings.

The scenario becomes even more complex when one considers that the enlistment terms of many men had ended while they were POWs. When they returned home, a majority of the GIs requested—and were granted—discharge. Although there are provisions for exception, as a rule the Armed Forces cannot court-martial a civilian for a crime committed while in the service. As a consequence, men who collaborated and then were discharged were immediately lost to the military justice system. Therefore, on July 3, 1953, shortly after Operation Little Switch, the adjutant general of the army ordered that "the army commander will submit

---

* Empowered to impose the most severe punishments, a general court-martial is the highest level of court-martial under the Uniform Code of Military Justice. Following in descending order is the special court-martial and the summary court-martial.

the case for appropriate action to the Special Agent in charge of the FBI in the army area." The "appropriate action" was to arrest the new civilians so they could be tried in federal court. But arrested and tried for what? Treason was the only civilian charge that could be placed, and not one former Korean POW-turned-civilian was arrested and brought to trial for that. Consequently, to be discharged was to be home free.[32]

Members of the Armed Services cannot be tried in a military court on an accusation of treason. That crime can only be brought in federal court. Therefore, what the army did was charge soldiers with collaboration, which carried the same potential penalty as treason. The army vigorously denied that collaboration and treason were identical, but many would say that it is a distinction without a difference.[33]

Once many Americans discovered that numbers of soldiers were going to be court-martialed for activities while prisoners of the enemy, there was a tremendous outburst of indignation. Newspapers editorialized, politicians preached, and thousands of letters poured into Washington, most of them denouncing the actions of the army. The North Carolina chapter of the Legion of Valor, for example—membership in which was limited to holders of the Medal of Honor, Distinguished Service Cross, and Navy Cross—passed a resolution that said, in part, "It is earnestly requested and prayerfully asked that the present procedure of handling these investigations be eliminated and if any of these people desire to remain in the service of the United States it is our recommendation that they be permitted to do so on an absolutely unprejudiced basis, and if they desire to return to civilian life, we believe, that they should be given honorable discharges without prejudices and bidden God speed." Rear Adm. Dan Gallery was somewhat less ceremonious when he unburdened himself: "We try our soldiers for cowardice—after a war we didn't have the guts to win."[34]

The populace could complain as much as they liked, but the army had decided on a course of action and was determined to proceed. All the *New York Times* could say was, "We simply don't know all the facts and may never know some of them. We can, however, try to be generous, humane and humble and hope to find wisdom."[35]

>«

The first—and only—arrest that was made in 1953 was of Rothwell "Tiny" Floyd. On October 30, two days after he was married, Floyd was taken into custody. When soldiers were arrested, they often were not immediately told of the charges; in some instances the accused would be locked up and forced to wait for months. Although the pretrial investigation against Floyd did not begin until January 10, 1954, the army wanted him in jail until it determined what to do with him. Eventually, he was indicted for striking a superior officer, mistreating other POWs, larceny, and murder. He was the only POW of the fourteen not to be charged with collaboration, and his was also the only case that received scant publicity. Why that was so constitutes fertile ground for speculation.[36]

The first collaboration arrest took place on January 22, 1954. The accused was Cpl. Edward Dickenson, the first of the twenty-three to walk out of the Neutral Zone. Arresting officers entered his living quarters at Walter Reed Army Hospital and took him to jail. The army had known of the arrest for some time, and January 22 marked the end of the 120-day custody period for the remaining twenty-one in the Neutral Zone. Had Dickenson been arrested before that date, it would have ended all hope of persuading the remaining nonrepatriates to return. Therefore, orders not to touch him until January 22 had been issued and signed by Col. Stanley Jones, chief of the Military Justice Division: "Presumably, the remaining Americans in such custody could be influenced by any punitive action initiated in Dickenson's case prior to determination of their custody. [Therefore], under no circumstances will Dickenson be given notice of [any charge] prior to 22 January, 1954."[37]

When Dickenson walked out of the Neutral Zone, CIC snapped him up. Eventually, as soon as it could, so did the military justice system. Two days after his announced arrest, the New York Times stated that "a reliable source here [in Tokyo] said Dickenson's case represented just the first step in an investigation of the whole sordid story of crimes committed by Americans against Americans behind the barbed wire of North Korean compounds." The Times's military correspondent, Hanson Baldwin, continued: "The army in the Dickenson case is completely right in principle; crimes by Americans against other Americans . . . must be investigated fully."[38] Such statements are flawed, however, in that most charges and investigations focused on crimes against America rather than individual Americans. Despite innumerable investigations, only twelve follow-up courts-martial for collaboration were held.

Five days after his arrest, Dickenson was moved from Walter Reed to a small cell at Fort Belvoir, Virginia, where he awaited the outcome of his pretrial investigation. In the meantime, complaints were flowing in from all over the country, most of them demanding that the corporal be released. Frances Bolton, a member of Congress from Ohio, was "deeply disturbed" and said, "Let's be human beings in these things." President Dwight Eisenhower told the army to think twice and at a news conference referred to the story of the Prodigal Son when asked about Dickenson. But the decision to try Dickenson had been made and would not be changed.[39]

The purpose of a pretrial investigation is to ascertain whether there is sufficient evidence to bring a person to trial. The investigator was often a well-trained lawyer, frequently a lieutenant colonel. For the most part, these men were intelligent and impartial; they interviewed, took affidavits from prospective witnesses, and made a written recommendation to the army commander. During these investigations, the defense was permitted to cross-examine each witness and draw out information supportive of the accused's side of the story. The investigator's task, however, was limited to determining whether sufficient grounds existed for a court-martial, not the guilt or innocence of the subject. In a few cases, the convening authority (the area commanding general) received an investigator's recommendation that no trial should be held as a consequence of insufficient evidence and adhered to that advice. It is also true that the convening authority sometimes concluded that the investigator was wrong and ordered a court-martial anyway. Some wondered why time and money was expended on such investigations in the first place, and one wag conjured up the Queen of Hearts, who demanded, "First the verdict, then the testimony."[40]

The records of the secret pretrial investigations are worth examining, because few normal courtroom rules needed to be followed in their preparation. If a former POW was ordered to submit a deposition on the actions of another, his deposition or oral testimony could ramble on for pages and cover almost every subject in the world, something that never would be allowed in a court of law. Although the documents are replete with hearsay, they provide an excellent synopsis of daily POW life.

Little more than two weeks after Dickenson's arrest, on February 8, 1954, Lt. Col. George Carter began a pretrial investigation of the corporal. In addition to personal interrogations, Carter had received twenty sworn affidavits, and "the contents of the affidavits presented during the pretrial investigation were in many instances ambiguous, often irrelevant and immaterial to the issues and the accused in this case, and generally contained more opinion, rumor, and hearsay than direct evidence." Nevertheless, in Dickenson's case there was more than ample testimony to warrant a trial, and on February 18 one was ordered. The news shocked his family, and his recent bride wept. Soon after Col. Norman Sprowl, the public relations officer of the Military District of Washington, announced the charges he began to receive threatening telephone calls. Things became so serious that he feared for his life and requested—and received—permission to carry his service pistol at all times.[41]*

Claude Batchelor did not like Edward Dickenson. When asked what he thought of the arrest, he did not mention Dickenson by name but replied, "Each of these cases will be judged on its own merits. I think I know why they are going to try the other man." On March 5, 1954, however, five weeks after Dickenson's arrest, Batchelor was put into the stockade at Fort Sam Houston, Texas, headquarters of the 4th Army.[42]

Although pretrial confinement is permitted only to assure the presence of the accused at trial or because of the seriousness of the allegations, there is no such thing as bail when a person is locked up by the army. Batchelor, for example, was kept in jail for nearly six months before his proceedings began. When the army was questioned about why Batchelor had been jailed for so long without a trial, Col. C. G. Schenken, staff judge advocate, 4th Army, replied that if he were released, "Defense counsel will undoubtedly capitalize on the fact—in publicity released—by implying that as soon as the investigating officer submitted his report, it became apparent that there wasn't much of a case so the convening authority turned the accused loose. Also, there is a possibility of accused stirring up public opinion by appearing on TV. Finally, if accused is released from confinement, defense counsel will undoubtedly use all of the tricks of the trade in getting postponements; he might be more interested in a prompt trial if accused is still in confinement."[43]

Four men from Camp 12 (Traitors Row) were also investigated and court-martialed: Paul Liles, Harry Fleming, Ambrose Nugent, and Jeff Er-

---

* It cannot be determined who made these calls, but it would not be too far-fetched to assume that some progressives in the United States were part of the campaign.

win. Two months after Batchelor was jailed, so was Fleming. He was arrested at Fort Leonard Wood and transferred to the confinement section of the U.S. Army Infirmary at Fort Sheridan, Illinois. There he was kept in virtual solitary confinement for three months before his trial. During that period, Fleming said, he was asked "many times" to retire in order to avoid the proceedings. He refused, however, because "I did nothing wrong. I am not going to run. It would have been a cowardly act not to go on trial." In other words, the army offered him an escape not afforded to any of the others, and no reason has been given for such proffered leniency. Completely rejected by Fleming, it would not be proposed again.[44]

The pretrial investigator in Fleming's case was Lt. Col. William Belser. It can be easily seen in the documents of this investigation that if an enlisted man wanted to "get" an officer, here was the opportunity. Opinions were permitted at this stage although not allowed in the courtroom. Sgt. Jose Mares, for example, made his opinions clear: "Liles was a bad one, as bad as Fleming if not worse." In another statement, Mares said that at Camp 12, "Fleming had a pass [issued by Colonel Kim] that would take him all over North Korea. If he wanted to go anywhere, he just took off."[45] That was untrue, but virtually all of the pretrial statements relating to the defendants contained similar allegations. It was difficult for investigating officers to separate truth from fiction.

Sometimes things happened that would have been hilarious had they not been ridiculous. In January 1951, for example, twenty men were moved by truck from Camp 5 south to Camp 12 (chapter 5). Over the winding, mountainous road, the truck bumped and swayed, and at one point during that freezing night Colonel Fleming sat on the foot of Cpl. Robert Gorr. There were words between Gorr and Fleming, and that minor incident in a tightly packed vehicle surfaced during the pretrial investigation. By a great stretch of the imagination it could be said that an officer had assaulted an enlisted man. Although potentially a court-martial offense, Colonel Belser recommended that the matter be dropped. "I do not believe," he said, "that the alleged offense committed under such circumstances was sufficiently serious to warrant trial." Belser was backed by the staff judge advocate of 5th Army in a memo to the commanding general. He, too, recommended that the charge "be withdrawn because the incident, under the circumstances, was not important enough to warrant trial in view of the other more serious charges." But the general refused to accept the recommendation, and one of the charges that Fleming had to defend himself against was sitting on Gorr's foot.[46]

Ambrose Nugent was investigated and recommended for trial largely because he had been president of the Central Peace Committee. When he heard he had to defend himself, Nugent said, "I do not feel I am guilty of any crime or transgression against any army regulations. I think and hope the army will give me a fair trial. That is all I ask."[47]

Liles's case was investigated by Col. James Lockett, and Jeff Erwin's by Maj. James Cassidy. Both investigators suggested that the evidence was insufficient to go to trial and recommended the army drop any and all charges. In both cases, however, the commanding general elected instead to convene courts-martial. That annoyed Liles's attorney, who complained that "Article 32 investigations are fast becoming a perfunctory and somewhat frivolous procedure if they are to be ignored completely by the convening authority."[48]

This also suggests that decentralization of authority was not the best way to handle the affair. The same charges had been placed against the four officers of Camp 12, and one of those men, Fleming, had been locked up for ninety days before trial whereas the other three were not. Furthermore, two were recommended for court-martial and the other two were not. There was reason to expect more consistency than was demonstrated. Why, for example, was it fitting for Fleming to be put into virtual solitary but not the others? And if the two senior officers of Camp 12 were slated for trial along with the president of the Central Peace Committee, why try Erwin? What about the other captains and majors of Camp 12 who stood between Lieutenant Erwin and Lieutenant Colonels Liles and Fleming?

Of the five officers court-martialed after the war, four were from Traitors Row and the fifth was Maj. Ronald Alley from Camp 5. The charge against him was a general one of collaboration, and he, too, had to prepare himself for trial. Surely these were not the only five officer POWs who cooperated with the enemy during the Korean War. Approximately sixty thousand pages of pretrial, trial, and appellate transcripts are packed with statements by officers who admitted under oath that they had cooperated with the Chinese and North Koreans. Yet only Liles, Fleming, Nugent, Erwin, and Alley were put through the ordeal of trial.

The army gives no reason for placing only those officers on trial (and, of course, does not have to). There is little doubt, however, that similar cases could have been made against others. Moreover, a strict interpretation of the law should have required that each individual be put in front of an impartial board of peers for judgment. That did not happen. Decisions on all other officers were made outside of the courtroom by various commands across the United States. The same argument holds true for the eight enlisted men (setting aside Floyd) court-martialed for collaboration. Hundreds of men admitted to cooperating with the enemy in some form or another. Either all of them should have been put on trial or none.

When Sgt. William Banghart heard about his pending court-martial, "he showed a noticeable increase in tension and became quite resentful about the necessity for psychiatric examination and the fact that he was being charged with offenses that he felt had been committed by others who were going unpunished." Banghart made an excellent point. When M. Sgt. William Olson heard of his court-martial he was "completely amazed" and said the charges had "no foundation." That may be debatable, but hundreds of other men could also have been charged. Sgt. John Tyler's pretrial investigation lasted only a day. He was tried because of a batch of written statements given to the investigator by former comrades. The sergeant could only remark that he was "dumbfounded" and "stupefied."[49]

With the permission of Washington, *Pageant Magazine* paid Cpl. Harold Dunn $800 to write an article on his experiences as a POW. In January 1954, his piece, "I Was a Progressive POW in Korea," appeared. A little more than a year later he was locked up in Castle William on Governors Island, New York. About the same time Dunn went to jail, James Gallagher was also sent to Castle William. His family made the trip from Brooklyn every Sunday to visit him, and Gallagher told them, "Don't worry, all these charges are lies. I didn't do anything like that."[50]

On January 21, 1954, the marines ordered that a court of inquiry be held for Col. Frank Schwable. An inquiry is similar to a grand jury proceeding, where members of the court do not judge guilt or innocence. Their responsibility is to gather facts and recommend whether a follow-up court-martial should take place. "I am very greatly relieved that the nerve racking period of waiting and uncertainty is over," Schwable remarked. "Now something definite is going to happen. Waiting is always the hardest part."[51]

The three services should have adopted a uniform policy on actions to be taken against returning POWs but they did not. Secretary of Defense Charles Wilson wrote a memo to the secretaries of the navy and air force to notify them that he wanted their branches of the service to adhere to the policies of the army. Yet the U.S. Navy wanted the Air Force to set up courts of inquiry to determine the facts, as they were doing with Colonel Schwable. The army stuck to its plan for courts-martial, however, and in the end each service went its own way. The army rushed helter-skelter in 1954 and 1955. Fourteen courts-martial meant fourteen separate prosecutors, fourteen separate defense attorneys, fourteen separate judges, and nearly 126 separate "jury" members all trying essentially the same charge but reaching fourteen separate decisions and penalties. The marines held their court of inquiry, and the air force established a board of review to determine what had happened and what, if anything, should be done. The lack of uniformity among the three branches of the Armed Forces created a public furor.[52]

Lt. Col. William Belser, who handled the pretrial process in the case of Harry Fleming, said, "As far as this investigator has been able to adduce from his [thirty-eight] contacts with prospective witnesses from the several armed services, the army is the only service which, as of this date, has adopted the policy of trying its members for alleged collaboration with the enemy while interned as POWs. Offenses which appear to be supported by the available evidence should not condoned, but justice should be even-handed throughout all the armed forces of our nation." The media and general public also clamored—sometimes loudly—for uniformity. Capt. Howard Vincent, an assistant defense counsel in the case of Cpl. Thomas Bayes, noted, "The future effect of these army prosecutions upon Air Force and navy personnel is problematical. Certainly, it will make them congratulate themselves upon choosing their branch of service over the army."[53]

When compliments are deserved they should be given, and the U.S. Air Force is more than worthy of praise for not decentralizing the decision-making process. Eighty-three of the 220 repatriated Air Force personnel were suspected of collaboration—almost half that number related to germ warfare confessions. On February 8, 1954, a board of review convened in

Washington, D.C., and the eighty-three were brought in front of the board to explain their actions. The five air force officers who composed the board were Lt. Gen. Idwal Edwards, president; Maj. Gen. Jarred Crabb; Maj. Gen. Glenn Barcus; Brig. Gen. Monro MacCloskey; and Brig. Gen. Richard Carmichael.

It was up to those five men—and only those men—to decide what to do with returned POWs. They were mandated to determine the extent of duress applied to the pilots, how far they had gone in collaborating, and what their preflight briefing instructions were. Finally, they were to take into account "the possible effects of the action of the board upon discipline and morale of the armed forces, both present and future."[54]

After five weeks of testimony the board returned its findings, which subsequently were approved by Gen. Nathan Twining, chief of staff, and Secretary of the Air Force Harold Talbott. As a result, sixty-nine men were immediately cleared of any allegations of wrong-doing and fourteen were held for further investigation. Six of the fourteen requested and were immediately granted honorable discharges. The other eight were given an additional hearing in July 1954 at Scott Field near Belleville, Illinois. This second board of review, also conducted by five generals, was a "show cause" hearing.[55]*

As the air force pointed out, "These individuals are not being charged with anything. They are simply being given the opportunity to show why they think they can still effectively serve their country in the USAF. It is emphasized that the procedures involved here are not trials and any discharge would be under honorable conditions." The result was that four officers left the service and the remaining four were retained. The air force officers were treated consistently. The worst that happened to any of them was receiving honorable discharges and having to find a new line of work. [56]

The air force board reached some startling conclusions; for example, "Voluminous military and personal information was disclosed to the enemy by POWs of all ranks during interrogation." It has been reported in army documents, for instance, that one pilot told the Chinese, to the

---

* The five generals who conducted the second board of review were Maj. Gen. George Finch, Brig. Gen. James Howard, Brig. Gen. Frank Robinson, Brig. Gen. George Schlatter, and Brig. Gen. Walter Wise.

best of his ability, how to build a B-29. The report went further and stated that "there was complete abandonment of the Name-Rank-Serial Number policy even in the absence of severe duress." That was because the air force, during preflight briefings, had permitted pilots to abandon the policy. "In the cases examined," the board concluded, "disclosure of military information to the enemy by USAF prisoners of war does not warrant further action. The act of making a false confession to germ warfare while under continued intimidation will not be considered a traitorous act and the fact that these men signed or made false statements re germ warfare will not influence any future assignments." The air force wanted pilots to forget the entire experience and go back to flying, for "if the Air Force stands behind its men and recognizes that we did not mentally prepare them for situations of this nature, then the men will possess an undying faith in their service and their leaders."[57]

Was the air force's philosophy fair? Most air force officers were better trained and educated than the vast majority of army privates, and yet they received not even a mild slap on their wrists. Some soldiers, however, were awarded severe punishments. As Hanson Baldwin wrote, "The armed services owe to their men, and soon, some unified concept of what the nation expects their conduct to be if they should be so unfortunate as to be captured by the communists." On May 19, 1954, the *Christian Century* summed up the issue in an editorial: "The need for the armed forces to attempt to reach a common policy on such matters was further highlighted when the Air Force, without a court-martial, cleared eighty-three former Korean War prisoners, freeing sixty-nine unconditionally and saying it proposed to give honorable discharges to the remainder. The quality of mercy should not vary between colonels and corporals or between the different branches of the services."[58]

>≪

The U.S. Air Force was less than cooperative in the research of this subject, and that lack of cooperation leaves many questions unanswered and raises others. The boards of review in Washington and at Scott Field were held in secret session, and much of what went on in those rooms is still unknown. The information that is available was declassified upon request from the files of the secretary of the air force and is lodged in the National

Archives. All requests for printed transcripts of the boards of review were replied to, but with no results.

When I requested records, I directed my correspondence to the highest levels of the air force, including but not limited to the chief of staff. For almost a year, letters flowed to all air force offices that had even a remote likelihood of possessing the transcripts. My final answer, however, pointed out that the records could not be declassified and forwarded because they could not be found.

Of course, the request was not for a single sheet of paper but rather for thousands of pages of some of the most important documents to come out of the Korean War concerning USAF prisoners. One way to avoid the Freedom of Information Act is to claim the inability to locate a file, but it is hard to understand how thousands of pages could disappear. Perhaps the papers were found—and read—and then not released because of the military or political ramifications they might have for the Air Force and the United States. If that were the case, the papers might contain one or two things (or perhaps both) that the air force does not want made public.

First, perhaps the Air Force still does not want the public to know that pilots were officially informed that they could furnish more than name, rank, and service number to the enemy. Right after the war, Col. James Dowling of the Air Force Office of Information Services was being pressured by Charles Corddry of the UPI about what the pilots were schooled to do in event of capture. "I don't think there is any information that should have a higher security classification than the instructions which we gave our people on how to conduct themselves as a POW," Dowling replied. "A compromise of this information would certainly affect the future welfare of POWs and give aid and comfort to the Russians." Dowling further recommended "that the Marines be requested to hold the hearings [in the Schwable case] in Executive Session concerning the specific instructions given to potential POWs."[59] If that is the reason for possibly holding back the transcripts, it is too late.

Whenever air force officers testified at army courts-martial, the room would be cleared and that part of the proceeding would be classified. Those portions of the transcripts were declassified by the army, however. Furthermore, documents obtained from files of the secretary of the air force indicate that the board of review in Washington reported, "Our

POWs almost unanimously stated, under oath, that premission briefings ranged from 'tell anything necessary to save your life or to avoid mistreatment' to 'tell only that which you consider already known to the enemy.'"[60] Therefore, if boards of review transcripts were intentionally withheld for that reason, they were withheld after the fact.

Second, could it be possible that American pilots, before the secret boards of review, admitted to committing germ warfare over North Korea, making communist allegations true? If that is what the phantom transcripts contain, the air force need only state that they are unavailable because they infringe upon national security. National security would probably not be invoked because of preflight briefings, however. That seems to leave open only the second reason: germ warfare. One way to solve the dilemma is to claim the inability to locate the documents.*

Was germ warfare committed during the Korean War? The North Koreans and Chinese have all types of "proof" that it was, from scientific commissions and photographs of the actual "bomb" to "confessions" by the pilots themselves. How, in turn, can the United States prove that it did not? Hidden in the files of the secretary of the air force is a sentence that demonstrates the demanding position in which the United States found itself. "The act of punishing returning prisoners of war for confessing to germ warfare can be used against the United States since this would, in effect, be a tacit admission of the employment of germ warfare by UN forces."[61]

Did the air force want to punish pilots but hold back because of the propaganda the communists could (or would) make out of its doing so? The argument is endless and one the United States cannot win. Whatever its reasons, the air force let all its people go unpunished for collaboration although ordinary soldiers who slogged through mud and dodged bullets were court-martialed for similar behavior. There are those who may consider what happened to some of these GIs during and after their trials a national disgrace.

---

* A possible third reason for not releasing the testimony is that questions were submitted to the pilots concerning the nonrepatriation of a relatively large number of air force pilots at the time of Operation Big Switch. The Chinese claimed they were not released because they were shot down over Chinese territory while on reconnaissance missions. Because the Chinese charged them with spying, they were not classified as prisoners of war and therefore not entitled to repatriation (Epilogue).

Notes

1. Maj. Ambrose Nugent, USA, Transcripts, 12:3546.
2. Pfc. Rothwell Floyd, USA, Transcripts, 1a:224.
3. Lt. Col. Paul Liles, USA, Transcripts, 2b:700–701, 708.
4. Cpl. Thomas Bayes, USA, Transcripts, 4:1138–39.
5. Liles Transcripts, 2b:706.
6. Liles Transcripts, 2b:701–2, 2b:707; Col. Frank Schwable, USMC, Transcripts, 2:496.
7. Lt. Jefferson Erwin, USA, Transcripts, 5:1499–50. The National Archives possesses 325 pages of documentation with classifications from "confidential" ("security information") to "secret" concerning POWs (specifically Air Force POWs) in Korea. These documents have been declassified, are contained in one volume, and will henceforth be referred to as "NA" followed by the page number. The documents are open and can be reviewed by referring to Decimal 383.6 for 1954, Decimal Correspondence File, Records of the Office of the Administrative Assistant, Records of the Secretary of the Air Force, record group 340, entry 15, box 1518, see also NA, 242.
8. M. Sgt. William Olson, USA, Transcripts, 5:143.
9. Lt. Col. Harry Fleming, USA, Transcripts, 2:84; Cpl. Edward Dickenson, USA, Transcripts, 6:631; see also Sgt. William Banghart, USA, Transcripts, 1:94.
10. Floyd Transcripts, 2:1036, 2a:1464; Erwin Transcripts, 6:1502–3.
11. Dickenson Transcripts, 5:284; Erwin Transcripts, 4:971.
12. Sgt. John Tyler, USA, Transcripts, 1:74, 1:147.
13. Dickenson Transcripts, 5:313.
14. Erwin Transcripts, 6:14.
15. Maj. Ronald Alley, USA, Transcripts, 7:675; Erwin Transcripts, 4:1005.
16. Schwable Transcripts, 1:385, 1:409, 1:431, 3:956, 3:1175; NA, 216–18; "The Dreadful Dilemma," 63; "Text of Inquiry Findings on Marine Col. Schwable," 16.
17. Fleming Transcripts, 4:112–13, 5:67, see also 11:1695–96 and 12:1780.
18. Alley Transcripts, 9:1297.
19. Erwin Transcripts, 6:14, see also 5:1244 and 6:37–40.
20. Floyd Transcripts, 1a:242; Pate, *Reactionary!* 144; "Two G.I.'s Here Seized for POW Crimes," 1; "Ex-P.O.W. Loses Fight over Trial," 3.
21. Olson Transcripts, 3:66, 5:5, 5:15–16; Liles Transcripts, 4b:2007; Banghart Transcripts, 1:146; Floyd Transcripts, 5c:16.
22. Dickenson Transcripts, 1:86, 2:13, 5:289.
23. Ibid., 5:289.
24. Ibid.
25. Ibid., 5:308, see also 4:222.
26. Ibid., 1:284, 3:4, 3:412, 4:79; Cpl. Claude Batchelor, USA, Transcripts, 12:20–21; "G.I. Who Chose Reds, Then Quit," 1.
27. "G.I. Changes Mind, Quits Reds' Camp for Repatriation," 1; Batchelor Transcripts, 5:483, see also 5:345–46 and 5:354.
28. Batchelor Transcripts, 5:486; 10:33, see also 10:58.
29. Ibid., 10:33, see also 5:413 and 8:1746.
30. NA, 224. Russell, a member of the Senate Armed Services Committee, wrote

this letter to Wilson on September 18, 1953. See also Kinkead, *In Every War but One,* 17.

31. Dickenson Transcripts, 4:256.

32. NA, 208.

33. Alley Transcripts, 5:188.

34. Olson Transcripts, 4:831–32.

35. "The Dickenson Case," 18.

36. Floyd Transcripts, 1:2.

37. Dickenson, secret volume, 12, see also 1:86, 1:284, 3:13, "Twenty-one Pro-Red G.I.s to Get Dishonorable Discharges," 1, and "Former Prisoner of War in Korea Appeals," 3.

38. "Army Challenged on P.O.W. Charges," 1; Baldwin, "The Army in the Dickenson Case," 2.

39. "Twenty-one Pro-Red G.I.'s to Get Dishonorable Discharges," 1; see also "Eisenhower Urges Tolerance," 1.

40. Dickenson Transcripts, 3:12.

41. Ibid., 1:287, see also 2:257, "Snafu and Showdown," 18, "Shift in Dickenson Case," 3, and "Army Orders Trial for Former P.O.W.," 1.

42. "Army Challenged on P.O.W. Charges," 1, see also "Second Ex-P.O.W. Arrested by Army," 2.

43. Batchelor Transcripts, 3:45, see also "Ex-P.O.W. to Be Tried," 51.

44. Fleming Transcripts, 3:290, see also 3:36, 3:208–9, 3:211, 3:217, "Ex-P.O.W. Colonel Denies Aid to Reds," 7, and "Ex-P.O.W. Chosen to Head Red Cell," 8.

45. Fleming Transcripts, 5:227, 5:231, see also 5:392.

46. Ibid., 5:10, 5:391.

47. "Ex-P.O.W. Major Accused by Army," 3.

48. Liles Transcripts, 2:31, see also 2:30 and 1:24 and Erwin Transcripts, 1:118–19.

49. Banghart Transcripts, 1:146, see also 1:74, Tyler Transcripts, 1:235a, "Veteran of Korea Faces Army Trial," 8, and "Held as Collaborator," 6.

50. "Two G.I.s Here Seized for P.O.W. Crimes," 1, see also Dunn Transcripts, 1:189–90, 1:285, 1:319–22, and Gallagher Transcripts, 2:1, 6:1174.

51. "Army Challenged on P.O.W. Charges," 1; see also Schwable Transcripts, 1:exhibit Q.

52. NA, 140, 207.

53. Fleming Transcripts, 5:387; Bayes Transcripts, 7:brief, 7:61.

54. NA, 64, see also 61–62.

55. Ibid., 55.

56. Ibid., 53, 59, see also 23, 51–52, 59, 61–62 and "Air Force Clears Four Ex-P.O.W. Pilots," 26.

57. NA, 58, 65, 182, 188.

58. Baldwin, "Reds and Prisoners," 3; "Quality of Mercy Is Strained," 603.

59. NA, 90.

60. Ibid., 65.

61. Ibid., 179.

TEN

And Justice for All?

The people demand a fair trial and a speedy execution.
—Editorial, East German newspaper

A military general court-martial is one of the fairest trials a person can receive. That is not to say that the Uniform Code of Military Justice (UCMJ) is fair and equitable, but the proceeding itself is. All officers in the courtroom, no matter who they are, appear to make every effort to see that the accused has the opportunity for self-defense.

The composition of a court is similar to that in a civilian proceeding: a prosecutor (trial counsel), defense counsel, and law officer. The jury is composed of members of the court, with the senior ranking member usually designated as president. The function of the law officer is to keep things running smoothly, rule on objections and evidence, and charge members by explaining the law to them. The number of members for each POW trial averaged about nine persons who had equal or higher grade than the accused and were permitted to question witnesses after attorneys had completed their examinations. As in all general courts-martial cases, it was their responsibility to determine guilt or innocence and decide the sentence. During the trials of the Korean War POWs, the prosecution, defense, and law officers were always attorneys—very good ones—who generally held the grade of lieutenant colonel or colonel. Many former GIs-turned-civilians were witnesses and thus were subpoenaed by the president of the United States. Failure to comply would result in a $500 fine and/or six months' imprisonment.[1]

Although each trial was fair, each law officer interpreted the law independently. That as well as the differing evidence resulted in members reaching sometimes opposing conclusions in various cases on essentially the same charges. Most discrepancies were minor, but over the course of a trial (about four weeks on average) they added up. In the case of Maj. Ronald Alley, for example, his defense counsel requested that Alley be permitted to leave the courtroom when his psychiatrist testified. The doctor, counsel reasoned, would feel freer to speak about his patient if Alley were not present. After a heated argument, however, the law officer ruled that Alley had to remain in the room. When the same request was made in the trial of M. Sgt. William Olson, the law officer permitted him to leave. Countless other inconsistencies begged for one judge and jury, such as the Air Force used, to handle the trials.[2]

Another clumsy matter concerned the charges. Some men were indicted under the old Articles of War and others under the UCMJ, which replaced the Articles of War on May 31, 1951. Complicating matters, a few area army commanders charged men under both the old and new laws. Defense attorneys also complained that clients should not have been indicted under the UCMJ. The men had been isolated along the Yalu River overlooking Manchuria when the new law came into effect and could not have known about the UCMJ. That objection did not stand, however. As the trial counsel in the Fleming case retorted, "The first and most obvious answer is the fact that ignorance of the law is no excuse."[3]

Some charges were quite specific and outlined the times when a particular offense was alleged to have been committed and precisely what that offense had been. In other trials that was not the case, and a soldier would only be charged with collaboration—the specifics apparently to surface during the course of the proceedings. Because they did not know what to prepare against, defense teams often were unable to ready themselves thoroughly. As Capt. Howard Vincent, one of the appellate defense attorneys for Cpl. Thomas Bayes, argued:

The specification charged that the accused did communicate, hold intercourse with, and aid the enemy by "unnecessarily cooperating" with him. This remarkable charge was soberly defended as being perfectly definite, concise, and certain, and the accused stands convicted of it, whatever it means. It provided as much guidance to the court and accused as the blank map Carroll described:

The Bellman himself they all praised
to the skies—
Such a carriage, such ease and such grace!
Such solemnity, too! One could see he was wise,
The moment one looked in his face!

He had brought a large map representing the sea,
Without the least vestige of land:
And the crew were much pleased
  when they found it to be,
A map they could all understand.

"What's the good of Mercator's
  North Poles and Equators,
Tropics, Zones, and Meridian Lines?"
So the Bellman would cry: and the crew would reply,
"They are merely conventional signs."

"Other maps are such shapes,
  with their islands and capes!
But we've got our brave Captain to thank."
(So the crew would protest)
"That he's brought *us* the best—
A perfect and absolute blank!"[4]*

The 1954 and 1955 trials for collaboration with the enemy were unique in the history of military jurisprudence. For the first time, former American prisoners of war were charged with collaboration.** An indignant

---

* From "The Bellman's Speech," in Lewis Carroll, *The Hunting of the Snark*.

** In World War I, charges of collaboration had been brought against a soldier who wrote to someone in Germany to say that he would desert when he reached the front lines. Five such cases occurred during World War II, four of which stemmed from the same incident. Four American soldiers were tried for helping German POWs in the United States escape to Mexico. In the fifth case, which went to court, it was charged that the defendant, while in a hospital in Bizerte, Tunisia, assisted German prisoners' escape plans by furnishing them with a compass. In none of these instances, however, were American POWs collaborating with their enemy while in the hands of that enemy.

public flooded the army with protest letters but to no avail. A typical re-action came from Charles Baxter of Hollywood, Florida, who wrote to the secretary of the army: "It is a rotten shame that any serviceman has to be tried for collaboration with the enemy during that 'police action' that we didn't have the 'guts' to win."[5] Although the army sent a boilerplate re-ply to every letter received, the complaints themselves fell on deaf ears.

The army made a feeble attempt in private correspondence to justify its actions, but some of those statements bordered on the absurd. Col. R. L. Lancefield, who was with the Office of the Judge Advocate General, wrote, "The vast majority of our soldiers never wavered in the face of com-munist mistreatment and torture," but even men who were there dis-agreed with that. Lt. Chester Van Orman remarked, "In my opinion, many of the POWs who came back have hands that are not entirely clean. If derogatory remarks were wanted to be made, there could be many of them against a lot of people." "Literally hundreds of Korean POWs made state-ments, oral and written, under pressure," Captain Vincent observed, "which can be construed as derogatory of the United States." Maj. Mike Lorenzo, who was at Camps 5 and 2, said, "I was not too proud of my own [actions] or any other prisoner of war living today. We are all guilty of certain deeds." Another army officer, also a defense attorney, blanketed all when he angrily observed, "The conduct of each and every one of our officers was shameful."[6]

On June 27, 1957, a year and a half after the last of the trials was over, Maj. Gen. J. H. Michaelis, chief of legislative liaison, wrote to Sen. Marga-ret Chase Smith: "The Department of the Army has made, and is making, every effort to insure that there is equality of justice and consistency of treatment of those individuals who were prisoners of war in the Korean conflict and who may have been guilty of misconduct." But that treat-ment was inconsistent, and justice far from equal. Many witnesses at the trials were themselves admitted collaborators; some were admitted pro-gressives and yet not court-martialed. "Every witness," said Lt. Col. James Scott, "who testified both for or against the accused [Master Sergeant Ol-son] admitted doing at least some of the things of which he has been found guilty. The only difference therefore in their positions and his is one of degree not kind." Even government lawyers such as Lt. Col. Andrew Kane pointed out, "It must be remembered that many of the witnesses at the Fleming trial admitted collaborating with the North Koreans." Some of the admitted collaborators became belligerent as witnesses and, when asked pointedly about their own activities, replied, "Am I on trial?" It is a valid question that deserves an answer, but in thousands upon thousands of pages of documents there is none.[7]

There can be only one of two answers to the question of why others were not court-martialed, and there is no documentation to prove either. First, the army was tired of the issue and no doubt wanted to put an end to it. Second, and more likely, was that for their testimonies, witnesses were granted immunity from prosecution. Whatever the case, to make an example of a few men—who had suffered terribly—and identify them as the "bad guys" was unfair, inconsistent, and untrue.

With each public statement about the trials the army dug its hole a little deeper. "No case involving a repatriated prisoner of war was referred to trial without an appreciation and painstaking consideration of all the conditions these men endured during their captivity," said Col. Richard Tibbs, chief of the Military Justice Division. Along the same lines, an advisory committee to Secretary of Defense Charles Wilson reported that "no case was brought for court-martial action in which there was evidence of duress, brainwashing, or any other type of coercion."[8] Although evidence of duress, "brainwashing," and coercion fairly spills from the documents, the advisory committee reported that it could find none regarding those placed on trial. It is incredible that they would expect Wilson—or the public—to believe that conclusion.

≫≪

Article III, section 3 of the U.S. Constitution states that "treason against the United States shall consist only in levying war against them or in adhering to their enemies, giving them aid and comfort." Furthermore, Title 18 of the Constitution rules that "whoever, owing allegiance to the United States, levies war against them or adheres to their enemies, giving them aid and comfort within the United States or elsewhere, is guilty of treason." The army's proceedings of 1954 and 1955 were de facto trials on the charge of treason, although a military court-martial cannot consider a charge or specification of treason. That charge may only be brought in a federal court. Instead, the army's charge was "collaboration," which carries the same penalty. In his appellate brief to the Court of Military Appeals in the case of Corporal Bayes, Capt. Howard Vincent said, "The prosecution throughout insisted that Bayes was a traitor, his acts traitorous, but that he was positively not being tried for treason, since that would require an intent to betray. No, he was being tried for the military counterpart of treason, a new and novel offense in which the specification reads word for word with a treason indictment but the proof is not required to correspond with and support the allegation."[9] The potential penalty, however, was the same—death.

To commit treason is to give the enemy aid and comfort. But "aid and comfort" can mean anything. In the Bayes trial, for example, a defense attorney stated, "The amazing proposition that one can aid the enemy by eating his food and smoking his cigarettes was charged and earnestly and sincerely prosecuted."[10] Technically, a POW may furnish only name, grade, and service number and at that point must stop. But as another army lawyer reasoned:

> I ask simply the question. How can a prisoner of war, in the situation he is in, be required to abide by the rule of absolute nonintercourse? It's simply impossible. Intercourse doesn't mean just speaking, it doesn't mean just talking; it means any exchange of ideas, any help, any contact with the enemy. You don't have to give them anything; you just talk with them. And in this connection, of course, the playing of chess with a Chinese guard [as Maj. Gen. William Dean was photographed doing] might be considered intercourse with the enemy; and certainly advising them about the Table of Organization strength, as we know Gen. Dean did in his book, is certainly intercourse with the enemy. But what did he get but the Congressional Medal of Honor.[11]

General Dean freely admitted providing more than name, grade, and service number to the North Koreans. He also admitted that he had no authority from the U.S. government to do so. Dean further stated that he ate at the same table and drank alcohol in the same room as North Koreans. "I urge you to impress upon the Air [Force] the necessity to confine their attacks to military targets," he had written to Lt. Gen Walton Walker at 8th Army in September 1950 while a POW and at the insistence of the enemy.[12] When General Dean came home, he held his nation's highest military award. Did he collaborate with the enemy and provide aid and comfort? If so, why wasn't he court-martialed?

The first and least publicized of the trials was that of Pfc. Rothwell Floyd. It began at Fort Leavenworth, Kansas, on February 10, 1954; cost nearly $200,000 to conduct; and was the only court-martial that did not also include a collaboration charge. Floyd, a twenty-eight-year-old black soldier and newly married, was from London, Kentucky. He was being tried for striking an officer, mistreating other POWs, and murder. Although entitled to have a certain quota of enlisted men sit as members, he elected to have the members' panel composed only of officers. He also conveyed his "desires that colored officers be appointed to sit on the court by which he is tried." The panel was composed of eleven officers, all of them white except for Maj. Jerry Vallory. The two-month trial introduced fifteen black witnesses and one white witness for the defense and seven black and seventeen white witnesses for the prosecution.[13]

Floyd continually proclaimed his innocence and offered to take a lie detector test and be administered truth serum. As he stated, "If I had been guilty of this stuff and thought that I was, do you think that I would come back here? Well, I wouldn't have. I'm not guilty and that's why I come back." Floyd apparently could not understand the need for a trial, although he'd given the matter much thought: "When I come here all I had to do was set down there and think, and I was wondering why these men made these [pretrial] statements against me and come in here and testify false. I know and God knows and those men that testified against me [know] that these things never did happen." When asked, "What does it mean to testify under oath?" he replied, "So help me God I will tell the truth or so help me God smack me dead."[14]

The prosecutor was unpersuaded by any claim of innocence, however, and said that Floyd "did more by his conduct to convince the Chinese of the inhumanity of the American than a million words of propaganda. . . . [Furthermore], he chose to travel a thorny path, reaping where he had not sown, and in which he appears to have chosen this path as his avocation. He preferred to pursue a devious course of outlawry in preference to that of being a good soldier and a good citizen, but he is the architect of his own misfortune and he must abide by the consequences of the acts taken in his own course."[15]

The defense fought hard to acquit their man and attacked the pretrial investigation. Capt. William Vinet, the assistant defense counsel, said, "Let's remember, too, that hearsay was desired by the Criminal Investigation Division in conducting their investigation in this case;* that some of the statements were not sworn to; that some of the witnesses didn't read their statements before they signed them but merely signed them and initialed at the places indicated to them by the agent interrogating. What a wonderful pretrial investigation this trial has been. I don't feel that the administration of justice is at all complimented by the proceedings that we have had here."[16]

Just as the trial began, Elisha Scott, an attorney working under the auspices of the NAACP, entered the proceedings. Some say that one should never bring a civilian lawyer into a military courtroom, especially for a general court-martial. There isn't a prejudice against that person, but military lawyers are far better practiced in the law that pertains only to the armed forces. The defense attorney in these POW cases, usually a lieutenant colonel, knew how to fight his counterpart, also a lieutenant colonel and was likely to give everything he had to the defense effort. It is also the case that in the military a defense attorney may act in that capacity in one case, in another case function as the trial counsel, and in a third, as the law officer. Such individuals know the law, and in many instances the Uniform Code of Military Justice differs from civilian law.

Scott's presence made Floyd's two military lawyers, Lt. Col. Thomas Cameron and Captain Vinet, his assistants, and Scott directed the defense. At times, he behaved as if he were standing at the pulpit on a Sunday morning rather than in a military court of law. He called one witness a "lying perjurer," for example, and exclaimed, "Never was a more damnable lie ever told! He didn't see it. He didn't see it. . . . Now, great God, have mercy on me. Have mercy, Jesus."[17] Scott also seemed to have no idea that his tactics were inappropriate.

Scott played on the black-white theme a number of times. He pointed out, for example, that "negro [POWs] were given priority over the whites. Why? Because the Chinese are trying to educate negroes to rebel against you in this country, poison you in your home, destroy your home. There isn't any argument to the contrary." He also warned members that communists were planning to overthrow the United States, using black

---

* This was true not only in Floyd's pretrial investigation but also in every other case.

men as their agents: "Give me Floyd and I will make some disclosures. The NAACP has the information where the common scheme [by communists] is to destroy the white man in this country by negroes, but it will not be done! I will never leave you. You stood by me. My parents were slaves. . . . Don't talk to me about hanging a man and hanging a negro when he shed the first blood on the Boston Commons for the perpetuation of the principles of this country."[18]

Sometimes Scott's rhetoric was moving and beautiful, but he also occasionally appeared to forget that he was defending a man against very serious charges, including murder. Although it was noble and possibly helpful to invoke God, Rothwell Floyd needed a better defense. "The clouds are now assembling out there in space," preached Scott. "Soon those somber clouds will cover the sun, the end of day. The end of day I say, but ere long there will be a brightening and that sun will thus appear, and I hope that the verdict in this case will be the greatest sunlight in the life of Rothwell Floyd. You have been a good soldier. You can do nothing else. Come back in the army. Join Elisha Scott. Let's uncover the communism in this country."[19] The time to pray came when the eleven officers walked out of court. Pfc. Rothwell Floyd, former prisoner of war, could hang.

≫≪

The first trial for "communicating, corresponding and holding intercourse with the enemy" (collaboration) was that of Cpl. Edward Dickenson, the first of the twenty-three to have walked out of the Neutral Zone. The trial began on April 19, 1954, on the third floor of an old, weathered-brick building at Fort McNair in Washington, D.C., and lasted until May 4. Not very far from Dickenson's court-martial the Army-McCarthy hearings were in session, and the army was defending itself for "coddling communists." The public thought differently. Hundreds of letters poured into various high-level offices, primarily President Eisenhower's, to denounce the army's actions.[20] The following are only a few examples:

> For the love of God, give Corporal Edward Dickenson a pardon.
> Patrick O'Keefe
> Northhampton, Mass.[21]

> I am only sixteen years old and maybe do not understand the procedure

taken by the army. You will probably read this letter and toss it away. However, it does me good to write this letter and ask you.

Mike Smith
Painesville, Ohio[22]

I am angry and I am ashamed.
Dr. T. W. Arnold[23]

Being the apparent scapegoat for the higher echelons is the supreme example of the expendability of the U.S. enlisted GI.
Robert Alferi
Kingsville, Texas[24]

Rear Adm. Dan Gallery wrote in the *Saturday Evening Post:* "In propaganda the Reds were always slick and we were clumsy. Through brainwashing they were able to broadcast peace appeals by our men. What kind of appeals did we broadcast? We pleaded with twenty-two of our men, 'Come home, all is forgiven!' When one of them (Dickenson) did come home, we court-martialed him—just as the Reds predicted we would. How stupid can we get? That blunder will be a windfall to the Communists' propaganda for years to come."[25] Such protests continued with every trial, but public opinion was ignored. The president, the secretary of defense, and the secretary of the army did not interfere with the decision to court-martial a certain number of returnees.

One valid point in Dickenson's defense was that, as he testified, "I was promised immunity if I would come back to the U.S. if I had committed any crimes against the U.S. government. But they didn't keep their promise." The army replied that it had never promised immunity to anyone.* If a hint of immunity was perceived, it was that the reluctant repatriates would not be charged with remaining behind while Big Switch was taking place. The army did not intend, however, for them to have immunity for crimes committed while a POW. It was the case, however, that Maj. Edward Moorer had said to the twenty-two, "Corporal Edward Dickenson returned home to his loved ones and enjoyed a combination thirty-day leave and honeymoon. *This fact explodes communist charges that you and your family will be harmed if you return.*"[26] As Major Moorer was giving that speech, the army already knew that it would arrest the young corporal

---

* If that is the case, why were admitted progressives, who were witnesses at the trials, not court-martialed?

(and to be arrested and court-martialed, many would state, is to be harmed). The immunity claim fell on deaf ears, and the trial went on.

The grades and experience of those who participated in the first of the thirteen collaboration trials reflected the seriousness of the charge. The members consisted of three colonels, one lieutenant colonel, three majors, and a captain. The law officer was a colonel; the trial counsel, a colonel (with a captain and lieutenant as assistants); and the defense counsel was a lieutenant colonel (assisted by a major and a captain). Finally, Guy Emery, a civilian but a retired colonel, was the "individual defense counsel." Compared to other civilians at other trials, Emery's credentials were impressive. A graduate of West Point, he had spent twenty years in the infantry, where he earned the Silver Star; had graduated from the University of Virginia Law School; and had been a professor of law at the U.S. Military Academy for three years. He was acting as counsel for no fee because he felt a wrong was taking place. The courtroom contained heavy artillery, arrayed for and against a somewhat naive, twenty-four-year-old corporal who was from Virginia and had a sixth-grade education.[27]

As witness after witness paraded into the courtroom, Corporal Dickenson seldom took his eyes off them. As long as they remained on the stand, he stared. "The only difference between me and a lot of others," he stated, "is the others have not been caught." That is not quite true. The others were caught; the army had the goods on everyone. The difference was that most of the others were not called to account. One witness, however, was not so fortunate and would himself be brought to trial a year later, although Harold Dunn didn't know that then. "My first impression of Dickenson," Dunn announced pompously, "was that he was a weak-willed individual who was not too intelligent. His general attitude was that of an escapist from reality. My personal opinion of Dickenson is that he is a coward." Such self-serving statements by witnesses whose own behavior was suspect were common in the trials. If a witness had a score to settle with someone, the trial setting was made to order. It became difficult to ascertain who was speaking the truth. "The men that swore against me . . . swore false," Dickenson remarked, "they have their own conscience to live with."[28]

Apparently the corporal's quartet of lawyers believed the army had not proven its case. As the trial neared its end, Dickenson did not testify in his behalf, saying to the court, "Sir, I wish to remain silent." With his deafening silence filling the room, the eight members of the court left to deliberate. Eleven hours later they returned.[29]

>«

The four officers who had the unenviable task of evaluating the merits of the case against Col. Frank Schwable were career professionals. Maj. Gen. Henry Linscott, a marine for thirty years, was an authority on military law and procedure; Maj. Gen. Christian Schilt was a veteran marine aviator and holder of the Congressional Medal of Honor; Maj. Gen. Robert Bare was director of the Marine Corps Development Center at Quantico, Virginia; and Rear Adm. Thomas Cooper was assistant chief of the Navy Bureau of Medicine and Surgery. The sole functions of these officers was to gather facts, formulate opinions, and offer recommendations. It was from their guidance that the commandant of the marine corps would determine whether to court-martial Frank Schwable.[30]

The inquiry began in mid-February 1954. On its the third day, Maj. Roy Bley was informed that he was an "interested party" (codefendant) and therefore entitled to remain in the courtroom and be represented by counsel. A parade of pilots marched into Building 4 of Henderson Hall in Arlington, Virginia, and told harrowing stories of their time of terror under the communists. They also detailed their preflight briefings by marine and air force officers. One star witness was Maj. Gen. William Dean, who outlined his own ordeal and then walked over to Frank Schwable and shook his hand. The colonel took the stand in his own behalf for six hours. "I want to emphasize," he explained, "I did not undergo physical torture in the sense of brutality. Perhaps I would have been more fortunate if I had because people nowadays seem to understand physical brutality. I didn't have that. Mine was the more subtle kind of torment. That kind is a little bit harder, I am afraid, for people to understand."[31]

The panel took six weeks to reach a verdict. The colonel was at home and had just completed putting up a fence around his yard when a call came to report to Marine Corps Headquarters. Looking fit again—his cheeks had filled out and the vacant look had left his eyes—he dashed around the house, cleaning up and getting his uniform together. Minutes after walking into headquarters, his blouse decorated with four rows of ribbons and gold wings, Schwable discovered that he had been cleared.[32]

The court concluded that "Colonel Schwable resisted this torture to the limit of his ability to resist [and he had] reasonable justification for entering into such acts." The members were also of the opinion that only one of three things could happen to those who undergo what the colonel experienced: "The victim's will to resist is broken and he responds as the enemy desires; the victim becomes insane; or the victim dies." Thus the court of inquiry recommended that no further action be taken against Frank Schwable.[33] Facts, opinions, and recommendations aside, Gen. Lemuel Shepherd had reached his own conclusions about what was appropriate treatment for a marine who had behaved as the colonel did.

>«

May, June, July, and most of August 1954 were quiet months. Toward the end of August, however, things started to heat up again when Cpl. Claude Batchelor and Lt. Col. Harry Fleming went on trial, both at about the same time. Batchelor's trial began on August 30, 1954, at Fort Sam Houston, Texas, and lasted exactly one month. Although two competent attorneys were appointed to represent him (Lt. Col. Kerlin Bragdon and Lt. Jack Oeffinger), Batchelor elected to have Joel Westbrook, a civilian from San Antonio, defend him. Once the corporal became his client, Westbrook wrote to Bishop Fulton J. Sheen and said, "Frankly, I approached the matter with considerable skepticism because of my strict and orthodox views respecting a soldier's responsibility and my firm belief in the incomparability of communism and God's grace. I was not mentally prepared for what I found in this case . . . but I do now realize that Claude Batchelor's tragic plight imports a great social problem and a stern ethical warning."[34]

Joel Westbrook was well intentioned but long-winded. Some of his individual questions to witnesses filled more than one legal-size, single-spaced, typewritten sheet. A number of his queries were so complicated that witnesses had no idea what he was talking about, and Westbrook would have to repeat everything over again. During the trial he was asked to shorten his questions, and the trial counsel (Lt. Col. Francis Boyles) once stood and said, "I suggest that if counsel is going to make a dissertation at some length before asking the question, that he be required to reduce it somewhat so that it is intelligible to the witness."[35] The fact that even members of the court seemed to have difficulty with Westbrook's approach could not have helped Batchelor.

During the trial, treason was mentioned more than once. That created a stir, because treason could only be tried in a federal court and not by the military. As the trial began, one member of the court, Lt. Edward Schowalter, who held the Congressional Medal of Honor, stood to announce, "Sir, I challenge myself on the grounds that I am hostile to the accused and that prior to the convening of the court, I formulated the opinion and expressed the opinion that the accused is a traitor." Schowalter was excused, but later in the trial even the trial counsel, who should have known better, used the word *treason*. When asked to explain himself, Boyles said, "I merely made the general statement that the acts with which Batchelor is being charged are treasonable in nature." At that, Westbrook attempted to have all charges dismissed, but the petition was overruled.[36] Nevertheless, if the acts Corporal Batchelor committed were "treasonable in nature," the case should have not been tried in a military courtroom.

When the two CIC officers interrogated Corporal Batchelor in Tokyo, he had furnished them with a 148-page statement of his activities as a POW. The information in that small book was solicited from him for intelligence purposes. The material also included many incriminating statements that virtually amounted to a confession. Unfortunately for Batchelor, and over the vehement protests of the defense, the written testimony was accepted as evidence of wrongdoing. It had an enormous impact on the members.[37]

One charge was that Batchelor had written to his hometown newspaper with the intent of promoting disloyalty among the civilian population. The prosecution seemed to imply that newspaper readers would have been swayed, but the defense reminded the court that the letter was never published. When Nev Evans, publisher of the *Winkler County News,* had received the letter, he forwarded it to a friend, Myer Donosky, in Dallas, saying:

> Enclosed is a letter from a local boy who is a prisoner of Red China. First, let me assure you I have no intention of giving it any publicity whatsoever. I am asking you what you would do with it. I am curious to know how this kind of stuff gets through the censors. Quite obviously, the words are not the boys as he only went two years to local high school and was a seventy-five student. He's either been converted or was forced to write the letter. Do you think it should be turned over to officialdom or what is your idea? Knowing the family as I do, and assuming their attitude, I have not mentioned the matter to them.[38]

The letter was turned over to the army and used against Batchelor at his trial.

In his defense, a respected psychiatrist, Leon Freedom, noted, "The case of Claude J. Batchelor presents one of the most outstanding examples of what I have chosen to call an induced political psychosis that I have seen. This lad actually was deluded into believing he was a potential savior of humanity and that his efforts were devoted to the good of his fellow man." After a month of testimony, the members of the court retired to determine the fate of Cpl. Claude Batchelor.[39]

≫≪

Harry Fleming was incarcerated at Fort Sheridan, Illinois, on May 20, 1954. His trial began three months later. He was the first army officer to be court-martialed for "unlawful collaboration with the enemy." According to the trial counsel, "The general nature of the charges in this case is conduct unbecoming an officer and gentleman, and conduct designed to bring discredit upon the armed forces." Those far less serious charges are at odds with an allegation of collaboration. Furthermore, the specifications against Fleming covered only the four-month period from February 1, 1951, to May 30, 1951, the time he led the men at Camp 12.[40]

The proceeding took place after the Schwable court of inquiry and the Air Force Board of Review. In noting that, Fleming's defense counsel Lt. Col. Rodham Routledge remarked, "We are forced to admit that this trial involves policy; there can be no question about that. That policy is between the Army on one side and the Air Force and the Navy on the other." Routledge also suggested to the eleven members (eight colonels and three lieutenant colonels) that "the accused is before a court-martial today because somebody thinks he does not have much value. That is why we are here today." According to the army, however, the purpose of the court-martial was not because Fleming had no value, for "the issue here is not what Fleming did but the justification for his actions and to some extent, his motives." Fleming, of course, maintained that the justification rested in his election—with the blessing of Colonel Liles—as the leader of the men. His sole motive was to save as many lives as possible. "I do not consider that Col. Fleming's activities at any time he was a prisoner were contrary to the best interests of the United States government," Paul Liles told the court. "I believe that he was doing the best he could, under the circumstances, to preserve the lives of his men, and he did just this."[41]

The collaboration trials provided a rostrum for former POWs to vent anger and frustration against their comrades and the accused. Because Fleming had been a tough leader and therefore resented by some of the men, his case was no exception. Lt. Chester Van Orman said, "I feel that there was a good deal of very strong feelings against Fleming and that there were several people who definitely planned to 'get him' when they were released from prison camp." Another former POW, Maj. Harry Gibb, observed, "Many POW stories are grossly exaggerated, oftentimes to the benefit of the author and to the detriment of innocent people."[42]

During any trial of a former POW, it is essential that other prisoners appear as witnesses. Such testimony must be weighed with extreme caution, however. It was not at all unusual for the lawyers to catch people in outright lies while under oath. An attorney from Madison, Wisconsin, John J. Jenswold, once a marine corps law officer, said:

> I feel very strongly that the testimony of any individual who has ever been subjected to the rigors of a prisoner of war compound, particularly the communist style, would be, by virtue of such experience, an extremely unreliable witness. We have learned in many of these cases that men who were imprisoned in such camps are subject, and most likely, to lose all perspective on many of the simple everyday situations of life because their entire outlook has been so distorted by such confinement and the extremely close contact between [other] prisoners under such undesirable conditions that it breeds prejudices and strong reactions which usually result from molehills being mountains.[43]

Nevertheless, hundreds upon hundreds of men told their stories during the trials and in some cases consciously committed perjury.

The government invested time and money trying to prove that Harry Fleming once sat on the foot of Cpl. Robert Gorr during the truck ride south from Camp 5 to P'yŏngyang. The prosecution pressed the allegation and placed the corporal on the stand to testify against the colonel. "I had my foot out," Gorr said, "and he sat on it and I told him to get off. Instead of getting off, he got rude about it. He bounced on it, I think. I told him to stop and got up and was going to knock him out of the truck. The other prisoners told me to sit down."[44]

The prosecution remarked, "Without overstating its case the Government can safely say that the record is replete with evidence from which the court-martial could reasonably have concluded that [Fleming] acted only in his own self-interest." Because he didn't want to die, it may be true that he considered his own interests; however the record is also replete with evidence that he had acted in the best interests of his men. The trial so angered one civilian observer that he took the time to send a telegram to Lt. Col. John Pritchard, the trial counsel: "By your blind prosecution regarding Col. Fleming, you've destroyed army and civilian public relations. You staunch, fearless hero; you jerk."[45]

Alfred LaFrance, a civilian and president-elect of the Wisconsin Bar Association, acted as individual defense counsel for Fleming without pay and tried every way he could to transform his client's image from villain to hero. "I saw in Col. Fleming a man of great courage," the noted lawyer said, "a man of firm convictions who did what he did not willfully . . . but sincerely for what he considered to be to the best interests of the men in his charge. . . . [His men] lived to see the day when they might return to their homes and their loved ones."[46]

After ten hours of deliberation, the eleven members made a decision about whether Lt. Col. Harry Fleming was indeed a hero.[47]

≫≪

Three weeks after the new year began, Maj. Ambrose Nugent, survivor of the Tiger's death march and former president of the Central Peace Committee, went on trial at Fort Sill, Oklahoma. Two colonels and seven lieutenant colonels listened for a month to harrowing recollections of the Tiger at Camp 7 and Colonel Kim at Camp 12. When Nugent took the stand, he began to cry when relating stories of the hardships and brutalities of POW life. "If there could be anything done to conserve the lives of the American prisoners over there," he said, "that would be well worth it. I don't think there was any thought of repercussions or anything else at that time."[48]

Five weeks after the proceedings began, Col. Ferdinand Unger, president of the court, ordered Nugent to step forward. With an attorney on each side, the major stood at attention in front of the members and saluted smartly. Colonel Unger then read the verdict.

At the time Major Nugent was on trial, across the country at Fort Bragg, North Carolina, M. Sgt. William Olson was also being tried for his life on the charge of collaboration with the enemy. While the court-martial was going on, his seven-year-old son was teased by schoolmates: "Your father killed a man." One day the boy came home and asked his mother, "Are they going to kill Daddy?" It was, after all, a possibility.[49]

During the heated trial, witnesses made no secret of their distain for the sergeant. In one instance, the trial counsel asked M. Sgt. Chester Mathis, USMC, "What is your opinion of Sgt. Olson?" "I despise him" was the reply. After reading of the charges in the *Washington Post,* Sgt. Paul Portee wrote the army: "If I am needed as a witness for the prosecution, I would be very happy to tell you what I know of this Chink Gong-so-yen rat."[50]

In support of the charge of collaboration, a major accusation against Olson was that he wrote articles for the camp newspaper. If that constituted collaboration, one might reasonably have expected hundreds of others to have been so charged. Olson admitted writing the articles but denied that they were pro-communist or anti-American. His defense counsel, Lt. Col. Bruce Gillaspey, told the ten members of the court to "compare the article carrying Olson's by-line [in *New Life*] with others in the same paper written by those who have testified against him. Then ask yourselves who should properly be the accused in this case." Gillaspey pointed out, "We are not so much proceeding with a trial under the UCMJ but with a sacrifice on the altar of some blood-thirsty pagan god." He and his client could only hope that the pagan god would be merciful at the time of the verdict.[51]

≫≪

Cpl. Harold Dunn, a witness against his fellow soldiers at other trials and an admitted progressive, had his day in court on June 28, 1955. The following day it was over, for at 1st Army Headquarters on Governors Island, New York, Dunn pleaded guilty to "aiding the enemy by making propaganda recordings while a prisoner of war." He also acknowledged that he did "willfully, unlawfully, unnecessarily and knowingly collaborate, communicate, and hold intercourse with the enemy." The trial counsel said, "He's a very cooperative man. He was first cooperative to the Koreans, cooperative to the Chinese, now he's cooperative with us."[52]

"I found I made a big mistake when I was a prisoner," said Dunn. "I did a lot of foolish things. I love my country and know that I am in a far better position than I was before the war to appreciate the wonderful things we have." He may have loved his country, but when the "large and rather rumpled figure" walked into the courtroom for sentencing he had to worry whether the feeling was reciprocal.[53]

≫≪

One month after the Dunn trial, Sgt. John Tyler had his turn at Fort Bragg, North Carolina. "Did you see Tyler walking around with a cigarette?" was one of the prosecution's questions to many witnesses. The defense counsel, Maj. C. V. Beimfohr, remarked to the court that the trial counsels were "fine trial lawyers—they've had a lot of experience; but I've never seen them groping for a case like they have here."[54]

The key witness against Tyler was John Allen, who after repatriation had reenlisted for an additional three years. Eleven months later he was discharged because of a purportedly low I.Q. test result. Allen had the reputation of being a fighter and was said to be in trouble more often than most other soldiers. Reflecting on his character, Sergeant Tyler's counsel addressed the court: "Now let's take an evaluation of Allen. He was picked up in downtown Fayetteville, charged, I believe, with profanity and drunkenness. He took exception to the fact that the cop kept calling him a punk and while he was testifying I, individually, could not help but think how accurately that policeman had evaluated the situation. So he shows up in court after having spent a night or so in jail and paid a fine, with a black eye."[55]

To many, the court-martial seemed a joke, albeit a serious one. After Tyler refused to testify, his defense counsel closed by saying, "I submit to you, gentlemen, that the government has tried desperately to convict John Tyler of something. I submit to you also that for a long time they didn't know what they were trying to convict him of."[56] The weakness (possibly absence) of the army's case aside, it was not up to the defense to render a verdict. That burden fell upon the eleven members of the court.

Nearly two years after his release by the communists, Sgt. James Gallagher was court-martialed at Fort Jay, Governors Island. He listened impassively while charges of throwing John Jones and Donald Baxter out in the cold, hanging the young soldier named Dunn on a peg, and general collaboration with the enemy were read. Only twice did he move, and then to look at his mother, Mary, and offer her a half-smile. Another interested spectator during those first warm two weeks of August in New York was Loretta Jones, the mother of John Jones. Ironically, neither the Jones or Baxter families had known what happened to their sons until a week before the proceeding. For two years after the war, both families had believed their boys had died of illness while POWs.[57]

As much as it was Gallagher's trial, it was also a trial of a different sort for Lloyd Pate. The twenty-one-year-old sergeant* from South Carolina had promised while a POW that his nemesis from Brooklyn would pay for his actions. Although Pate was reluctant to give evidence about what had happened to Dunn, he did so because he had made a vow while at Camp 5. Otherwise, he said, "I would have walked out and gone home and not testified." While Sergeant Pate recalled the incident, Gallagher sat only ten feet from him and stared, betraying no sign of emotion. Pate stared back and saw a sharp-looking soldier but pitied him because of his eyes, which "had the look of a little whipped puppy in them." According to defense counsel Lt. Col. William Walsh, "Getting Gallagher must have become almost an obsession with Sgt. Pate."[58] Whatever his motivation, Lloyd Pate appeared to be doing a good job.

"All the time I was a prisoner of war, I was accused of murdering [Jones]," said the handsome blond in his own defense, and he further denied ever murdering anyone. Sergeant Gallagher stated that when he came off kitchen duty and entered the room, he had noticed that Jones had defecated all over his sleeping bag. He told Jones to go outside and clean himself off, but Jones refused. Then the squad leader ordered him put out, and he and Gallagher carried Jones outside, where they left him for about fifteen minutes. Gallagher said that Baxter was not in the room at the time, but when he brought Jones indoors he saw Baxter and brought

---

* Pate was only fifteen when he joined the army by falsifying his enlistment documents.

him as well. About a half hour later, a Chinese medic entered and pronounced both men dead, although Jones, Gallagher testified, was still alive. The Chinese then gave him an injection under the heart, and an hour later he was dead. It was then that both Jones and Baxter were permanently removed from the room.[59]

"I do not believe myself guilty," declared Gallagher. "I have often wondered, since that day, whether if I left [Jones] in the room he may have lived or not, but I believe with all the men dying as they did that the man would have died anyway." With respect to the second man, the sergeant said, "As far as I'm concerned, there was no Baxter incident."[60]

Concerning Dunn, Sergeant Gallagher claimed that he was trying to help him live by hanging him on the peg. "The doctor came in and told [Dunn] either he gets up and gets fifteen minutes exercise, at least, and try to get two or three hours of sun a day, or he would die," remembered the sergeant. "Dunn wasn't sick. He was lazy." Therefore, Gallagher took a scarf and hung Dunn from the wall because "he could move his body around. It was much better than laying on the floor and not moving at all." The sergeant further pointed out that Dunn was very much alive when removed from the peg and did not die until two or three weeks later. As to Pate's testimony that he had witnessed the incident through a window, Gallagher maintained that there were no windows in the building.[61]

Nearing the close of the proceeding, the trial counsel said, "This man was God unto himself. . . . The Good Samaritan? God preserve me, and God preserve each and every soldier from such a samaritan. . . . This pitiful scene in the annals of history is perhaps the most loathsome and certainly the most gruesome that you or I will ever hear one American prisoner, one American soldier do to his buddy. A soldier, much less a man?"[62] With accusations and denials ringing in their ears, the members of the court withdrew to determine the fate of Sgt. James Gallagher.

≫≪

While Gallagher was on trial for his life in New York, Lt. Jeff Erwin faced a court-martial at Fort Lewis, Washington. He was charged with making statements disloyal to the United States in that he allegedly lead discussion groups, signed petitions, was a member of the peace committee, and communicated with the enemy while at Camp 5 between January and May 1951. He was also forced to defend himself against similar charges growing out of his purported behavior while at Camp 12 between June and December of that same year. In every collaboration case the defense attempted—some counsels more strongly than others—to invoke duress as a cause of any illegal actions. During the Erwin proceedings that justification was strenuously advanced.[63]

As a general rule, duress is not an acceptable defense in a military court of law. Indeed, if duress were a complete defense, there might well have been no courts-martial. Any compassionate person might conclude that being a POW under the thumb of a ruthless enemy would create stress sufficient to lead captives to do things they normally would not. Still, Col. Richard Tibbs, chief of the Military Justice Division, said, "No case was tried by court-martial in which there was credible evidence of duress or other types of coercion."[64] Although Congress has recognized that the maintenance of military discipline has its own logic, Tibbs's words fail the civilian test.

According to the dictionary, duress is "imprisonment" or "the use of force or threats; compulsion." The military, however, will not accept that, and during the various courts-martial the army maintained that "nothing short of a showing of an immediate danger of death will qualify as a legal defense [for duress]." In the Nugent case, "duress" was defined to members of the court in the following manner: "It must be a reasonable belief that death or serious bodily harm will occur immediately upon a refusal to act." To overcome that strict interpretation was virtually impossible, but defense attorneys did make an effort. Lt. Col. Leslie Dixon, Erwin's counsel, said, "There is nothing more ridiculous than trying to say that it is the law that every time you do something under duress, someone has to be standing there with a loaded pistol pointed at your head." "The communists, in short," another defense counsel angrily insisted, "used starvation and deliberate degradation to bend the prisoners to their will and not to recognize this as legal duress is to indulge in unreality."[65]

The POWs were not lawyers, and they had to act immediately in what they considered to be life or death situations. Erwin was accused of making a disloyal assertion at Camp 5 in front of his company. When asked why, he responded that the Chinese had spoken to him the previous evening and stated "if I didn't stand up the next day and make a statement, that I wouldn't go back to the squad, that I would be killed and I thought that it would be easy to do because all they had to do was tell the other prisoners that they had removed me to another camp and if the war ever did end, they could say that I died in transit."[66] In early 1951 the Chinese were indeed systematically killing thousands of American POWs, and under such conditions Lieutenant Erwin would have felt that the threat on his life was legitimate.

Capt. Clifford Allen, the black officer who assumed leadership of Camp 12 from Colonel Fleming, had his own definition of duress:

> We were reduced to the state where we were suspicious and jealous and envious and mistrustful of one another—fighting, scrapping, bickering among ourselves. Any move that any man made brought the question— Why did he do that? What was he doing? And what for? Because we always felt that someone was getting a morsel of food from some other place; was getting a grain of salt in which we had no opportunity to share. It was through these conditions of life—these predatory conditions of life, I should say—that the communists reduced us to a very, very servile state; where they almost got us to the point that we would do anything they wanted us to do because we had no—we had nothing to fall back on, no strength left and no source of strength. Duress? That is duress; that is the way I saw it.[67]

One of the more ludicrous cross-examinations of the POW trials took place during Erwin's testimony. He had admitted doing something the army considered collaboration, but he had done so because a gun was pointed at him. Yet that act, the prosecution attempted to convince the court, did not constitute duress:

> Q. Now, with regard to this pistol, did this Chinaman ever show you that it was loaded at any time?
> A. He didn't show me that it was loaded, no, sir.
> Q. Then as far as you know, the pistol was unloaded or could have been unloaded just as easily?
> A. I am absolutely certain, sir, that the pistol was loaded.
> Q. Would you tell us how you know that or did he show you a loaded clip, or what?
> A. Sir, the pistol was in the hands of the enemy.
> Q. Did he show you a loaded clip?
> A. I can see no reason for carrying around an unloaded pistol, sir.
> Q. You have made a statement that that weapon was loaded and I want to know how you know it was loaded.
> A. Frankly, sir, I don't know whether it was loaded or not.
> Q. That's all I wanted you to say.[68]

It was nearly impossible to sustain a duress defense in an army courtroom.

In closing on Erwin's behalf, Colonel Dixon said to the court, "Today, we are all sitting here in this courtroom, fat and well fed, but let us project ourselves back a few years ago and see these boys lying on these hard floors, freezing to death, and let's try to picture what would I have done—what would you have done?"[69] It would not take very long for Lt. Jeff Erwin to get the court's answer.

≫≪

Of the five officers court-martialed after the war, only Ronald Alley was not part of the group that traveled south to what was known as Traitors Row (Camp 12). Most charges against him were for his activities while a POW at Camp 5. Many other officers had admitted to doing the same things. Yet no other officer who remained in the Yalu camps and admitted to some of the wrongs charged to Alley ever was prosecuted.[70]

"This is a tragic case whatever way you look at it," inveighed defense counsel Lt. Col. William Logan. "We do not realize just how tragic it is for Major Alley. . . . And it is tragic too for the witnesses who must relive for a time the dreadful first few months of their captivity; . . . and finally, this case is tragic for our country." Yet a court of ten officers convened in a courtroom at Fort George G. Meade, Maryland, on August 22, 1955, and for weeks listened to eighty-six witnesses describe what went on in the officers' compound at Camp 5 during the early days of imprisonment.[71]

Ronald Alley, whose "character of service" had been graded excellent during much of his career and who had above-average intelligence, likely did more harm to his cause than anyone else. He refused, for example, to answer any questions during his pretrial investigation, would not testify in his own defense, and remained mute when asked to plead, thereby forcing the court to enter a not guilty plea on his behalf. Maj. Ralph Potter, an army psychiatrist, said, "At times he rushes impulsively into things, tends to be somewhat too outspoken, and at times makes blunders in judgment because of his impulsive need to get things done, to organize, to, in a way, be a big man." Because of his personality, Major Alley was not well-liked, and that became obvious at the trial as witness after witness, either consciously or unconsciously, displayed contempt toward him. Another psychiatrist, Bernard Glueck, said, "I cannot escape the conviction that the common denominator underlying the testimony of one and all of the witnesses is a hatred of the accused."[72] Not surprisingly, quite a few officer witnesses at Alley's proceeding admitted under oath to doing some of the things for which the major was being court-martialed.

Ronald Alley had grown up in Bar Harbor, Maine, and when a group of prominent citizens there heard of the pending court-martial they set to work raising money for his defense. C. Edward Shea, chair of the Ronald E. Alley Defense Fund Committee, said, "Indeed, those who knew him as a boy and young man find it impossible to imagine that such an upright individual, so devoted to the service of his country as to make the army his career, could, in any way, be guilty of any actions aimed against his country or countrymen." Alley, however, refused to recognize the committee. "He became very suspicious at once," Glueck reported, "and wanted to know what their motives were. Did they seek notoriety; did they seek some financial return from the publication of the story in the newspaper? And in spite of the fact that these people on, I imagine, a spontaneous feeling of generosity, had contributed funds to assist in his defense, I understand that Maj. Alley never communicated with them."[73]*

In April 1951, the Chinese had mandated forced study. Because the captors could not possibly be everywhere at once, however, one group of "students" set up a system whereby a lookout would signal an instructor's arrival to check their progress. Thus everyone would appear to be reading earnestly and discussing the subject matter when the instructor entered the room. When he left, they stopped. Alley was accused of reporting the existence of that system to the enemy, but, mysteriously, the Chinese did nothing about it for three months. In attempting to reason with the court, Alley's counsel, Lieutenant Colonel Logan, said, "Whatever the faults of the Chinese Communist Forces, stupidity was certainly not among them and it passes the utmost bounds of credulity to suppose that having learned all about the signal system in April, they would nevertheless have allowed it to go on working and fooling them until they learned about it a second time in July or August." The trial counsel retorted that because "the system may have worked for some time after [the information was given] to the enemy is probably due to the initiative, imagination and

---

* Capt. Robert Howell said, "It is a well known fact, but never proven, that the communists supplied a rather large amount of financial aid in Alley's trial." Such off-the-cuff remarks were common throughout the trials. Statements of this nature had no basis in fact, but because the army asked for opinions, it received them.

perseverance of the American prisoners. With numerical advantage on their side, it requires but little imagination to see how the prisoners could continue to thwart the efforts of the captors in this relatively small segment of the overall indoctrination program."[74] He did not, however, satisfactorily explain what happened to the imagination and initiative of the POWs when the enemy permanently terminated the system three months after Alley had allegedly reported it.

In July 1951, all prisoners from the various compounds in Camp 5 had been gathered to listen to speeches delivered by several American officers. According to Richard Jones, "In his speech, Alley stated that the United States was the aggressor in Korea and, in general, implied that the Chinese communists were right and that the United States had no business in Korea."[75] Major Alley stood trial on charges arising from this incident, yet signatures of hundreds of officers and enlisted men attest to similar digressions. The issue may be one of selective enforcement. Almost two decades later, many citizens expressed the belief that the United States was the aggressor and had no business in Vietnam. The fact that Alley's speech in 1951 was made in the context of a military prison camp constituted, authorities insisted, a major difference.

"I deny ever advocating communism," Alley claimed, but he apparently did not deny an affinity for socialism. That, in the early 1950s, was grounds for many to ostracize him, even though communism and socialism were not analogous. The legacy of McCarthyism was still strong, however, and Alley's apparent socialist leanings worked against him. Capt. Robert Howell said of him, "On numerous occasions, he had stated that he was a—he believed in socialism and the like." "We all knew he was a socialist and he made no bones about it," Maj. David MacGhee, USAF, caustically noted. "I do not believe that Alley was a communist but was a rank opportunist of the lowest form. He was a selfish individual who put himself before anyone else and seemed completely lacking in ethics." Lt. Henry Lang stated, somewhat in support of the major, that he "was always making certain it was understood that his beliefs were socialistic and not communistic."[76]

The well-respected Lt. Col. John McLaughlin, USMC, did not particularly care for Alley, but he set his feelings aside and supported him during the trial. McLaughlin, a senior officer at Camp 5 during the early months of starvation and death, said, "Major Alley was rather friendly, I thought, with the Chinese indoctrinators . . . and he seemed to be rather eager about studying this material and deceiving the Chinese into feeling he believed them. I did feel it was a deception. I did not believe he believed them. . . . I don't recall any specific derogatory statements made by Major Alley."[77] As in all the courts-martial, it came down to a question of whom the members believed.

As had other defense counsels, Logan insisted that the army was charging Alley with treason. His arguments were strong on that point, and he maintained that because of the nature of the charges his client must be tried in federal court:

> Major Alley is no less a citizen of the United States because he has on a uniform of the United States Army. We come to you with the argument that, if he is a citizen of the United States, first you should dismiss this entire proceeding, because he is charged here only with treason—exclusively with treason. This can't be anything else in the light of the English language—the construction of the English language from the earliest times of Chaucer and Bacon down to Funk and Wagnall's Dictionary. . . . [The charges] spell out treason, if anything; and I don't mean to be humorous, but an egg, if it is scrambled or hard boiled or soft boiled or poached, it is still an egg. Now, there is nothing here on this sheet of paper that is not treason.[78]

The members of the court were as receptive to this argument as others had been.

Alley's refusal to take the stand in his own defense prompted Col. Albert Glass, an army psychiatrist, to plead with him to do so: "You are just like a puppet in there. Everybody is pulling the strings and you aren't doing anything. You have a damn good story to tell. Get in there and tell the world. You are not just telling the court, you are telling the world." In lieu of heeding that advice, Alley, together with his wife, Erna, who was present throughout the proceeding, took notes. Bernard Glueck said, "I think it's a terrifically important thing; his vigilance, his preoccupation in taking notes—he cannot trust anybody. And I regret this very exceedingly because I have no other relation to him except to try and help and I have become convinced . . . that he has included me in this hostile world in which he thinks he lives." When Erna Alley was asked why she was taking notes when Alley would be furnished with a copy of the complete transcript, she replied, "We must do that. My husband and I decided we must do that so we can bring the truth to higher authorities."[79] The Alleys seemed to have concluded that they were alone. They were alone but not forgotten; the members were prepared to remind them of reality.

>«

On September 2, 1955, two years after his repatriation, Cpl. Thomas Bayes was court-martialed for allegedly aiding and communicating with the enemy and making statements disloyal to the United States. The trial was held at the Presidio of San Francisco, headquarters of the 6th Army. Why Bayes was singled out for trial while so many others were not remains a mystery. Also unexplained is why the army waited two full years before convening a court. The Air Force and marines had completed their investigations a year and a half earlier, but the army's effort was still strong. Capt. Howard Vincent, Bayes's assistant defense counsel, pointed out, "All personnel of the Air Force and navy are apparently immune from prosecution for their acts as prisoners of war; army personnel are not."[80]

A line of witnesses unpunished for similar behavior waited to testify against Corporal Bayes. After they had finished, Vincent told the court, "The case was treated as if this miserable forced mouthing of the communist litany from the lips of a stinking, starving prisoner of war in the wilds of Korea proved the accused soldier was a highly dangerous secret agent roughly comparable to Aaron Burr and Dr. Goebells combined."[81]

Before the seven members of the court withdrew to determine the fate of the thirty-two-year-old Kentuckian, defense attorney Col. Max Hazelhurst admonished them: "Remember this—this case interests you—it interests all of us today. Tomorrow, next week—it may be only a passing interest; six months from now it will be largely forgotten but the accused must live with your decision for a lifetime."[82] Whether the officers would heed that advice Corporal Bayes would know shortly.

>«

The fifth and final army officer to be placed on trial was Lt. Col. Paul Liles. As November winds whipped through Fort Lewis, Washington, Liles wrote to a prospective witness: "Dear Tony: I hope you enjoy the big reunion to be held here at Ft. Lewis. Looks like I'm the goat. See you."[83]

Lt. Col. William Cohen, the trial counsel, was especially vehement in his comments about Liles, whom he characterized as being gutless. Of the incident at Valley Camp when Fleming was in command because Liles was ill, Cohen remarked, "This alleged physical disability was a cover-up to evade assumption of leadership and was used to throw the burden on [Colonel] Fleming. This made Fleming the scapegoat, even though Liles was especially trained to assume leadership, more so than any other officer present. Liles just did not have what it takes. He had no backbone." As to Liles's activities at Camp 12, Cohen referred to him—without using the word—as a traitor. "This conduct of Liles is indeed a black page in the military history of the United States," said the trial counsel. "It ranks worse than the plot of Benedict Arnold, for this was carried out. It was actually executed." Even the office of the judge advocate of 6th Army, through Maj. Donald Young, noted, "It is incredible that an officer of the United States Army with the accused's background and experience could have so utterly failed in his duties, responsibilities, and obligations to his country at such a critical time."[84]

In his own defense, Liles said, "It may be difficult to understand why these things were done unless you transport yourself into the desperate days of 1951 behind the communist lines when we had undergone a winter of starvation, did not expect to survive the next winter, and we took what appeared to be a desperate chance. If we had succeeded [in our escape attempt], well and good, and if we failed—well, you know the result." Most actions Liles and his group took at Camp 12 were to put into effect the escape plan, which required getting at least two men out of camp. In that regard, the defense attorney at Lieutenant Erwin's trial told the court, "Had [Liles] been successful in this, he would have been the greatest hero in the United States today. He would have been, absolutely, the greatest hero in the United States today. He would have been absolutely the greatest because his plan had worked. But, what are they trying to paint him today? He didn't get an opportunity to find out whether that plan would work or not, so here they are, trying to flaunt the word around here that he must be a traitor."[85]

Many character witnesses appeared in Liles's behalf. One, Lt. Col. Leslie Bailey, said of him, "I feel that his past character indicates that in dealing with a ruthless and treacherous enemy, the Chinese Communists, Lieutenant Colonel Liles would have acted in the best interests of his fellow prisoners and his country, and that having once decided upon a specific course of action, he would have pursued it with vigorous physical and moral courage, irrespective of whether or not his actions were approved, criticized, or misconstrued by those who possessed only a 'worm's eye' view of his actions and but a nebulous understanding of their long-range purpose and objectives." But what does the word *character* mean? As Col. Robert Ingersoll said before the U.S. District Court of Northern Illinois in 1876:

> Good character, gentlemen, is not made in a day. The walls of that grand edifice have to be worked at during life. All the good deeds, all the good words, every right and true and honest thing that one does goes into this edifice, and it is domed and pinnacled with lofty aspirations and grand ambitions. It is not made in a day, nor can it be crumbled into blackened dust by a word from the putrid mouth of a perjurer. . . . And yet we are told that splendid fabric called good character cannot stand for a moment against a word from a gratuitous villain. . . . A good character will stand against the testimony of all the thieves on earth. A good character, like a Gibraltar, will stand against all the testimony of all the rascals in the universe, no matter how they assail it. It will stand and it will stand firmer and grander the more it is assaulted.[86]

>«

The ninth and final enlisted man to be placed on trial was Sgt. William Banghart. It was a fast proceeding at Fort Meade, Maryland, for the sergeant pleaded guilty to the general charge of "knowingly communicating, corresponding, and holding intercourse with the enemy."* Attached to the charge were ten specifications for which Banghart acknowledged guilt:

1. Participated in a Camp 5 propaganda play, *Doctor Dubois.*
2. Participated in a Camp 5 play about germ warfare.
3. Made a recording describing the "Olympics" at Camp 5 in 1952 and saying that he had spoken with an Air Force lieutenant who confessed to germ warfare.
4. Made a recording addressed to the president of the United States.
5. Wrote articles.
6. Acted as a public address announcer.

---

* Banghart and Cpl. Harold Dunn were the only two of the fourteen men court-martialed to enter guilty pleas.

7. Acted as Camp 3 librarian.
8. Spoke to and associated himself with the enemy.
9. Was a monitor.
10. Signed a germ warfare document.[87]

Still, Banghart repeatedly proclaimed that his behavior "was not essentially different from many others and that many had committed worse crimes and yet were going unpunished."[88] Indeed, the weight of evidence suggests that a great many former Korean War POWs committed at least one of the same crimes. The "crime" of being a squad monitor, for example, does not take into account a turnover of monitors within the same squad. Assuming that each monitor was responsible for a squad of ten men and that there were four thousand POWs, there would have been approximately four hundred monitors. Neither was Banghart the only camp librarian. The documents contain hundreds of articles written by hundreds of men. If signing a germ warfare document was a crime, the pilots who signed actual confessions, according to the army, committed crimes—at least according to Specification 10 of Banghart's indictment.

》《

On January 25, 1954, three days after the arrest of Edward Dickenson, Secretary of Defense Charles Wilson handed a memo to Assistant Secretary of the Army John Slezak that ordered him to dishonorably discharge the twenty-one American soldiers who decided to remain with the Chinese. Because the cooling-off and grace periods in the Neutral Zone were over, it seemed apparent that none would return. Wilson's rash step had no precedent, because a dishonorable discharge must follow or be the sentence of a court-martial or military commission. It may not be ordered by administrative fiat. In justifying his angry move, the secretary of defense said, "You can't court-martial a man when he is not in your control."[89]

On the afternoon of July 29, 1955, a year and a half after their dishonorable discharges had been ordered and while the eighth trial was being held (that of Sgt. John Tyler), the *President Cleveland* docked in San Francisco. Aboard were William Cowart, Lewis Griggs, and Otho Bell, three of the twenty-one who had decided to remain in China. As soon as they set foot on U.S. soil, Capt. Walter Leahy placed them under arrest, saying,

"Court-martial charges have been preferred against each of you." Leahy read the collaboration charges, which were at least as ominous as those that had been placed against the men who'd previously returned and were tried. The three were then taken to the stockade at Fort Baxter, San Francisco. Speaking for the group, Cowart said, "I know we'll get justice in our country. We have faith in our country and our government. Any punishment we receive we will gladly accept. We came out because we feel we now are true Americans. Being true Americans, we'll take whatever punishment is coming to us."[90]

Lawyers for the three immediately set to work, and on November 8, 1955, five days after Major Alley's verdict and two weeks before the trial of Lt. Col. Paul Liles was to commence, Cowart, Griggs, and Bell walked out of jail as free men. The civilian courts had ruled that the army had no jurisdiction over a civilian, even if that civilian committed crimes while in the service. Such crimes can be tried only in a federal court. The men were civilians not because they had wanted to be but because Secretary Wilson had automatically placed them in that category by issuing dishonorable discharges.* While American soldiers were being tried for collaboration, men who had elected to remain and live with their captors were free American citizens.[91]

Notes

1. Cpl. Claude Batchelor, USA, Transcripts, 3:74.
2. M. Sgt. William Olson, USA, Transcripts, 3:46.
3. Lt. Col. Harry Fleming, USA, Transcripts, 6:24–26; see also Olson Transcripts, 3:79, and Sgt. James Gallagher, USA, Transcripts, 1b:89.
4. Cpl. Thomas Bayes, USA, Transcripts, 7:brief, 12.
5. Lt. Col. Paul Liles, USA, Transcripts, 6:440; Cpl. Edward Dickenson, USA, Transcripts, 4:159–66.
6. Fleming Transcripts, 3:64, 5:264; Bayes Transcripts, 7:brief, 28; Maj. Ronald Alley, USA, Transcripts, 4:158, 9:1408.
7. Alley Transcripts, 1:191; Olson Transcripts, 1:164; Fleming Transcripts, 1:346–47; Dickenson Transcripts, 5:182.
8. Alley Transcripts, 1:67; Fleming Transcripts, 2:42.
9. Dickenson Transcripts, 1:362, 5:65; Bayes Transcripts, 7:brief, 9.
10. Bayes Transcripts, 7:brief, 10.
11. Sgt. John Tyler, USA, Transcripts, 1:251a.

---

* Based upon available records, sixteen of the twenty-one in China eventually returned to the United States.

12. Col. Frank Schwable, USMC, Transcripts, 2:813; see also Bayes Transcripts, 7:appellate exhibit 7, 26.

13. Pfc. Rothwell Floyd, USA, Transcripts, 1a:271, see also 1:11–12, 1:74, 1b:14, 4a:3557–58, 5b:5217, and 5c:255–57.

14. Ibid., 4:4787, 5a:4830–31, 5:4899, 5c:26, see also 4a:3610.

15. Ibid., 5b:5118, 5b:5238.

16. Ibid., 5b:5195, see also 5b:5193.

17. Ibid., 5b:5222–23.

18. Ibid., 5b:5220, 5b:5522.

19. Ibid., 5b:5522.

20. Dickenson Transcripts, 1:36, 1:276, 2:155, 3:3, 4:23; "Defendent Dickenson," 2. When I examined the original sixteen cartons of court-martial transcripts, I found that many volumes had missing pages. In some cases, entire volumes were kept back. During the trials, whenever sensitive or classified material was discussed the room was cleared. That part of the proceeding was then held behind closed doors and that portion of the transcript classified. In the Dickenson case, for example, one volume out of a total of seven, about four hundred pages, was not provided to me because "the classified portions contain information affecting the national defense of the United States within the meaning of the Espionage Laws." After extensive correspondence, all classified materials of all the trials were declassified and for the first time are made public in this book.

21. Dickenson Transcripts, 3:337.

22. Ibid., 3:331.

23. Ibid., 3:181.

24. Ibid., 3:182.

25. Ibid., 3:124.

26. Dickenson Transcripts, 3:412, emphasis added.

27. Ibid., 1:281, 2:322, 3:2, 3:123, 5:2.

28. "Korea Turncoat Ends Jail Term," 2; Dickenson Transcripts, 4:79, 4:374; see also "Former Comrades Accuse Corporal," 12.

29. "Dickenson Waives Right," 10; see also "Army Convicts Dickenson," 1 and Dickenson Transcripts, 5:2, 6:818.

30. Schwable Transcripts, 1:1.

31. Ibid., 3:960–61, see also 1:1 and 1:111, exhibit S.

32. "The Dreadful Dilemma," 63.

33. Schwable Transcripts, 3:1176.

34. Batchelor Transcripts, 12:26, see also 1:45, 5:489, and 12:23.

35. Ibid., 5:442.

36. Ibid., 5:8, 5:196.

37. Ibid., 3:124.

38. Ibid., 4:53.

39. Ibid., 10:53, 10:57.

40. Fleming Transcripts, 6:5, see also 1:1, 1:177, 1:234, 1:250, 2:1, 13:2136 and "Officer Convicted of Collaboration," 1.

41. Fleming Transcripts, 2:3, 4:120, 5:285, 11:1692, see also 6:2.

42. Ibid., 5:263–64, 5:350.

43. Ibid., 1:152.

44. Ibid., 5:305, see also 5:60.

45. Ibid., 1:19, 4:148.

46. Ibid., 1:235, see also 1:159 and 13:2081.

47. "Officer Convicted of Collaboration," 1.

48. Nugent Transcripts, 12:3519, see also 2:1, 2:1a and "Major Acquitted of Helping Reds," 12.

49. Olson Transcripts, 5:15.

50. Ibid., 2:483, 3:245.

51. Ibid., 4:830, 4:832, see also 4:779.

52. Dunn Transcripts, 1:280, see also 1:40.

53. Ibid., 1:199, 1:330; "Corporal Admits He Helped Enemy." 3.

54. Tyler Transcripts, 1:217a, see also 1:1.

55. Ibid., 1:212a-13a, see also 1:73-74.

56. Ibid., 1:212a, see also 1:216a.

57. Gallagher Transcripts, 1:3, 1a:1; "G.I. Goes on Trial in Three Korea Deaths," 3.

58. Pate, *Reactionary!* 145; Gallagher Transcripts, 6:1083-84, 6:1144; see also "G.I. Avenger Names Gallagher," 1.

59. Gallagher Transcripts, 5:888, see also 5:832-34 and 5:837.

60. Ibid., 6:928, 6:940.

61. Ibid., 5:840-41, 5:899, 5:920.

62. Ibid., 6:1123-25.

63. Erwin Transcripts, 1:1, 1:30, 1:41a.

64. Alley Transcripts, 1:68.

65. Ibid., 3:75, 3:170; Nugent Transcripts, 13:3795; Erwin Transcripts, 6:1532.

66. Erwin Transcripts, 5:1266-67.

67. Fleming Transcripts, 9:972.

68. Erwin Transcripts, 5:1372-73.

69. Ibid., 6:1537.

70. Alley Transcripts, 1:218, 1:311-12, 3:37.

71. Ibid., 7:741, see also 1:2, 5:138-39, and 5:142.

72. Ibid., 9:1207, 9:1239, see also 4:48 and 4:89.

73. Ibid., 1:149, 3:31, 8:1098.

74. Ibid., 3:71, 3:158.

75. Ibid., 5:25.

76. Ibid., 1:148, 1:362, 5:42, 5:53, 10:58-59, see also 4:171. A partial listing of organizations that the government considered suspect includes the Socialist Worker's Party, Federation of Italian War Veterans in the USA, Congress of American Women, George Washington Carver School (in New York City), Jefferson School of Social Science (in New York City), Jewish Peoples Committee, League of American Writers, National Negro Congress, Philadelphia School of Social Science and Art, School of Jewish Studies (in New York City), United Harlem Tenants and Consumers Organization, and the Protestant War Veterans of the USA. U.S. Department of the Army, *Organizations Considered by the Attorney General to Have Interests in Conflict with Those of the United States.*

77. Ibid., 4:110, 4:112.

78. Ibid., 5:185-87.

79. Ibid., 8:1106, 8:1109, 9:1222.

80. Bayes Transcripts, 7:brief, 61, see also 2:1 and 2:3.

81. Ibid., 7:brief, 12.

82. Ibid., 5:1546, see also 2:130 and 4:1156.

83. Liles Transcripts, 6:67.

84. Ibid., 1:16, 4c:2127, 4c:2147.

85. Ibid., 4c:2035; Erwin, 6:1549.

86. Liles Transcripts, 7:defense exhibit ooo, 4b:1807. Ingersoll's definition of character is contained in *United States v. Munn* (1876).

87. Banghart, 1:45–47.

88. Ibid., 1:145, see also 1:53.

89. "Twenty-one Pro-Red G.I.s to Get Dishonorable Discharges," 1; "Statement by Pro-Red Korea Captives," 2.

90. "Three Ex-G.I. Turncoats Land in San Francisco," 1.

91. "Eisenhower Gets Turncoats Plea," 7; "'Turncoat' Trial Scheduled," 36; "Court Frees Toth," 1; "Army Releases Turncoat P.O.W.'s," 14; Middleton, *Compact History of the Korean War,* 211; "Handwashing," 14.

ELEVEN

Again Prisoners

For the punishments set down in the law are to subjects, not to enemies; such as are they that, having been by their own act subjects, deliberately revolting, deny the sovereign power.

—Thomas Hobbes, "Of Commonwealth"

Of the fourteen soldiers chosen for court-martial, three were found not guilty of collaboration with the enemy and the remainder were punished. Maj. Ambrose Nugent, former president of the Central Peace Committee; Lt. Jeff Erwin; and Sgt. John Tyler were permitted to go free and return to duty.

With the exception of Tyler, whose trial had been initiated on slim evidence, both Nugent and Erwin had been at Traitors Row. The question is, Why were the two officers found not guilty although both freely admitted to making broadcasts, signing documents, or in one way or another cooperating with the enemy? It appears reasonable to assume that the members of the respective courts-martial felt Nugent and Erwin had justification for committing any acts that resulted in cooperation with the enemy. If their actions were justified, however, why weren't those of at least some others? If the Nugent and Erwin courts had judged the other defendants, would a number of those men also have been found not guilty? The innocent verdicts for Nugent and Erwin highlight the inequity of the decentralized system of justice by which returned prisoners were tried.

≫≪

Rothwell Floyd was found not guilty of murder but was convicted of striking a superior officer (Lieutenant Colonel Keith at Bean Camp), mistreatment of other POWs, and larceny. The members of the court showed no pity and sentenced him to forty years' imprisonment at hard labor.* He was then taken to the U.S. Disciplinary Barracks at Lompoc, California.[1]

The review process in the military is extensive. The first mandatory step is for the sentence to be evaluated by the convening authority, who in all the trials was the lieutenant general who controlled that particular zone of command within the continental United States and had initially ordered the proceeding. The general, after reading the transcript, could on his own authority lower the sentence the members of the court had imposed. In Floyd's case, the general allowed everything to stand.

The next *required* step in the process is for a case to be brought before the Army Board of Review. That body, primarily consisting of lawyers from the Office of the Judge Advocate General, reads the transcript, listens to arguments from appellate attorneys from both sides, and determines whether the findings and sentence are correct. On March 24, 1955, a year after the court-martial reached its verdict, the board of review, taking all circumstances into consideration, upheld the conviction but reduced Floyd's forty-year sentence to ten years at hard labor.[2]

The final move in the review process (which is not mandatory) is for the case to be brought before the Court of Military Appeals—the only place in the entire process where a panel of three civilian judges, appointed by the president with the consent of the Senate, sits. On July 25, 1955, while Sgt. John Tyler was being court-martialed, the Court of Military Appeals, "the GIs' Supreme Court," refused to hear the case of Rothwell B. Floyd. The final decision, therefore, stood at ten years' hard labor.[3]

---

* According to the Office of the Judge Advocate General, "We recognize, of course, that the term 'hard labor' has its origin in historic penology and that the labor required of present day prisoners is often no more strenuous than the cutting of grass or leaf raking."

Cpl. Edward Dickenson and his attorney Guy Emery were stunned when they heard the verdict of guilty. The corporal's wife Lottie could be seen desperately holding back tears. For collaborating with the enemy, Dickenson received ten years in prison. The case went all the way to the Court of Military Appeals. Although that body said, "We take judicial notice of the fact that many prisoners were subjected to severe brutality or to tremendous psychological pressures which made them do and say things which they would otherwise have avoided," the court refused to reverse any part of the verdict or lower the sentence.[4]

On September 8, 1956, while Dickenson was serving time, the law firm of Kauffman and Kauffman of Pennington Gap, Virginia, wrote to the judge advocate general. "We have been employed by Lottie Kate Dickenson, wife of the above named ex-soldier," the firm advised, "to file a divorce action for her against the subject. The fact that Cpl. Dickenson was convicted of a crime against the United States is the grounds of divorce relied upon by our client."[5]

On March 25, 1957, almost three years after the trial and subsequent to all appellate reviews upholding the verdict and sentence, the secretary of the army reduced Dickenson's sentence to five years, thus making him eligible for early parole.[6] "I sure am glad to get out of here," he said as he walked to freedom from Fort Leavenworth, Kansas, on November 23, 1957. After serving three and a half years, he announced that he would study for the Baptist ministry. Concerning his future, the former corporal noted, "According to our religion, you have to be called by God before you can really be a minister. I feel I have had that call since I have been in the disciplinary barracks."[7]

≫≪

Although the court of inquiry recommended that no further action be instituted against Frank Schwable, his military career had been seriously impaired. "I will not resign or retire now," he announced, but his commandant, Gen. Lemuel Shepherd, would not place him in a command position. As far as the commandant was concerned, the colonel was a nonentity. General Shepherd noted that he did not care about the colonel's preflight briefing because, based upon Schwable's experience, "There was no real requirement for detailed elementary guidance."[8]

After the inquiry, Frank Schwable served in the Aviation Division, Headquarters of the Marine Corps. In February 1955 he was put out to pasture and given the title of aviation safety officer, Fleet Marine Force, Atlantic, based in Norfolk, Virginia. On June 30, 1959, Schwable retired and on the same date was promoted to brigadier general.* Compared to many soldiers, however, he and his Air Force counterparts got off easily.[9]

>«

The members of the court were unsympathetic toward Claude Batchelor, and on Thursday evening, September 30, 1954, announced their verdict. The panel of army officers had decided that he should be locked away for the remainder of his life. His mother, Clara Mae Batchelor, was in the courtroom at the time and broke down. In an attempt to comfort her, he said in a low voice, "I can take it." His attorney's comment was, "I'm not worried about Corporal Batchelor's future, nor is he. I'm only worried about the army's lack of understanding of the evil insanity of communism."[10]

When the twenty-one in China heard of the trial and sentence of their former leader and nonrepatriate, they sent a letter to his mother, saying, "This trial and sentence of your son must go down as a black page in the history of American justice. After knowing your son as we have, and reviewing the particular conditions surrounding his trial—with its trumped up charges, fixed jury, and atmosphere of hate and mistrust whipped up by the government through the press—we can only conclude that Claude was unjustly tried and for a definite political purpose."[11]

Upon completion of the trial, Col. C. G. Schenken, a lawyer on the staff of Lt. Gen. I. D. White, the commanding general of the 4th Army, reviewed the transcript. Batchelor, he reported, had "a strong desire to make a good impression and to show that he was merely an innocent young boy who was mislead by communist propaganda. He seems more like an immature opportunist. It is my opinion that he refused repatriation initially because he thought that he could be a big shot with the communists." Yet Schen-

---

* The increase in grade was what was known at the time as a "graveyard" or "tombstone" promotion. The practice is no longer followed in the armed forces.

ken felt that the penalty imposed was excessive and recommended that General White, the convening authority, reduce the life sentence to twenty years. A month after the trial, White concurred and approved the recommendation. He said he hoped that Batchelor "appreciates [that] the American way of life is worth many sacrifices and privation." O. L. Batchelor, father of the convicted collaborator, noted that he was encouraged by the general's action, "but we will not be satisfied until they turn him loose and give him an honorable discharge."[12]

After hearing the case, the Court of Military Appeals upheld the conviction and twenty-year sentence. "It is not a pleasant task to sit in judgment on a young man who yields to temptation while a prisoner of war," the court observed. "However, at best, he was a victim of his own selfish desire to improve his internment at the expense of other servicemen; at worst, he was a soldier who betrayed his cause."[13]

After he had served four and a half years in jail, the U.S. Parole Board granted Batchelor his freedom. On March 18, 1959, he walked out of prison a free man and began the attempt to glue together the shattered pieces of his life.[14]

>«

As Lt. Col. Harry Fleming stood at attention in the sunlit room, he knew he could receive life imprisonment at hard labor. When the president of the court announced the finding of guilty, Fleming accepted it "without a visible trace of emotion." His sentence for collaborating with the enemy was dismissal from the service (involuntary discharge) and forfeiture of all pay and allowances, which came to about $700 per month.[15]* "I will do everything to clear my name," he said.[16]

> My conscience is clear, and I can live with myself because it is. Without exception, the prisoners who were with me in camp are back home with their mothers, wives, and families. That to me is a very important thing.
>
> The little picture just affects me, my wife, and a few friends. The big picture affects many Americans. I've lost the battle so far. In the end, if right is to prevail, American justice will come out of it, not only for me but for the thousands who came out of the North Korean prison camps under suspicion.

---

* Only an enlisted person can receive a dishonorable discharge; the equivalent for an officer is dismissal.

They are just as good Americans, just as good soldiers, as we've ever had in this country.[17]

Because no person wants to be labeled a convicted collaborator, Harry Fleming took his case through the entire review process. The convening authority, board of review, and Court of Military Appeals, however, upheld everything. The Court of Military Appeals in Washington said, "Good motives are not a defense to a crime. . . . Our sympathy goes out to the men who were, unfortunately, forced to endure the inhuman treatment foisted on them by their barbaric captors. However, war is a harsh business and Col. Fleming was a field-grade officer in the United States Army. Due to his superior rank and senior position, he was called upon to exercise a conduct more exemplary than the other prisoners."[18]

One of the court's statements may be difficult to agree with: "Although by civilized standards, conditions in the prisoner of war camp were deplorable, we cannot conclude, as a matter of law, that the threat of duress or coercion was so immediate as to legally justify [Fleming's] acts." Apparently, when Colonel Kim took the colonel to the Caves each day, exhibited the young men dying off one by one, and threatened him with the same fate, those actions did not constitute sufficient duress. Chief Judge Quinn, however, said, "[I disagree] with the majority's conclusion that, as a matter of law, a threat of confinement in the Caves did not constitute a sufficient threat of, at least, grievous bodily harm." A two-to-one decision, however, meant that it was all over for Harry Fleming.[19]

On September 12, 1957, after the entire appellate process had been completed, Fleming was drummed out of the army. "I intend to go into a business I've been interested in for twenty years—the marine sporting supply business," he said. "Motorboating is my hobby."[20]

≫≪

Although eight specifications were placed against M. Sgt. William Olson, he was only found guilty of making speeches, which, of course, hundreds of POWs did as well. Olson, however, received a sentence of two years' hard labor.* Even the Court of Military Appeals noted, "When the record is

---

* Every sentence was also accompanied by a dishonorable discharge and forfeiture of all pay and allowances.

considered in its entirety, it is clear that his behavior was less offensive than that of other collaborators who have been before us."[21]

In 1946 "Pop" Olson had received a divorce complaint from his wife, Dorothy, to end a marriage that had produced two children. During the summer of 1954, less than a year after his return from North Korea, he had wed Mabel Hardin, and they had a child. Olson claimed to be legally divorced from Dorothy Olson thereby free to marry Mabel Hardin. Dorothy Olson had not gone through with the divorce, however, and Olson had two wives.

Army authorities had heard about the matter but were disinclined to prosecute because of Olson's three years in prison in North Korea and the additional sentence of two years' hard labor in the United States. Joseph P. Cleland, commanding general of Fort Bragg, was not going to let the issue drop, however, and forwarded a handwritten note to his judge advocate: "This man will be tried by CM for this. JPC." A month after his collaboration trial, Olson pleaded guilty to bigamy in front of a second court-martial and received an additional six months' hard labor.[22] He was released from prison on January 19, 1957, and died in 1959.[23]

≫≪

Standing in a very hot room on June 29, 1955, Cpl. Harold Dunn, wearing a Combat Infantryman's Badge, Purple Heart, Good Conduct Medal, and various theater ribbons, heard the president of the court tell him that in return for his guilty plea he was to serve eight years' hard labor. Dunn was unconcerned about this, however. He knew something the court did not. The day before he had made a deal with the army: "In the hope of securing a lenient final sentence, I hereby freely and voluntarily offer to plead guilty to the specifications and charges at my forthcoming trial if you will recommend to the commanding general, First Army, that he approve a sentence not in excess of dishonorable discharge, forfeiture of all pay and allowances, and confinement at hard labor for two-and-one-half years."[24] A month later, Lt. Gen. Thomas Herren, the convening authority, kept his part of the bargain and reduced the eight years to two and a half.[25]

"How much does a soldier for the United States have to endure?" Mildred Fontano of Alameda, California, wrote to Dwight Eisenhower when she heard of the sentence. "Have you looked at the pictures of those prisoners of war? The haggard thin flesh, the hollow haunted vacant eyes? Oh, God, have mercy on us and help us as a nation to not heap any more indignities on suffering humanity and especially on our own loved ones."[26] Around the same time, Eisenhower received another letter, this one from Ellen Dunn, mother of Harold Dunn. One of Dunn's friends in the POW camp had been a boy nicknamed Major, and Dunn had cared for him until Major died. Ellen Dunn had many things to say to the president. Among them were:

> When Harold came home it was still on his mind he would cry out in his sleep "You have got to eat Major you have got to eat." I would go sit by him and he would say "talk to me mother so I can forget." Harolds nerves were in terrible shape when he came home. . . . Must he spend the next eight years of this fast changing world in prison the lost of a good name by a dishonorable discharge, the lost of anything he might receive from the Gov't such as allotments, rights under the G.I. Bill, or for a pension should he need one because of leg wounds. . . . I, Harold Dunn's Mother am asking you please give Harold a chance to rehabilate himself and then an Honorable Discharge so disgrace will not follow him, his brothers, his mother, wife, & his Son the rest of our lives. Neither Harold or his Attorney do not know that I have written this letter, please do not make it public.[27]

Eisenhower turned the simple yet moving handwritten letter from Ellen Dunn over to his military aide, Col. Robert Schultz, who forwarded it to the army "for necessary action." The army replied with a standard boilerplate description of the review process, exactly the same reply thousands of uninvolved strangers across the country also received to their own pleas.[28] Harold Dunn was released from Leavenworth on July 1, 1957.[29]

>«

Looking fit and trim in his starched khakis, Sgt. Jim Gallagher heard the court announce that he was going to spend the remainder of his life in prison at hard labor. Lloyd Pate, upon hearing the sentence, remarked, "I hope the kid, whoever he is, is resting easier over there. Maybe now he's happy."[30]

The convening authority placed his seal of approval upon the findings and sentence. When the record reached the board of review, however, everything was thrown out—charges, findings, and sentence—and Gallagher was freed. On October 27, 1953, he was discharged from the service, but he reenlisted the next day. The board noted that during those intervening few hours the sergeant had become a civilian, therefore the army lacked court-martial jurisdiction over him.[31]

The army refused to release Gallagher from custody, however, and on the same day the board overruled the court, the army made preparations to bring the case before the Court of Military Appeals. This highest appellate court ordered the board of review to examine the case again and this time not to come to the conclusion that the sergeant was a civilian. The court further noted that there was only a nine-hour hiatus between his discharge and reenlistment and stated:

> Certainly we are not as easily convinced as was the Board of Review that there is no basis on which to be found court-martial jurisdiction over the accused. . . . Gallagher elected to cast his lot with the military a second time. . . . What, then, are we to say to those who did thwart the enemy and his designs while in captivity? Must they serve side by side with others such as [Gallagher] who informed, collaborated, and murdered—and benefited thereby? Should the authority of military justice to punish the wrong done depend upon the illogical and fortuitous contingency of an intervening honorable discharge when it is delivered only after the accused has reenlisted in the service? The answer should be obvious—and is to us.[32]

When the board of review received the case a second time, it set aside the murder conviction but upheld the original court's sentence. In November 1965 the secretary of the army remitted the life term so the total sentence did not exceed thirty-three years, and in 1966 Gallagher was approved for parole.[33]

≫≪

Maj. Ronald Alley held the highest hopes of remaining in the army and eventually retiring as a colonel. Instead, in November 1955 he heard that he was to remain in jail for ten years at hard labor. The findings of the court-martial were upheld throughout the entire review process, but on August 14, 1958, almost three years after the trial, Assistant Secretary of the Army Hugh Milton showed mercy and reduced the prison term to five years.[34]

After the trial, Alley was transferred to the U.S. Disciplinary Barracks at Leavenworth, where his mental condition slowly deteriorated. He was examined during the summer of 1956, and a psychiatric evaluation followed: "DIAGNOSIS: Paranoid personality, chronic, severe, manifested by conspicuous tendency to utilize the projection mechanism, expressed by suspiciousness, stubbornness, unsociability, seclusiveness, serious-mindedness, inability to adapt to new and different situations of stress, poor judgment, marked paranoid delusions, and latent schizophrenic tendencies."[35] A few months later, another psychiatrist, Merrill Eaton, Jr., from the University of Kansas, wrote to the commandant of Leavenworth and said, "On examination, I find this man to be mentally ill. My diagnosis is Paranoid State (000–X32)."[36]

While incarcerated, Ronald Alley placed charges against practically every officer who testified against him, saying, in effect, that if he were a collaborator, so were many others. The army, however, replied, "There is no basis for any of the charges. They are groundless and an apparent attempt by Alley to keep 're-trying' his case for an indefinite period of time." Furthermore, according to the army, even if some other officers did collaborate it had been on a small scale. Additional trials would not be called for because they "would involve an unwarranted substantial expenditure of time and money."[37] Apparently, then, the authorities did recognize degrees of collaboration.

Erna Alley was heartbroken and in late 1957 wrote to the defense counsel:

> Although my two children, aged eight and nine, hardly know their father, they cannot understand why he is not with them as other fathers are. It is difficult for me to bring them up as normal, happy children, growing into useful, healthy citizens. My personal life is naturally full of worry and loneliness. I am deeply concerned with my husband's current welfare and with the outlook for his future. At no time have I inflicted him with useless worries about home affairs; however, our financial affairs are serious. I realize these factors do not affect the legal aspects of the case but I feel that the army should be aware of the hardship inflicted on the family of a man who was proud to serve seventeen years with the army.[38]

Although Alley had refused to speak at his pretrial investigation and during the court-martial, after the sentence he became a prolific letter-writer, claiming that someone from the officer corps had to hang and that was him. The reason he had been chosen, according to the major, was because he was a reserve officer, whereas West Point graduates and other regular officers were protected:

I was made the scapegoat for the officer POWs in Korea.[39]

I have not really done wrong. If I had to do it all over again, I would do it the same way.[40]

The sentence was [so] excessive as to be absurd when compared to the sentences adjudged against the other . . . officers convicted on charges similar to [my own].[41]

I have one great fault and that is of placing too much faith in the U.S. Army which, up until some months ago, I believed the sun rised and set on it and found it hard to believe that such injustices could happen. I have taken as the gospel truth advice and opinions of senior officers of whom I held a great respect but of late, I find my faith in the great U.S. Army and its officer corps shaken beyond the point of repair.[42]

The different policies used by the Army, Navy and Air Force to handle the returning POWs from Korea has led to some officers receiving the Medal of Honor, the Legion of Merit, Silver Stars, etc., while others must take the rap for these officers misgivings and their failure as officers.[43]

I urge and request that you [Sen. Margaret Chase Smith] use your good office to get to the bottom of the POW trials and assist to bring about a little justice for those of us who have been made the example and "scapegoats" for, what I believe and contend is, the result of gross negligence of duty on the part of our senior officers while POWs.[44]

The government took the position in the prosecution of the case against me that the law requires absolute non-intercourse with the enemy while in a prisoner of war status and that any communication whatsoever, and no matter what its intent, was denounced. Now, if in fact the government intends to uphold this interpretation of the law regarding communication with the enemy while a prisoner of war, it is my contention that every former prisoner of war in the Korean conflict did, on one or more occasions, communicate with the enemy and all should be tried for their unauthorized and unlawful communication. If those who have admitted their unauthorized and unlawful communication at the trials of others are allowed to go unprosecuted or are exonerated, then I and others so tried and convicted should likewise be allowed to go unprosecuted or be exonerated.[45]

After serving his term, a very bitter Ronald Alley was allowed his freedom.

≫≪

Cpl. Thomas Bayes received a sentence of five years at hard labor, which the board of review later reduced to two and a half years. One of his "crimes" was "criticizing living conditions, discrimination, and unemployment in the United States." Even one of his defense lawyers, Capt. Howard Vincent, noted that Bayes "has the unique distinction of being the first man in the history of United States jurisprudence to be convicted of this 'crime.'"[46] Vincent concluded:

> [Bayes] was charged with treason, found guilty of treason, and punished for treason, all without the necessity of proving an intent on his part to betray the United States, and the overt acts by two witnesses. His conviction no doubt served as an example to future prisoners of war and might provide a motive for them to resist being so used, provided that they heard of Bayes' trial and were *not* cognizant of the results of the trials of the officer POWs. However, it is difficult, if not impossible, to find the exact crime which the ventriloquists dummy commits in such circumstances, under our criminal code. It would appear that new legislation is necessary.[47]

Thomas Bayes was released from confinement on September 14, 1957.[48]

≫≪

Lt. Col. Paul Liles, found guilty of aiding, communicating with, and holding intercourse with the enemy, received a twenty-four-month suspension in rank coupled with a reprimand.* When he left the courtroom with his wife, Harriet, he was smiling and said that he would appeal to win "complete vindication." Another reason to smile was because most military people agreed that his sentence was the next best thing to acquittal.[49]

Sen. Hubert Humphrey was annoyed when he heard of the punishment accorded the West Pointer and wrote to Wilber Brucker, secretary of the army, for an explanation. "I do not recall the army having been quite so lenient with other personnel who were convicted of collaboration with the enemy in Korea," Humphrey said. "I would be very interested in hearing the reasons why a convicted collaborator should be let off at so light a sentence when others were fined, discharged, or imprisoned, if I am not mistaken." The army, however, was not required—and was unable—to provide reasons why the court, in secret deliberation, had arrived at the punishment it did. According to the reply to Humphrey, "The principal effects of the sentence suspending Liles from rank necessarily include

---

* For the caustic reprimand that was made part of his service record, see Appendix E.

suspension from command. This deprives him of authority to exercise military command and, consequently, of authority to give orders to his juniors and to perform any duty involving the exercise of command."[50]

Although it may be true that the colonel had lost command authority for two years, he did not lose his pay or allowances. While Harry Fleming lost his job, career, money, and benefits, Paul Liles went back to work. Again, what would have happened if both men had the same jury?

≫≪

For collaboration with the enemy, Sgt. William Banghart was sentenced to fifteen years at hard labor. When the convening authority, Lt. Gen. Floyd Parks at 2d Army, received the papers, he concluded that the sentence was too harsh and mercifully reduced the prison term to one year. Banghart was interned at the U.S. Disciplinary Barracks at New Cumberland, Pennsylvania, until his release.[51]

≫≪

Upon being taken to the stockade, Cpl. Tom Bayes remarked, "Well, I guess the Chinks scored another victory."[52] That derogatory epithet not withstanding, a great many of his fellow citizens believed he was right.

Notes

1. Pfc. Rothwell Floyd, USA, Transcripts, 1:11–12, 1:224; Maj. Ronald Alley, USA, Transcripts, 1:349.

2. Floyd Transcripts, 1:3, 1:106; "P.O.W. Conviction Upheld," 5.

3. Floyd Transcripts, 1:54; Cpl. Edward Dickenson, USA, Transcripts, 3:116.

4. Dickenson Transcripts, 1:84, see also 1:23, 2:155, "Army Convicts Dickenson," 1, and "Former Prisoner of War in Korea Appeals," 3.

5. Dickenson Transcripts, 3:49.

6. Ibid., 1:10, 1:16; "Turncoat's Sentence Halved," 27.

7. "Korea Turncoat Ends Jail Term," 21.

8. "Schwable Freed," 1; Lt. Col. Frank Schwable, USMC, Transcripts, 1:exhibit E.

9. "Schwable Freed," 1.

10. "Batchelor Guilty," 8; "Batchelor Awaits Review," 8.

11. Cpl. Claude Batchelor, USA, Transcripts, secret volume, 428.

12. Ibid., 1:480–81; "Batchelor's Life Term Reduced," 12; see also Batchelor Transcripts, 1:140.

13. Batchelor Transcripts, 1:27–28.

14. Floyd Trascripts, 1:5; Batchelor Transcripts, secret volume, 734; "Parole for Turncoat," 7.

15. "Officer Convicted as Collaborator," 1; see also Lt. Col. Harry Fleming, USA, Transcripts, 1:7, 2:68, 2:351 and "For 'Aiding the Enemy,'" 28.

16. "Ex-P.O.W. Colonel to Be Cashiered," 11.

17. Fleming Transcripts, 3:205–6; "Officer Convicted as Collaborator," 1.

18. Fleming Transcripts, 1:90, 1:108, see also 1:74.

19. Ibid., 1:92, 1:109.

20. "Drawing the Line," 28; see also Fleming Transcripts, 1:322.

21. M. Sgt. William Olson, USA, Transcripts, 1:39, see also 1:35 and 1:235–36.

22. Ibid., 1a:1, see also 1a:10, 1:5, 1:9, and 1:22.

23. Ibid., 1:4.

24. Cpl. Harold Dunn, USA, Transcripts, 1:200.

25. Ibid., 1:143, 1:281–82; "Sentence of Ex-P.O.W. Reduced," 3.

26. Dunn Transcripts, 1:72–74.

27. Ibid., 1:62–63, 1:60–61, 1:68–69.

28. Ibid., 1:57–59.

29. Ibid., 1:4; Olson Transcripts, 1:23.

30. Pate, *Reactionary!* 150; see also "Gallagher Gets a Life Sentence," 1.

31. Gallagher Transcripts, 1:1–2, 1a:112.

32. Ibid., 1a:199, 1a:203, 1a:205–6, see also 1a:40 and 1a:112.

33. Ibid., 1a:8, 1a:112.

34. Alley Transcripts, 1:229, 1:311, 1:242, 2:73–81, 2:84, 2:91, 2:289.

35. Ibid., 1:219.

36. Ibid., 1:228.

37. Ibid., 1:79, 1:228, see also 1:94.

38. Ibid., 1:53–55.

39. Ibid., 1:61.

40. Ibid., 9:1401.

41. Ibid., 2:270.

42. Ibid., 1:363.

43. Ibid., 1:361.

44. Ibid., 1:359.

45. Ibid., 1:176. Alley wrote this from the U.S. Disciplinary Barracks at Fort Leavenworth, Kansas, on May 31, 1957.

46. Bayes Transcripts, 7:brief, 29, see also 1:54 and "Ex-P.O.W.'s Sentence Reduced," 24.

47. Bayes Transcripts, 7:brief, 28, 38.

48. Ibid., 1:4.

49. Liles Transcripts, 1:522; "Colonel Guilty," 11.

50. Liles Transcripts, 6:393, 6:404, see also 1:5.

51. Banghart Transcripts, 1:29, 1:38, 1:48, 1:53; "Korea G.I.'s Term Is Reduced," 3.

52. Banghart Transcripts, 2:66, see also 2:70.

EPILOGUE

We do have certain evidence that indicates there are additional prisoners alive who should be returned.

　　—Gen. Mark Clark, 1953

There are no intelligence indicators that U.S. personnel from the Korean Conflict were not returned to U.S. control at the end of the war.

　　—Rear Adm. Donald Marryott, 1990

"New Account Adds to the Mystery about the Fate of American P.O.W.'s in North Korea."

　　—*New York Times*, 1996

Operations Little Switch and Big Switch* made former captives free men, and by air and sea GIs made their way back to the United States. Through documents, I made the return as well. Four million dead (half of them civilians) were left behind, along with destroyed cities, and, according to recently declassified papers, sixty-six of their comrades. I have not conducted research concerning nonrepatriates because that topic was

---

* Between April 20 and April 26, 1953, Operation Little Switch took place, wherein sick and wounded UN prisoners were released. Of these, 149 were Americans. Operation Big Switch commenced on August 5, 1953, took a month to complete, and returned an additional 3,597 U.S. soldiers, sailors, and airmen to UN control.

not the focus of this book. Many knowledgeable people, however, testify that hundreds, even thousands, of American men were left behind. Although limited on that topic, previously classified records reveal beyond doubt that at least sixty-six men were held back by the Chinese.[1]

After the war, some eight thousand GIs were unaccounted for, a number that first appeared in early August 1953 at the beginning of Operation Big Switch. The *New York Times* reported on August 8 that "Gen. James A. Van Fleet, retired commander of the United States Eighth Army in Korea, estimated tonight that a large percentage of the eight thousand American soldiers listed as missing in Korea were alive." That estimate seems premature, however, because Operation Big Switch was not completed until a month later. General Van Fleet was apparently trusting prisoner lists that were swapped between the parties before the actual transfer of captives. The eight thousand number still appears and with no reduction. Col. Harry Summers, a military historian, has concluded that the majority of the eight thousand missing in action were due to combat conditions. Some bodies could not be recovered because of explosions; others were lost on the battlefield. Furthermore, in a war such as that in Korea (a country with rugged terrain), heavy casualties and unexplained losses can result from rapid retreats and advances. Still, American men were left behind.[2]

>≪

No U.S. Army personnel are among the sixty-six government-documented, nonvoluntary, nonrepatriates. All were air force, with the exception of twelve civilians and eleven from the U.S. Navy and Coast Guard. Possibly excepting civilians, the men were considered by the Chinese as spies on intelligence-gathering missions. If, as the Chinese say, Americans in airplanes did engage in intelligence-gathering over China and the former Soviet Union's territory, then, under the terms of the armistice, those individuals did not qualify to be released with men captured either fighting on Korean soil or flying above it.

But an airman did not have to be in the intelligence arena to be retained; it was enough that the Chinese suspected intelligence-gathering. No matter whether officers or enlisted personnel, aviators, both air force and marine, were held. In one case, a U.S. Army artillery officer, a passenger in a downed airplane, was roundly interrogated. If you fell from the sky, you had a problem. Capt. John Patrick Flynn, USMC, had been shot down in mid–1952, for example, and was questioned at Col. Frank Schwable's court of inquiry:

A. I was pulled out of the compound on 16 July, 1953 and taken to a camp. I think it was Camp 3 and remained under interrogation [by the Chinese] until 16 August, 1953.
Q. That being after the war was over, 16 August?
A. Yes, that was three weeks or so after the war was over, I believe.
Q. During this period, how did they interrogate you?
A. This period it was intensive germ warfare. They wanted my confession and that they were going to get it, whether they got it within a month, a year, or twenty years.[3]

Flynn did not confess to his interrogators and was later repatriated.

It would seem beyond reason that the Chinese (or North Koreans) could retain hundreds of men without being confronted. When Captain Flynn was removed from his compound, for example, others no doubt witnessed that event. At least they knew he was missing the following day. Paul Liles had insisted just before release that names of the missing be memorized and then secreted the names so he could report them when he reached UN jurisdiction.

The testimony of Lt. Col. John McLaughlin, USMC, at the Schwable inquiry further supports the fact that the captors could not take a man away unnoticed: "One of our major complaints at [the] time [of Little Switch] was the method in which [the Chinese] carried out the repatriation of sick and wounded. There was a one-legged Air Force officer in our camp who had been taken out of the camp presumably to be repatriated and he was not repatriated as we knew it. At least we had sufficient reason to think he was not."[4]

Upon release, the names of men known to be alive, such as the Air Force officer, were furnished to the proper authorities for further investigation. Although record-keeping in POW camps was minimal, it would still appear unlikely that the enemy could keep hundreds upon hundreds of prisoners (some say thousands) without challenge.

On March 5, 1954 (seven months after the armistice), an important confidential letter addressed to a Mr. Nash, assistant secretary of defense, from Walter S. Robertson, assistant secretary of state, confirmed that eighteen Air Force and eleven U.S. Navy and Coast Guard personnel still remained Chinese prisoners. Robertson said, "On September 12, 1953, communist correspondent Burchett indicated that the Chinese Communists continue to retain in a non-prisoner of war status certain United States Air Force personnel, alleged to have overflown Chinese territory, and stated that their return must be sought through diplomatic negotiations. Subsequent Peiping radio broadcasts have given similar indications."[5]

If eleven U.S. Navy and Coast Guard captives were not repatriated and continued to be prisoners in 1954, where had they come from and why were they not repatriated? The UN command in Korea consisted of all ground and air forces but not naval. The navy was coordinated operationally with, but totally independent of, the UN command structure. The only major exception was Colonel Schwable's 1st Marine Aircraft Wing, which was under operational command and control of the 5th Air Force, Korea.

A 5th Air Force "Operation Order and Task Organization" document previously classified as "Secret: Security Information," states in a section on naval forces that one aircraft carrier (either a CVL or CVE), with one squadron of aircraft aboard, was always in operation as a task element "of the West Coast Blockade and Patrol Group." Further, "Navy PBMs, P2Vs, P4Ys, and RAF Sunderlands furnish[ed] air patrol reconnaissance of the SEA OF JAPAN, the YELLOW SEA, TSUSHIMA STRAITS, and waters off the CHINA COAST and FORMOSA." Why naval forces were so close to the Chinese mainland can possibly be explained by another "Secret: Security Information" paper. According to "Naval Forces Far East, Operation Order and Task Organization," "United Nations operations have so far been limited to KOREA and its territorial waters, but the possibility exists that such operations may be directed against Communist forces on the mainland of CHINA. (No information is currently available as to possible modification of the directive if and when UN action against Communist forces in China is initiated.)"[6]

Because the document was a contingency plan for a direct attack on China, naval forces had to be in place, and continual reconnaissance of proposed attack areas was necessary. In flying over an enemy's sovereign territory, however, one can expect an attack. If shot down, a crew must hope to be rescued by friendly forces.

According to one scenario, on January 18, 1953, a Navy P2V patrol aircraft was shot down near Swatow, a coastal city on the Chinese mainland directly across the South China Sea from the southern half of Formosa (now Taiwan).* A U.S. Coast Guard seaplane crashed while attempting to rescue the navy crew. Both crews were captured, and those eleven sailors were not repatriated—the navy crew of the P2V and the Coast Guard crew of the downed seaplane.[7] The March 5, 1954, letter to Nash of the Department of Defense from Walter Robertson of the State Department described a plan to have the eleven sailors released. The British government should negotiate with China on behalf of the United States and "on behalf of eleven non-United Nations command United States Naval and Coast Guard personnel missing as a result of two plane crashes off Swatow on January 18, 1953."[8]

><

During 1954 the United States seemed to be focused on eighteen airmen who were not released; the eleven sailors and twelve civilians were virtually ignored (and remained ignored) in the documents. Forty-one unaccounted-for U.S. citizens were thus known with a fair degree of certainty to be alive.

1st Lt. Roland Parks, flying an F-86 Sabrejet, was shot down over "MiG Alley" (south of the Yalu River) on September 4, 1952. China, however, would not release him and claimed that he flew over the Yalu River into Manchuria and was downed in Chinese territory. The same goes for 1st Lt. Lyle W. Cameron, shot down on October 26, 1952; Lt. Col. Edwin Heller, shot down on January 23, 1953; and Capt. Harold Fischer, downed on April 7, 1953. Whatever the circumstances, the four fighter pilots were not repatriated. The Chinese contended that all four had overflown Chinese territory and been captured; thus they were not considered legitimate prisoners of war. To complete the total of eighteen, the remaining fourteen airmen apparently came from one aircraft, a B-29 commanded by Col. John K. Arnold on a "weather reconnaissance mission" when

---

* Some accounts say off Formosa, which is incorrect.

shot down over northeastern China on January 13, 1953. The total crew numbered fourteen. Three were killed during the shoot-down, but eleven survived.[9]

>«

Forty-one Americans remained in captivity: twelve civilians, eleven U.S. Navy/Coast Guard personnel, and eighteen from the air force. The government's focus, however, was to negotiate for the eighteen airmen: four fighter pilots and the crew of the B-29. The crew, however, had only eleven survivors. It is uncertain whether the three additional names in the documents are those of the three men killed during the B-29 shoot-down or three other individuals. They were two first lieutenants and an airman first class and most likely part of Arnold's crew. What was of concern was how to negotiate for the men. The United States had no diplomatic relations with China at the time, so a conduit (the British) had to be used. The Chinese would have welcomed a U.S. overture, which would have signaled tacit recognition of communist China as a diplomatic equal.

On April 6, 1954, a short memorandum from the Office of the Secretary of the Air Force to an assistant secretary of defense stated, "The Department of the Air Force concurs in the proposal to accept the offer of the British Government to approach the Chinese Government in an effort to secure the release of all United Nations personnel held as political prisoners. The persons on the attached list have been propagandized as political prisoners in China." The list contained the name, grade, and service number of the four fighter pilots (Heller, Parks, Fischer, and Cameron) and the crew of Colonel Arnold's B-29—twelve officers and six enlisted men. Why the list did not contain the names of civilians (most likely diplomats) and navy and coast guard personnel is unexplained other than the fact they were not under UN command. The names were handed over to the British, who then attempted to negotiate the release of the men at the Geneva Conference in 1954.[10]

The eighteen-name list was not made public but was declassified on February 1, 1985, at my request. Somehow, however, word got out to *Air Force Magazine* that fifteen air force personnel were known to be alive. The periodical went public with the story in November 1954. The publication seemed furious about the manner in which the men were being handled. One reason they remained in captivity, according to *Air Force Magazine,* was because the Chinese wanted "to force the United States to recognize the Peiping government and to support its bid for admission to the UN in exchange for giving up our men. . . . There is little doubt but that our government could buy them back immediately by recognizing Red China and supporting its admission to the UN. Is this price too high? The United States position has been that it is too expensive." In a final volley, the article concluded, "In a sense, the fifteen are victims of our national dilemma. We have only ourselves to blame for their imprisonment."[11]

>«

On January 2, 1953, about a week and a half before Colonel Arnold went down, either a B-29 or B-50 was destroyed, apparently over China.* There were thirteen survivors. Almost two years later a message arrived in Washington. An "announcement [had been made] by Peiping Radio this morning [November 4, 1954] that thirteen Americans, including Far East Air Force (FEAF) personnel, had been sentenced to prison terms for espionage." The Chinese said that the aircraft had been assigned to "the 581st Aerial Resupply and Communications Wing, FEAF." The wing, based on Okinawa, had the primary mission of resupplying outlying FEAF units, and such aircraft never overfly "enemy or unfriendly territory." On January 2, 1953, however, the crew of the huge aircraft had been "on [a] leaflet dropping mission."[12]

Primary documents show that one other airplane was downed, which brings the known total to sixty-six captured and unrepatriated.** On July 29, 1953, an RB-50 attached to the 343d Strategic Reconnaissance Squadron with a crew of seventeen was downed over Vladivostok. Five men were rescued by friendly craft. The remaining twelve crewmen were last seen huddled in two groups, with nine Russian patrol craft heading toward them at full speed. Frederick Ayer, Jr., special assistant to the secretary of the air force, stated that the information about the shoot-down "was to be handled with great delicacy."[13]

---

* This aircraft is unmentioned in any secondary source used herein. The only information is contained in an incoming message from Far East Air Force through the Staff Message Division, Department of the Air Force, and directed to a Brig. Gen. Brooke Allen (Nov. 24, 1954).

** "Known total" only relates to the primary documents in my possession and not to possible other sources. There may be many more.

According to a Rand Corporation study, "The United States conducted routine peripheral surveillance of the Soviet Union using a variety of aircraft and intelligence collection techniques." Not until April 8, 1950, however, just a little over two months before the outbreak of hostilities, did the Soviet Union (and apparently China) "adopt . . . a more hostile and aggressive air defense policy" that continued throughout the conflict.[14]

The British, acting as a conduit for the release of prisoners in China (and possibly the Soviet Union) in 1954, created a problem, however, in classifying the men.* They could not be labeled "prisoners of war," because all negotiations for repatriation of POWs had to be funneled through the facility of the Military Armistice Commission. Nor would "missing in action" do because they were not missing and that label continued to keep them as members of the Armed Forces, although the Chinese considered them spies. The United States also contemplated "paper killing" them. In a memorandum of January 16, 1954, to the secretary of the army from an assistant secretary on the topic of "The Unaccounted-For Americans Believed to Be Still Held Illegally by the Communists," it was stated "to continue to carry these personnel in a 'missing' status is costing over one million dollars annually. It may become necessary at some future date to drop them from our records as 'missing and presumed dead.'"[15]

The confusion had been straightened out by July 8, 1954, when Frederick Ayer, Jr., special assistant to the secretary of the air force, wrote to Sen. Charles Potter, enclosing "a brief (not complete case histories and investigations) of circumstances surrounding the missing in action status and subsequent change of status under the provisions of Public Law 490 as amended (The Missing Persons Act)."[16] The men were now "missing persons," a category apparently acceptable to all concerned.

≫≪

All seemed quiet as the summer of 1954 passed into fall. Negotiations were taking place behind closed doors for the release of the airmen and likely

---

* "The men" refers to the list of eighteen air force personnel. All documents, with the exception of the March 5, 1954, Robertson to Nash letter, only mention UN Command people whom the British would be negotiating for and not civilians or U.S. Navy/Coast Guard personnel, who were not within that command structure.

for others still remaining in captivity. In November, however, came a bombshell: "Forgotten Fifteen: American Eagles in a Bamboo Cage" was published in *Air Force Magazine*. Edmund Hogan, the author, somehow (no doubt covertly) garnered through confidential sources within the Department of the Air Force that four fighter pilots and most of Colonel Arnold's crew were still alive. He did not know about the civilians and navy people, or about the other twenty-eight Air Force personnel, but he went public with what he had. Doing so created a storm of activity within the Pentagon. Although the vast majority of the article was background material about the fifteen airmen, the cat was out of the bag. There was positive proof that nonvoluntary nonrepatriates were being held in bamboo cages. The Air Force Association, which publishes *Air Force Magazine,* sent a telegram to the secretary of the Air Force:

> Date/Time Stamp
> 1954 Nov 26 PM 4 52
>
> LDDOO3 DL PD
> Washington DC 26
>
> Hon Harold E. Talbott
> Secretary of the Air Force WashDC 4
>
> In behalf of the Air Force Association, I have sent today the following telegram to President Eisenhower, with copies to the press, all members of Congress, and the governors of each state. Text follows:
>
>> The Air Force Association has been deeply concerned about United States Air Force personnel and other Americans still held as prisoners by Red China. As evidence of this concern the association printed in the November issue of *Air Force* magazine, its official journal, a special report including pictures of the eleven airmen who have in the last few days been given long and severe prison sentences by Red China. We have been informed through sources which we believe to be correct that these men were shot down over Korea, not Red China. The motto of a famous Air Force fighter group is "We Take Care of Our Own." The Air Force Association believes that this is an appropriate motto for our nation at this time. We know you share our feeling that these men must be released. This message is to assure you that the Air Force Association stands behind whatever action, no matter how strong, you may take to obtain the release of every American held in the prisons of Red China. We believe time is of the essence.

We respectfully enlist your support in efforts to obtain the release of these Americans.

John R Allison President Air Force Assn.[17]

The leak (or leaks) at the Pentagon had to stop, and a few weeks after the telegram and article President Dwight D. Eisenhower gave a direct order:

CONFIDENTIAL

THE SECRETARY OF DEFENSE
WASHINGTON

December 16, 1954

MEMORANDUM FOR: The Secretary of the Army
The Secretary of the Navy
The Secretary of the Air Force

I have just received a memorandum from the President which I will quote below:

"I would like to suggest that there be the least possible talking about the 'captive airmen' until all of the negotiations in which the State Department and the United Nations are now engaged can have reached fruition. Anything said now by any individual in authority could easily so exacerbate the situation as to damage the efforts being made for the recovery of these airmen."

Please inform all of the senior civilian and military in your Department of the substance of this memorandum and direct that they take appropriate action in any public statements that they might make on this, and govern themselves accordingly.

Signed
C. E. Wilson

cc: Assistant Secretary of Defense
(Legislative and Public Affairs)

CONFIDENTIAL[18]

It was over. At this point the documents stopped, and from 1956 on nothing appeared. There may be, however, yet another carton continuing the paper trail from January 1956, possibly in a dusty corner of the National Archives. An energetic reseacher may not have too much trouble contacting the archives and continuing the search for Americans who may possibly still remain in bamboo cages.

>«

Since 1954 the families of many missing from the Korean War have looked for loved ones. Private organizations have cropped up, Congress has investigated, government-sponsored departments have been established, and American citizens have visited North Korea—all, it appears, for naught.[19] It seems that the United States has taken the position of "let's get on with our lives," and both China and North Korea have consistently denied holding anyone with the exception of those accused of spying.

In 1991 apparently four different government agencies shared responsibility in the search for missing servicemen, not only in Korea but also in Vietnam. In a "Dear Colleague" letter dated May 23, 1991, Sen. Jesse Helms of North Carolina, having completed a report entitled *An Examination of U. S. Policy toward POW/MIAs,* blasted the agencies involved in the MIA search:

> On October 29, [1990], I released an interim report prepared by the Minority Staff of the Senate Committee on Foreign Relations based upon an ongoing investigation of the POW/MIA issue. . . . [This report] was an attempt to ascertain whether the agencies of the U.S. government responsible for POW/MIAs were doing the job they were supposed to do—that is, to find any POW/MIAs who might still be alive.
>
> The interim conclusions are very disturbing. After examining hundreds of documents relating to the raw intelligence, and interviewing many families and friends of POW/MIAs, the Minority Staff concluded that, despite public pronouncements to the contrary, the real, internal policy of the U.S. government was to act upon the presumption that all MIAs were dead.
>
> As a result, the Minority Staff found, any evidence that suggested an MIA might be alive was uniformly and arbitrarily rejected, and all efforts were directed towards finding and identifying remains of dead personnel, even though the U.S. government's techniques of identification were inadequate and deeply flawed.[20]

One innocent person caught in the web of intrigue concerning missing servicemen was Col. Millard A. Peck, Infantry, U.S. Army. Colonel Peck, a Vietnam veteran, was chief of the Special Office for Prisoners of War and Missing in Action (POW-MIA). Although he attempted to do his best, he was frustrated. On February 12, 1991, he not only resigned his position but also resigned from the army. Some comments in the colonel's letter of resignation were scathing:

Motivation. My initial acceptance of this posting was based upon . . . persistent rumors of American servicemen having been abandoned in Indochina, and that the Government was conducting a "cover-up" so as not to be embarrassed. I was curious about this and thought that serving as the Chief of POW-MIA would be an opportunity to satisfy my own interest and help clear the Government's name. . . .

Highest National Priority. That National leaders continue to address the prisoner of war and missing in action issue as the "highest national priority" is a travesty. . . .

The Mindset to Debunk. . . . Rarely has there been any effective, active follow through on any of the sightings, nor is there a responsive "action arm" to routinely and aggressively pursue leads. . . .

Duty, Honor and Integrity. It appears that the entire issue is being manipulated by unscrupulous people in the Government, or associated with the Government. Some are using the issue [of MIAs] for personal or political advantage and others use it as a forum to perform and feel important, or worse. The sad fact, however, is that this issue is being controlled and a cover-up may be in progress. The entire charade [of attempting to find MIAs] does not appear to be an honest effort, and may never have been.

POW-MIA Officers Abandoned. . . . Any military officer expected to survive in this environment [as chief of the POW-MIA Office] would have to be myopic, an accomplished sycophant, or totally insouciant. . . .

One Final Vietnam Casualty. So ends the war and my last grand crusade, like it actually did end, I guess. However, as they say in the Legion, "je ne regrette rien." For all of the above, I respectfully request to be relieved of my duties as Chief of the Special Office for Prisoners of War and Missing in Action.

A Farewell to Arms. So as to avoid the annoyance of being shipped off to some remote corner, out of sight and out of the way, in my own "bamboo cage" of silence somewhere, I further request that the Defense Intelligence Agency, which I have attempted to serve loyally and with honor, assist me in being retired immediately from active military service.[21]

In July 1993 a single office was established and charged with the responsibility for all missing service personnel: the Defense Prisoner of War/ Missing in Action Office (DPMO). Edward W. Ross, the acting deputy assistant secretary of defense (POW/MIA affairs), described the function of DPMO as "designed to offer more efficient and effective control over

POW/MIA affairs worldwide."[22] Hundreds upon hundreds of families took a wait-and-see attitude.

≫≪

During the hot summer of 1952, Sgt. Philip Mandra, USMC, was on duty at Outpost Bronco, ready to alert the main entrenchment on a mountain in North Korea (code-named Hook) of any enemy activity within his area. On August 7, 1952, his family was formally notified by the Department of the Navy that Mandra was missing in action. For decades, Irene Mandra, his sister, has searched for him.

A number of private organizations have been founded for the purpose of locating missing loved ones. One of the larger groups in the United States is the Coalition of Families of Korean and Cold War POW/MIAs. The group's mission statement stresses that the coalition is "dedicated to the fullest possible accounting for our missing servicemen." Irene Mandra has been an officer of the organization. The coalition is a fine source of information about missing service personnel and has details on who was, or was not, released. For example, from Irene Mandra's material, I discovered that three of the four fighter pilots (Parks, Heller, and Fischer) were repatriated on May 31, 1955.[23] The group can be contacted at Coalition Headquarters, P.O. Box 7152, Roanoke, VA 24019-0152. The telephone numbers are (540) 366-6681 or (516) 694-0989, and the Fax numbers are (540) 366-5893 or (516) 694-8438. The coalition can be reached online at info@coalitionoffamilies.org, and a large Web site is at <http://www.coalitionoffamilies.org>.

≫≪

They answered the call.
They were willing to fight for their country.
They knew they might die.
They never imagined they might be left behind.
    —Coalition of Families

To walk on another country's land—armed and unescorted—is an invasion. To fly over its territory—armed and uninvited—is an invasion. To sail on its seas—armed and unannounced—is an invasion. Scripture tells us "that the way of the transgressor is hard." It is equally hard for the families of those lost men and for the citizens of a nation, who send troops into battle not knowing. Many would say that it would be easier to know whether they were dead than to know nothing. Imagination grows ripe picturing a then-twenty-year-old son now an old, gray-haired man, stooped and wearing black pajamas, walking through a rice field somewhere in China or North Korea. Is he married? Does he have children? Is he fluent in Mandarin? Can he still speak English? Does he remember his mother or father, his sister or brother? Does he cry? I know they do.

Notes

1. Office of Sen. Bob Smith, "Chronology of Policy and Intelligence Matters."

2. U.S. Senate Committee on Foreign Relations Republican Staff, *An Examination of U.S. Policy toward POW/MIAs,* sec. 4–1; Joint Commission Support Branch, Research and Analysis Division, DPMO, *Transfer of U.S. Korean War POWs to the Soviet Union,* 56; Summers, *Korean War Almanac,* 165; "Eight Thousand Missing, Van Fleet Says."

3. Col. Frank Schwable, USMC, Transcripts, 2:527–28. Many pages of the three-volume Schwable transcript, as with the army transcripts, were missing because they were classified. The Schwable citations in this Epilogue are from the previously classified pages.

4. Ibid., 1:370–71.

5. NA, 76, 88–89; Office of Sen. Bob Smith, "Chronology," 13. The letter from Robertson to Nash was declassified on February 1, 1985, at my request.

6. Schwable Transcripts, 3:1189–90, 3:1192.

7. Cole, "World War II, Korean War, and Early Cold War MIA-POW Issues," 109; Office of Sen. Bob Smith, "Chronology," 9, 26.

8. NA, 88–89.

9. Hogan, "Forgotten Fifteen," 23–28. Schwable Transcripts, 1:787.

10. NA, 81–82.

11. Hogan, "Forgotten Fifteen," 28. The author of the study was not privy to the list of eighteen, which was not declassified until nearly twenty-eight years later. The information in the article came from contacts within the Pentagon.

12. NA, 8; Schwable Trascripts, 2:787. During the Schwable investigation, Col. Arthur F. Binney, chief of staff of the 1st Marine Aircraft Wing until May 1952, had testified: "Q. How about leaflets dropped? A. I think those that were made there were made in the small OY or OE types, those are the only ones I had knowledge of immediately in front of the lines" (ibid.).

13. NA, 46; Office of Sen. Bob Smith, "Chronology," 11; Cole, "World War II, Korean War, and Early Cold War MIA-POW Issues," 109, 120, 122.

14. Cole, "World War II, Korean War, and Early Cold War MIA-POW Issues," 103.

15. Office of Sen. Bob Smith, "Chronology," 18.

16. NA, 45. Sen. Charles Potter held a brief investigation on nonrepatriated POWs and was chair of what was commonly known as the Potter Committee. His

official function was "Chairman, Special Subcommittee on Korean Atrocities, Committee on Government Operations, United States Senate." Potter had threatened to go public with the information he had, which Washington did not want him to do. From primary documents, it is evident that the Air Force successfully attempted to stonewall his efforts.

17. Ibid., 6.

18. Ibid., 132.

19. Why the focus should be on North Korea rather than China is puzzling. The United States had been essentially at war with China since November 1950, and China (not North Korea) held the prisoners. Although North Korea has allowed Americans to dig into North Korean soil to seek the bodies of the missing, that digging has been conducted at the wrong place. North Koreans, meanwhile, have become angrier and angrier with each new investigation. According to the *New York Times* (Sept. 8, 1996, 10), North Korea has said that "the accusation[s] 'has seriously gotten on our nerves.' . . . if America pursues the issue, North Korea might revoke its permission for joint excavations now under way to search for bodies of American flyers killed during the war." Perhaps further investigation should center on China.

20. U.S. Senate Committee on Foreign Relations Republican Staff, *An Examination of U.S. Policy toward POW/MIAs,* Introduction; Peters, "Endless Search," 26–31.

21. U.S. Senate Committee on Foreign Relations Republican Staff, *An Examination of U.S. Policy toward POW/MIAs,* secs. 10–1 through 10–5.

22. Peters, "Endless Search," 26; Joint Commission Support Branch, Research and Analysis Division, *Transfer of U.S. Korean War POWs to the Soviet Union,* Edward W. Ross letter.

23. Joint Commission Support Branch, Research and Analysis Division, *Transfer of U.S. Korean War POWs to the Soviet Union,* 68. Irene Mandra must be thanked separately for her cooperation—and patience—in helping with this section of the book.

APPENDIX A

Transcript of a Written Appeal Allegedly Made by M. Sgt. William Olson in New Life *at Camp 10 (ca. Jan. 19, 1951)*

Friends, members of the Korean People's Army, the Chinese Volunteers, and British and Americans.

We are gathered here to celebrate our liberation by the North Korean Forces.

We were led to believe by our propaganda that capture meant being crippled, blinded, or, at least death. Instead, we have been given kind treatment—good food and warm clothing—to help us withstand the bitter cold of the North Korean winter. Our wounds and sickness have been given good medical care and the badly wounded were sent to hospitals. All we were told about capture was lies made by the warmongers and imperialists of the U.S.

Our hands are stained with blood, the blood of an innocent people. I am ashamed of this. We were told by the capitalists and imperialists of our government that we were to fight to preserve peace in the Pacific. Instead we brought ruin, death, and destruction to a peace-loving people. We destroyed their homes and caused them untold misery and unhappiness.

Who is to blame? I say we, the men here who have been liberated, are to blame. We listened to the warmongers and their lies and let them lead us blindly into a war that was none of our business. It is true the actual blame lies with the capitalists and imperialists of the US but we are equally guilty.

We were lied to, cheated, and deceived by our government but thanks to the kindness and generosity of our captors, we have learned the truth. They have taught us the facts and have shown us the true state of affairs.

Now, how can we repay the Chinese and Korean people for what they have done for us? We can never pay the price of their misery and unhappiness, but we can in some small measure do our part to make amends.

We can study their teachings and learn all there is to learn about the truth. One big thing we can do is this—we can draw up an appeal to the United Nations to accept the three-point proposal of the Chinese Peoples' Government. This is the only thing that can bring complete peace to the Pacific. It is the only way to end this war and permit the Korean People to have their right to peace and happiness.

We should all sign the appeal and send it to the United Nations Security Council. In this way we can in a small way repay the Korean and Chinese people. This is all. I thank you.

Source: M. Sgt. William Olson, USA, Transcripts, 1:27–28.

APPENDIX B

Code of Conduct of the United States of America

Article I

I am an American, fighting in the forces which guard my country and our way of life. I am prepared to give my life in their defense.

Article II

I will never surrender of my own free will. If in command, I will never surrender the members of my command while they still have the means to resist.

Article III

If I am captured I will continue to resist by all means available. I will make every effort to escape and to aid others to escape. I will accept neither parole nor special favors from the enemy.

Article IV

If I become a prisoner of war, I will keep faith with my fellow prisoners. I will give no information nor take part in any action which might be harmful to my comrades. If I am senior, I will take command. If not, I will obey lawful orders of those appointed over me and will back them in every way.

Article V

When questioned, should I become a prisoner of war, I am required to give name, rank, service number, and date of birth. I will evade answering further questions to the utmost of my ability. I will make no oral or written statements disloyal to my country or its allies or harmful to their cause.

Article VI

I will never forget that I am an American, fighting for freedom, responsible for my actions, and dedicated to the principles which made my country free. I will trust in my God and in the United States of America.

»«

The massive indoctrination and subsequent collaboration of Korean War POWs mandated that the education of servicemen be more intense than the usual training to furnish only name, rank, and service number to the enemy. Statistics have underlined the fact that very few can successfully stave off a captor with only name, rank, and service number while under acute mental and physical torture. Something better, something more tangible and realistic, had to be put in place. Hence, the Code of Conduct.

On August 17, 1955, about the time the last of the U.S. Army courts-martial proceedings were winding down, Dwight D. Eisenhower signed the Code into law. In 1977 Jimmy Carter modified it somewhat by changing one word in Article V and deleting another. Article V had initially read "I am bound to only give." The word *bound* was changed to *required,* and the word *only* was omitted. The president and the services agreed that these two subtle revisions made the Code "more reasonable."

The Code is self-explanatory, and the military is divided over whether it serves a purpose. It should be remembered, however, that the one-page document is given to frightened eighteen-year-olds in boot camp. They are told to read and attend a class on it and likely will never see (or remember) it again during the rest of their military careers. There must be a foundation, however, on behavior as a prisoner, and the Code of Conduct is the best that has been developed up to this time.

Finally, the officer corps is responsible for the behavior of troops in captivity. Officers must be thoroughly versed in what can and cannot be done under the guidance of the Code. That, of course, is easier said than done, but that is why they are officers.

APPENDIX C

Transcript of Deposition by
Col. Frank H. Schwable

I am Colonel Frank H. Schwable, 04429, and was Chief of Staff of the First Marine Aircraft Wing until shot down and captured on July 8, 1952.

My service with the Marine Corps began in 1929 and I was designated an aviator in 1931, seeing duty in many parts of the world. Just before I came to Korea, I completed a tour of duty in the Division of Aviation at Marine Corps headquarters.

Directive of the Joint Chiefs of Staff

I arrived in Korea on April 10, 1952, to take over my duties as Chief of Staff of the First Marine Aircraft Wing. All my instructions and decisions were subject to confirmation by the Assistant Commanding General, Lamson-Scribner. Just as I assumed full responsibility for the duties of Chief of Staff, General Lamson-Scribner called me into his office to talk over various problems of the wing. During this conversation he said: "Has Binney given you all the background on the special mission run by V.M.F. 513?" I asked him if he meant "Suprop" (our code name for bacteriological bombs) and he confirmed this. I told him I had been given all of the background by Colonel Binney.

Colonel Arthur F. Binney, the officer I relieved as Chief of Staff, had given me, as his duties required that he should, an outline of the general plan of bacteriological warfare in Korea and the details of the part played, up to that time, by the First Marine Aircraft Wing.

The general plan for bacteriological warfare in Korea was directed by the United States Joint Chiefs of Staff in October, 1951. In that month the Joint Chiefs of Staff sent a directive, by hand, to the Commanding General, Far East Command (at that time General Ridgway), directing the initiation of bacteriological warfare in Korea on an initially small experimental stage, but in expanding proportions.

This directive was passed to the Commanding General, Far East Air Force, General Weyland, in Tokyo. General Weyland then called into personal conference General Everest, Commanding General of the Fifth Air Force in Korea, and also the Commander of the 19th Bomb Wing in Okinawa, which unit operates directly under F.E.A.F.

The plan that I shall now outline was gone over, the broad aspects of the problem were agreed upon and the following information was brought back to Korea by General Everest, personally and verbally, since for security purposes, it was decided not to have anything in writing on this matter in Korea.

Objectives

The basic objective was at that time to test, under field conditions, the various elements of bacteriological warfare, and gradually to expand the field tests, at a later date, into an element of the regular combat operations, depending on the results obtained and the situation in Korea.

The effectiveness of the different diseases available was to be tested, especially for their spreading of epidemic qualities under various circumstances, and to test whether each disease caused a serious disruption to enemy operations and civilian routine or just minor inconveniences, or was contained completely, causing no difficulties.

Various types of armament or containers were to be tried out under field conditions and various types of aircraft were to be used to test their suitability as bacteriological bomb vehicles.

Terrain types to be tested included high areas, sea coast areas, open spaces, areas enclosed by mountains, isolated areas, areas relatively adjacent to one another, large and small towns and cities, congested cities and those relatively spread out. Every possible type or combination of areas was to be tested.

These experiments were to continue for an indefinite period which would make it possible to carry them out in the most diversified meteorological conditions found in Korea.

All possible methods of delivery were to be tested as well as tactics developed to include initially, night attacks and then expanding into day attacks by specialized squadrons. Various types of bombing were to be tried out and various combinations of bombing, from single planes up to and including formations of planes, were to be tried out with bacteriological bombs used in conjunction with conventional bombs. Enemy reactions were particularly to be tested or observed by any means available to ascertain what his counter-measures would be, what propaganda steps he would take, and to what extent his military operations would be affected by this type of warfare.

Security measures were to be thoroughly tested—both friendly and enemy. On the friendly side, all possible steps were to be taken to confine knowledge of the use of this weapon and to control information on the subject. On the enemy side, every possible means were to be used to deceive the enemy and prevent his actual proof that the weapon was being used.

Finally, if the situation warranted, while continuing the experimental phase of bacteriological warfare according to the Joint Chiefs of Staff directive, it might be expanded to become part of the military or tactical effort in Korea.

Initial Stage

The B.29s from Okinawa began using bacteriological bombs in November 1951, covering targets all over North Korea in what might be called random bombing. One night the target might be in Northeast Korea and the next night, Northwest Korea. Their bacteriological bomb operations were conducted in combination with normal night armed reconnaissance as a measure of economy and security.

Early in January 1952, General Schilt, then Commanding General of the First Marine Aircraft Wing, was called to the Fifth Air Force H.Q. in Seoul, where General Everest told him of the directive issued by the joint C.G.S. and ordered him to have V.M.F. 513—Marine Night Fighter Squadron 513 of the Marine Aircraft Group 33 of the First Marine Aircraft Wing—participate in the germ warfare programme. V.M.F. 513 was based on K8, the air force base at Kunsan of the Third Bomb Wing, whose B.26s had already begun bacteriological operations. V.M.F. 513 was to be serviced by the Third Bomb Wing.

At that time, all the aircraft of the Marine Corps (combat type) based on the Korean coast were under the direct command of the Fifth Air Force and the First Marine Aircraft Wing was constantly informed of all their operations; whenever new flights were undertaken or old ones continued in connexion with the programme for bacterial warfare, the Fifth Air Force Command usually informed the Aircraft Wing beforehand.

By the end of January 1952, night fighters of the 513th Squadron making isolated night reconnaissance flights and conducting operations in connexion with bacterial bombs shared their targets and objectives with the B–26 bombers, which operated in the southern part of North Korea and concentrated mainly on its western regions. The 513th Squadron co-ordinated its operations in all these flights with the Third Bomb Wing, using "F7F" (Tiger Cat) aircraft for these operations, because of their twin-engine safety.

K.8 (Kunsan) offered the advantage of a take-off directly over the water, in the event of engine failure, and both the safety and security of over-water flights to enemy territory.

For security reasons, no information on the types of bacteria being used was given to the First Marine Aircraft Wing.

In March 1952, General Schilt was again called to the Fifth Air Force headquarters and verbally directed by General Everest to prepare Marine Photographic Squadron One (V.M.J. 1 Squadron) of Marine Aircraft Group 33 to enter the programme. V.M.J. 1 based at K.3, Marine Aircraft Group 33's base at Pohang, Korea, was to use F2H–2P Photographic Reconnaissance Aircraft (Banshees).

The missions would be intermittent and combined with normal photographic missions and would be scheduled by the Fifth Air Force in separate, top secret orders.

The Banshees were brought into the programme because of their specialized operations, equipment facilities and isolated area of operations at K.3. They could penetrate further into North Korea as far as the enemy counter-action was concerned and worked in two plane sections involving a minimum of crews and disturbance of normal missions. They could also try out bombing from high altitudes in horizontal flight in conjunction with photographic runs.

During March 1952, the Banshees of the Marine Photographic Squadron One, commenced bacteriological operations, continuing and expanding the bacteriological bombing of North Korean towns, always combining these operations with normal photographic missions. Only a minimum of bomb supplies were kept on hand to reduce storage problems and the Fifth Air Force sent a team of two officers and several men to K.3 (Pohang) to instruct the marine specialists in handing the bombs.

The Navy's part in the programme was with the F.9F (Panthers) AD (Skyraiders) and standard-type F2H (Banshees) aircraft, which, unlike the aircraft of the type used for photographic reconnaissance, were based on aircraft carriers operating along the east coast of Korea.

The Air Force also extended its operations, using squadrons of various types of aircraft, using various operational methods and tactics of bacterial warfare.

Such was the situation on the eve of my arrival in Korea. The important events described below then took place.

Operational Stage

In the second half of May, the new Commanding General of the First Marine Aircraft Wing, General Jerome, was called to the Fifth Air Force Headquarters and given a directive for expanding bacteriological operations. The directive was given personally and verbally by the new Commanding General of the Fifth Air Force, General Barcus.

On May 25, General Jerome outlined the new stage of bacteriological operations to the wing staff at a meeting in his office at which I was present in my capacity as Chief of Staff. The other staff members of the First Marine Aircraft Wing present were: General Lamson-Scribner, Assistant Commanding General; Colonel Stage, intelligence officer (G.2); Colonel Wendt, operations officer (G.3) and Colonel Clark, logistics officer (G.4).

The directive from General Barcus, transmitted to and discussed by us that morning was as follows: A contamination belt was to be established across Korea in an effort to make the interdiction programme effective in stopping enemy supplies from reaching the front lines. The Marines would take the left flank of this belt, to include the two cities of Sinanju and Kunuri and the area between and around them. The remainder of the belt would be handled by the Air Force in the centre and the navy in the east or right flank.

Marine Squadron 513 would be diverted from its random targets to the concentrated target, operating from K.8 (Kunsan), still serviced by the Third Bomb Wing using F.7F's (Tiger Cats). The squadron was short of these aircraft but more were promised.

The responsibility for contaminating the left flank and maintaining the contamination was assigned to the commander of squadron 513 and the schedule of operations left to the squadron's discretion, subject to the limitations that: the initial contamination of the area was to be completed as soon as possible and the areas must then be replenished, at periods not to exceed ten days.

The crews of the aircraft carrying out these operations were to be given orders for the regular night reconnaissance carried out over Haeju peninsula.

On the way to the target, however, the aircraft were to fly over Sonanchu or Kunuri, drop their bacterial bombs there and then carry out their regular tasks. That was done for greater security and also to interfere as little as possible with the regular operations.

Reports on this programme of maintaining the contamination belt would go direct to the Fifth Air Force, reporting normal mission number so and so had been completed "via Sinanju" or "Via Kanuri" and stating how many "superpropaganda" bombs had been dropped.

Squadron 513 was directed to make a more accurate "truck count" at night than had been customary in order to determine or detect any significant change in the flow of traffic through its operating area.

General Barcus also directed that Marine Aircraft Group 12 of the First Marine Aircraft Wing was to prepare to enter the bacteriological programme. First the A.Ds (Skyraiders) and then the F.4Us (Corsairs) were to take part in the expanded programme, initially, however, only as substitutes for the F.7Fs.

General Jerome further reported that the air force required Marine Photographic Squadron One to continue their current bacteriological operations, operating from K.3 (Pohang). At the same time, Marine Aircraft Group 33 at

K.3 was placed on a standby, last resort, basis. Owing to the distance of K.3 from the target area, large-scale participation in the programme by Marine Aircraft Group 33 was not desired. Because the F.9Fs (Panthers) would only be used in an emergency, no special bomb supply would be established over and above that needed to supply the photographic reconnaissance aircraft. Bombs could be brought up from Ulsan in a few hours if necessary.

These plans and the ramifications thereof were discussed at General Jerome's conference and arrangements made to transmit the directive to the officers concerned with carrying out the new programme.

It was decided that Colonel Wendt would initially transmit this information to the commanders concerned and that details could be discussed by the cognizant staff officers as soon as they were worked out.

First M.A.Ws Operations

Marine Night Fighter Squadron 513

The next day then, May 26, Colonel Wendt held a conference with the Commanding Officer of Squadron 513 and I believe, the K.8 Air Base Commander and the Commanding Officer of the Third Bomb Wing and discussed the details.

The personnel of the Fifth Air Force were already cognizant of the plan, having been directly informed by Fifth Air Force Headquarters.

Since the plan constituted, for Squadron 513, merely a change of target and additional responsibility to maintain their own schedule of contamination of their area, these were no real problems to be solved.

During the week of June, Squadron 513 started operations on the concentrated contamination belt, using cholera bombs. (The plan given to General Jerome indicated that at a later, unspecified date—depending on the results, or lack of results—yellow fever and then typhus in that order would probably be tried out in the contamination belt.)

Squadron 513 operated in this manner throughout June and during the first week in July that I was with the Wing, without any incidents of an unusual nature.

An average of five aircraft a night normally covered the main supply routes along the western coast of Korea up to the Chong Chon River but with emphasis on the area from Pyongyang southwards. They diverted as necessary to Sinanju or Kunuri and the area between in order to maintain the ten-day bacteriological replenishment cycle.

We estimated that if each airplane carried two bacteriological bombs, two good nights were ample to cover both Sinanju and Kunuri and a third night would cover the area around and between these cities.

About the middle of June, as best I remember, the squadron received a modification to the plan from the Fifth Air Force via the Third Bomb Wing. This new directive included an area of about ten miles surrounding the two principal cities in the squadron's schedule, with particular emphasis on towns or hamlets on the lines of supply and any bypass roads.

Marine Aircraft Group 12

Colonel Wendt later held a conference at K.6 (Pyongtaek) at which were present the commanding officer, Colonel Gaylor, the executive officer and the operations officer of Marine Aircraft Group 12. Colonel Wendt informed them that they were to make preparations to take part in the bacteriological operations and to work out security problems which would become serious if they got into daylight operations and had to bomb up at their own base, K.6. They were to inform the squadron commanders concerned, but only the absolute barest number of additional personnel, and were to have a list of a limited number of handpicked pilots ready to be used on short notice. Colonel Wendt informed them that an air force team would soon be provided to assist with logistic problems, this team actually arriving the last week in June.

Before my capture on July 8, both the A.Ds (Skyraiders) and the F.4U's (Corsairs) or Marine Aircraft Group 12 had participated in very small numbers, once or twice, in daylight bacteriological operations as part of regular scheduled, normal, day missions, bombing up at K.8 (Kunsan) and rendezvousing with the rest of the formation on the way to the target. These missions were directed at small towns in Western Korea along the main road leading south from Kunuri and were a part of the normal interdiction programme.

Marine Aircraft Group 33

Colonel Wendt passed the plan for the Wing's participation in bacteriological operations to Colonel Condon, commanding officer of Marine Aircraft Group 33 on approximately May 27–28.

Since the Panthers (F.9Fs) at the group's base at Pohang would only be used as last resort aircraft, it was left to Colonel Condon's discretion as to just what personnel he would pass the information on to, but it was to be an absolute minimum.

During the time I was with the Wing, none of these aircraft had been scheduled for bacteriological missions though the photographic reconnaissance planes of the group's V.M.J. One Squadron continued their missions from that base.

Scheduling and Security

Security was far the most pressing problem affecting the First Marine Aircraft Wing, since the operational phase of bacteriological warfare, as well as other type combat operations, is controlled by the Fifth Air Force.

Absolutely nothing could appear in writing on the subject. The word "bacteria" was not to be mentioned in any circumstances in Korea, except initially to identify "superpropaganda" or "Suprop."

Apart from the routine replenishment operations of Squadron 513, which required no scheduling, bacteriological missions were scheduled by separate, top secret mission orders (or frag orders). These stated only to include "Super Propaganda" or "Suprop" on mission number so and so of the routine, secret "frag" order for the day's operations. Mission reports went back the same way, by separate, top secret dispatch, stating the number of "Suprop" bombs dropped on a specified, specially numbered mission.

Other than this, Squadron 513 reported their bacteriological mission by adding "via Kunuri" or "via Sinanju" to their normal mission reports.

Every means was taken to deceive the enemy and to deny knowledge of these operations even to friendly personnel, the latter being most important since 300 to 400 men of the wing are rotated back to the United States each month.

Orders were issued that bacteriological bombs were only to be dropped in conjunction with ordinary bombs or napalm, to give the attack the appearance of a normal attack against enemy supply lines. For added security over enemy territory, a napalm bomb was to remain on aircraft until after the release of the bacteriological bombs so that if the aircraft crashed it would almost certainly burn and destroy the evidence.

All officers were prohibited from discussing the subject except officially and behind closed doors. Every briefing was to emphasize that this was not only a military secret, but a matter of national policy.

Personally I have never once heard the subject mentioned or even referred to outside of the office, and I ate all of my meals in the commanding general's small private mess where many classified matters were discussed.

Assessment of Results

In the Wing, our consensus of opinion was that the results of these bacteriological operations could not be accurately assessed. Routine methods of assessment are by presumably spies, by questioning prisoners of war, by watching the nightly truck count very carefully to observe variations from the normal traffic, and by observing public announcements of Korean and Chinese authorities, upon which very heavy dependence was placed, since it was felt that no large epidemic could occur without news leaking to the outside and that the authorities would announce it.

Information from the above sources is correlated at the base commander-in-chief's Far East level in Tokyo but the overall assessment of results is not passed down to the wing level. Hence the complete lack of knowledge of the results.

When I took over from Colonel Binney, I asked him for results. And he specifically said, "Not worth a damn."

No one that I knew of has indicated that the results are anywhere near commensurate with the effort, danger and dishonesty involved, although the Korean and Chinese authorities have made quite a public report of early bacteriological bomb efforts. The sum total of results known to me are that they are disappointing and no good.

Personal Impressions

I do not say the following in defense of anyone, myself included, I merely say it as an absolute direct observation that every officer when first informed that the U.S. is using bacteriological warfare in Korea is both shocked and ashamed.

I believe, without exception, that we come to Korea as officers who had always been told about bacteriological warfare—that it is being developed only for use in retaliation in the third world war.

Those officers who arrived in Korea and there learned that the Government was deceiving them so crudely by announcing to the whole world that it was not using bacterial weapons, are now forced to doubt the truth of everything else that the Government states about war in general and about the Korean war in particular.

None of us considered that bacterial weapons could be given any given place in war, since the main purpose of bacterial bombs was the mass annihilation of the civilian population, which is absolutely contrary to the human conscience. The spread of diseases cannot be foreseen and there are probably no limits to the development of an epidemic. Furthermore, a feeling of cowardice and dishonestly is engendered in any one who realized that he is dealing with a weapon which is being used surreptitiously against an unarmed and unwarned people.

I remember specifically asking Colonel Wendt what were Colonel Gaylor's reactions, when he was first informed and he reported to me that: Colonel Gaylor was both horrified and stupified. Everyone felt like that when they first heard of it, and their reactions are what might well be expected from a fair-minded, self-respecting nation of people.

Tactically, this type of weapon is totally unwarranted—it is not even a Marine Corps weapon—morally it is damnation itself: administratively and logistically as planned for use, it is hopeless: and from the point of view of self-respect and loyalty, it is shameful.

F. H. Schwable, 04429, Colonel, U.S.M.C.
December 6, 1952, North Korea

Source: Col. Frank A. Schwable, USMC, Transcripts, 3:exhibit 10.

APPENDIX D

Counter Intelligence Corps
Interrogation Questionnaire

COUNTERINTELLIGENCE INTERROGATION
of

NAME _____

RANK _____

ASN _____

HOME ADDRESS _____

CITY _____

"INFORMATION CONTAINED HEREIN IS
NOT TO BE RECORDED IN ANY OTHER
INTERROGATION REPORT."

Attention is invited to par 43, SR 380–320–10

CONFIDENTIAL
(Declassified on 29 Mar 85)

Article 31

Compulsory Self-incrimination Prohibited

(a) No person subject to this code shall compel any person to incriminate himself or to answer any question the answer to which may tend to incriminate him.

(b) No person subject to this code shall interrogate, or request any statement from, an accused or a person suspected of an offense without first informing him of the nature of the accusation and advising him that he does not have to make any statement regarding the offense of which he is accused or suspected and that any statement made by him may be used as evidence against him in a trial by court-martial.

(c) No person subject to this code shall compel any person to make a statement or produce evidence before any military tribunal if the statement or evidence is not material to the issue and may tend to degrade him.

(d) No statement obtained from any person in violation of this article, or through the use of coercion, unlawful influence, or unlawful inducement, shall be received in evidence against him in trial by court-martial.

Read and explained to: _____

By: _____ , Date: _____

An inquiry to determine to what extent, if any, this Returnee was subjected to a foreign ideology, his response to such, his observations of methods and techniques employed by his captors in attempting to indoctrinate American Prisoners of War during their periods of captivity in Communist-Controlled North Korea, and to what degree, if any, he believes or embraces this foreign ideology.

1. Explanation of the 31st Article of the Uniform Code of Military Justice.

2. Ascertain how soon after his arrival at camp, were squad and unit leaders selected, by whom, for what qualifications, and how long did they serve?

3. Determine who was responsible for calling the rolls of prisoners, who received such reports, and whether this responsibility was delegated to prisoners?

4. Determine which prisoners, if any, attempted to influence other prisoners to follow and accept theories of a foreign ideology (Communism), and what were the methods used?

5. Ascertain which prisoners held offices, special jobs, and performed special duties for camp authorities. Who selected them and what were their qualifications?

6. Determine which prisoners served as leaders, speakers, liaison representatives in camps to which he was assigned, whether they were selected or volunteered for such duties?

7. Ascertain which prisoners had occasions to report to camp officials frequently, whether such visits were made during night or day-light hours, and whether such visits were voluntary or by invitation from camp authorities?

7.a. Did any American prisoners have the privilege of living outside the prison compound? Who were they? What did they do?

7.b. Were any prisoners invited to go for walks with camp officials? Who were they? What were their jobs?

8. Determine whether any prisoners were absent from any camps for unusual periods of time, and for what reason?

8.a. Ascertain which prisoners, if any, were held at places and under circumstances which afforded camp authorities an opportunity to influence them to accept a foreign ideology (Communism).

9. Determine which prisoners were sent outside of North Korea? What was their destination, and for what purpose?

10. Ascertain to what extent prisoners were photographed in groups? Was still or movie camera used, and for what purpose?

11. Determine which prisoners were photographed and fingerprinted at the camps to which he was assigned, when, where and by whom?

a. Did any prisoners use an alias?

12. Ascertain which prisoners joined his group from another camp, and for what reason.

13. Determine which prisoners were transferred from camps to which he was assigned, and for what purpose?

14. Determine to what extent American prisoners cultivated friendship with Chinese or North Koreans during their periods of captivity, and whether addresses were exchanged for future use? Which prisoners exchanged addresses?

15. Determine which prisoners were required to perform duties outside of camp, type of duty and how far from camp?

16. Ascertain which prisoners received special treatment (easy jobs, better food than others, better clothing than others, better sleeping quarters, and better medical treatment), and the reason for such preferential treatment?

17. Determine which prisoners received mistreatment, under what circumstances, and why?

18. Determine whether any prisoners received safe-conduct passes for return to United Nations Lines, and why?

19. Ascertain names of organizations formed within camps to which he was assigned? Who sponsored them, their objectives, size of following, and how disciplined?

20. Determine whether study group meetings were part of required camp training, or whether attendance was voluntary? Who were the study group leaders, and how were the study group leaders, and how were they selected?

21. Determine how long after he arrived at camps did camp officials begin

orientation and indoctrination for the new arrivals? Of what did the first orientation lecture consist? Was it given by a fellow-prisoner?

22. Ascertain means employed by camp authorities in conducting indoctrination? Did they use movies, pictures, charts, personal contacts, books? Which means proved most effective?

23. Determine if special instructions or training was given to any prisoners, where were instructions given, who were the instructors, and what were the subjects?

24. Ascertain in which type of prisoner did camp authorities appear to be the most interested? (Education, rank, age). Why?

24.a. In which branch of service in the United States Army did camp authorities show most interest? (Signal, Military Police, Engineers, Intelligence)

24.b. In which type of U.S. Air Force activity did camp authorities show most interest? (Communications, radar, intelligence, armament, flying personnel and activities, non flying activities, logistical support, guided missiles, other scientific developments, etc.)

What information was sought regarding each activity?

To what extent was it obtained and how?

25. Determine which prisoners in camps to which he was assigned, appeared to have leanings toward Communism or other foreign ideology?

25.a. Did they appear sincere in supporting Communism, or were they merely pretending they were in sympathy with Communism in order to gain favors for themselves?

25.b. What did they do beyond the duty requirements at camps to which they were assigned.

26. Ascertain what consideration was shown prisoners who applied themselves to the programs given by camp officials? Were they considered leaders by the camp authorities? Were they called "progressives" or "reactionaries"?

27. Determine whether any American prisoner collaborated with camp authorities? In what way?

28. Ascertain which prisoner mistreated or abused any other prisoner? Why? Did he do it in the presence of camp officials?

29. Determine the identity of intelligence and political officers at the camps to which he was assigned during his captivity?

30. Determine to what extent prisoners acted as informants on other prisoners? Did they do so for personal favors, or did they do it as a matter of loyalty to camp authorities?

30.a. Was any prisoner mistreated as a result of some other prisoner informing camp officials of his conduct?

31. Ascertain to what extent, if any, camp officials encouraged prisoners to use alcohol, narcotics, or women? How did the prisoners obtain these items?

32. Determine how frequently prisoners were subjected to interrogation by

camp authorities? Were they conducted verbally or in writing? Who was questioned, and for how long?

32.a. Were prisoners required to sign confessions or statements and were the prisoners required to read such confessions or statements before formations? Why?

33. Determine the existence of camp newspapers at camps to which he was assigned? Who were the staff members? Who contributed articles to the camp papers? Who selected the staff? Where did staff members live, and how were they treated compared with other prisoners?

34. Determine the existence of the publication or magazine called, "New Life" at camps to which he was assigned. Ascertain what other newspapers were distributed to camps?

a. What other means did prisoners have for receiving news and information? Were they authorized to listen to U.S. broadcasts?

35. Determine the existence of a group of prisoners at camps who were called "Workers" (Yun-So-Yen)? What did they do? Did they wear a special uniform?

36. Determine the existence of diaries among prisoners at camps, the reason for keeping them, and whether camp officials discovered them at any time?

37. Determine how frequently Soviet personnel visited camps. What duties did they perform while there?

38. Ascertain which prisoners, if any, deliberately avoided a chance to escape.

a. Did any prisoner attempt to interfere with other prisoners who planned for, and tried to escape? How and why?

b. Do you know of any prisoners released by camp officials before repatriation, or given an opportunity to escape?

39. Ascertain which prisoners spoke a foreign language. Were they used by camp officials? What did they do? Do you know that the prisoner could speak the language before he was captured?

a. Did any prisoners show special aptitude in learning Korean, Chinese, or other languages, while in camp? Why?

40. Determine the number of American prisoners or other United Nations personnel still in Communist hands? Why are they detained?

a. Were these prisoners friendly with camp officials before repatriation? Did they volunteer for any special duty with the Chinese or North Koreans?

b. Did these prisoners want to return to their own country?

41. Ascertain those Americans who tried to be taken prisoner? How and why? Do you have a personal knowledge of their efforts to be taken prisoner?

42. Determine whether any prisoners were given any kind of mission by their captors upon their release?

a. Were prisoners told that they had contacts in the United States? Who were these contacts?

43. Determine what incidents occurred during his captivity which seemed unusual. Explain.

44. Ascertain his primary duties prior to his capture. (MOS, etc). (specialties).

45. Determine his position in his PW unit. (Interpreter, clerk, liaison, committeeman, speaker, writer).

46. Ascertain which American prisoners had pro-communist leanings. How did they reflect such leanings?

a. Did there appear pro-communists among other United Nations prisoners? What countries did they represent?

47. Ascertain which Americans, if any, acted in a pro-communist manner prior to capture? How did they reflect such actions?

48. Determine what he thinks of Communism. Would it work in the United States? Why?

49. Determine methods and techniques used in obtaining signatures of prisoners to confessions, sworn statements, letters, etc.

a. Were prisoners subject to duress and intimidation before signing such documents?

b. Did any prisoners refuse to sign such documents under duress? What was the nature of punishment if a prisoner refused to sign such documents?

50. Determine which Americans circulated petitions in camps to which he was assigned? Did such action benefit them in any way?

a. What Americans made recordings for camp officials? Were these recordings made voluntarily or by request from camp officials? How were the recordings used?

51. Determine if any Americans were betrayed in any manner to the enemy during combat, or to camp officials during captivity. Explain.

52. Determine which Americans made anti-communist speeches in camps, or expressed opposition to Communism. Were they punished for such actions?

53. Who were the camp officials who had daily contact with the prisoners? (casual, official or otherwise).

54. Determine the missions, if any, assigned to American prisoners before they were repatriated.

55. Determine which American prisoners were encouraged to remain in North Korea, go to Red China or to the Soviet Union.

56. Determine how he spent his off-duty time.

57. Ascertain what information camp officials had concerning his family in the United States. How was that information obtained?

58. Determine what information he has which he thinks will be of importance to the United States.

59. Ascertain the names of other American returnees who might have in-

formation concerning atrocities committed against American prisoners by Americans, Chinese, and Korean communists.

60. Ascertain whether prisoner personally heard any lectures on USAF participation in bacteriological warfare. Where? Who gave them?

60.a. Did the prisoner personally talk with U.S. Personnel who were lecturing on bacteriological warfare or Communism?

Who were they? Did they appear to lecture and talk freely or appear to be under the influence of narcotics, drugs, or undue pressure of some kind? Describe any indications of this.

61. Was there any difference between the treatment of prisoners by the Chinese Communists and the treatment by North Koreans?

If so, what were the differences and what seemed to be the objectives of each group?

62. What physical security and counterintelligence systems were in effect at the camps in which you were a prisoner?

If informant nets were used, who were the informants and to whom did they report? What did they report?

63. What interest was shown regarding counterintelligence systems of the U.S.? Who showed this interest (names and whether Chinese or Koreans) and what information did they secure? From whom was the information secured?

64. What publications were suggested to the prisoners as reading material for use after their release? Where were the publications to be obtained?

65. What organizations were the prisoners encouraged to join or attend after their release? Where are these organizations located (addresses) and/or how were the prisoners to get in touch with them?

66. Were all captured personnel of your platoon (barracks, hospitals, labor camp, group, special detail etc.) (Interrogator to select suitable word) repatriated?

Yes _____ No _____

67. (If answer to 66 above was Yes) Do you know of any captured personnel in any other group who for any reason you suspect may not be repatriated, or who expressed belief they were not to be repatriated?

Yes _____ No _____

(If answer to 67 above is No cease interrogation on this subject)

68. (If answer to 66 above was No) Do you have any reason for believing that there may be captured personnel remaining behind who may not be returned to UNC control?

Yes _____ No _____

69. Do you know of any other captured personnel in any other group or camp who you believe may not be repatriated, or who have expressed a fear that they will not be repatriated?

Yes _____ No _____

(If answer to both 68 and 69 above was NO, cease interrogation on this subject)

70. If answer to either 68 or 69 above is YES then develop your interrogation along the following lines.

a. Names of non-repatriates (if known).

b. Nationality (if known).

c. Branch of service if US or other affiliation.

d. Location where seen.

e. Number (if more than one).

f. Reason or reasons for non-repatriation (if known).

g. Any other pertinent details which may assist in identifying non-repatriates, or of substantiating the above information.

Source: Cpl. Claude Batchelor, USA, Transcripts: secret volume, prosecution exhibit 2.

APPENDIX E

*Transcript of Reprimand Issued to
Lt. Col. Paul V. Liles*

ACTION
HEADQUARTERS SIXTH ARMY
Presidio of San Francisco, California

21 February 1956

In the foregoing case of Lieutenant Colonel Paul V Liles, 023876, U S Army, 6006 Area Service Unit, Station Complement, Fort Lewis, Washington, the sentence is approved and will be duly executed.

The following reprimand is hereby administered:

You, Lieutenant Colonel Paul V Liles, having been found guilty by a general court-martial of the offenses of aiding and of knowingly communicating, corresponding, and holding intercourse with the enemy, while a prisoner of war during the Korean conflict, by making recordings which were inimical to the interests of the United States, and having, by said court-marital, been sentenced, among other things, to a reprimand, are hereby reprimanded.

The court-martial, by its sentence, could have sentenced you to dismissal, imprisonment, and forfeiture of all pay and allowances. It is your good fortune that the court-martial limited its punishment to suspension from rank for twenty-four months and to a reprimand. Your conduct, as reflected in the findings of the court-martial, and as fully supported by the record of your trial, discloses that you, an officer of the Regular Army, with the advantage of an education tendered you by the people of the United States in the United States Military Academy at West Point, with a background of many years of service in various ranks and assignments in the United States Army, and in spite of the full and positive knowledge you must have gained by your education and experience, as above outlined, of the conduct expected and required of an officer, supinely complied with the dictates of your captors and otherwise conducted yourself in a servile, craven, and unsoldierly manner for the obvious purpose of securing favored treatment for yourself while a prisoner of war. Although you well knew that your participation in the armed conflict did not end when you were taken prisoner, and that it was your positive duty to carry on the conflict to the best of your ability as a prisoner of war, offering only that degree of cooperation contemplated by international law and holding yourself ever in readiness to escape and resume the fight, you chose to damn your country and its representatives, to hold the American way of life up to ridicule and contempt, and to extol the practices and the concepts of a deadly enemy. In committing this heinous crime you made recordings at the request of said enemy, the purpose of which was fully known to you, namely, use as a psychological warfare weapon against your country and its forces. The odiousness of your actions and of your philosophy is clearly evidenced when compared with the steadfastness and the fortitude displayed by many other officers and enlisted men, including many of very limited service, in refusing information to, or cooperation of any kind or description with, their unprincipled captors. Furthermore, the conduct of which you stand convicted occurred at a time when other, and loyal, American soldiers and officers were fighting and dying in the defense of the United States. You have held personal safety and comfort above duty, honor, and country, and, in so doing, have deliberately violated your oath as a citizen of the United States and as an officer of the United States Army. Your actions have not only brought disgrace upon yourself, but upon the Army and upon all of those who wear its uniform, and have caused me to harbor the gravest doubts as to your fitness for continued membership and service in the United States Army.

s/Robert N Young
ROBERT N YOUNG
Lieutenant General, USA
Commanding

Source: Lt. Col. Paul Liles, USA, Transcripts, 1:37–38.

BIBLIOGRAPHY

In addition to using the primary sources previously mentioned, a number of secondary sources were reviewed for background data. Most works on the Korean War generally will contain a chapter or two offering an overview on prisoners of war during that conflict. There are, however, three excellent books entirely devoted to POWs: Albert D. Biderman, *March to Calumny: The Story of American POWs in the Korean War* (New York: MacMillan, 1963); Eugene Kinkead, *In Every War but One* (New York: W. W. Norton, 1959); and William Lindsay White, *The Captives of Korea: An Unofficial White Paper on the Treatment of War Prisoners* (New York: Charles Scribner's Sons, 1957). The most recent of these works was published in 1963, and although they all exhibit a knowledge of the POW experience in Korea, the authors were not privy to the vast documentation available through the exercise of the Feedom of Information Act, which was not codified until 1967.

≫≪

"For 'Aiding the Enemy.'" *Newsweek,* Oct. 4, 1954, 28.
"Air Force Clears Four Ex-P.O.W. Pilots." *New York Times,* July 24, 1955, 26.
"Army Challenged on P.O.W. Charges." *New York Times,* Jan. 24, 1954, 1.
"Army Convicts Dickenson of Collaborating with Reds." *New York Times,* May 5, 1954, 1.
"Army Orders Trial for Former P.O.W." *New York Times,* Feb. 19, 1954, 1.
"Army Releases Turncoat P.O.W.s." *New York Times,* Nov. 9, 1955, 14.
Baldwin, Hanson W. "The Prisoner Issue II: Crimes of American against American in Korean Camps Call for Investigation." *New York Times,* Jan. 27, 1954, 2.

———. "Reds and Prisoners." *New York Times,* Aug. 12, 1955, 3.

"Batchelor Awaits Review of Sentence." *New York Times,* Oct. 2, 1954, 8.

"Batchelor Guilty, Sentenced to Life." *New York Times,* Oct. 1, 1954, 8.

"Batchelor's Life Term Reduced to Twenty Years." *New York Times,* Oct. 29, 1954, 11.

Carroll, Lewis. *Lewis Carroll's* The Hunting of the Snark: An Agony, in Eight Fits. Berkeley: University of California Press, 1983.

Cole, Paul M. "World War II, Korean War, and Early Cold War MIA-POW Issues." Typescript, Santa Monica, Calif., 1993.

"Colonel Guilty in P.O.W. Trial." *New York Times,* Dec. 22, 1955, 11.

"Corporal Admits He Helped Enemy." *New York Times,* June 29, 1955, 3.

"Court Frees Toth and Bars Military Trials." *New York Times,* Nov. 18, 1955, 1.

Dean, William F. *General Dean's Story.* New York: Viking Press, 1954.

"Defendant Dickenson." *New York Times,* April 25, 1954, 2.

"The Dickenson Case." *New York Times,* Jan. 29, 1954, 18.

"Dickenson Waives Right to Testify." *New York Times,* April 30, 1954, 10.

"Drawing the Line." *Time* magazine, Oct. 4, 1954, 28.

"The Dreadful Dilemma." *Time* magazine, March 22, 1954, 63.

Dunn, Harold M. "I Was a Progressive POW in Korea." *Pageant,* Jan. 25, 1954, 84–88.

"Eight Thousand Missing, Van Fleet Says." *New York Times,* Aug. 8, 1953.

"Eisenhower Gets Turncoats' Plea." *New York Times,* Sept. 16, 1955, 7.

"Eisenhower Urges Tolerance for G.I." *New York Times,* Jan. 28, 1954, 1.

"Ex-P.O.W. to Be Tried." *New York Times,* June 22, 1954, 51.

"Ex-P.O.W. Chosen to Head Red Cell." *New York Times,* Sept. 17, 1954, 8.

"Ex-P.O.W. Colonel to Be Cashiered." *New York Times,* Sept. 24, 1954, 11.

"Ex-P.O.W. Colonel Denies Aid to Reds." *New York Times,* Aug. 21, 1954.

"Ex-P.O.W. Loses Fight over Trial." *New York Times,* Aug. 4, 1955, 3.

"Ex-P.O.W. Major Accused by Army." *New York Times,* Nov. 13, 1954, 3.

"Ex-P.O.W.'s Sentence Reduced." *New York Times,* Nov. 9, 1956, 24.

Fehrenbach, T. R. *This Kind of War: A Study in Unpreparedness.* New York: MacMillan, 1963.

"Former Comrades Accuse Corporal." *New York Times,* April 21, 1954, 12.

"Former Prisoner of War in Korea Appeals Ten-Year Sentence to Military High Court." *New York Times,* June 18, 1955, 3.

"Gallagher Gets a Life Sentence." *New York Times,* Aug. 20, 1955, 1.

"G.I. Avenger Names Gallagher as Slayer." *New York Times,* Aug. 9, 1955, 1.

"G.I. Changes Mind, Quits Reds' Camp for Repatriation." *New York Times,* Jan. 1, 1954, 1.

"G.I. Goes on Trial in Three Korea Deaths." *New York Times,* Aug. 2, 1955, 3.

"G.I. Who Chose Reds, Then Quit, Is Seized in Court-Martial Case." *New York Times,* Jan. 23, 1954, 1.

Goulden, Joseph C. *Korea: The Untold Story of the War.* New York: Times Books, 1982.

"Handwashing." *Time* magazine, Feb. 1, 1954, 14.

"Held as Collaborator." *New York Times,* June 21, 1955, 6.

Hermes, William G. *United States Army in the Korean War: Truce Tent and Fighting Front.* Vol. 2. Washington: Office of the Chief of Military History, 1966.

Hogan, Edmund F. "Forgotten Fifteen: American Eagles in a Bamboo Cage." *Air Force Magazine* 37 (Nov. 1954): 23–28.

Joint Commission Support Branch, Research and Analysis Division, DPMO. *The Transfer of U.S. Korean War POWs to the Soviet Union.* Aug. 26, 1993.

Kinkead, Eugene. *In Every War but One.* New York: W. W. Norton, 1959.

"Korea G.I.'s Term Is Reduced." *New York Times,* Feb. 22, 1956, 3.

"Korea Turncoat Ends Jail Term." *New York Times,* Nov. 24, 1957, 21.

Leckie, Robert. *Conflict: The History of the Korean War, 1950–1953.* New York: G. P. Putnam's Sons, 1962.

"Major Acquitted of Helping Reds." *New York Times,* March 8, 1955, 12.

Middleton, Harry J. *The Compact History of the Korean War.* New York: Hawthorn Books, 1965.

Moskin, J. Robert, and Morris R. Wills. *Turncoat: An American's Twelve Years in Communist China.* Englewood Cliffs: Prentice-Hall, 1966.

Office of Sen. Bob Smith. "Chronology of Policy and Intelligence Matters Concerning Unaccounted For U.S. Military Personnel at the End of the Korean Conflict and during the Cold War." Nov. 10, 1992.

"Officer Convicted as Collaborator." *New York Times,* Sept. 23, 1954, 1.

"Parole for Turncoat." *New York Times,* Jan. 14, 1959, 7.

Pate, Lloyd W. *Reactionary!* New York: Harper and Brothers, 1955.

Peters, Katherine McIntire. "The Endless Search." *Government Executive* 28 (April 1996): 26–31.

"P.O.W. Conviction Upheld." *New York Times,* March 31, 1955, 5.

"Quality of Mercy Is Strained by Rank." *New York Times,* May 19, 1954, 603.

"Red 'Brain Washing.'" *Look* magazine, June 2, 1953, 80.

Rees, David. *Korea: The Limited War.* Baltimore: Penguin Books, 1970.

"Schwable Freed but Is Criticized." *New York Times,* April 28, 1954, 1.

"Second Ex-P.O.W. Arrested by Army." *New York Times,* March 6, 1954, 2.

"Sentence of Ex-P.O.W. Reduced to Two and a Half Years." *New York Times,* Aug. 21, 1955, 3.

"Shift in Dickenson Case." *New York Times,* Feb. 6, 1954, 3.

"Snafu and Showdown." *Newsweek,* Feb. 1, 1954, 18.

Sommers, Stan. *The Korea Story.* Packet no. 9, American Ex-Prisoners of War, Inc. (National Research Committee). Tampa: National Headquarters.

"Statement of Pro-Red Korea Captives." *New York Times,* Jan. 27, 1954, 2.

Summers, Harry. *Korean War Almanac.* New York: Facts on File, 1987.

"Text of Inquiry Findings on Marine Col. Schwable and Comments of Defense Officials." *New York Times,* April 28, 1954, 16.

"Three Ex-G.I. Turncoats Land in San Francisco and Are Jailed by Army." *New York Times,* July 30, 1955, 1.

Toland, John. *In Mortal Combat: Korea, 1950–1953.* New York: William Morrow, 1991.

"A Tough Task." *Newsweek,* March 22, 1954, 33.

"Turncoat's Sentence Halved." *New York Times,* April 17, 1957, 27.

"'Turncoat' Trial Scheduled." *New York Times,* Oct. 10, 1955, 36.

"Twenty-one Pro-Red G.I.s to Get Dishonorable Discharges." *New York Times,* Jan. 26, 1954, 1.

"Two G.I.'s Here Seized for POW Crimes." *New York Times,* May 12, 1955, 1.

U.S. Department of the Army.*Organizations Considered by the Attorney General to Have Interests in Conflict with Those of the United States.* Circular no. 338. Washington, D.C.: U.S. Department of the Army, 1948.

U.S. Senate Committee on Foreign Relations Republican Staff. *An Examination of U.S. Policy toward POW/MIAs.* Washington, D.C.: Government Printing Office, 1991.

"Veteran of Korea Faces Army Trial." *New York Times,* Jan. 13, 1955, 8.

INDEX

Logan, Lt. Col. William, 252, 253, 255
London Daily Worker, 42, 94
Lord, Commissioner Herbert, 22
Lorenzo, Maj. Mike, 107, 108, 232
Lunn, Pfc. Roosevelt, 50, 53, 57

MacGhee, Maj. David, 147, 254; the Caves and, 126
Maffioli, S. Sgt. Leonard, 85, 86
Magnant, Lt. Joseph, 100
Mares, Sgt. Jose, 124
Marlatt, Capt. Herb, 19, 130
Mathis, M. Sgt. Chester, 83, 246
McAbee, Maj. Filmore, 148
McCool, CWO Felix, 69, 93
McLaughlin, Lt. Col. John, 155, 254–55, 281; threat to, 100–101
McShan, Cpl. Laurence, 58, 80
Michaelis, Maj. Gen. J. H., 232
Miller, Capt. Lawrence, 116, 164
Millward, S. Sgt. George, 125–26
Milton, Hugh, 272
Moore, Cpl. Johnnie, 159
Moorer, Maj. Edward, 199, 238
Mountain Camp. *See* Pike's Peak

Name, rank, and service number, 104–6, 107, 149, 163, 164, 225, 298; abandonment by pilots, 223–24; confusion over, 164–65; impossibility of using, 234; instructions to ignore, 163–65, 225–26
Nardella, Capt. Ralph, 104
Narvin, Pvt. John, 117
Navy (U.S.), 280, 281–82, 284; "Operation Order and Task Organization," 282; P2V patrol aircraft incident, 282
Neel, Sgt. Clifford, 114, 127, 129, 136n, 138; plan to murder Cocks, 133
New Korea, 119
New Life, 246; contents of, 84–85
New York Daily Worker, 94
Nugent, Maj. Ambrose, 9, 10, 23, 130, 133, 179n, 220; arrival in Korea, 10–11; beating, 14–15; Camp 12 and, 132; capture, 13–15; Central Peace Committee and, 130, 137, 139–40; as collaborator, 147; combat experience in Korea, 11–13; court-martial, 220, 245, 264; on death march, 21–24; on escape, 15; hatred of captors, 148; around Manp'o, 20–21; march through P'yongyang, 19; military

interrogation of, 15–16; no retreat order and, 12; physical condition, 132, 137; preparation for Korea and, 10; return home, 203; Seoul experience, 15–17, 19; at "the shacks," 24–25; shipment to Manp'o from P'yongyang, 20–21; signature on blank paper, 16, 16n; torture, 14, 16, 17

Olson, M. Sgt. William, 83, 85n, 209, 232, 295–96; capture, 37; court-martial for bigamy, 270; court-martial, 221, 230, 232, 246, 269–70; as *gong-so-yen,* 87–88; propaganda speech at Camp 10, 83; on repatriation, 185
O'Neil, Lt. Floyd, 159, 160
Operation Big Switch, 184, 203–4, 226n, 238, 279, 279n, 280
Operation Little Switch, 184, 207, 214, 279, 279n, 281
Overholser, Dr. Winfred, 175

"Pak's Palace," 116, 169n
Parks, Lt. Gen. Floyd, 276
Parks, Lt. Roland, 283, 284, 291
Pate, Lloyd: Dunn incident and, 75–77; Gallagher conversation with instructor and, 154; at Gallagher court-martial, 248; jail term from Chinese, 154–55; as reactionary leader in Camp 3, 153–55, 271
"Peaceful Valley," 86
Peck, Col. Millard, 289; resignation letter, 289–90
Peking Daily Release, 84
People's China, 94
People's Guardian, 119
Pick-up Camp. *See* Pike's Peak
Pike's Peak interrogation center, 169, 169n
Portee, Sgt. Paul, 246
Porter, M. Sgt. John, 108, 130n, 136n
Potter, Maj. (Dr.) Ralph, 252
Potter, Sen. Charles, 286, 292n16
Preece, Cpl. Ellas, 79–80
Prisoners of War (Korea), 3; aboard ships returning home, 205–7; activities upon return to United States, 185, 186, 187–88, 190, 193–94, 195; apathy upon returning home, 204; atrocities against, 13, 14, 15, 21–25; 31, 32, 33, 59, 60–61, 75–76, 124–26; attitude about repatriation, 185; captors' rules for, 148–49; in Chinese uni-

Raymond B. Lech is director of commercial mortgages for a realty corporation in Brooklyn, New York. A past national director of the Navy League of the United States as well as its New York Council, he has also served in the marine corps and is the author of *All the Drowned Sailors: The Coverup of America's Greatest Wartime Disaster at Sea, the Sinking of the* Indianapolis, *with the Loss of 880 Lives Because of the Incompetence of Admirals, Officers, and Gentlemen.*

Typeset in 8.5/14 Stone Serif
with Moonshine display
Designed by Paula Newcomb
Composed by Jim Proefrock
at the University of Illinois Press
Manufactured by Thomson-Shore, Inc.

University of Illinois Press
1325 South Oak Street
Champaign, IL 61820-6903
www.press.uillinois.edu